GUARDIAN OF AMERICA

The Life of James Martin Gillis, CSP

Richard Gribble, CSC

PAULIST PRESS
New York, N.Y. • Mahwah, N.J.

Library of Congress Cataloging-in-Publication Data

Gribble, Richard.
    Guardian of America : the life of James Martin Gillis, CSP / Richard Gribble.
        p.   cm.
    Includes bibliographical references and index.
    ISBN 0-8091-3751-8 (alk. paper)
    1. Gillis, James M. (James Martin), 1876–1957. 2. Paulist Fathers—Biography. I. Title.
BX4705.G54G75   1998
271′.79—dc21
[B]   97-44822
                                                                                              CIP

Published by Paulist Press
997 Macarthur Boulevard
Mahwah, New Jersey 07430

Printed and bound in the
United States of America

Contents

DEDICATION

This book is dedicated to the man who initially suggested its genesis and guided its completion—Dr. Christopher J. Kauffman—mentor, teacher, and friend.

ACKNOWLEDGMENT

I would like to express my sincere thanks to several people who have aided and guided me in the completion of this book. My religious community, the Congregation of Holy Cross, Indiana Province, gave me the time, opportunity and economic support to pursue this project. Special thanks are given to Professor Christopher J. Kauffman of The Catholic University of America, who read various drafts, gave insightful suggestions, and provided invaluable criticism. Reverend Monsignor Robert Trisco, Professor of Church History at Catholic University, was also extremely helpful in his thorough reading and critique of the penultimate draft of the manuscript. Their expertise was instructive and valuable in the completion of this book. The archives staff at St. Paul's College in Washington, D.C., especially Reverend Paul Robichaud, CSP, archivist, and his assistants Nick Creary and Patrick McNamara, gave me every possible assistance in obtaining material in the James Gillis Papers and other collections. The assistance of The Paulist Fathers, the Congregation of Holy Cross and Stonehill College in North Easton, Massachusetts was invaluable in the publication of this book.

I am greatly blessed with family and friends whose care and support makes all my endeavors more fruitful. It is my family—my parents, Richard and Dorothy Gribble; my sisters, Judy and Barbara and her family, and good friends, especially Mary, whose ever present love and caring ways have been my rock foundation. They have been the source of my inspiration and have always been present in my life to lend an ear and give a word or two of advice. They deserve my deepest thanks for being themselves and sharing their lives with me.

Introduction

Catholic Authors of 1948 described James Martin Gillis, Irish-American, Paulist priest, and editor as a man with "the zeal of a modern Savonarola attacking political corruption and religious and moral indifference." Judging from the historical record of the fifteenth-century Dominican reformer, who considered himself a prophet sent to pronounce severe judgment on Italy and the Church, the description is apt and accurate. Through editorials, essays, and lectures, Gillis for over thirty years decried modernity's tendencies toward relativism and called for a return to the one absolute—God. Like Savonarola he preached reform with zeal in a campaign which called for moral reform in a society given to economic greed and over-dependence upon the ever expanding spheres of the federal government, which engendered a dangerous diminution of individual responsibility and made the nation vulnerable to atheism, socialism, and Communism.

Gillis's significance in twentieth-century American Catholic history has not been thoroughly explored by biographers or historians. As a conservative who edited the Paulist journal *The Catholic World* from 1922 to 1948, he stood as the most vocal Catholic agent for those Americans who perceived that the nation's values and principles were in jeopardy of collapse. In an effort to publicize his career, James Finley, CSP, who lived with Gillis the last ten years of the latter's life in New York, preached missions, and wrote movie reviews for *The Catholic World,* produced in 1958 an interesting and highly readable account of the Paulist editor's life. In this biography Finley utilized data from the public life of Gillis, including his editorials, syndicated column *Sursum Corda,* essays, books, and radio addresses to describe the opinions he voiced during his career as a Catholic

1

journalist. Additionally, Finley interviewed members of Gillis's family (one sister and one brother) and his lifelong friend, Monsignor Joseph Gibbons, and consulted diaries of the editor's early life to round out his life picture and provide some background to his personal thought and self-understanding.

Finley's book portrays the life of James Gillis and conjectures as to the basis of his thought, following a chronological format with special emphasis placed on Gillis as preacher and editor. He used the data available to him to describe Gillis's life and work, but the objective distance and appreciation of contexts necessary to effectively analyze the editor's contribution to American Catholic life are missing. Finley's work was severely criticized as derogatory to Gillis by those close to the editor;[1] moreover, it lacks scholarly criticism and does not give an accurate description of the James Gillis of history. Written shortly after the editor's death and under the constraints of a publisher's deadline, Finley's book makes no attempt to document sources, place Gillis within Catholic thought of his time, or analyze his writings and talks in search for inconsistencies, shortsightedness or patterns over the span of his career. Because of his proximity to and friendship with Gillis and his membership in the Paulist community, it is likely that Finley was to some extent biased in his analysis, manifested most notably in his failure to compare or critique Gillis against contemporary Catholic editorial comment on the principal issues of the day and to criticize his polemical and unbending style. It must be noted, however, that Finley did not possess all the primary data now available for research, nor was his intent to produce a scholarly work. Rather, he produced a popular account, written at the behest of the publisher, which served the important function of telling the life story of one who, without question, was a household word in many Catholic homes of mid-twentieth-century America.

This book's contribution to the historical record is dependent upon an evaluation of the reasons for Gillis's opinions and places the editor within the greater scope of contemporary American Catholic life by analyzing the course of his thought and its formative influences. Gillis held a dualistic world view which was professed through a conservative understanding of

American society. Though certainly outdated, Clinton Rossiter's *Conservatism in America* (1955) describes characteristics of the conservative mindset that illuminate the world view of James Gillis, who died two years after the publication of the book. Rossiter lists the characteristics of this world view: conviction of the freedom and dignity of the individual, opposition to expanding and centralized government, duty-consciousness, and the belief that humans are a composite of good and evil. Conservatives believed government must be constitutional, diffused and balanced, representative, and limited. In his analysis Rossiter places in the category of "ultra-conservatives" the likes of the newspaper columnist George Sokolsky, the authors John T. Flynn, William F. Buckley, Jr., Westbrook Pegler, and James Burnham, and the essayist Erik von Kuehnelt-Leddihn.[2]

Gillis fits the mold of Rossiter's conservativism in almost every aspect. Throughout his career Gillis wrote and spoke against big government (statism as he called it) in its manipulation and defeat of the individual. The political career of Franklin Delano Roosevelt, particularly his New Deal, became the principal object of his critique. Gillis perceived Roosevelt as unprincipled in his efforts to "railroad" the country to his way of thinking, ignoring the will of the people in the process. Gillis viewed himself as the guardian of the nation against those who ignored Abraham Lincoln's dictum, "government by the people," which echoed the beliefs of the founding fathers. Gillis applied to society his own value system, which emphasized duty and moral righteousness, developed in his youth and early years as a priest, and he viewed the world in dualistic terms as a contest between the forces of God and Satan. These ideas were foundational to his conservative mindset and represented the thought of a significant body of American Catholics. Gillis discussed and argued these ideas with the likes of Sokolsky, McCarthy, Pegler, and von Kuehnelt-Leddihn in correspondence and essays during a long and at times tumultuous journalistic career.

Gillis applied his conservative understanding of Church and society to his role as editor of *The Catholic World,* a major Catholic monthly. He began his work in Catholic journalism during a period that William Halsey and other historians have described as a time of disillusionment for much of the nation. In the post-World War I years American Catholics filled the vacuum caused by evangelist Protestant descent into disillusionment by promoting America's innocence, namely, "the belief in a rational and predictable cosmos, the belief in a moral structure inherent in the universe, the belief in progress and a didactic or 'genteel' rendering of cultural, especially literary, art forms."[3] Catholics set out to defend the values and principles of American idealism, which were threatened by various forms of irrationalism, including probability in scientific thought, skepticism in literature, and relativism in law and morality. Although never articulated in precise terms of time, Gillis called for America's return to a period in which the concepts of moral righteousness, smaller government, and personal accountability were significant values. Time, issues, and enemies would change, but Gillis's message that America had lost its way in its failure to maintain what he perceived as the nation's foundational virtues never wavered. Through the public media of editorials, essays, books, addresses, and radio broadcasts the Paulist editor voiced his tightly held convictions in his perceived role as guardian of America.

The public persona of James Gillis, which has received some comment in the historical literature,[4] is best understood, however, in light of the private man, a dimension unexplored by historians. One year before his death Gillis wrote, "The heart and soul of man is a battleground of Titans, supernatural Titans. And what is worse—if anything can be worse than the conflict of God and Satan—is that man is at odds with himself as to which side he shall take."[5] In these words Gillis captured the essence of his interior struggle and search for reconciliation and conversion which constituted the dynamic of his formative years. Raised in Boston's Irish-Catholic community, he came to understand himself, God, and society through multiple influences. His father fostered in him a strong sense of duty and commitment while the New England environment of his childhood imbued him with moral beliefs characteristic of "Yankee Puritanism," especially total abstinence from alcohol. His first experiences in ministry as a preacher of missions to non-Catholics solidified and aided the development of his dualistic world view where God and society were constantly at odds.

In his formative years Gillis often wrote of his unworthiness and worried about his close proximity to sin and damnation. He once stated,

> I am not contented. Why? It's the tearing and the struggling, the reviling and pulling of the good and the bad in me, of the noble and the depraved, of the ideal and the actual.[6]

He referred to the dualism of his spirituality as the Jekyll and Hyde of his personality, a condition he could never escape and which, in his early years, produced much pain as he recorded in retreat logs, diaries, and meditation books. Gillis's spirituality was steeped in asceticism,[7] which he found useful as a means to control his Mr. Hyde, who sought to run his spiritual ship aground.

Unable to achieve inner peace because of a self-imposed goal of spiritual perfection, Gillis projected his need for moral rigorism and absolutism onto society, voicing his world view, developed from his spirituality, which pitted the forces of darkness against the righteousness of God. The Jekyll and Hyde duality which Gillis claimed existed in every person was equally present in the world. It was his persistent challenge, in line with his Paulist identity as a preacher, to deliver his message that the forces of evil, representative of the monster Hyde, were jeopardizing the possibility for the individual to freely discover repentance and conversion. He used his strongly held convictions as the basis upon which he would critique the world's manifestations of Hyde, its leaders, institutions, ideologies, and programs, for more than three decades through the varied public media. Gillis never rested from his self-assigned task as guardian of America. In general Gillis viewed God as distant; there was no apparent understanding of the immanent presence of God's Spirit active in the world. As a Paulist and thus a spiritual disciple of Isaac Hecker, who believed in the active presence of the Spirit in the world, especially the United States, Gillis's spirituality and his Jekyll-and-Hyde dualism, which ran contrary to that of the founder's, demonstrates what Joseph Chinnici, OFM, has described as a "fractured inheritance."[8] Hecker's spirituality was based upon the integration of the internal life of the Spirit and the experience of the Church and society. Gillis, in contrast, understood his religious meaning in terms of internal conflict and his external experience with society.

This book is built on a chronology which can be separated into two sections. Part I, chapters one through three, covering the period from Gillis's birth until he was appointed as editor (1876–1922), describes the formation of his dualistic world view as derived from a reading of his extensive diaries, retreat notes, sermons, and meditation books. His understanding of society became the base upon which his public life as editor and commentator would rest and from which it would grow. Gillis's spiritual journey encompassed three seminaries: St. Charles, a minor seminary, St. John's in Brighton, Massachusetts, and St. Thomas, the Paulist house of formation in Washington, D.C. Along the road his greatest influences were his father, the Paulist evangelist Walter Elliott, and certain educators, including Francis Gigot and Thomas Shahan. Preaching missions to non-Catholics for fifteen years reinforced his self-understanding and led to the redirection of his inner conflict onto society.

Part II of this book, chapters four through seven, comprising the years of Gillis's work as a Catholic journalist (1922–1957), narrates and analyzes his editorial opinions and their contexts in overall American Catholic thought in an effort to demonstrate how he continued the Paulist mission to non-Catholics and exercised his own identity as a preacher in a new accumulation of forums. Gillis's arrival at the editor's desk of *The Catholic World* in September 1922 was the major shift in his life as a Paulist; this required an equally significant change in historical method. The record of his internal conflict is not extant after 1922, but the public defender of America emerges. The voluminous extant sources including editorials, weekly columns, essays, books, radio addresses on the Paulist station WLWL as well as NBC's "Catholic Hour," additional sermons, and extensive correspondence provide the historian with a wealth of material that reveals the character of the public man. Over the decades the face of the enemy changed: apparent moral laxity, greed, and the demise of family life in the 1920s; the leviathan state and interventionist politics in the 1930s; and Communism, deceptive government, and imperialism in the 1940s and 1950s. Yet, Gillis's basic conflict, which pitted good against evil and placed Church and society constantly at odds, remained the driving force of the articulation of his polemical stance.

During his tenure as editor James Gillis was *The Catholic World.* He wrote the editorial comment each month, made all decisions pertinent to essays published and advertisements run, and represented the journal to the Paulist community during general chapters and other community decision-making meetings. *The Catholic World* did carry essays which differed from Gillis's opinion, but they were generally matched by articles supportive of his stance. His commentary seldom touched on topics pertinent to the Church, a fact which at first glance seems odd for a priest editor. Closer examination, however, reveals that Gillis perceived the Catholic faith as filled with God's presence, integrated, and complete; thus, it required no reform. American society, on the other hand, with its atheistic and self-serving culture makers, who rejected personal duty, moral righteousness, and God, was in desperate need of spiritual renewal on all levels. Thus, Gillis viewed his editorial role as an extension of the Paulist mission to non-Catholics. He defended the United States and its formative values against all perceived threats. As a conservative he promoted personal renewal, while liberal Catholics, such as John A. Ryan, supported social reform. James Gillis's thought may be identified with "Catholic innocence," particularly in his extolling the foundational values of the nation.

James Martin Gillis was a modern Savonarola in his efforts to preach to a world bent on self-destruction. In concert with other conservative voices he fearlessly expressed his convictions derived from a dualistic view of the world. The private man of inner turmoil and the public person of conservative opinion produced one significant and heretofore unappreciated voice of twentieth-century American Catholic life and thought.

CHAPTER 1

Toward the Priesthood—1876–1901

Irish textures are deeply woven into the life and culture of America's people. The spirit of celebration, evident from the almost universal appeal to identify oneself by heritage or association as Irish on St. Patrick's Day, reveals the widespread influence of Irish culture in the United States. The Irish immigrants who flocked to America's shores in the early to mid-nineteenth century brought their Catholic faith with them. Irish Catholicism was steeped in moral rigorism and dogmatism, and it emphasized the letter of the religious law over its spirit. By force of numbers and assumptions of positions of authority, in Church and society, Irish Catholics, as Lawrence McCaffrey has stated, "have played...an important role in directing the American Church, urban politics, and the labor movement."[1]

Irish influence in the American Church was present from the outset and grew over time. English-speaking Irish men and women were better able to assimilate into American life, compared with Germans, Italians, and Eastern Europeans, during the era of immigration. More important, the American hierarchy was dominated by Irish or Irish-American prelates, many of whom fostered American values of liberal democracy, popular sovereignty, and the separation of Church and State. It is this ethnic understanding of Catholicism which formed and influenced James Martin Gillis, Irish-American, Paulist priest, and commentator on world affairs. Gillis brought his ethnicity, Boston roots, foundational influences, and life experience to his work as a missionary in defense of America, exercised through the unusual "pulpits" of editor, essayist, radio evangelist, and lecturer. His mission, controversial to many, yet loyal to his youthful influences and Paulist identity, established him as a significant personality in twentieth-century American Catholicism.

The Nineteenth-Century American Catholic Experience

American Catholicism of the nineteenth century was characterized by an apologetic defense against nativists, by massive migration, and by a quest for self-understanding in a new land of opportunity. The era experienced waves of nativism and anti-Catholicism. The forms varied but the persistent message was that Catholics could not make good Americans. At times the animus was manifest in violence, such as the burning of the Ursuline Convent in Charlestown, Massachusetts in 1834, the Philadelphia riots of 1844, and the riotous behavior that met the visit of the Papal representative, Archbishop Gaetano Bedini, in 1853. Anti-Catholic literature abounded including the lurid tales of women religious published as *Six Months in a Convent* (1835) by Rebecca Reed and the infamous *Awful Disclosures of the Hotel Dieu Nunnery in Montreal* (1836) ostensibly by "Maria Monk" but actually written by a group of Protestant ministers. Numerous other books, periodicals, newspapers, and countless pamphlets, published in this same period, described Rome as the whore of Babylon.[2] Politically the Know-Nothing Party, a derivative of the Order of the Star-Spangled Banner, founded by Charles B. Allen in 1849, was active in an anti-Catholic campaign from 1852 to 1856. The party swept to many local, state, and congressional victories while supporting as one of its principles that no Catholic should hold public office.[3]

Massive waves of immigration to America's shores in the nineteenth century added to the anti-Catholic animus of the nation. The first significant period of immigration, 1830 to 1860, was dominated by an influx of Irish and Germans, many of whom were Catholic. The Irish in general were poorly educated with no marketable skills. Native-born Americans, including some Catholics, argued against their presence because they served as competition for unskilled labor jobs. Additionally, many Irish immigrants landed on the rolls of government assistance, which placed a drain on the limited resources of the community. Many Germans, because of the language barrier, were more resistant to assimilation, both within the Catholic community[4] and in the nation as a whole. The second wave of immigration, 1880 to 1920, brought many Eastern and Southern European Catholics to America with the problems of assimilation, job competition, and religion again bringing anti-Catholicism to the forefront with the formation of the American Protective Association (APA).[5]

While American Catholics searched for acceptance in their newly adopted land, they also were absorbed in a quest for self-understanding. All the aforementioned factors which pushed Catholicism to create a defensive apologetic in spirit and action also accelerated its need to establish an identity within American society. If the myriad peoples, heritages, and nationalities with the common bond of the Catholic faith were to persevere and be successful, they would have to find comfort with an identity. Nativists habitually stated that Catholics could not be good Americans, since their fealty to Rome as a foreign power conflicted with loyalty to the United States. Immigrant Catholics were stereotyped with old-world priest-ridden monarchists or paradoxically anarchists fomenting revolution. To counter such arguments, many other Catholics stressed the close compatibility of American principles with those of Catholicism. Catholic converts Orestes Brownson and Isaac Hecker, the latter the founder of the Congregation of Missionary Priests of St. Paul the Apostle (the Paulists, 1858), made every effort to show that not only could Catholics be good Americans, but it was Catholicism that provided the most compatible religious match with the democratic principles upon which the nation was founded and which its people held in highest esteem.

According to Hecker and his followers among the Americanists, an incarnational concept of Church, with its concentration upon divine immanence in the history of Catholicism in the United States, was central to their self-understanding.[6] Amid a growing middle class with a vast array of charitable and educational institutions, parish and diocesan societies, these assimilated Catholics stressed the positive character of American society. The contribution of American Catholics would, in the mind of many, be significant and formative as the nation began to gain international status and prestige.

Youth and Influences—1876–1895

The Irish immigrant community in Boston was one expression of the nineteenth-century American Catholic experience. The diocese was established in 1808 with the first creation of new episcopal sees since Baltimore in 1789. A French priest, Jean Lefebvre de Cheverus, was selected as the first bishop. The Church grew slowly but steadily under the guidance of Cheverus but increased significantly under his successors. The immigrant church was dominant during the administration of John Williams, who became the fourth bishop of Boston in March 1866. Donna Merwick has characterized the Williams episcopal administration as one of "sheer drift, a kind of intellectual paralysis" with respect to immigrants and the problems which accompanied their arrival. The diocese was disorganized as the bishop established no ecclesiastical court, made no requirement for parish reports, and failed to establish a seminary until 1884.[7] Williams seems to have feared that any outward demonstration of faith would lessen Catholicism's acceptability. Irish immigrants in Boston society were expected to uphold patterns of social behavior that were acceptable to the upper realms of society. Social deference was demanded of the new arrivals despite an on-going transition in power and dominance from the descendants of the Puritans to Catholics. One measure of this shift was the rate of immigration in the city which increased fifteenfold while the number of Catholics in the city rose to almost one-half million by 1875.[8]

Merwick uses the writing career of John Roddan (d. 1888) to illustrate the haphazard and inconsistent solutions which were proposed for social and religious problems. As priest-editor of the Boston *Pilot* from 1848 to 1858, Roddan promoted Williams' Catholic "invisibility" through his inconsistent opinions in editorials. Catholics could be easily ignored if they took no definite positions nor made waves in the political and social order.[9] There was no recognized plan for Catholic life in Boston.

Williams' response to the perceived need to protect the faithful was to raise an intellectual elite in his clergy who could represent the Catholic laity to the "Yankee" establishment. The founding of Boston College by the Jesuits in 1864 was instrumental in his educational scheme. Jesuit ideas became "a decided factor in the mentality of younger Boston clergy." Since the Jesuits accepted the prevailing American vision of Catholicism, Boston College graduates developed the conviction that a culturally educated Catholic could equal any Protestant in America.[10]

Catholics became more noticeable in Boston after 1875 when their numbers and the importance of the city in American society were recognized by the Holy See and brought about its elevation to the status of an archdiocese. A sense of optimism began to course through the veins of the Boston Church. The Irish lost their traditional pietism, a triptych of race, creed, and nationality, and became more assimilationist in their view of society, a shift which Merwick sees in stampede proportions.[11] A new sense of Irish Catholic presence and power would wait its ultimate champion in William O'Connell, who succeeded Williams as archbishop in 1907.[12]

The Boston-Irish mentality was influential in the development of the young James Martin Gillis, who was born on November 12, 1876, the second of four surviving children of James Gillis and Catherine Roche. His paternal grandparents, natives of Enniskillen County Fermanagh in Northern Ireland, had emigrated to Canada shortly after their marriage. The senior Gillis, born in Montreal, was the eldest of three children born in a ten-year period before his mother died at the age of twenty-nine. This woman, known to James Martin Gillis and his siblings as "Grandmother Greene," was influential in the lives of her children, especially her first-born, James. Young James' paternal grandmother was well educated, a rare opportunity for her day, as a result of her father's position as a tutor to the family of the Duke of Enniskillen. She passed on what she could to her son James before her death. James Gillis, Sr. would later claim that his whole demeanor and way of life came from his mother.[13]

The older Gillis grew to maturity in Canada. Trained as a machinist, he used his skills to work his way from Montreal through northern New England to Boston, arriving in 1870; he became a citizen one year later. It was soon after this that he met Catherine Roche, another first-generation Irish-American. The two courted but Catherine was not initially impressed with the senior Gillis; he seemed too youthful to her. James quickly remedied this situation as he grew a beard, a feature of his appearance which never left him. The couple produced four children who reached maturity, Mary the eldest, James Martin, John, and Katherine. A fifth child, a boy, lived only ten days after birth.

James, Sr. worked hard and received average compensation for a worker of his trade. Catherine maintained things at home as was typical for Irish-American women of her day.[14] John and Mary Gillis stated that their father was the responsible person in the house. Although Catherine Gillis assisted her husband, James Gillis, Sr. was the dominant authority figure. He was one who was exacting in his demands and expectations; yet it appears that he seldom reproached his children. His abiding affection and solid character were the overriding qualities which permeated the Gillis home. Unlike most Irish men of his day, the elder Gillis was closely involved in the religious formation of his children. He listened to them recite their prayers and quizzed them on their religious lessons as well as their courses from the public schools which the Gillis children attended.[15]

James Martin Gillis took after his father in many ways. Physically he followed the Gillis line: short, medium build, and fair. He also possessed many of the mannerisms and actions of his father. The younger Gillis was impressed with the stories of Grandmother Greene and her thirst for knowledge. The desire to learn, combined with native intellectual ability and a strong drive for excellence, made Gillis a candidate for the best schools. Besides physical traits and his academic drive, James also inherited a good sense of humor from his father. Though no court-jester, he did enjoy a good laugh and readily told jokes. Witticisms were part of Gillis's life from his school days to his years of retirement in New York City at the Paulist mother parish, St. Paul the Apostle.[16]

The senior Gillis also bequeathed to his children a sense of moral responsibility and personal duty. Gillis demonstrated little sense of the affective side of religion; there is no evidence that pietism, devotionalism or an emphasis on God's providence was fostered in the Gillis home. Rather, a sense of rugged individualism which James Gillis, Sr. had developed as an immigrant to the United States prevailed. Individuals contributed to society through their own initiative and effort; there was no place for laziness or inattention to duty. James Gillis, Sr. inculcated this belief in his children, a view which was manifest by his namesake in numerous oral and written platforms in a long career as editor and commentator.[17]

Throughout his life Gillis expressed appreciation for his family along his journey to self-understanding. His diaries, retreat notes, and meditation books are replete with anecdotes on family relationships. Throughout his seminary formation he referred to his family whenever they came to visit or wrote to him. He considered himself privileged to have such a family which supported him in so many ways; he was especially grateful for his parents' guidance, concern, and Christian example.

As was common for the majority of Boston's Irish-Catholic population, James Gillis attended public school in the primary and secondary grades.[18] After one year at English High School, he transferred to Boston Latin School, one of the most prestigious secondary schools in the country. Established in 1635, Boston Latin had graduated many famous Americans including the prominent Protestant divines Cotton Mather, Charles Chauncy, and Henry Ward Beecher, founding fathers Benjamin Franklin, Samuel Adams, and John Hancock, and the philosopher and essayist Ralph Waldo Emerson. Matthew Harkins, Bishop of Providence (1887–1921), was also an alumnus. Under the tutelage of Headmaster Moses Merrill, Gillis followed a classical education which included English, Latin, Greek, French, science, mathematics, and classical history.[19] He was an outstanding baseball player. During his senior year he was elected captain of the team and was named to the Massachusetts State High School squad as the best third baseman in the Commonwealth. Upon graduation in June 1895, a year early, Gillis collected numerous other awards, including the prestigious Franklin History Medal and other scholastic accolades.

Gillis possessed a zealous work ethic, the desire to excel, a sense of moral responsibility and personal duty, the ability to achieve, and a drive for perfection. Though he was proud to be a member of Boston's Irish-Catholic community, he seems to have exhibited, as Donna Merwick claims, the traits of "Yankee" society and to have at times distanced himself from his Irish-Catholic culture.[20] One noticeable nod to the Yankee ideal was his prim and proper manner, in dress, decorum, and personal behavior.[21] Gillis also absorbed some ideas of New England Puritanism, such as his strong belief in temperance. Overall, the eighteen-year-old James Gillis was academically quite mature, but he sensed the need to pursue his religious growth. He had been raised in an environment which stressed personal initiative and duty; he now turned to his need to find God.

Following a Vocation—St. Charles College, 1895–1896

Father James J. O'Brien, pastor of St. Catherine's Church in Somerville, Massachusetts, son of Boston mayor Hugh O'Brien, and a Gillis family friend, advised the youth to go to St. Charles College, a minor seminary in Ellicott City, Maryland, to determine whether he had a religious vocation. No minor seminary was present in the archdiocese of Boston. St. Charles, the institution closest to Boston, had served as a primary center to start theological training for Boston priest candidates (including Cardinal William O'Connell) before the establishment of St. John's Seminary in 1884. This pattern continued into the twentieth century.[22] O'Brien had seen Gillis grow and mature from the days when he first taught him and his siblings the doctrines of the faith. The cleric had suggested the possibility of priesthood to Gillis when he was a boy and thus, now as a young adult, James sought assistance and advice from O'Brien. The priest's belief that St. Charles was the place for Gillis, who matriculated there in the fall of 1895, was verified in his personal payment of the tuition costs during his stay.[23] Priesthood at this point, however, was only an idea for the youth. He wrote, "I decided on going to college [St. Charles], not with a sure choice of priesthood, but to find out whether I should like that life."[24]

Gillis's journey from his home to St. Charles became an event of significant revelation to the young man. On September 8, 1895 he traveled from Boston to Fall River by train with fellow Bostonians Will Grant and Jim McCue; Gillis was never again to spend more than summers with his family. There the three met four other young men who were also bound for the Maryland college. Together the youths boarded the steamer *Pilgrim* and continued their trip to Baltimore. Aboard the vessel, Gillis met a man who claimed that he was a priest. This cleric was intoxicated and invited the boys to imbibe with him in drink. In his diary Gillis expounded on how the incident mortified him and moved him forcefully to swear off drinking for his entire life.[25] He would later campaign often and zealously for personal temperance by means of parish missions, editorials, syndicated columns, radio addresses, and speeches, and through membership in the Catholic Total Abstinence Union of America. Along the road to priesthood James Gillis clearly placed himself in the "dry" camp; he never abandoned this opinion.[26]

Various opinions as to the source of Gillis's belief in personal abstinence exist. Merwick claims that he saw drinking as a general problem for the whole generation of Boston's clergy born twenty years before him. Finley believes that Gillis's opinion and later outward campaign for temperance were generated in his family, especially his father, and his association with New England's residual Puritanism. James Gillis, Sr. was raised in the rigorism of French Canada and he never drank. The residue of Boston Puritanism as well as the remains and the presence of Irish rigorists in the Boston area also must have influenced the young Gillis. Mary Gillis thought that her brother's aversion to alcohol was as a result of observing its destructive effects in the lives of neighbors. The incident on the *Pilgrim* would be evidence to this effect.[27]

The ideas of his father, as noted earlier, were important to the St. Charles student in these early years. Gillis quoted him, "The great curse of the Catholic priesthood in this country is drink." A lecture at St. Charles in November 1895 against the vices of drink, impurity, and love of money prompted the youth to state, "This talk caused me to take a strong resolution to continue total abstinence from liquor and to avoid the other sins." Gillis's arguments against liquor encompassed both the physical and spiritual realms. Late in the school year he wrote,

> Even if it were not a moral curse, alcohol is fully worthy of being banished as a physical curse. With God's help, I fully resolve never to take a drop of liquor beyond necessity.

From his personal papers it is clear that he was faithful to his pledge.[28]

When Gillis arrived at St. Charles in mid-September 1895 he found a well ordered and established program of study in place. The institution had opened on October 31, 1848 under the guidance of Father Oliver Jenkins. The Society of Saint Sulpice, a community of diocesan clergy who specialized in the religious formation of young men for the priesthood, had obtained 250 acres of land in January 1830 near Ellicott City, Maryland from a donation by Charles Carroll of Carrollton. The Sulpicians hoped to open a *petit seminaire* to serve as a feeder school for St. Mary's, the original national seminary established and run by the Society in Baltimore since October 1791.[29]

The question of his religious vocation became a primary source of meditation and concern for the first-year student. A daily regimen of prayer, meditation, physical exercise, and spiritual reading, in line with the Sulpician model of religious formation, paralleled the rigorous academic schedule that one might expect in a college. To discern his religious vocation caused concern for Gillis, who sensed periods of anxiety. He wrote, "The immense responsibility which a decision [about the priesthood] entails frightens me, makes me see I am incapable of doing anything myself and forces me to trust wholly in the guidance of God."[30]

The academic program which he followed at St. Charles complemented the classical education he had received at Boston Latin. The curriculum was a modified form of the Jesuits' *ratio studiorum*, but put less emphasis on philosophy and science and more on English composition, grammar, and literature.[31] Gillis's diaries abound with comments about his academic performance, comparisons of his work with others, and fears that he would not gain top honors. Gillis not only wanted to do well for himself, he wanted to outshine others. He lists the scores of specific tests, refers to those who "rushed" (received the highest mark on) the exams, and compares his performance to that of his classmates.[32] He was obsessed with the idea of achievement to the point that he had almost a compulsive drive for perfection. For example, he felt anguish over his score on a history examination that he considered too long and intricate. His frustration with the examination was transformed to fear when he considered the possibility that he might lose the "summa." Gillis's competitive spirit drove him to work toward "'the' first honor," on graduation day.[33]

Gillis's experience at St. Charles was flavored with many special events and people. Although present for only a brief period at the outset of the year, Charles B. Rex made a deep and permanent impression on the youth from Boston. Rex had been the rector at St. John's Seminary in Brighton, the regional seminary for the Boston archdiocese, established in 1884. He was scheduled to be the founding rector for St. Joseph's Seminary at Dunwoodie for the archdiocese of New York, but complications from the early stages of consumption brought him to St. Charles as president. Gillis's laudatory comments about Rex were extensive. He described the Sulpician as "a model man," "a man in a million," one "beyond praise."[34] Rex's influence on Gillis was remarkable for so short an acquaintance; the priest was forced to leave his post at the college in early November 1895 due to illness. He was sent to Colorado Springs with hope for recovery but died there in February 1897.

James Gillis's year at St. Charles was formative in the development of his political ideas as well. In January 1895 the entire student body went to Baltimore to attend special ceremonies in honor of Archbishop Francesco Satolli, apostolic delegate in the United States. Gillis wrote that the homily delivered at Mass by Archbishop John Kain of St. Louis "contained nothing extraordinarily fine." Yet, his diary entry specifically mentions how the sermon spoke of the similarity in governance between the Church and the United States, an idea that would complement his Paulist formation and charism, and the support he gave to individual freedom in his later editorial opinion.[35]

In May 1896 Father Elias Younan, a Paulist priest, came to St.

Charles to give a presentation on India. Gillis described the talk as a "most excellent lecture, in fact, a lecture that astonished me."[36] One can reason in hindsight that the lecture meant more to Gillis than an interesting presentation about a culture on the other side of the globe. It is probable that Younan's missionary vision was the principal attraction to Gillis. Seeds were planted in the youth's mind on the need for evangelization, not only overseas but, at least equally important, at home. Younan was the first Paulist he had met, and less than ten years later these two would be matched to preach missions to non-Catholics in Chicago.

Joseph Gibbons, a man who became a lifelong friend, companion, and confidant, also entered Gillis's life at St. Charles. The two shared what James F. Finley has described as a "chosen friendship."[37] Since Gillis was individualistic and competitive and did not make friends readily, it is significant that he spoke of Joseph Gibbons in respectful and laudatory terms, describing him as "a mighty good fellow."[38] Over the years Gillis and Gibbons spent many vacation periods together and gained mutual trust. When Gillis experienced one of his many bouts with illness Gibbons came to visit him. Later, Gillis wrote to his friend as if he were a brother:

> I have sent a note of thanks to everybody who was so wonderful and who helped me so much in my illness. I've saved you for the end and thanking you seems out of place. I mean by that, that it is impossible to really thank your own flesh and blood.[39]

Gibbons knew Gillis well, describing him as "a serious type" who seemed older than his contemporaries in ideas, attitudes, manners, and purpose. He further characterized Gillis as "Bostonese" from head to toe, a confirmation of his manifest "Yankee" character. His proper manner in appearance and speech made him appear to some as aloof and standoffish, but Gibbons discounted this idea, saying it was a false perception.[40] Gillis was a difficult man to get to know and understand, but once his rather stiff and formal personality was accepted, friends appreciated his humor and wit.

St. John's Seminary, Brighton—1896–1898

St. John's Seminary opened on September 22, 1884 and functioned as a regional seminary for the New England area.[41] John Hogan served as the first superior and rector from 1884 to 1889. Hogan, described by Christopher Kauffman as a major figure in Catholic progressive thought, possessed liberal ecclesial views, endorsed much of Modernist Scripture scholarship, and was in sympathy to the Americanist cause.[42]

The liberal tendencies present at St. John's were continued and amplified by Charles B. Rex, the second rector, who served from 1889 to 1895. Rex promoted modern methods which were very American in flavor. He initiated affiliation of St. John's with The Catholic University of America so that seminary students could achieve bachelor degrees in philosophy and theology. Although the plan was never formally instituted, several fourth-year students at St. John's were able to attend the University and obtain degrees. Rex promoted new intellectual and social trends and he stocked the seminary library and reading room with scholarly reviews and newspapers. Additionally, he advocated physical conditioning for all seminarians.[43]

St. John's provided traditional formation for priesthood as influenced by its American environment. The reforms which Rex initiated were departures from Sulpician tradition, but in themselves were not rooted in any "ideological relation to Americanism." Rather the progressive methods at St. John's were simply American in nature. This is evident when one considers that the anti-Americanist Bishop Bernard McQuaid (Rochester) fashioned his new St. Bernard's Seminary, established in 1893, on a strong American model.[44] Robert Sullivan has characterized St. John's during this period as a place where academic preparation took a subordinate role to religious formation. Sullivan says this was particularly true after Cardinal O'Connell removed the Sulpicians from St. John's in 1911.[45]

Gillis arrived at St. John's in September 1896 to study for the archdiocese of Boston. Finley claims that he came to the seminary with no particular agenda other than "to look at the priesthood and go where the archbishop might place him."[46] There was no formal commitment at this time to the priesthood; yet he was a man who weighed his options, made clear decisions, and held to his convictions with tenacity. Gillis's option for priesthood would be transformed during his two-year stay at the Brighton seminary into a quest for personal worthiness to participate in the sacerdotal life, which satisfied his sense of duty and brought him to the exalted state of "perfection" he sought.

The academic life at St. John's initially appealed to Gillis and he attacked it with characteristic fervor. His desire to excel was always at the forefront; it was a mainstay of his personal understanding which he developed during this period of education and formation. Gillis's diaries again speak of his motivation to excel, his lofty academic goals, and his achievement as the top student of his class.[47] He began to expect this as his normal course of events.

As at St. Charles, Gillis developed important personal relationships while at St. John's. Francis Gigot (1859–1920), a noted Scripture scholar and graduate of the Institut Catholique de Paris, taught at St. John's from 1885 to 1899. Kauffman states that Gigot and his colleague James Driscoll "represented the most advanced thought on Scripture studies at the [Catholic] university."[48] Gigot was Gillis's professor and advisor, but more important he was his friend. Gillis described him as "perfectly incomparable in his efforts to help me with any director I have formerly had."[49] The spiritual direction which Gillis received in the sacrament of penance inspired the youth to write of Gigot's "wonderful interest in penitents" and his "kind heart." Gillis already possessed much of the French Sulpician's work ethic which he quoted, "Do not be satisfied with superficiality....Permit no slovenly work. Do things with energy and interest, not half-hearted." He was struck by Gigot's personal qualities as a teacher, preacher, and also a tennis player.[50]

Despite his admiration for Gigot and Rex, Gillis complained many times in his diary about the methods used at the seminary dominated by a regimen which provided no room for individual responsibility and choice, basic tenets of Gillis's emerging world view. The community was seldom open to constructive criticism when suggestions came from the outside. He wrote in disgust about how the examination schedule was destructive of health and incompatible with one's ability to gain knowledge: "It is a marvel to me that men who have spent their whole lives in teaching should show such absolute ignorance as to hygiene and even as to the best methods to get good results."[51]

Gillis's condescending criticism of the Sulpicians illustrates the passion with which he would later express his views on national and international events in several media forms. He began to understand himself as a man of conviction along the lines suggested by his father's example. He did not merely voice his opinion, but rather tended to state his views in uncompromising, patronizing, and sarcastic ways. James Gillis possessed great tenacity in his thought; he never backed down from his opinions or what he knew to be right.

Gillis's personal understanding of priesthood took a significant step forward during his first year at Brighton when he observed his first ordination. The experience electrified him and ignited an intense meditation on his progress toward ordination. He wrote, "God grant that when my time come [*sic*], if it be His will that it come, I may take the step [of orders] without hesitation, feeling confident that I am doing what is God's will." At the time he only asked "to be directed by God during the coming year." Father James O'Brien, who continued to serve as mentor and to give financial support, wrote to the youth in January 1897 with encouragement on his progress and direction toward understanding his vocation which O'Brien seemed to convey as a certitude.[52]

Gillis was profoundly affected when he attended a talk by Walter Elliott, the Paulist evangelist:

> The impression left on me by his address was wonderful,— for some time after I could hardly speak, being filled with admiration for the man and for his work, and with the feeling of my own littleness and unworthiness.[53]

His chance meeting of Walter Elliott was transformative in a way that would only be seen in retrospect. For the moment, however, it is apparent that Gillis was attracted not only by what Elliott said, his personality and missionary spirit, but also to the society of priests of which he was a member, and their apostolate of evangelization.

He described the "inextinguishable enthusiasm of Fr. Elliott and his community....It is like enjoying a refreshing breeze to listen to them [the Paulists] and the results are far more beneficial from such [a] talk than from a thousand 'spiritual readings,' etc." Gillis was also impressed with the "splendid optimism" of the Paulists. He wrote, "Never a hopeless word escapes them. They seem to be carried along in a blast of enthusiasm that permits them no time for pessimism and discouragement." Gillis concluded his long reflection, "Oh, how I should like to be such a priest!"[54]

His enthusiasm for Walter Elliott and the other Paulists seems to have ignited further criticism of the Sulpicians and St. John's in general. He referred to insufficient life and vigor in the seminary environment to adequately nurture and cultivate his religious vocation; it was not the place where a Walter Elliott, a man he considered to possess boundless energy and deep and varied knowledge, could have thrived.

> There is too little opportunity to advance, too much waste of time and energy and (though I may be rash, and perhaps should not say so after only one year's experience) too much misguided effort. I long for something better and I would gladly grasp a proffered chance at improvement.[55]

William Laurence Sullivan, a Bostonian who followed the route from St. John's to the Paulists and was a contemporary of Gillis, also complained about the formation at the Brighton seminary. He referred to the teaching staff as "of no blazing brilliance" and rejected the "incessant rounds of memory recitations."[56]

Walter Elliott's religious community, the Congregation of Missionary Priests of St. Paul the Apostle, commonly known as the Paulists, was organized in 1858 under the guidance of Isaac Thomas Hecker and three associates, Augustine Hewit, George Deshon, and Francis Baker, all converts. Hecker had converted to Catholicism after searching for a religious practice and charism in accord with his personal spirituality. He was ordained a Redemptorist priest on October 23, 1849 at the hands of Bishop (later Cardinal Archbishop of Westminster) Nicholas Wiseman in England. Hecker's missionary commitment as a

Redemptorist was soon manifested in his ministry in the United States. He became convinced that what America needed was a new foundation of the Redemptorists aimed toward mission work in the United States. When Hecker went to Rome in August 1857 to plead for such a wing of the community, he was promptly expelled from the order for his unauthorized trip.

Hecker found friends in high places in Rome, however, in the person of Alessandro Barnabò, prefect of the Congregation of the Propaganda, which supervised American affairs. Barnabò spoke with Pius IX, who released Hecker and his associates from their vows and suggested that they form a new community. Back in the United States, Hecker discussed his plan with his friends. A "Programme Rule" was drawn up and approved by Archbishop John Hughes of New York on July 10, 1858. Hecker believed that America needed the new religious community to carry the message of Catholicism to non-Catholics.[57]

Although he might not have realized it, Gillis was clearly accurate when he described Walter Elliott as "the celebrated Paulist." Elliott was a Civil War veteran, who, after that national conflict, attended the University of Notre Dame. In the late 1860s, when he was living in Detroit and practicing law, Elliott heard Hecker speak; the impression made was deep and permanent. Elliott saw the Paulist founder as one who stamped the label of "American" on every Catholic argument. After this 1868 encounter, with little thought and no formal introduction, Elliott traveled to New York City to present himself as a candidate for the Paulist Fathers. Thomas Jonas considers Elliott "the heir of Hecker's religious vision and vocation"; he was to carry the mantle of the founder.[58]

Elliott had distinguished himself in the Paulist community. He took care of Hecker the last four years of the founder's life and wrote his biography, *The Life of Father Hecker,* which appeared in 1891. By the time Gillis heard him speak at St. John's he was a well-known evangelist, particularly devoted to the cause of missions to non-Catholics. In 1893 he gave a stirring speech at Chicago's Catholic Congress (part of the World's Columbian Exposition) on the need to evangelize America's non-Catholic population. This led to the initiation of missions to non-Catholics in the Midwest. In 1896, along with a fellow Paulist, Alexander P. Doyle, he established the Catholic Missionary Union and its organ *The Missionary* for the promotion of missionary zeal in the American Catholic community.[59]

In his ministry and theological vision, Walter Elliott typified the Paulist tradition.[60] He believed that God had acted in America to resolve divisions within Christendom and to provide a model of Catholicism compatible with an age of social individualism and political liberalism. Additionally, he believed the Paulist community's mission was to promote the personal sanctity of the faithful and to labor for the salvation of souls. He was the principal Hecker disciple who took up the task of fulfilling the work which the founder envisioned and proclaimed.[61]

Along with his friend, colleague, and fellow convert Orestes Brownson, Hecker preached the total compatibility between democracy and Catholicism. He once stated, "I have the conviction that I can be all the better Catholic because I am an American: and all the better American because I am Catholic."[62] This in essence became the Paulist philosophy of mission and evangelization. The spirituality which Hecker bequeathed to his followers was rooted in the pluralism of America which he had experienced. Combining Protestant and Catholic influences he promoted a spirituality emphasizing submission to God's Spirit, focus on the interior life, and self-abandonment to the will of Divine Providence. The Paulist spirituality was distinctly American in its belief that God had chosen the United States for a special mission. She was the city on the hill of Protestant theology, but she was not to shine this concept of faith, but the glories of a renewed Catholicism.[63]

Hecker's earlier writings demonstrate these themes. *Questions of the Soul* (1855) was written to non-Catholics to show them that only the Catholic Church could satisfy the cravings of the human heart. In *Aspirations of Nature* (1858) Hecker took an intellectual tack to show how both philosophy and Protestantism failed to answer humanity's quest of the mind—only Catholicism could so function. *The Church and the Age* (1887) was composed with a double theme: (1) America is most congenial to Christianity, and (2) the mission of the American

Church is to show both its citizens and Europeans that only Catholicism can properly effect the needed synthesis between Christianity and republicanism.[64]

With the seed of his Paulist vocation and its missionary spirit sown, Gillis returned to St. John's in September 1897 for the opening retreat. He seemed to have softened his competitive edge. He concluded that there were many intelligent men at Brighton and thus he must learn "to resign the honors if necessary with grace and without harm to myself from discouragement or lapse of earnestness." However, he continued to refer to his classmates as his "rivals" and always maintained his personal standard of excellence.[65]

The summer also provided him with time and space to reflect upon his vocation with a sense of certitude. The seminary had become for him "the most natural thing in the world." On his twenty-first birthday he reflected on how often he had looked forward to this day, but his thoughts were more pointed to the possibility of priesthood than personal maturity when he wrote, "God grant me that I may see that [ordination] day."[66]

In the spring Gillis again began to review his call to a religious vocation. In April he accepted tonsure as a first step toward his goal. He realized that priesthood has a dignity that he was unworthy to attain, but he was determined to climb from the depths of unworthiness to the plane of reconciliation, his personal ideal of "perfection."[67]

St. Thomas Seminary—1898–1901

The summer of 1898 was a turning point in the life of James Martin Gillis. James O'Brien suggested that his protégé should speak with Paulist Father Peter O'Callaghan about his future and the decision which ultimately needed to be made. O'Callaghan, a Massachusetts native who had graduated from Harvard in 1888 and attended St. John's for one year, was ordained in 1893. For three days, August 14–16, Gillis met with O'Callaghan at St. Paul the Apostle Church in New York City. The Paulist suggested that Gillis abandon himself totally to God so as to discover his vocation.

Gillis, who expressed his unworthiness, reported the results of daily conferences:

> He [O'Callaghan] asked me to put before him all the objections I could think of which might prevent my becoming a Paulist. I did so, he countered them, considered them as unimportant, and then said flatly that he believed I am called to be a Paulist.[68]

Gillis returned home to Boston and contemplated his future. He was certain that the Paulists would provide endless activity which would be welcome by his aggressive nature, but it was the missionary spirit of evangelization which he observed in Younan and, especially, Elliott, that he found most attractive. Additionally, he began to feel the diocesan priesthood would not provide the variety or challenge that he sought; the "underpinnings of his resistance [began to] melt away." Gillis finally decided that he would take Father O'Callaghan's advice as the will of God in his life.[69] He left Boston on September 7, 1898 and two days later arrived in Washington where on September 11 James Gillis officially matriculated at St. Thomas College, the Paulist novitiate and formation house in Washington, D.C.[70]

The Paulists were the first congregation to accept John Keane's 1887 general offer for religious communities to relocate their houses of formation at or near the new Catholic University of America, which was authorized by the American hierarchy at the Third Plenary Council of Baltimore (1884) and approved by Pope Leo XIII in April 1887. The University opened in November 1889 with Keane as the first rector.[71] The Paulists negotiated a twenty-five-year lease of the Middleton mansion on the University grounds, at an annual rent of $600, for use as a formation house. The Society occupied this building until October 1914 when St. Paul's College was opened on ground purchased from the Stuart family behind the Dominican House of Studies.[72]

Gillis thrived in the environment at St. Thomas which possessed a progressive spirit tempered with discipline.[73] Peter O'Callaghan introduced several reforms when he took the reins as novice master. Students were granted many freedoms including permission to read newspapers and to smoke at designated times. Walks were permitted on study days and music and athletics were promoted for general participation.[74]

The progressive administration of O'Callaghan was balanced, in contrast to St. John's, by the Paulist traditionalist Constitution of 1898. A regular routine of prayer, meditation, and study was enforced. Students were required to practice daily two thirty-minute meditations, spiritual reading, rosary recitation, particular examen, thanksgiving, Mass, and a visit to the Blessed Sacrament. All were also required to observe house silence, receive weekly confession, and attend an annual week-long retreat.[75]

More important for Gillis, in his steady climb from the depths of personal unworthiness and his quest for self-understanding, the rule stated that Paulists were to "labor in the Society for their own perfection." Perfection was to be fostered by observance of the evangelical counsels of poverty, chastity, and obedience—these being the foundation of the constitutions and, thus, of the community's life and ministry.[76] This quest for spiritual perfection was nearly insatiable for James Gillis and caused him severe internal conflict for a number of years. He understood himself as one who must attain perfection as the only possible means to respond to the exalted position of ordained life.[77] Gillis was not able to see the providence of God in his life, but rather, refuting Luther's adage *sola fide,* believed it was necessary for him (all society for that matter) to save himself. The positive anthropology of Isaac Hecker was not present; Gillis's search for God was never fulfilled.

Like the other religious houses in the area, St. Thomas enjoyed an affiliation with Catholic University which allowed seminary students to utilize the greater resources of a larger school. During his student days Gillis was taught by some of the best minds in the country including Thomas Shahan in history, Charles Grannan in Scripture, and William Kerby in sociology. Gillis was educated in the neo-scholastic tradition, as mandated by the Pope, with its strong emphasis on moral absolutes. He utilized the academic opportunities afforded him to stimulate his mind, form his conscience, and aid his mental preparation for ministry.[78]

As he started his new life as a Paulist, the American nation experienced its own renewal, in both domestic and international affairs. The economic depression of 1893 to 1897 and the trend toward trusts and monopoly engendered widespread discontent and a spirit of reform. The depression in agriculture created the environment for the emergence of Populism, an energetic but localized (principally in the South, Great Plains, and West) movement that aimed to restore farm profits in the face of much exploitation and under unfavorable market and price conditions. Cooperatives recruited farmers for an alliance which became the organizational structure of the movement. Populists blamed the government and its 1873 adoption of the gold standard for the many problems in agriculture. While the Populist (People's) Party in the 1892 and 1896 national elections promoted reasonable political reform, such as a graduated income tax and popular election of senators, the movement was dominated by free silverites who poisoned its potential. Still, the party provided a service in calling attention to growing monopolies and problems which agriculture suffered.[79]

On the international scene the short-lived Spanish-American War placed the United States at center stage in the world. Almost overnight, with the defeat of the old world power Spain, the United States advanced to international recognition. America's global presence was strengthened and broadened with the annexation of the Philippine Islands, a spoil of the War.[80]

Gillis was an anti-imperialist. He favored the avoidance of conflict with Spain at all costs, writing that the war sentiment was carried by, "a group of warriors in the U[nited] S[tates] Senate who would delight in a safe encounter with unfortunate Spain." He commented that America's actions were "a poor pretext for waging war."[81] Gillis had two years earlier concluded about war, "I should much prefer to live in an age of peace. If it be glorious to be even a mere contemporary of great war, how much more so must it be to live in an age rewardable for its acts of peace."[82]

Gillis fully entered into the life of his new community of St. Thomas. Although he was far from home and lamented the fact that he would not be able to regularly see his family, as in the past two years, he was happy at the Paulist house of studies.[83] His parents' approval of his decision to enter the Paulists made the transition easier. On November 1, 1898 he and nine others received the Paulist habit from Superior General George Deshon, in a ceremony witnessed by representatives of several religious communities and William Kerby.[84]

In January 1899 the American Catholic Church found itself on the plane of ascendancy as evidenced in many areas. Although the APA had recently been active, its nativist animus was in decline. Forty years earlier, Catholicism had become the largest religious denomination in the country. The Church was established from East to West with its (unofficial) primate, Cardinal James Gibbons, in residence in Baltimore. The Catholic University of America had been established and would be recognized for its scholarship.

The Paulist community also enjoyed growth and a sense of accomplishment as the twentieth century beckoned. Under Deshon the new Paulist Constitution of 1898 made the election of community superior more democratic through the institution of a popular vote and a reduction in the term of office from nine years to five. Paulist publications, *The Catholic World* and *The Missionary,* were well respected and widely read in their presentation of a wide spectrum of issues. The missionary spirit of the community was expanded with the opening of a parish in Winchester, Tennessee and the Apostolic Mission House in Washington, D.C. in 1902, as well as the assumption in 1903 of Old Saint Mary's parish in downtown Chicago. Thus, at the dawn of the new century, the Paulists were in possession of mission bases in the north, south, east, and west (Old Saint Mary's in San Francisco had been obtained in 1894) sections of the country, plus a school of missiology. The community was poised to pursue Hecker's dream of the conversion of America.

However, the publication of *Testem Benevolentiae,* an apostolic letter addressed to Cardinal Gibbons on January 22, 1899, sent the American Church and the Paulist community into a tailspin which took several years to halt before a restoration could begin. The letter said that an end must be put "to certain tendencies which have arisen lately among you, and which disturb the minds if not of all, at least of many, to the no slight detriment of peace."[85] The Pope referred to what has become known in history as Americanism. A detailed analysis of this major American

Catholic controversy is beyond the scope of this work; yet it is important to understand its impact on the Paulist community and the life of James Martin Gillis.[86]

In the United States the controversy pitted traditionalist bishops, championed by Michael Corrigan, Bernard McQuaid, and Frederick Katzer, against the transformationist leaders John Ireland, John Keane, and Denis O'Connell. James Gibbons played a supporting role for the progressives. The Paulist community became embroiled in the affair in a rather unforseeable way. After the death of Isaac Hecker, community Superior Augustine Hewit asked Walter Elliott to write a biography of the founder. Since Elliott had been at Hecker's side for the last four years of his life, the assignment was natural and welcomed. In 1898 a French translation of Elliott's monograph, *La Vie du Père Hecker*, was published with a new introduction by Abbé Felix Klein. Klein characterized Hecker as a man of action, the ideal contemporary priest, gifted with all the virtues characteristic of an American, including the belief in the compatibility of democracy with Catholicism.

French Catholics who supported the monarchy associated Hecker with the evils of anticlericalism, liberalism, and subjectivism, a blend of the twin evils of the Protestant Reformation and the French Revolution.[87] Abbé Charles Maignen, the French monarchist champion, wrote a series of essays in the Parisian daily *La Verité* which were later collected and published as a book, *Le Père Hecker, est-il un Saint?* This polemical work condemned many of Hecker's ideas, as outlined by Klein, and attacked Ireland, O'Connell, and other leaders of the American progressives.

Testem was an effort to calm the stormy waters threatening the Church. The apostolic letter became, however, in the minds of some,[88] including James Gillis and George Deshon, an indictment of Isaac Hecker and the charism of the Paulist Fathers. As was the custom of the period, spiritual reading was conducted during meals at St. Thomas. The publication of *Testem Benevolentiae*, which included the association of "Heckerism" with Americanism, altered the pattern for two days as the letter was read and repeated for all to hear in the seminary refectory. Gillis considered *Testem* "an insidious attack on Heckerism," the Paulist community, and its philosophy. He called these accusations and insinuations "little short of wicked," concluding, "Our Holy Father the Pope is in evident ignorance concerning what true Americanism is."[89] Deshon called upon his ordinary, Michael Corrigan of New York, who had granted the original *imprimatur* for the biography, to aid in clearing the Paulists' name, which had been besmirched in the controversy. The archbishop, however, refused to act, which demonstrated his traditionalist stance and kept a pall of suspicion over the Society.[90]

While the traditionalist bishops welcomed *Testem*, the reaction of the Americanists was denial.[91] Gillis maintained that Americanism could be labeled as a "phantom heresy." This view was consistent from his days as a student to his retirement over half a century later. His foreword to the fourth volume of the memoirs of Abbé Klein is illustrative,

> The storm of "Americanism" ought never to have happened. It was artificially produced. Its sound and fury signified nothing. There was no heresy and no schism.[92]

The storm which raged over *Testem Benevolentiae* at this time was one element of a larger issue of the period which questioned the compatibility of Catholicism and the American principles of government. The issue was raised at the Third Plenary Council of Baltimore (1884) where the bishops concluded:

> We repudiate with equal earnestness the assertion that we need to lay aside any of our devotedness to our Church, to be true Americans; the insinuation that we need to abate any of our love for our country's principles and institutions, to be faithful Catholics. To argue that the Catholic Church is hostile to our great republic...is evidently so illogical and contradictory an accusation, that we are astonished to hear it advanced by persons of ordinary intelligence.[93]

The leading Americanists pushed the argument one step further and claimed a connection existed between Catholicism and the principles of democratic government. John Keane, while rector of The Catholic University, wrote, "The Constitution of the United States has innovated nothing, differs in nothing from the principles ever held by the Catholic Church."[94] In a similar view, John Ireland stated, "By the terms of the Federal Constitution as by the teachings of the Catholic Church, no room is given in America for discord between Catholicism and Americanism, between my Catholic faith and my civic and political allegiance."[95]

The view which linked American democracy and Catholicism was not confined to the frontline progressives. James McFaul, Bishop of Trenton, wrote of the support which American Catholics had always shown to the Constitution. The Harvard-educated attorney Henry Sedgwick claimed that the "Church has been the greatest democratic power in the western world." A third author concluded, "Indeed, between the American Constitution and that of the Roman Church analogies meet us at all points."[96] As editor of *The Catholic World*, Gillis would many times comment and always uphold what he perceived as the unity of American democracy and Catholic moral principles.[97]

Four months after *Testem* was published, James Gillis and seven others received minor orders at the hands of Alfred Curtis, Bishop of Wilmington. At the same time his friends William Laurence Sullivan and John J. Burke were ordained to the diaconate. Gillis reflected that the community would be well served by such members.[98]

His second year at St. Thomas opened, as was the common practice, with a community retreat led by Walter Elliott, the new novice master at the seminary. Although the experience of *Testem* would make Elliott more pessimistic, Gillis was again mesmerized by the man whose presence and missionary spirit had struck him so powerfully in his first year at Brighton. The retreat proved to be a major step for Gillis in his self-understanding as priest. He contemplated the cost of priesthood and his ill-preparedness,

> What is the cost? It will cost *work*, it will cost *self-denial*, it will cost *mortification*, it will cost mental and spiritual anguish, it will cost *patience*, it will cost *prayer* [Gillis's emphases], which I am beginning to understand is, with its accessions and preparations, the supreme mortification. There's not one of these things in the attempt to secure evidence which I have been in any way conspicuously successful.[99]

Elliott's retreat also ignited in Gillis a near-stifling view of the justice of God and eternal punishment. He spoke to the novices of the life of a missionary and the cautions one must always observe in such an environment. Priests must be constantly aware of their roles and their responsibilities. Gillis reflected on Elliott's warning, "The fear of the Justice of God, the terror of Hell, must never be banished from the Spiritual Life."[100] Gillis sensed his imminent association with the forces of evil, the absence of God's providence, and ultimately his inability to achieve spiritual reconciliation or as he termed it "perfection."

Gillis closed the retreat by receiving the sacrament of penance from his mentor, an experience that rekindled the fire which had blazed in their first meeting. "It [confession] was the most apparent and sensible manifestation I have ever experienced of God's mercy and love to me and of his [Elliott's] request that I give myself to Him in love." If Elliott had changed it was not evident to Gillis, whose idealistic admiration for him had not dimmed:

> He certainly is a saintly man and [possesses] a grand robust character. The love of God is all over him and inside and above him, so that he seems to be carried along in his duties by a supernatural grace for zeal.[101]

Walter Elliott had a reciprocal feeling for Gillis when he wrote, "Gillis is a star. He's as bright as he can be and he is so pious he shames me."[102]

Gillis's experience as a penitent was consistent with the theory of reconciliation which Elliott promoted in his later writings. An advocate of Salesian spirituality,[103] Elliott perceived the sacrament of penance as a condition in which "fraternal love is most deliberate and its highest activity"; it is "the most human of the sacraments." Elliott believed that the purgative way must lead to self-abnegation; confession brings the penitent to this state of humility.[104] For Gillis, however, this experience was formative in a way that would only be fully revealed as his Paulist identity as a missionary preacher emerged. Confession provided the opportunity to exercise free choice in one's desire to experience repentance and a change of heart. Gillis believed that the individual choice of conversion was a golden kernel of good which all had the possibility to possess. Personal conversion, as experienced through confession, was the first step required in the transformation of society.

As the time for Gillis's ordination to the diaconate approached, the internal struggle between his personal call to spiritual perfection and the reality of the broken world he experienced was a prominent theme of reflection. He firmly believed that to identify himself as priest he had to attain spiritual perfection. He wrote that such a lofty goal was possible with the help of Christ:

> How impossible for me ever to begin to approach to the perfection that is required. Impossible? No! Because my God is also man. The divine perfections that are my standard have been humanized, tempered to my needs and my comprehension by their passage through human flesh in Jesus my Savior.[105]

This concept of depending upon Christ for perfection was, however, more theoretical than experiential for Gillis. In practice his existential belief of God's response and the need to perform one's duty seem to have precluded a sense of God's presence in his life, although he held hope for its possibility. The sense of duty was imbedded in his vocation. On December 20, 1900 he and five classmates were received into the community by Father Elliott; the next day they were ordained deacons by Bishop Curtis. The proximity of the culmination of his long-standing goal precipitated a series of reflections in his meditation books where he continued to emphasize his personal need for spiritual perfection. He realized that the priest must achieve the highest sanctity "that is attainable," possess a spirit of love so as "to lighten the burdens of a priest's life," and live purely in every way.

> There—that frightening word perfection. Can I escape it? Has God called me to perfection? He surely has, for He has called me to the priesthood. There can be no doubt about that. The state of the priesthood is the state of perfection.[106]

Gillis's concept of perfection was derived from several sources. The Paulist Constitution, based on Jesus' exhortation to His disciples, "You must be perfect as your heavenly Father is perfect" (Matthew 5:48), called for spiritual perfection as the primary goal for community members. Another source of his understanding was the writing of Cardinal Henry Edward Manning. In his diaries, retreat notes, and meditation books, Gillis often quoted from Manning's *The Eternal Priesthood.* The English prelate saw no greater vocation than the priesthood and its two great powers and privileges, consecration of the Body and Blood of Christ and absolution. Guided by the scholastic thought of Thomas Aquinas and Albertus Magnus, Manning said the priest must attain the greatest sanctity and spiritual perfection. One should not be ordained until this is possible. For Manning spiritual perfection meant "freedom from the power of sin," not the attainment of a sinless state. Gillis constantly feared that he could not escape the power of sin and thus felt unworthy. Yet, his faith yielded a positive assessment of his call to the priesthood and the hope of God's love.[107]

The day of a priest's ordination is a special rite of passage and so it was for James Martin Gillis. His family came to New York City for the great event. The ordination took place on December 21, 1901 at St. Paul the Apostle Church. Archbishop Michael Corrigan presided at the ordination of James Gillis and his classmates Thomas Verner Moore, Thomas Healy, and Dennis Devine.[108] That day the new priest wrote in his diary, "I resolve, God aiding me—to pray with constancy and fidelity—to give myself to the best kind of prayer that God shall make possible for me."[109]

Boston-born Irish Catholic James Gillis spent the early years of his life in a quest for personal understanding as a priest. Along the road of his early life journey Gillis was introduced to people, ideas, and movements which meshed together to form a hybrid set of influences that ultimately created in him a dualistic world view. This understanding became the foundation to a long period of internal conflict and was integral to his public life as a preacher to various peoples, under multiple media, and at different times. The path also provided numerous occasions for personal growth through educational opportunities, friendships, and the time to reflect on his life as priest and Paulist.

Personal relationships played a significant role in this formative time of Gillis's life. From his father he gained a sense of moral responsibility and personal duty that became constituent to his self-understanding. The famed Paulist evangelist, Walter Elliott, planted the seed of his religious vocation and made an impression on the youth that was deep and permanent. Gillis was attracted by Elliott's personality, rugged individualism, pastoral presence, missionary spirit and membership in the Paulist community. Additionally, he discovered through Elliott the need for conversion, a process which all people could experience through the exercise of one's free choice. Gillis's youth experience also provided him with a lifelong friend and confidant in Joseph Gibbons.

Events and movements also played a major role in the formation of Gillis's identity as priest and Paulist. The Spanish-American War initiated a thought process which would later lead to a complete rejection of war. Gillis answered the condemnation of Americanism in 1899 with a spirited denial of its presence in the American Church and an equally strong defense of the Paulist community which felt the full force of the attack.

Seeds for James Gillis's dualistic world view and his Paulist identity as a missionary to America were planted early in his life. Nurtured by people, movements, and events, the seeds germinated and grew roots which anchored themselves deep into the fertile soil of his impressionable heart and mind. Ordained for service to God, the Church, and the Paulist community, Gillis was ready to enter fully into his role as priest and Paulist.

CHAPTER 2

The Young Paulist—1902–1910

The dawn of the twentieth century brought many opportunities and challenges for the American people. Victory in the war with Spain brought international recognition and acceptance; no longer would the United States be characterized by Europeans as a distant nation of the new world. Respect from the international community brought with it certain responsibilities to safeguard America's new status. President Theodore Roosevelt, believing that strong and virile nations survive, while the weak disappear or are conquered, strengthened America's military forces, extended the Monroe Doctrine through the 1904 Roosevelt Corollary, and built the Panama Canal to aid international trade. Roosevelt also skillfully used the nation's more respected status to aid in negotiating peace following the Russo-Japanese War of 1904. In domestic affairs the Federal government, which had heretofore been basically blind to the precepts of the Sherman Anti-Trust Act of 1890, reinvigorated its efforts to control the growing power of industry and financial monopoly. Regulation of business through the reinterpretation and application of the Interstate Commerce Act of 1887 and a balanced approach in the labor-capital struggle were also trademarks of the first decade of the twentieth century.

American Catholicism lived in a state of contradiction. "Americanism" and the 1899 publication of *Testem* threw progressives into disarray. As the first decade of the new century progressed the intellectual life of Catholics worldwide was dampened even further with the condemnation of Modernism in 1907. Despite these setbacks, the American Church made progress in other ways. In 1903 Cardinal Gibbons became the first American ever to vote in a papal election. Five years later, through the apostolic constitution *Sapienti Consilio,* the Church in the United States was removed from mission status and dependence upon the Sacred Congregation for the Propagation of the Faith. The Church continued to grow with thirteen new dioceses being created between 1903 and 1914. The ecumenical spirit demonstrated in the corporate reception into the Roman Catholic Church in 1909 of the American Episcopalians Paul Lewis Wattson and Lurana May White and their associates as the Franciscan Friars and Sisters of the Atonement was another notable event in the progress of the turn-of-the-century American Church.

Student Priest and Professor of Church History—1902–1903

Between 1902 and 1903 James Gillis studied at The Catholic University in the departments of dogmatics and historical science within the School of Sacred Sciences. Although he was not impressed with the Sulpicians and the program at St. John's, he had earned a Ph.B. from the Boston seminary in 1898. This degree qualified him to pursue the licentiate's degree. Gillis's professors were well respected in their disciplines and included Thomas Bouquillon in moral theology, William Kerby in sociology, and Thomas Shahan, whom he called "the most enthusiastic and inspiring of teachers," in Church history.[1] On June 4, 1902 he was awarded the baccalaureate in Sacred Theology (STB) as a stepping stone to his goal of the licentiate's degree.

During the summer interlude between classes Gillis found time for himself, his family, and friends. He was particularly gratified to renew his friendship with Joseph Gibbons, who had attended Saint Sulpice in Paris to complete his theological training. After his 1902 ordination he returned home immediately and went to St. Paul's in New York where Gillis was in residence for a summer rest. He prevailed upon his friend to accompany him to New Bedford, Massachusetts and to preach at his first Mass. Gillis considered it an honor but thought it quite presumptuous for one ordained less than a year to preach at another's first Mass. Gibbons later recalled Gillis's sermon that day, "Never a word, never a gesture out of place. He was all preacher, even in 1902, only seven months out of the seminary...almost perfect I'd say."[2] James

Gillis's gifts as a preacher were recognized early and would be exercised often and in multiple ways in his future mission to return America to moral rigorism and personal duty.

Gillis's second year at The Catholic University proceeded smoothly and he was awarded the licentiate's degree on June 10, 1903. He wrote his thesis in the field of historical theology, "The Agape: Its Existence and Its Relation with the Holy Eucharist," a work which described the historical origins of the agape (love feast) and contrasted the opinions of two leading contemporary scholars on the possible connection of this celebration to the Eucharistic liturgy. He attempted to answer two questions: (1) Does the historical record support the idea that the agape was a primitive institution of the Christian Church? (2) Was the agape, primitive or non-primitive, a liturgical custom? Gillis used historical criticism in his analysis but was quite cautious in his use of sources and the wording of his thoughts. He made no challenges to traditional beliefs and concluded that although *lacunae* do exist in the the historical record, there is sufficient evidence to conclude that the agape did exist in the early Church and that it was a primary part of the Eucharistic liturgy.[3]

Gillis was a student at The Catholic University at a critical time in the history of theological scholarship. Concepts, born in Europe and publicized principally in the writings of George Tyrrell, SJ, Alfred Loisy, and Baron Friedrich von Hugel,[4] and later condemned in the 1907 encyclical *Pascendi dominici gregis* of Pius X, circulated amongst the faculty and students. Gillis and fellow Paulists William Laurence Sullivan and Joseph McSorley all studied at the university and thus received similar influences. Later events, including Sullivan's self-proclamation as a modernist and accusations against McSorley's orthodoxy, led to the natural question of what Gillis learned in his studies. His STL thesis gives evidence of his public orthodoxy. Later, however, his private reflections would reveal his sympathy for many of the movement's ideas.

Gillis's degree earned him an appointment as professor of church history at St. Thomas for the academic year 1903–1904. Besides Gillis, the seminary staff consisted of some of the best and brightest in the Paulist community and the Catholic academic world. In January 1902, immediately after Gillis's ordination, Joseph McSorley was appointed the new superior and novice director at the seminary. This appointment commenced a long and fruitful relationship between the confreres. Both would serve in the Paulist administration, stand together as proponents of personal rigorism in the Society and wield great influence upon the community. William Laurence Sullivan, Gillis's friend from his student days, had also returned to St. Thomas in 1902 from the Texas missions to teach moral theology. The academic staff was rounded out with Francis Gigot, Gillis's former Sulpician mentor and friend from St. John's.[5]

The first years of the new century were a time of significant development for the Paulists in Washington, D.C. In September 1902 ground was broken on the construction of the Apostolic Mission House. An outgrowth of the Catholic Missionary Union, started by Elliott and Alexander P. Doyle in 1896, the House was established to train diocesan priests for mission work in their home dioceses. Affiliated with Catholic University but administered by the Paulist Fathers, the school offered a nine-month program in missiology and Paulist mission techniques. Although the primary purpose of the House was to prepare clergy for domestic missions to non-Catholics, Elliott and Doyle hoped that the school might one day double as a training center for foreign missionaries. In concert with the mission-to-America theme of Americanist ecclesiology, Cardinal James Gibbons and Archbishop John Keane of Dubuque were featured guests at the dedication of the cornerstone.

The death of George Deshon on December 30, 1903 marked the end of the age of the founders and the beginning of a new direction for the Paulists. George Mary Searle was elected as the first Superior General (under the terms of the 1898 Constitution) on June 15, 1904. At the age of sixty-five, Searle was the youngest Paulist leader in decades, yet he seemed out of touch with the pulse of the community's progressive members, who, inspired with modernist theology, clashed with others who underwent an internal conversion to conservatism.[6] Searle was not the strong leader needed to evoke confidence and establish unity in these troublesome times for the Society and the American Church in general following the publication of *Testem*. Searle's administration (1904–1909), while promoting the Society's tradition of missionary preaching, is remembered as the time when campus ministry became an apostolic work of the community, with the opening of Newman Halls at Berkeley (1907) and Austin (1908).

During the summer of 1903 Gillis received his first mission experience. Teamed with the future Superior General Thomas Burke, he preached missions in Williamsport, Pennsylvania and Waverly, New Jersey.[7] This same summer Gillis, McSorley, and Elliott combined to preach a mission at the Convent of the Good Shepherd in Georgetown.[8] He also started his extra-ecclesial speaking engagements, with a series of lectures to the Christ Child Society of Washington on the "Life of Christ." His experience in the STL program at The Catholic University produced an invitation for a series of talks on the "Catholic Church in History" for a group of Knights of Columbus councils in Baltimore.[9] Preaching became fundamental to Gillis's Paulist identity as a missionary to America and would be practiced throughout his life as his career evolved and took on different faces.

In accordance with the Paulist Constitution, Gillis spent his annual retreats in reflection upon his interior life and his relationship with God. Retreat notes on his twice-daily meditations are extant but discontinuous for the period 1902 to 1927. The first years' notes evince a pattern of resolutions made in order to live better and more fully the apostolic religious life. His personal reflections indicate self-chastisement and subsequent internal anguish for violating retreat resolutions. The topics for meditations, such as zeal, sin, death, judgment, hell, and fidelity to God, are indicative of the pessimistic mood so prevalent in his spirituality.[10]

The period 1902 to 1904 was characterized by him as one of personal strife, inner turmoil, and spiritual stagnation. In a somber mood he wrote,

> As I enter this retreat, I find myself in a mental and spiritual condition that is perhaps the climax of a growing sentiment or sense of evil, restlessness, dissatisfaction, almost discouragement. My spiritual life has never been particularly buoy-

ant for any length of time. I am continually haunted by a conviction—too well founded—of my sinfulness, of my weakness and cowardice. But of late things have been worse than ever.[11]

His inner conflict as well continued to challenge his peace of mind: "I am not contented. Why? It's the tearing and the struggling, the reviling and the pulling of the good and the bad in me, of the noble and the depraved, of the ideal and the actual." He called himself a "brute beast...[a] disgrace."[12]

Though Gillis felt a deep sense of personal unworthiness, he was able to express some belief in God's love in his life. He wrote, "It might be said that when once the love of God comes into a soul, it never departs."[13] However, he never manifested to others God's presence in his own life nor in his general world view. Gillis felt unworthy of God's favorable judgment:

Life's a fearfully tragic drama. My soul is destined for judgment. I am not far removed from the danger of hell. I am nearer to it than I can well understand. These things are true. Before God they are true and I must not forget them.[14]

On the same retreat he wrote, "I have the elements of hell in my bones."[15] He insisted, however, at the conclusion of the retreat, that he could achieve his spiritual goal when he resolved to again seek perfection instead of "the wicked ingratitude" with which he had repaid God's "mercy and long suffering patience."[16] Gillis's persistent feeling of self-worthlessness was countered by his deep-seated faith which professed hope in God's action in his life.

Gillis's internal sense of unworthiness characterized his life and colored his outlook on the outside world. The dissatisfaction he discovered in himself and his need for spiritual perfection created in him a dualistic perception of the world where life was a continual battle between the forces of good and evil. Unable to find personal peace, Gillis projected his internal battle onto society in his first full-time opportunity to experience the mission band and to exercise his Paulist identity.

Catholic Revivalism and the Paulist Mission Heritage

The apostolic mission had a long history in American Christianity, Catholicism, and the Paulist community. Revivalism had been part of the American scene since the time of Jonathan Edwards and the first "Great Awakening" in the 1730s. Evangelists such as George Whitefield and Methodist founder John Wesley rode thousands of miles on horseback and preached to hundreds of thousands of people. Charles Wesley, John's brother, composed more than 6,000 hymns plus hundreds of occasional poems to be used in the revivals.[17] Camp revivals of a week's duration or longer were quite common and drew people from an entire region. In the mid-nineteenth century Charles Finney (1792–1875) transformed the Protestant revivalist tradition through his use of dual preaching platforms, the Broadway Tabernacle in New York and a professorship at Oberlin College in Ohio.

As Jay Dolan has noted, revivalism was not exclusively Protestant as presupposed by most people; Roman Catholicism also promoted religious revivals in the form of parish missions.[18] Indeed, Catholic revivals, which had their own form, flavor, and function, shaped the piety of the people and strengthened the institutional Church; they were the key to the revitalization of the Church in nineteenth-century America. Missions (Dolan uses the terms mission and revival interchangeably) became a primary means to stem the tide of "leakage" of Catholics to Protestant denominations. Missions were also a key ingredient to the renewal of personal piety so central to Catholic practice and worship. Dolan sees a transformation of Catholicism through the mission movement from a Church which stressed ritualism to one that was equally guided by evangelical fervor; its manifestation in confession and Holy Communion were signs of one's conversion. Thus, Catholic revivals influenced religious practice while religion, in turn, wielded a powerful hammer in the process of social change in the latter half of nineteenth-century America.[19] Dolan summarizes the principal thrust of Catholic revivalism in America, "Morality, not dogma; right doing, not correct believing was the thrust of the revival message."[20]

Many religious orders participated in parish missions such

as the Jesuits, Redemptorists, and Paulists. Generally, traveling bands of religious made circuits with some regularity in many parishes. Rural Catholics, who might only have the opportunity to attend Mass and receive the sacraments infrequently, flocked to missions as their one chance to participate in the liturgical rites and experience the communal piety of their Faith.

The vision and understanding of Isaac Hecker formed the cornerstone upon which the Paulist mission apostolate was constructed with an emphasis on reaching non-Catholics. As a Redemptorist Hecker had given missions as early as 1856. In 1863 the Paulist founder and his colleagues began to lecture to non-Catholics usually from Sunday to Sunday in locales ranging from Connecticut to Missouri. Between the founding of the community in 1858 and the death of Francis Baker, one of the founding members, in April 1865, Paulists preached eighty-one missions.[21] The success of these missions was communicated by Hecker to his friend Cardinal Alessandro Barnabò, Prefect of the Propaganda, in an 1863 communiqué: "The interest shown [in the missions] was remarkable, and the effect was equal to my hopes. My experience convinces me that if this work were continued, it would prepare the way for a great change of religion in this country."[22]

For non-Catholic missions certain topics were considered essential. The American Catholic understanding of the relationship between Church and State was explained in sermons on "The Church and the Republic," "Church and Society," and "The State of Religion in the United States." Church doctrine was explained in such lectures as "Luther and the Reformation" and "A Search for Rational Christianity." Motivation to seek Catholicism and to learn more was always part of a mission and was presented in a lecture entitled, "How and Why I Became a Catholic."[23]

Like Hecker, Walter Elliott believed that America had a providential role in the history of salvation. He saw the expansion of the mission effort and the production of converts as confirmation of God's blessing and sanction upon the apostolate. Elliott was the one man primarily responsible for the revival of missions to non-Catholics. The 1893 Catholic Congress held in conjunction with Chicago's Columbian Exposition provided the platform for initiating this shift in emphasis. In his speech, "The Missionary Outlook in the United States," Elliott stated, "Every diocese should have at least one or two priests who shall be exclusively missionary—I mean, of course, secular priests, and missionaries to non-Catholics."[24] This speech precipitated events which led to the aforementioned foundation, along with a fellow Paulist, Alexander P. Doyle, of the Catholic Missionary Union and its organ, *The Missionary*. The inauguration of the Apostolic Mission House on the grounds of The Catholic University in April 1904 was Elliott's crowning achievement in his efforts to promote diocesan priests as leaders of local missions to non-Catholics.

Walter Elliott's approach to the non-Catholic mission was a combination of theology and strategy based on a synthesis of Hecker's ideas and a Salesian model of spirituality. The theological foundation for evangelization rested on a positive image of the human person, the centrality of the Incarnation, and a reliance on the inner working of the Holy Spirit. Elliott's method was irenic and non-controversial with emphasis on the practical and concrete aspects of the Faith.[25] He made every effort to contextualize the teachings of the Church within a positive assessment of the American experience and the accessibility of grace. For example, in an explanation of the Latin dictum *extra ecclesiam nulla salus* (outside the Church [there is] no salvation), Elliott proposed the positive doctrine of "invincible ignorance" which claimed that under certain conditions all had the possibility of salvation. This was the Paulist's effort to refute the common Protestant charge that the Catholic Church was intolerant.[26]

The mission format Elliott adopted become almost standard for the Paulist community. In imitation of Hecker's method, a typical mission would begin on Sunday morning with an introductory sermon preached at the high Mass. The mission would progress the entire week and conclude the next Sunday. Early morning Mass, followed by a short thirty-minute instruction, scheduled to allow working people to attend, eat breakfast, and still begin work on time, was held each day. Later in the morning Mass was again celebrated without instruction. The principal events of the mission were held in the evening beginning at 7:30 PM with the missionary, for fifteen to twenty min-

utes, answering questions randomly and anonymously submitted on any and all aspects of the Faith. After the rosary came
the highlight of the evening, the mission sermon, usually forty-
five minutes in duration. Elliott underscored the importance of
the sermon:

> Remember that (apart from the workings of Divine grace)
> all success [in the mission] depends on good preaching—a
> superior kind of persuasiveness. There may be some lack of
> elegant composition, but the whole effect must be excep-
> tionally *powerful* [Elliott's emphasis].[27]

The evening's service generally concluded with Benediction and
the opportunity to receive the sacrament of penance.

The question box, described by Elliott as "the lungs of a
non-Catholic mission," was first utilized at the 1893 World Par-
liament of Religions held in Chicago.[28] It provided the best
means for inquirers to have their questions answered in a non-
threatening environment. The method was quite popular and
questions came forward in every possible area. Over 1,000 questions were collected by the veteran Paulist evangelist Bertrand
Conway in his book, *The Question Box* (1929), which sold over
three million copies and was a staple for free distribution at
Paulist-preached missions.[29]

Elliott gave more specifics than Hecker in his description of
required topics in missions. With recommendations for their
preferred order in presentation, he listed the following as necessary subjects in all missions: salvation, mortal sin, death, eternal
punishment (or particular judgment), and the mercy of God.
Missions to non-Catholics necessitated additional requirements
such as the rule of faith, doctrinal indifferentism, confession,
real presence, infallibility of the Pope, and, borrowing from
Hecker, a closing sermon, "Why I am a Catholic."[30]

Elliott also bequeathed to the mission effort a format to
record what transpired. All missionaries were encouraged to
keep accurate records of their ministry and to record the place
of the mission, whether it was to Catholics or non-Catholics, the
pastor's name, and a list of the sermons and who preached
them. The results of the mission were also to be reported with

data on the number of confessions (listed in categories of men, women, and children), converts, temperance pledges, inquirers, and baptisms to be recorded.[31] Gillis followed this format closely in the preaching log that he maintained for the whole of his ministerial life.

The Chicago Mission Band—1904–1907

In March 1904 Gillis left St. Thomas apparently because his interior conflict and his work affected his health, "which had been poor for some time."[32] He spent the summer at Lake George in relaxation and retreat and prepared for his new assignment with the Chicago mission band. This was the work for which he had been trained; it was the apostolate he considered central to the Society's charism. Persistent feelings of self-worthlessness and fear of damnation[33] continued to hound Gillis which prompted him to seek counsel from Walter Elliott, to whom he could trace the origin of his Paulist vocation. He recalled how Elliott once said, "After a few years' experience in the priesthood it becomes impossible for a priest, without a miracle, to make a new start."[34] His prospective entry into full-time apostolic life worried him; he was certain that his shaky spiritual life would be tested further. Thus, he realized that some change was immediately required. Elliott's advice helped Gillis to gain personal insight, make a realistic assessment of his own human frailty, and initiate steps to reduce his expectation for spiritual perfection.[35] This led eventually to a transfer of his need for perfection onto society, resulting in better self-acceptance.

Gillis entered the Paulist mission band in Chicago at Old St. Mary's in the heart of the city on September 1, 1904. His diary entry that day read, "Prepared for the worst, didn't find it." When he arrived he encountered several familiar faces which compensated for the loneliness he felt from his physical separation from his family.[36] The young Paulist began his ministry as a full-time evangelist in October 1904. He traveled through Illinois, Indiana, and Missouri in his first mission tour culminating in December when he preached to black Catholics at St. Monica's parish in Chicago amidst much enthusiasm and apparent gratitude.[37] Gillis labored long and hard in his new work but such expenditure of energy often resulted in illness. Preaching was central to his Paulist identity, however, and thus he entertained a radical remedy, a "whiskey punch," to meet his commitments. He felt he was successful despite his ailment and completed his work "with the affection of a good many of the people."[38] From the outset Gillis began a life-long pattern which today would be classified as "workaholism." He continued his missionary apostolate with such fervor that it would later result in forced rests of some length.

Not all was perfect on the mission band for Gillis on at least two fronts. His preaching log recounts many incidents, some rather humorous and others grimmer, where the cooperation he received from the local pastor was less than helpful. In Plattsburg, Missouri, for example, he came "face to face with the queerest situation I have yet encountered." The pastor who hosted Gillis was an ascetic who lived in one room of the church sacristy. The priest had no shower; meals provided by the nuns in the parish convent were placed on a tray outside the sacristy door.[39] More important, however, Gillis began to experience disagreements with his superior Peter O'Callaghan. Although the latter was a principal influence in Gillis's decision to enter the Paulists, it is apparent at this point that he was disappointed with his young protégé. Gillis stated that O'Callaghan "apparently disapproves of my sermons....[He] acts and looks unsympathetic."[40] Gillis's differences with others in the Paulist community would continue in the ensuing years.

Gillis considered his first year in the Chicago mission band to have been ambiguous at best. He boasted that he had been involved in fifteen missions and retreats. Yet, despite this record of achievement, the young priest felt wronged by O'Callaghan and the callous methods he used to indict him by means of public criticism of his sermons and assignments to the least desirable towns and parishes. The positive aspects of the year were obscured by this conflict with his superior. Gillis felt alienated and stated, "I am weary of the situation—chagrined, disappointed."[41]

This period was also a test of his relationship with his family. During an August home visit he became deeply concerned about his mother's health which he described as "failing considerably," while his father was perceived as "working too hard." The family's financial status coupled with his life as a religious caused him to lament, "I can be of no financial help to them." Still, the young Paulist sought some solution to the crisis which "demands an answer."[42] His fellow Paulist James Finley, his biographer, claims that this situation almost drove Gillis from the community, so tortured was his mind because of the unsettled condition of his family.[43]

After Gillis returned to Chicago, following his annual retreat, he spent numerous hours in reflection on the utter depravity of humanity, particularly the weaknesses of "the flesh":

> The world is horribly bad, sin is almost universally rampant—in congregations of the well-to-do as much perhaps as the poor unfortunate toilers who are only too apt to make their few pleasures known. Everybody knows, in general, that the world is vicious and rotten, but the missionary day after day and week after week has its vice and uncleanness poured into his ears and his soul is steeped in it.[44]

> I am not anxious to go back, not to the shedding of my blood, not to the confessional and the filth and the stupidity and the folly and the rest of it—or the dirty tenements or the houses of moral and physical uncleanliness.[45]

Gillis was disillusioned by unfulfilled expectations on the mission circuit. His own precarious self-esteem was in jeopardy of being overcome by the "power of sin in a brutal world."[46]

Gillis's second year in Chicago was equally as hectic as the first. He was teamed with Edward Mullaly, Oliver Welsh, John Harney, and Peter O'Callaghan in various mission undertakings. Disappointments and successes with the apostolate were described in his diary. He lamented the fact that his preaching partners seemed to always assign him more difficult areas so congregations saw him as "the 'cross priest' of the missions." He was concerned particularly with abuses of alcohol that predisposed people against the mission message.[47] On a more positive note, however, a mission preached in three rural parishes outside Chicago (Polo, Byron, and Oregon) was described as "one of the missions of a lifetime!"[48] One has the impression that Gillis was given to fits of despair and feelings of exaltation.

The personal highlight of this mission season for Gillis was a retreat he gave at his favored Loreto Academy near Niagara Falls. The change of pace provided much satisfaction for the weary preacher. Extolling women religious as providing a pure domestic refuge from the evil world, he wrote,

> This is the time of my life. Like a foretaste of heaven after the drudgery and dirt of the missions....All this reveals life worth while [sic] and is a solace for many weary days of mission work and a relief after many bitter disappointments in human nature.[49]

The mission grind, community disappointments, and family concerns all weighed upon him as he entered his annual retreat at Lake George where he hoped to experience a "second conversion." The spiritual renewal he so deeply desired had actually been in progress now for two years. His deep need to achieve spiritual reconciliation was transformed into a quest to call society to a life of perfection. The world was made perfect by the active presence of God; without God society would fall into corruption and depravity. He perceived that the purpose of religious life was to manifest the presence of God in the world while his mission was to admonish society to adopt moral rigorism, personal responsibility, and duty. This was the goal he thrust upon society, an end which allowed him to conclude, "I am not so bad after all."[50] His projection of his own unworthiness upon society helped to free Gillis from his own sense of depravity.

Gillis's mission preaching at this time emphasized the dutiful life of Christians. At St. Mary's in Chicago he stated, "The Church asks you, demands you, Her people, Her laity, to convert the nation to God."[51] This concept of personal responsibility and initiative in the promotion of God's work, which arose from his own interior struggle, became a common theme throughout his public life. God must be present; without God all is lost. Gillis expressed this idea in several different ways and situations by criticizing the modern world for its displacing the wisdom of God for narrow national self-interests. Borrowing the thought of

Cardinal Manning, he viewed such human folly as "the revolt of the intellect against God."[52]

He preached that the interior human struggle to avoid sin and live in the way of God could be described as the "Jekyll and Hyde, the angel and the animal, the man and the brute-beast," which exists in every person.[53] This inner conflict, which would later be projected onto society as a world view pitting light against darkness in his analysis of events, peoples (especially world leaders), and movements, could only be settled by one's total faith in the presence of God in the world. Those ideas which supported Gillis's nineteenth-century belief in the power of individual choice became the Dr. Jekyll of his society. Peoples, bureaucracies, organizations, and governments, which imperiled one's free choice to seek conversion, became the Mr. Hyde monster of Stevenson's classic novel. For Gillis the world was not an easy place; Christ never made any such claim or promise. Rather he said, "The life of Christ was inevitably destined to be a cross and a martyrdom, and, therefore, we who call ourselves by His name must not expect unbroken peace and joy and comfort."[54] Gillis's need for perfection in society was to be manifest in the need to welcome and recognize the presence of God in the world. When philosophical relativism challenged any need for God it was James Gillis who would serve as a contemporary prophet of doom by blasting society for its moral degradation and pleading for a return to a God-centered world community.

St. Thomas College—1907–1910

The personal and ministerial development of James Martin Gillis mirrored concurrent changes in American Catholic life and thought. Like many nations, the United States experienced the rise of socialism as the twentieth century dawned. An import from Europe, socialist thought was introduced in the United States through the Socialist political party and through the International Workers of the World (IWW), an industrial union movement. In 1912 Eugene V. Debs (1855–1926) ran for President as the Socialist party candidate and gained some notoriety.

Trade unionists, including the Catholic Socialist Movement of Chicago, were sympathetic to the socialist philosophy.[55]

Generally Catholics attacked socialism as a great moral evil. The 1891 publication of Leo XIII's classic encyclical, *Rerum Novarum*, engendered much anti-socialist literature, some of which was Catholic in origin. William Kerby and John A. Ryan, leading Catholic intellectuals of the period, were reformers who promoted social change, in accordance with Papal teaching (principally *Rerum Novarum*), as a challenge and alternative to socialism. Kerby, professor of sociology at The Catholic University of America, called for full Catholic opposition to socialism, "for it is a menace, immediately to our institutions and remotely to our faith."[56] Ryan, the principal Catholic voice for social issues, characterized the American socialist movement as "predominantly anti-Christian."[57] David Goldstein and Martha Moore Avery, former socialists who converted to Catholicism, led a more overt crusade through their popular book, *Socialism: The Nation of Fatherless Children* (1903), which stirred anti-socialist animus. Additionally, Goldstein and Avery toured the nation making speeches which derided the dictates of socialism while a Paulist, William S. Kress, leader of the Cleveland mission band, struck out against socialism in sermons based on *Rerum Novarum.*

While James Gillis toured the country and gave missions, social Catholicism was spreading. John Ryan's doctoral dissertation at The Catholic University, published in 1906 as *A Living Wage*, stressed the dignity of the individual by arguing that since all God's people were destined for a reasonable life, the dignity of the worker had to be protected and nourished. Just compensation was one means to assure equal economic protection for all. With the banner of *Rerum Novarum* raised before them, labor priests, such as Peter Dietz in the Midwest and Peter C. Yorke in California, worked tirelessly for the rights of workers and the cause of organized labor in general. The German Central Verein, through the inspiration of Dietz and Frederick P. Kenkel, expanded its organ *Central Blatt* to *Central Blatt and Social Justice* in 1909. The magazine was well received by the public and praised by Ryan. Francis Clement Kelley, in his establishment of the Catholic Church Extension Society (1905), indirectly struck another note in the Church's efforts to meet the social needs of society. This body was formed to economically support rural parishes and priests so that the Catholic message could be preached throughout the nation.

Such was the state of affairs in the American Church when James Gillis's career took a radical shift in the summer of 1907. On June 28 he recorded in his preaching log, "Appointed novice master!! God have mercy on me!" Earlier the same month Joseph McSorley, who was "in anguish from the position of novice master," left his post as superior and director of novices at St. Thomas College. His resignation was accepted by the Paulist Superior General, George Searle. Thus, a new director of novices was needed. Searle recommended Gillis to the consultors (assistants to the Superior General) who concurred in the nomination; he was appointed by the General. He arrived at Lake George, the novices' summer home, on July 20, 1907 and "immediately assumed his office as novice master."[58]

The summer of 1907 saw the publication of two papal documents, a decree of the Holy Office, *Lamentabili sane exitu* (July 3) and an encyclical *Pascendi dominici gregis* (September 8). *Lamentabili* was a syllabus of sixty-five errors related to the aforementioned Modernist movement; *Pascendi* condemned Modernism as "the synthesis of all heresies." Modernism was a diffuse Catholic movement of the late nineteenth and early twentieth centuries which endorsed contemporary Biblical scholarship, accepted historical development in Christianity, strongly opposed neo-scholasticism, and was thoroughly receptive to progress in science and philosophy. Although the influence of these documents was not immediately felt in the United States, a pall was cast on intellectual activity in the American Church due to the combination of the aforementioned *Testem Benevolentiae* (1899) and *Pascendi*.[59]

The specter of Americanism and the earlier publication of *Testem* had placed the Paulists under the bright lights of Vatican scrutiny. The Modernism controversy created a situation where the Society could again be thrust into the spotlight. The story of the American Church and Modernism has been told and is beyond the scope of this work,[60] but the fears which the controversy raised in the Paulist community affected James Gillis. The timing of McSorley's resignation and Gillis's assignment appear to be related to Pius X's anti-Modernism campaign. Essays written by McSorley and William Laurence Sullivan, who also left St. Thomas, were printed in the *New York Review*,[61] a journal which was suspect because of its publication of works by Alfred Loisy and George Tyrrell, theologians condemned by the Vatican as Modernists. Additionally, McSorley had served as Tyrrell's agent in the United States. The Paulist administration avoided all possible conflict through the transfers. Finley states that the appointment of Gillis was due to the Modernist crisis: "Gillis was a candidate who possessed rectitude. His assignment was a clear message to Rome that the Paulists were 'cleaning up their act.'"[62]

Certainly Gillis's public record gave no indication of heterodoxy in his theological approach. As mentioned earlier, his STL thesis used contemporary methods but challenged nothing of traditional theological or historical interpretations. The theological perspective which he presented must have been safe for in 1907 Thomas Shahan, Gillis's former professor and one of the editors of the on-going project to publish *The Catholic Encyclopedia*, asked him to contribute three essays to the effort. Gillis's submissions, "Agony of Christ," "Areopagus," and "Bible Societies," verified his guarded traditionalism. In fact, a contemporary reading of "Bible Societies" demonstrates the sharp pen which Gillis used at times to criticize Protestants who violated Catholic principles.[63]

When Gillis referred to the Jekyll and Hyde in every person, he well described not only the inner conflict which he had painfully experienced, but additionally how the public and private James Gillis could in many ways be so different. This contrast of appearance can be illustrated when we compare the public evangelist and the private retreatant. Gillis's public image and private meditations, as we have seen, were many times in conflict, demonstrating both his inner discord and complex personality.

The Jekyll and Hyde mentality applied as well to his relationship with Modernism. While he publicly denounced the "New Theology," his private papers reveal a strong sympathy to the movement. Comments made several years after the Modernism issue had came to a head reveal another side of Gillis which challenged the anti-modernist mentality, and argued against the death sentence handed to theological dissent. In 1915 he privately wrote,

> When I came [to the Paulist community] I found a group of men, within the community, whose spirit of earnestness and eagerness in the cause of truth and virtue I came to value highly.—Now it happened that they too were deeply interested in what was then called the 'New Theology'. They were heart and soul in favor of new methods of teaching and a new manner of setting methods of teaching and [a] new manner of setting forth dogma to the people. There was mental life—and intellectual enthusiasm among them. They were our leaders and teachers and they imbued me with something of their own earnestness in the 'cause'. The group grew in numbers. It was allied in spirit with other groups in the larger sphere of the [Catholic] University— new life in the old bones of theology.
>
> Then came the [in]quisitors. The 'New Theology' developed dangerously, was branded modernism and condemned. All of us—like lambs from the fold—were made to feel the pain, and we have not been allowed to wander again from the safe enclosure of the intellectual fold.
>
> It is taken for granted that all who are puzzled and worried are *ipso facto* modernists or modernistic, and they must drop everything, shut their books and submit their minds, with their question still unanswered—under penalty of damnation. And is it true that there can be no questioning? Is every indication of interest in these matters fatal? Is the acceptable attitude that of complete submission to the Church without so much as asking for information?[64]

Gillis challenged several accepted theological norms of the day. In questioning the "apparent legends in Sacred Scripture," he asked whether Genesis was in any way historically accurate. He accepted the validity of the Canon of Scripture as decreed by the Council of Trent, but he wondered if any truth could be found in the apocryphal gospels.[65] Additionally, he privately described neo-scholasticism, the prevailing theological synthesis, as "upon the period of its final disgrace—yet we are riveted to it by the authorities."[66] Paul Robichaud appears to be on the mark when he says that Gillis "was not infected with the Modernist virus."[67] This was the public man, the Dr. Jekyll, the one who preached missions and was seen as "safe" to the Paulist administration. The private man, the Mr. Hyde, however, was sympathetic to the movement.

Although the majority of public sources demonstrated his commitment to the Paulist apostolate of parish-mission preaching, in 1915 he pondered how the condemnation of Modernism altered his career. He reflected upon the life of scholarship and wondered whether the actions of the Vatican against the "New Theology" had pushed his life in a different direction. He wrote, "What might have been a scholarly life was summarily directed in another channel."[68] One cannot conclude from a single reference that James Gillis spent his life as a frustrated academic. Yet, his reflections on Modernism are significant for they represent a rare view at his anger and disappointment at the Church he loved so fervently, an aspect rarely demonstrated by this prim and proper Boston-bred Irish-American Catholic.[69]

Gillis was able to control his inner thoughts so as to always appear "safe" in his theological perspective. Dr. Jekyll, the public man, prevailed while Mr. Hyde was kept far from view. For example, Gillis's first official conference as novice master, given to all students, save those newly arrived, was on "The 'New Theology' and its Danger." His preaching log reports that it was "necessary in view of recent happenings." Obviously the Paulist community and Gillis himself wanted no taint of Modernism to be present in the halls of St. Thomas College.[70]

In many ways the routine at the seminary during Gillis's tenure as superior was the same as when he was a novice. First Friday days of recollection found Gillis giving conferences which covered the subjects of poverty, obedience, and the precepts of the Paulist rule. His ability as a teacher was recognized by his students such as John Carter Smyth, a future teammate with Gillis on missions, who said of him,

> He was one of the finest teachers we had in my time at the scholasticate. I thought in after years that Father Gillis had

taken over a pretty desperate situation and pulled it together manfully. He handled our theology with a surety and confidence that were needed at that period.[71]

Gillis's role as novice master provided him the forum to instruct new members of the community in his understanding of the Paulist mission to America. As he wrote later, Gillis believed the Society's work to be the Church's work, "to make known the Catholic Truth: to tell it honestly, completely, without minimizing or without compromise, and also without intemperance of speech or offensive dogmatism." Gillis preached Hecker's belief that the Paulist, as a self-directed man, was to be a missionary. Walking in the footsteps of Isaiah, John the Baptist, and St. Paul, disciples of Hecker must be trained to preach a tough message to hostile, alien, and many times unresponsive audiences. Gillis also promoted the compatibility of Catholicism and the Paulist tradition with the democratic principles of America.[72]

The remainder of Gillis's first year as novice master found him busy on many fronts. Although actively engaged in Washington, Gillis felt the need to preach beyond the immediate purview of St. Thomas College. His Paulist identity as missionary and need to seek conversion for himself and the world impelled him to preach to others. His Chicago experience and the needs of the local Church made parish missions a natural platform for the expression of his views. Mission engagements took him to Chicago, Baltimore, Niagara Falls and a Lenten series at St. Paul's in New York.

The summer passed swiftly as Gillis interspersed formation work with a few invitations to preach. In September he asked his friend, colleague, and mentor, Walter Elliott, to preach the student retreat at St. Thomas. This opportunity to revisit his conflicted inner life, the Mr. Hyde, produced another outburst of frustration from his pen. His idealism and high expectations of his fellow Paulists were in disarray as he considered that the rule was abused, common exercises were ignored, the spiritual life was lax, and the observance of poverty and obedience was challenged. Angrily he wrote, "We must have revolution or a dissolution [of the community]—and no revolution is in sight."[73]

Disappointed with the lack of moral rigorism in the community, Gillis, in desperation turned to Elliott, who informed him that his feelings were part of the pessimism that others observed in him. The counsel pulled Gillis from despair and allowed him to write, "I was blue-blue—and almost in full rebellion about being here, but thank God I have absorbed a little Christian charity."[74]

After completing his second year at St. Thomas, Gillis was elected to the 1909 General Chapter of the Congregation of St. Paul the Apostle. That summer he discovered his personal power and limitations in the Paulist society, was introduced to community controversies, and participated in the election of a new general administration.[75] Apparently he had achieved some level of approval of the community in accepting election and the responsibility to serve as a delegate. Gillis's disappointment with his fellow Paulists was not publicized, but, as has been shown, others recognized a negative attitude in his persistent pessimism.

During the recess of the Chapter, Gillis went to the new Paulist summer house at Rehoboth Beach, Delaware, where he received word that his mother, who had been in failing health for some time, had grown worse still. Following the close of the Chapter he traveled to Boston where she died on August 9, 1909, fourteen years after he left home for St. Charles College. He recorded about the day, "*Mother died* [Gillis's emphasis]. The passing of the heart and the soul is to God. Grant her immediate rest. Mother, pray for me!"[76]

In June 1910, James Gillis tendered his resignation as director of novices at St. Thomas College. Without evidence Finley has inferred that Gillis suffered from "occupational fatigue." He wanted more than St. Thomas could offer; he desired a more active ministry.[77] Gillis's need to seek conversion coupled with his desire to exercise his Paulist identity as a preacher "forced" him to move beyond the confines of St. Thomas College to seek a greater audience for his message. Spiritually, however, Gillis had grown in learning to accept imperfection in himself:

> I am stupid if I do not learn [from] experience that 'perfection' is beyond my scope. And why be quixotic? Why play the fool in the spiritual life? Be reasonable. Decide what I

can achieve—and try for that. Don't rhapsodize about myself![78]

He left Washington late in the month and reported to St. Paul's parish as a member of the New York mission band.

James Gillis's first decade as a Paulist priest initiated practices and solidified beliefs which would be instrumental in his later career as a mission preacher and editor. As a student priest Gillis was introduced to the theological concepts later condemned as Modernism. Although there is no taint of heterodoxy in Gillis's writings, public statements, or sermons, his private correspondence demonstrates his sympathy for the movement and the theologians who were ill-affected by its condemnation. Gillis's attitude is important because it serves to illustrate the dualism which he experienced between his private inner turmoil and public appearance. In describing this contrasting dualism as the Dr. Jekyll and Mr. Hyde which exists in each person, Gillis powerfully articulated the persistent theme of his own life which, through his need to find inner peace, was projected onto society. Over time Gillis grew into the belief that his inner conflict could not be resolved; only the transfer of his view of the battle between good and evil which he experienced on to society would allow him to live within himself. It was a slow process, but once Gillis moved his conflict beyond himself he began to break the descending spiral of his spiritual journey and return a sense of calm and peace to his tortured soul.

Gillis's first years after ordination were also critical in the solidification of his Paulist identity as a preacher. From his time at St. Thomas College, as a student, professor, and novice master, Gillis was imbued with the charism of Isaac Hecker, who believed his vocation to be the evangelization of America. Gillis's own preaching began with himself in the form of diaries, retreat notes, and meditation books where he many times excoriated himself for failures and lamented a deep-seated belief in his unworthiness and his inability to achieve spiritual perfection. Through the mission band Gillis was able to preach to others about the need to freely choose repentance and conversion. In general Gillis saw God as distant; an understanding of the immanent presence of

God's spirit active in the world was missing. As a son of Isaac Hecker, who believed in the active presence of the Spirit in the world and especially the American nation, Gillis's spirituality, which emphasized God's absence within himself and from society, demonstrates a "fractured inheritance" between his spiritual formation as a Paulist and the reality of the world from which he could not escape. James Gillis moved from St. Thomas College and joined the New York mission band with a secure world view and a stable Paulist identity. His projection of his inner conflict onto society would become the latest manifestation of his mission to America.

CHAPTER 3

Missionary to America—1911–1922

Historians have classified the years 1900 to 1918 as the Progressive Era in America. This period of reform was concurrent with the Social Gospel Movement, where Christian church leaders responded to the social evils that abounded in society. The Social Gospelers sought institutional change over personal and more individual-based solutions to problems. Josiah Strong (1847–1916) has been described as "the dynamo, the revivalist, the organizer and altogether the most irrepressible spirit of the Social Gospel movement."[1] This popular Christian leader centered his reform efforts on sweat shop factories and the horrors of packing houses that were graphically depicted in Upton Sinclair's *The Jungle.* Political corruption which bred many disorders in municipal governments was also the target of Strong. He served as the organizer and mobilizer of the Christian Churches in their efforts to alleviate the suffering and pain of workers.

Washington Gladden (1836–1918) used the teachings of Jesus in his two books, *Who Wrote the Bible ?* (1891) and *Present Day Theology* (1913), to emphasize theological dimensions to the social dilemma of the day. Gladden perceived the labor-capital struggle in terms of social justice, a view that was manifested in the twentieth-century Catholic champions of social thought. Like John A. Ryan, Gladden was a great critic of the American free-enterprise system. He never claimed membership in any socialist organization, but did advocate public ownership of utilities and cooperative management of industries.

Walter Rauschenbusch (1861–1918), a third and possibly the most influential voice of the Social Gospel leaders, typified the soul and passion of the movement. His experience as a pastor in the "Hell's Kitchen" section of Manhattan changed his perspective on life. From this formative period he developed his "out of work, out of clothes and out of hope" critique of social reality. Rauschenbusch used this philosophy as a professor at Rochester Theological Seminary and as an author of several books, all of which were successful and are still referenced today.[2]

By the time James Gillis arrived in New York to preach missions, public policies were influenced not only by the Social Gospel but by a new wave of political, economic, and moral reform. As characterized by Sean Cashman, the Progressive era was an age of "titans."[3] There was President Theodore Roosevelt's New Nationalism and Woodrow Wilson's New Freedom. Thomas Edison (1847–1931) was the man of invention while John Pierpont Morgan (1867–1943) was the nation's foremost banker and investor. This was also the era of Henry Ford (1863–1947) and the Wright Brothers.

The Progressive era stood as the middle ground of a long period of social reform in America; populism preceded it and the New Deal followed it. The moral traditions of rural evangelical Protestantism produced in Progressive leaders an ethos of personal responsibility; the propertied and educated classes promoted Progressive reform. Some sympathizers and proponents of Progressive ideas were by most standards wealthy, but such members allied themselves to the main body of the movement by distinguishing themselves as people of "responsible" wealth against the irresponsible who used their economic fortune as a weapon in industrial conflict.

Progressive era leaders in general fought against the monopolistic tendencies of big business and debated contemporary moral issues "in a comprehensive effort to grapple with the ills of a modern urban-industrial society."[4] Improvement in the quality of life for the laboring class and the creation of social stability were goals Progressives sought. Consolidation of large corporations was rejected by most Progressives; they believed that "bigness was badness." In response some reform leaders promoted Wilson's "New Freedom" which fostered free markets and suspected any efforts at consolidation. Not all Progressives agreed, however, as at least two leading voices of reform, Theodore Roosevelt and Herbert Croly, accepted bigness and promoted the regulation of monopolies. Progressive efforts to strike down corrupt municipal governments, such as New York's Tammany Hall and the political machine organized in San Francisco, were prominent instances of political reform.[5] The moral issues of women's suffrage, temperance and prohibition, and immigration restriction were single-issue crusades in the general ethos of social reform.

As described in the previous chapter, American Catholic leaders in the pre-World War I era concentrated their efforts on social justice rather than curbing monopolies and democratizing politics. Father John A. Ryan, the principal figure of Catholic reform, was professor of moral theology at The Catholic University of America, and later head of the Social Action Department of the National Catholic Welfare Conference (NCWC). These positions gave him two significant forums from which he could initiate and help implement social reforms.[6]

Early Missionary Years—1910–1914

The Progressive era forms the background to the mission ministry which James Martin Gillis resumed in the fall of 1910. Gillis entered upon his work after his annual retreat which brought forth a more positive and enthusiastic attitude. The topics of his meditations illustrate the positive nature of his thought: "Incarnation," "Love of God," "Love of Jesus," "Love of People," "The Encouraging Side of the Consideration of Sin." He saw his retreat as a "time to plant" and the opportunity to "fill the reservoir" which has been depleted over the last year. This renewed attitude was also reflected in his positive understanding of the faith. He wrote, "Religion means enthusiasm. It is not mere obedience or regularity or cold fidelity. There must be love, else there is no *religion* [Gillis's emphasis]."[7]

A new spirit of hope was present in Gillis as he re-entered the mission field to once again preach his message of personal conversion to a wider audience. He realized that a need to strive for self-improvement would always be present. Yet, he was able to write, "I am convinced particularly as a result of this retreat—that there is a better man in me than anything that has yet appeared."[8]

St. Paul's Church, which Finley calls the "pulpit of the day,"[9] became the base of operation for Gillis as he entered fully into the apostolate of mission preaching. As time would show, Gillis's first entry into mission life in Chicago had provided experience, but represented only a foreshadowing of the pace and energy which he would demonstrate as a member of the New York mission band. He traveled extensively, coast to coast, and included missions in the southern sections of the country where hostility to Catholics had long persisted.

As Gillis again changed direction in his ministry, so the Paulist community began to refocus its sights after the pall of Modernism was cast upon the American Church. John J. Hughes, elected Superior General in the extended chapter of 1909, responded to the issue at hand by requiring all Paulists to take the oath against Modernism, a move which led to several resignations from the community. Under Hughes the community expanded its foundation with four new parishes, Good Shepherd in New York (1911), St. Philip Neri in Portland, Oregon (1912), St. Peter's in Toronto (1914), and St. Lawrence in Minneapolis (1915). While the latter two were Newman Centers, the move appears to be one into parish work and away from the mission apostolate. Hughes was the first Superior General who had never been a missionary, spending his entire ministerial life at the mother church of St. Paul the Apostle. The Paulist historian, Paul Robichaud, believes that many men ordained for the Society in this era preferred parish work, which suggests one possible reason for Hughes's decision.[10]

Hughes attempted to impose more discipline on the Society but he he did not possess the personality for such a leadership style. Gracious, mild-mannered, and soft spoken, he was extremely popular both within the community and with parishioners. His ten years as Superior General did, however, provide the stability necessary to lead the community in the wake of the Americanism and Modernism crises.

Throughout his years as a mission preacher, Gillis utilized his summer retreats to retool his spiritual life which he appeared to deny or at best ignore during his public ministry. While he continued to experience feelings of depravity, pessimism, and depression, the summers provided him with the opportunity to rejuvenate and refill his emotionally drained spirit. Most times he wrote long reflections on two topics per day; on other occasions he used his retreat time to read and meditate utilizing such books as Frederic William Farrar's *Life of Christ, Ecce Homo* by Sir John Seeley, Elliott's *The Life of Father Hecker,* and *The Confessions* by St. Augustine. Although the retreats resulted in peaks and valleys along his spiritual journey, he was able near the end of his mission-preaching career to echo Newman, "Begin! Lead Thou me on....Jesus blind me—or let me see but the next step. One step enough for me. Lead Thou me on."[11]

The Catholic Church in general did not vigorously promote missions to non-Catholics. Several factors inhibited the effectiveness of such Catholic missions: the use of Latin in the liturgy projected an image of mysticism which made the faith incomprehensible to some; sacramental and devotional practices further isolated Catholics from other Christians. Additionally, many Protestants felt alienated from the poor social standing of many Catholics. Yet, as Thomas Jonas points out, these same factors which isolated Catholics from other Christian denominations were the express reasons why some people were attracted to the Catholic faith.[12] Many of the Catholic faithful objected to missions to non-Catholics because priests, who were needed in parochial ministry, were siphoned off for the mission apostolate. The number of clergy could not adequately support this new apostolate except at the expense of neglecting their own parish communities.

Apathy toward the mission effort to non-Catholics was seen in the absence of publicity about this apostolate, especially in the dearth of information in Catholic periodicals. In his analysis of Catholic journalism between 1896 and 1912, Jonas notes that few published essays supported the non-Catholic mission effort. Besides essays published by Paulists or other communities of missionaries, the *American Ecclesiastical Review* and the *American Catholic Quarterly,* two leading voices of American Catholic opinion, published during this period only one article between them which dealt with non-Catholic missions.[13]

Paulists were known to arouse fear, reverence, awe, hatred of sin, and love of God in their mission sermons. Missionaries often freely distributed apologetic literature such as Cardinal Gibbons' *Faith of Our Fathers,* Bertrand Conway's *The Question Box,* and George Searle's *Plain Facts for Fair Minds.* Missionaries learned that they had to be lions in the pulpits, but act as lambs in the confessional. For Gillis aiding people to discover repentance and conversion in confession, with its product of God's forgiveness, was the primary objective of the mission. Preaching was aimed to convince people of their need to remove sin from their lives and be transformed. Gillis's own sense of sin was projected in his mission strategy:

> The pity of it is that—the priest *has* [Gillis's emphasis] to judge his brethren—in the pulpit and in the confessional. And he dare not compromise with a sin because he is a sinner himself. He must preach as if he were John the Baptist.[14]

During his first year on the New York mission band, Gillis demonstrated zeal for his work, a drive which bordered on obsession. Finley sees Gillis as one not satisfied with the ordinary, the routine or mundane; he was driven to do more than the average person. While it is probable that Gillis felt more was required of him and thus persisted in his call for personal change of heart, it is equally probable that he was running away from his personal struggle through a busy lifestyle. If he remained active, there would be no time for introspection; he could satisfy his idealism by focusing on the ills in society. Whatever the reason, the record is clear that Gillis was an incessant worker, both as a missionary and later as editor, columnist, and commentator.

Gillis's fall 1910 schedule was tortuous. In October he preached the Forty Hours Devotion in Wilmington, Delaware, then traveled to Peterborough, Canada, where he preached an eleven-day retreat to the local temperance society. The month closed with a mission preached to Catholics in St. Ann's parish in Washington, D.C. The following month he teamed with Conway and William Cartwright to give a two-week mission at St. Mary's parish in Rondout, New York.[15] From November 20 to December 18 Gillis returned north to Toronto where he preached successive two-week missions for Catholics and non-Catholics.[16]

The spring proceeded in a pattern similar to the fall. He

traveled to fifteen cities and preached retreats, missions, Forty Hours, and a handful of extra-ecclesial temperance lectures. His accomplishments were recorded: A two-week mission to Catholics and non-Catholics resulted in nineteen baptisms, seventy enrolled in an inquiry class, 220 "pledges" of voluntary abstinence from alcohol, and over 2,250 confessions.[17]

During the next three years Gillis continued to travel widely and preach missions to Catholics and non-Catholics. He gave missions up and down the west coast in 1912, including the "major pulpit" of Old St. Mary's in San Francisco. In 1913 he teamed with several different Paulists and preached fourteen missions, but was forced for the first time to curtail his activity for any significant amount of time due to excessive fatigue. In January 1914 Gillis, along with fellow Paulists William Cartwright and James Towey, entered the jaws of the lion of anti-Catholicism in a mission sweep through Arkansas. The area was "deliberately chosen as perhaps the most uncompromising field in the U.S. and the most benighted and bigoted," a tour Gillis referred to as "a real penance."[18]

There is no question that Gillis was a good preacher and it is apparent that as his New York ministry progressed, he became more and more satisfied with his apostolate. The Society's move into more parish-based ministries did not dampen in the least the fire of his mission spirit. His sermons included: "True Spirit of Inquiry," "Is One Religion as Good as Another?", "The Church and Fidelity," "Confessions of Sins to a Priest," "The Pope on Church and State," "The Catholic Church in Principle," "Marriage and Divorce," "The True Meaning of Holy Communion," and "Why I Am a Catholic." Some sermons were catechetical; others were apologetic or explanatory. Whatever the mission or the topic, however, Gillis always told his congregations that people must come to a mission with an open and proper attitude; it is not a time to be entertained. For Gillis the sole good mission was conversion to the path of righteousness of Catholic duty: "Beloved brethren, this is the mission, this and nothing else—a chance to stand face to face with God and to listen to the demands of your own soul."[19]

Gillis continued to emphasize personal moral responsibility in his missionary preaching. The Atonement of Christ made salvation a personal choice for all; blindness to this fact was no excuse for irresponsible behavior. God has called all but some refuse to answer. Others want to answer but they are sidetracked by the horrible reality of sin in the world. Gillis referred to sin as "the most glaring and hideous fact in human history"—a personal rejection of God. He believed sin to be one's personal choice—a person can accept or reject God at any time.[20] Gillis also believed that the personal choices we make against God must be seen for what they are. Most people can be convinced that sin is disastrous for them personally, but few can see that sin offends God. Thus, he taught that the only remedy to sin was to see how destructive it is to God. Gillis never spoke of God's grace, especially as manifest in the sacraments, as a remedy to sin or a means which draws one closer to God. Rather, he believed that human effort was fundamental and necessary to achieve spiritual reconciliation.

When asked why so few converts were drawn from the great efforts of Catholic evangelists, he answered that the problem lay with bad Catholics, as if the errant ways of Catholics led non-Catholics to scoff and blaspheme. Honest Protestants were scandalized by the actions of the Catholics they saw. Gillis synthesized his frustration:

> There is scarcely any department of vice or crime that is not represented largely by Catholics....If there is a difference between the morality of Catholic men and of Protestant men, and of men of no religion, the difference is so small that you have to get a microscope to see it.[21]

The solution to the lack of responsibility in the present generation was found for Gillis in the return to greater zeal for Catholicism. People had for too long thought that it was possible to do nothing, to "stagnate in the faith" and things would be fine. Gillis retorted that Catholics had lost the zeal, the spirit of the apostolic age: "The fire that our Lord came to kindle upon the earth does not burn in our hearts."[22] In his preaching Gillis taught that Catholics needed the spirit of the age which drove Isaac

Hecker in his efforts to convert the nation to the faith. Interiorly, however, he continued to question the activity of the Spirit in himself and in society.

In his description of Christianity as a battle, James Gillis argued strongly against the tendency of modern society toward secularism. Almost as a puritan divine he spoke of the legions of Satan under three banners, the world, the flesh, and the devil. He wrote, "Of all the members of the ungodly trinity, the world is the strongest, the most shameless, the most arrogant." The world had lost its sense of morality in its rejection of God. Another time he commented, "Of all theories of life, material-ism is the lowest, the coarsest, the crudest."[23] Christians forget that warfare exists between God and God's enemies. If worldli-ness is to be conquered and truth restored then a battle is nec-essary. For Gillis if a Christian valued truth highly, he would be willing to fight for it. He stated, "No! We cannot, we dare not stand aloof from any kind of battle for fear of soiling our hands or having our sensitive feelings wounded. A man that is a man will leap in and do what he can."[24] The battles for restoration of morality, censure of Protestants, and rejection of secularism became a total war between righteousness and the forces of darkness.

Gillis's projection of his dualistic interior struggle onto the world placed American society in a Jekyll-Hyde conflict. The forces of good, which promoted the free choice of individual and ultimately national conversion, represented Dr. Jekyll while the forces of evil, which jeopardized or rejected freedom and change of heart, stood as the monstrous Mr. Hyde of society. Gillis's personal conflict was played out in the world through people, organizations, and events.

An uncompromising attitude against Protestants was never abandoned by Gillis. In contrast to Isaac Hecker, he rejected religious tolerance, which "leads to indifference," and called such an idea "a curse." He openly accused Protestants of denying the divinity of Christ in their rejection of Catholic teaching. In a sermon preached to non-Catholics in Chicago, he stated:

> I have said before—I repeat it now, and I stand prepared to
> prove my statement, that here in America Congregationalist,
> Presbyterian and Baptist, if not Lutheran clergymen, in spite
> of the gospel, in spite of the creeds of their churches, in defi-
> ance of all the disastrous consequences of this belief, have
> rejected the cornerstone of Christian doctrine, the Divinity
> of Jesus Christ our Savior.[25]

For Gillis this epidemic of unbelief was present in varying
degrees in all institutions, such as schools and churches. Only
the Catholic Church rejected such heresy.

Gillis preached a muscular Catholicism animated by the
determination to battle the evils of the age. Despite the gentleness which Jesus displayed, He "was the strongest, ruggedest
character of man that was ever existent."[26] Gillis professed that
those whose character was soft and flabby were not ready for
Christianity. The priest as the personification of Christ, the *alter
Christus,* represented the virility of the faith and was responsible
for its promulgation and life.[27]

Both inside and outside Catholicism preachers were criss-
crossing the nation in efforts to promote certain causes, or,
like Gillis and his colleagues, to extol the general path of faith
and righteousness. The Progressive era marked the beginning
of lay evangelism in Catholic America. In 1917 the Catholic
Truth Guild was launched by David Goldstein, who had begun
his preaching ministry earlier in 1910. That year, at the invitation of Cardinal William Henry O'Connell of Boston, Goldstein gave lectures to workers on Church social teaching. In
1911 and again in 1914 the German Central Verein sponsored
Goldstein for similar work. In 1917, as mentioned previously,
he joined with his long-time friend, Martha Moore Avery, to
preach against socialism in a series of talks across the nation
that were sponsored by the Knights of Columbus.[28] A Presby-
terian minister and former professional baseball player, Billy
Sunday, was the most influential preacher of the Progressive
era. His urban revivals and support for temperance played "no
small role in the passage of the eighteenth amendment to the
U. S. Constitution."[29]

Mission and Community—1915–1919

It is the theory of some who operate mechanical equipment that such devices should be used as needed until they break with a ready spare at hand; preventive maintenance is not a consideration under such a theory of operation. The brutal schedule which James Gillis kept as a preacher would lead one to believe that he considered himself above physical limitations; he worked until he could no longer function. He refused to heed the warning signs that the 1913 mission year had brought, but rather continued to maintain a full slate of missions and other preaching engagements. He again traveled extensively, reporting many successes as well as disappointments. His frenzied activity masked his feelings of self-doubt.

Possibly because of his hectic lifestyle, Gillis in 1917 waged the first of many battles during his life with the painful skin disease, psoriasis. Although this outbreak was relatively mild compared with later years, the pain and embarrassment he felt from the flakiness of his skin forced him to curtail his activity. He was ordered to California to rest. However, as soon as he arrived he began to preach, traveling up and down the west coast in a reprise of his 1912 campaign.[30]

In the summer of 1919, James Gillis was once again called upon by his brother Paulists to attend the General Chapter of the Society, this time as a delegate from the New York house. The meeting opened on June 25 at St. Paul's in New York. Archbishop Patrick Hayes opened the chapter with a speech to the twenty-eight assembled delegates. Hayes and other bishops were disappointed in the work of the community and called its members to reform. The archbishop, in traveling throughout the country in support of the war effort, had been asked by many religious and clerics, "What's wrong with the Paulists?" Observers felt the community's spiritual life and mission work were at a low ebb. Hayes, believing that the questions were symptomatic of some problem, suggested that the community evaluate itself, diagnose any problems, and conduct internal reform as needed. He also recommended that the community choose a superior general who would require discipline and would enact any reforms suggested by the assembled body. In the course of the discussions delegates agreed to speak with Hayes and make every effort to rectify the defects which he and other members of the hierarchy saw in the Society.[31]

At the 1919 General Chapter Thomas Burke was elected superior general, Joseph McSorley first consultor, and Gillis second consultor, but on the ninth ballot. The Paulist administration was rounded out by the addition of Charles Powers as third consultor.[32] Burke, who at forty-seven was the youngest superior general since Hecker, was a missionary considered by many Paulists to be the best preacher in the community. It was hoped that his disciplined work ethic and understanding of religious life would bring order to the erratic house discipline present under Searle and apparently not corrected under Hughes, as evidenced by Hayes's outburst. Burke's election thus reaffirmed the call for reform in the Society. One Paulist's reaction to the new administration seemed typical for many, "The old guard has met its Waterloo!"[33] Ever engaged in battles, Gillis would have identified with this call for change and reform in the community.

A member of the mission band and now second consultor in the Society, Gillis was granted the authority by Joseph McSorley, the Superior at St. Paul the Apostle, to make assignments for the mission apostolate.[34] With his commission in hand, he asked the General for a list of "sure missionaries" from which to make assignments.[35] This new responsibility inevitably led to some disagreements, ruffled feathers, and wounded egos.[36] Yet, despite the added weight of community responsibilities or perhaps because he was in control, Gillis was never happier as a Paulist. He wrote to the Superior General,

> With regard to your recent letter asking for an indication of preference in regard to work, permit me to say that personally I am happiest when engaged in the missions, and most especially, the missions to non-Catholics. I shall consider myself favored by God and my superiors if I am permitted to engage in the apostolate to non-Catholics as long as my health and strength will last.[37] .

James Gillis found his identity and self-worth in his role as a preacher, to himself, mission congregations, and later the world. He continued to support the Paulist mission effort throughout his career.

In the summer of 1919 Gillis joined the Catholic Unity League, a Paulist-founded New York City foundation, established by Bertrand Conway and three Knights of Columbus, James A. Beha, Charles A. Rush, and Joseph Boldt, and committed to supporting missions to non-Catholics.[38] Gillis recommended to the Superior General that the League be expanded to a national organization with branches initially in each archdiocese and then, with further expansion, to each diocese. New York would be the national headquarters. He also proposed that the National Board of Directors should consist of clergy, laity, "and always at least two members of the Paulist community." The coordination of the League's expansion could be done through the fledgling Bishops' Sub-committee on Reconstruction (formed from the Committee on Special War Activities [CSWA] of the NCWC) headed by Monsignor Michael Splaine. Conway served as the League's director while Gillis volunteered to edit the group's organ once it began to publish.[39]

The advent of the war provided the catalyst for the nation and Church to unite in a common cause. Initially the American Catholic response was provided by the Knights of Columbus in their efforts to set up camps in Europe for the recreational and spiritual needs of soldiers.[40] In June 1917 John J. Burke, CSP, editor of the *Catholic World*, William Kerby of The Catholic University, Lewis O'Hern, CSP, who had assigned Catholic chaplains during the war, and Charles O'Neill, a layman and former Secretary of Labor, met to discuss a more formal response to the war. This initial meeting, together with the subsequent support of Cardinal James Gibbons led in August to the formation of the National Catholic War Council, an organization which was to represent the official Catholic response to the war. By the end of 1917 Burke was able to establish an administrative committee with Bishop Peter Muldoon of Rockford, Illinois as chairman to oversee the work of the Council.[41]

When the armistice was signed in November 1918 reconstruction plans were developed by several different organizations.

The NCWC felt the need to produce a document which would speak of the Catholic response to America's post-war needs. Monsignor Michael Splaine's subcommittee to the CSWA persuaded John Ryan to prepare a plan for the approval of the NCWC administrative committee. Actually Ryan had already developed a program which was to be presented in a scheduled address to a group of Knights of Columbus in New Orleans. Splaine pressed Ryan to revise and expand the talk so it could be submitted to the administrative committee. This work was published on February 19, 1919 as the "Bishops' Program for Social Reconstruction."[42] With Progressivism on the decline, this program of liberal non-politically oriented principles would not be enacted until the New Deal was initiated to raise the nation from the depths of the Depression.

With the war over, the armistice signed, and reconstruction in progress, Americans were faced with another challenge. The 1917 Bolshevik Revolution caused people to see the influence of Lenin everywhere. America's "Red Scare" of 1919 to 1920, which, according to Robert Murray, "unleashed a wave of hatred and hysteria unmatched in modern history,"[43] was fueled by the local presence of the socialist and communist parties and the International Workers of the World (IWW) or "Wobblies." United States Attorney General Matthew Palmer waged a brief but virulent attack on all suspect peoples and groups. His effort played on nativist fears and appealed to "100 percent Americanism."[44]

Transformation and Transition–1920–1922

The 1919 to 1920 mission year was one of great personal trial for James Gillis due to his poor health; his psoriasis had reached the point of severity. He requested from Superior General Thomas Burke that he be relieved of his present duties so he could attend to this ailment. In a series of letters from July through November Gillis asked for release from his preaching assignments, but received no response. He worried that delays would become dangerous to his overall health as well as make the skin disease itself difficult to control.[45]

The physical rest which Gillis desired and needed to restore himself to full health did not come until the summer of

1920. It was decided that he should take a cruise to South America for the summer months. He left Baltimore on June 23 and returned to Philadelphia on September 20. In this three-month period he traveled to Bahía Blanca, Argentina by ship, overland via Buenos Aires to Valparaiso, Chile, and then again by ship through the Panama Canal back to the United States. The trip provided Gillis with the opportunity to rest while he regained his health. The experience would prove, however, to be much more important in the development of his political ideas and his antipathy to war.[46]

Never to be idle, even during a period of rest, Gillis committed himself to reading and to the study of Spanish. In his log for the cruise Gillis listed thirty-four books he had read, including British journalist Philip Gibbs's *Now It Can Be Told, Inside History of the Peace Conference* by E. T. Dillan, and *Biology of War* by Nicolai Georg Friedrich. It is Finley's opinion that Gillis's reading produced "the turning point in his life."[47] What Gillis took from these books solidified his attitude against armed conflict, bolstered his belief in the world's need for conversion and renewal, and became integral to his support for non-intervention which appeared in numerous editorials and essays prior to World War II. War became another manifestation of the monstrous Mr. Hyde against which Gillis would persistently muster his forces and do battle.

Gillis's log kept during the cruise indicates that Gibbs's monograph, *Now It Can Be Told,* made a deep impression on him. In blunt fashion Gibbs presented a dark picture of the war gained from his personal experience as a journalist. He believed that greed and lust for power on both sides had created an environment that produced the initiation and prosecution of war. World leaders had become corrupted by Europe's penchant for war and in the process disregarded what Gibbs believed to be the will of the people. There was no effort to make peace or beg forgiveness; Christ had been placed aside for personal gain. Europe's long history of war and travail had generated a feeling of revolution on the continent; society would never be the same again. Gibbs's ideas must have influenced Gillis in the Paulist's future call for the reform of society.

During the prosecution of the war Gillis made limited comments about the conflict. In a general Christian sense he
bemoaned the pain and suffering which the war created. However, after reading Gibbs's book, he wrote,

> I have read the book principally because I am convinced that
> I must henceforth preach against war as long as I live and
> can speak....All who have voice or pen should at long
> advance argue against war.[48]

Gibbs warned his readers of a tragic future unless "a heritage of
evil and folly is not cut out of the hearts of people."[49] Gillis,
although he did not adopt the Christian pacifist position as articulated by A. J. Muste or later by Dorothy Day and her Catholic
Worker Movement, never retreated from this newly-discovered
moral conviction of the insanity of war.

When he returned to the United States, Gillis continued his
period of recuperation. In the fall he traveled to Hot Springs,
Arkansas to use the baths in order to alleviate the discomfort
and unsightliness of his skin condition. Such treatments would
become a regular part of his life. After the baths, he journeyed to
Los Angeles where he stayed for two months and ministered in
St. Paul the Apostle parish.[50]

Gillis returned to his full schedule of mission preaching in the
fall of 1921. The high point of the season was the various series he
offered during the season of Advent. He preached a set of four
talks at three different parishes. The topics included "Optimism vs.
Pessimism," "Evolution vs. Retrogression," "Reason and Faith,"
plus a four-week course on marriage.[51] In January 1922 he returned
to the South, this time to Alabama. He gave short missions in eight
towns including Tuscaloosa and Mobile. Gillis did not encounter
the bigotry he expected, but few attended his sermons. His report
was mixed: "The winter is not the time for missions in the
south....All in all, [however], a much easier and pleasanter experience than in Arkansas a few years ago."[52] He concluded the season
with a trip to McGill University in Montreal, where, it was reported,
"The students enjoyed [his] retreat immensely."[53]

During the summer months of 1922 Gillis was again active
in community affairs, a sign of positive growth in his attitude

toward fellow Paulists. As second consultor he attended the General Chapter as an *ex officio* delegate. He told the delegates that "The spiritual condition of the community has improved," in response to the critical remarks made by Archbishop Hayes to the Chapter in 1919. More important, he expressed his concern about the lack of interest in the mission apostolate, particularly missions to non-Catholics. He critically questioned the methods used in the novitiate to train men for the missions. For Gillis a return to the training methods of Elliott and McSorley, namely, sermon classes and constant exhortation in conferences, "could hardly be improved upon."[54]

The 1922 Chapter debated the question of the Paulists' future status: were they religious or a band of diocesan priests? Paulists, like most apostolic religious communities, engaged in various ministries, including parochial work, missions, publishing, and campus ministry. The nature of community life would provide a common thread of identity. For Paulists such as Gillis, Elliott, and McSorley the common thread was a deep spiritual life. Burke's administration promoted this understanding, arguing that one's failure to keep common exercises and the temperance pledge indicated a failure in community life. Sides were thus drawn on a future Paulist debate which would posit personal rigorism against a more lax form of religious life.[55]

James Gillis's identity as priest and Paulist was understood and manifest most significantly in his role as a preacher. For over twelve years as a member of the New York mission band he crisscrossed the United States proclaiming his message of the need to freely seek conversion and renewal. Gillis's ministry continued the tradition of the Paulist community as initiated in the thought and work of its founder, Isaac Hecker. More important, however, Gillis's need to find personal peace, which had projected his interior struggle onto society, necessitated his call for reform. The conflict between good and evil, the metaphor of Dr. Jekyll and Mr. Hyde, was present in the world as well as his person. Gillis viewed American society in a dualistic fight for superiority; the survival of the nation's founding principles was in jeopardy and needed to be safeguarded. Experience on the mission platform and in the confessional convinced Gillis that society was evil and needed to return to a period (which he never specified) when the absolute of God and its concept of standards reigned supreme. In Gillis's mind relativism in all forms was a many-headed hydra that needed to be slain; he believed his task was to attack each head one by one with his persistent message of the need to freely discover and accept repentance, renewal, and change of heart.

Gillis's dualistic world view, formed from the influences of family, environment, and experiences in ministry, was in place as the private man is lost from history and replaced by the public image of editor. The forces of evil, which challenged Gillis's beliefs and jeopardized his picture of the proper function of society, could not be ignored by the scrupulous Paulist. He had preached the message of renewal to himself through diaries, retreat notes, and meditation books; the mission circuit allowed him to deliver his thoughts to parish congregations, Catholics and non-Catholics alike. The end of World War I, the decline of Progressivism, and the rise of personal prosperity at the dawn of the 1920s were signals of change in the nation. Gillis also transitioned to continue his work as a preacher and to stand poised to safeguard the nation. Through the transfer of his idealism to society James Gillis gained more inner peace and provided the battle plan for his next thirty years as editor, columnist, and commentator.

CHAPTER 4

"What Price Prosperity?"—
1923–1932

The United States emerged from World War I in an advantageous
global position. While Europe floundered in economic depression and political chaos, American interests were expanding and
on the rise. The decade of the 1920s saw per capita American
income climb by one-third and manufacturing output soar by
greater than sixty-seven percent. Modern conveniences such as
electric lights and appliances, telephones, and especially motor
vehicles became part of everyday life for the majority of Americans. Another indicator of the prosperity of the country was a
100% rise in the number of students attending secondary schools
and colleges. By 1930 almost one-half of the United States population between the ages of fourteen and eighteen was in school as
modern inventions and greater economic prosperity freed youth
from their traditional need to economically aid the family.[1] Most
Americans lived better in the 1920s then they ever had before.

For business, politics, and international prestige, the buzz
word for the "roaring twenties" in the United States was "prosperity," while Warren Harding's simplistic slogan "A return to
normalcy" was an introduction to the bland politics of the twenties. Although small financial downturns did occur after the war
and for brief periods during the decade, the overall economic
growth of the country generated a false sense of security in a system which like an expanding balloon was bound to burst.

This period of American history was a time when twentieth-
century society and the prevailing political system dominated by
nineteenth-century liberalism collided with great force. A collision
course had been developing since the Populist reform movement

81

of the later nineteenth century with impact occurring during the Progressive Era. Liberalism, which emphasized constitutional checks and balances, began to be challenged by the arbitrary power of centralized government. A contradiction was visible between the needs of society and the existing political system, and in the emerging "imperial posture" of America against its cherished principles of self-government. Certainly the 1920s was a time when a dynamic society came to reckon with the existing liberal state. The historian Alan Dawley has accurately summarized the state of the nation in the post-World War I period, "Driven by necessity of circumstance, the United States shifted from the industrial toward the social, from personal liberty toward social security, from less government toward more government."[2]

During the decade of the 1920s James Gillis entered the national scene as an editor, radio personality, and syndicated columnist. His mission to America and identity as a Paulist preacher moved beyond the limits of the parish mission and reached the general citizen; the world became his audience. Gillis attacked the manifestations of darkness, the Mr. Hyde of his world view, which he perceived in people, events, programs, and institutions. He believed that the United States, in its enjoyment of the fatted calf of prosperity, was living an illusionary sense of security that would lead America to ruin. For him the price of prosperity was quite high—the loss of the moral fiber of the nation. Society's rejection of God had yielded the loss of moral absolutism, a condition of "creedless Christianity." He berated "the mental drovers, the moral cowards [who] glorify their laziness with the holy name of toleration and brand as bigots and fanatics those who are hungry and thirsty and battling for Truth!"[3] This state of affairs, combined with his dualistic world view, by which he tended to demonize Godless prosperity and sanctify the traditional American values of home and community in a nation originally conceived in light of divine providence, ignited in Gillis the spirit of a modern-day prophet who argued against the evils of society and for a return to God. The Paulist's world view forcefully collided with the changing American society, a fact which he could not appreciate or refused to recognize.

Editor of The Catholic World—1922-1932

In September 1922 Superior General Thomas Burke appointed Gillis editor of *The Catholic World,* the Paulist monthly magazine of literature and opinion. The move altered the focus of his life and dictated his future until his retirement from active ministry over thirty years later. Gillis's appointment had been determined during the previous summer when the National Catholic Welfare Council had requested the full-time service of John J. Burke, who since 1919 had held the position of General Secretary as well as editor of *The Catholic World.* There is no extant documentation that Gillis was consulted on the appointment, but the well-experienced mission preacher was given a letter of introduction to the Catholic Press Association in July in preparation for his new assignment.[4]

Gillis inherited a significant tradition when he took the helm as editor. *The Catholic World* was first published in April 1865 under the direction of Isaac Hecker, who believed that the journal would allow the Paulists to reach the cultural and intellectual elite and elevate their religious consciousness.[5] Initially identified as an "eclectic magazine of general literature and science," the journal published articles of scholarly and literary merit from the outset. Early issues included reprints from such respected publications as the *Dublin Review, The Month, Civiltà Cattolica, Der Katholik,* and *Le Correspondant.* Fiction, historical essays, poems, items of contemporary interest, book reviews, and a "miscellany" section of short notices and scientific-news items were published in *The Catholic World.* Many prominent American Catholics published their essays in Hecker's journal, including his close friend Orestes Brownson, the Church historian John Gilmary Shea, and Church prelates such as James Gibbons, John Ireland, and John Lancaster Spalding.

Hecker was one of the pioneers of Catholic publishing in the United States. *The Catholic World* joined *Brownson's Quarterly Review* (1844-1875) in the publication of scholarly essays on theology and philosophy. Later the *American Catholic Quarterly Review* (1876-1924) and *The American Ecclesiastical Review* (1889-1975) began to publish articles of academic significance.

In a more popular vein, the weekly *Ave Maria* (founded 1865) found a workable medium between devotional and family literature while the Jesuit periodical *Messenger of the Sacred Heart* (founded 1866) offered devotional literature, serious articles, fiction, poetry, and editorials.[6]

James Gillis was the fifth editor of *The Catholic World.* Augustine Hewit, who formally succeeded the founder as editor upon his death in 1888,[7] mounted a strong attack in the magazine against anti-Catholic forces, especially the American Protective Association (APA), which was at its peak of activity in the mid-1890s. Hewit kept Hecker's format for the magazine and was able to maintain its high standard of quality. Under Alexander P. Doyle, the third editor of *The Catholic World* (1897–1904), the magazine became more pietistic in tone and lost some of the literary quality it had previously enjoyed. To his credit, however, Doyle made efforts to publicize the social dilemmas of the day.[8]

John J. Burke returned the magazine to its former high intellectual plane. Burke and all Catholic editors were forced by the "modernist pall" to steer a safe and conservative course in the turbulent theological waters of the first two decades of the twentieth century. John Sheerin notes that Burke wanted to publish essays which showed the Church to be alive, alert, and attuned to the times, but with bishops instructed by *Pascendi* to seek out suspect writers, he was wary of any essays which did not use Thomistic thought or profess the traditional teachings of the Church. Under Burke's leadership *The Catholic World* published essays and editorials on social action and reform, including articles by William Kerby and John A. Ryan. Burke believed that America should avoid the war in Europe; however, when the United States entered in 1917 he wrote the lead article on patriotism and supported the nation's efforts. Later he cited, as had Gillis, Philip Gibbs's *Now It Can Be Told* and referenced it in a general argument against war.[9]

The Catholic World had always focused on the interaction of Catholicism and American culture, with its editor's vision of this interplay conditioning the content and spirit of the journal. Hecker and Hewit produced a scholarly magazine which avoided controversy; Doyle concentrated on apologetics, and Burke challenged

Catholics by returning the journal to its former scholarly level. James Gillis brought his need for perfection and consequent highly critical view of society to his position as editor, which became his new "pulpit" in the mission to non-Catholics. Using a polemical style, he preached that the bridge between Catholicism and American culture was being undermined by statism, godlessness, and moral irresponsibility; the safeguarding of America was paramount. The journal carried a broad scope of essays ranging from an expose on the Ku Klux Klan, to a discussion of prohibition, to an article on the need to end segregation and promote the cause of black Americans. Thus, *The Catholic World* took on a new more critical face which became apparent in short order.

Gillis placed himself in the conservative camp, politically and socially;[10] the reform he sought was not progressivism but a restoration of the American pioneer mentality, fusing neo-Thomism, medievalism, and classicism with traditional modes of American thought. Gillis's world view continued to perceive society in shades of black and white. He believed that the nation needed to be restored to the nineteenth-century emphasis on individual liberty in the face of a growing reform mentality. Gillis never seemed to understand this shift in American society's attitude. In his conservative mindset he maintained a strong aversion to change and remained firm in his convictions which held the past in high regard. William Halsey describes a three-tier Catholic edifice of intellectual life in the decade of the 1920s. The top of the pyramid, inhabited by progressive thinkers such as George Shuster, Robert C. Pollock, and Russell Wilbur (and to a certain extent *The Commonweal*), sought fresh and expansive ways of understanding the interaction of American culture and Catholicity. John A. Ryan, William Kerby, and John J. Burke were examples of those who occupied the second level, which encouraged interaction between Church and society. A third group, known as "100 percent Catholics," promoted a complete Catholic ethos that was opposed to society in their belief that Catholicism was in "a constant state of cultural conflict and contradiction" in America.[11] Gillis, whose conservative voice yet strong belief in the compatibility of Catholicism and American political values placed him between levels two and three, marked his first years as editor with opinions consistent with mainstream Catholic thought. The absence of any significant criticism to his editorials is indicative of his acceptance by America's Catholic readers.

The Catholic World was only one of several well-recognized Catholic "voices" of the period. The Jesuits' long-standing *Messenger of the Sacred Heart* gave way in the United States in 1909 to *America* and its founder John Wynne, SJ, the distinguished organizer and editor of the *Catholic Encyclopedia*. *America* was established to fulfill in the United States the role which the London *Tablet* filled in England, namely, to "give information and suggest principles that may help in the solution of the vital problems constantly thrust upon our people."[12] In 1925 Wilfrid Parsons was made the fourth editor of *America,* succeeding Richard H. Tierney. The aforementioned *American Ecclesiastical Review* and its legendary editor Herman Heuser, and, after 1927, William Kerby, also published scholarly essays. *The NCWC News Service,* headed by Michael Williams, was established in 1919 as a voice for the bishops, as well as a source of news for the American Catholic population at large.

The Commonweal, first published on November 12, 1924, was organized under the direction of the Calvert Associates headed by Michael Williams. The magazine was lay-operated and served as an independent Catholic voice of its editor and contributors, not a mouthpiece for the Church. Additionally, as Martin Bredeck has written, the journal was the one Catholic periodical "capable of initiating a serious intellectual dialogue with non-Catholic Americans."[13] The managing editor, George Shuster (1925–1937), like Gillis at *The Catholic World,* solicited articles from recognized intellectuals and scholars, including G.K. Chesterton, Jacques Maritain, John LaFarge, SJ, Carlton J.H. Hayes, John A. Ryan, Paul Hanly Furfey, Joseph Fichter, Leo R. Ward, CSC, John Tracy Ellis, and Fulton Sheen.[14] Shuster's biographer, Thomas Blantz, CSC, has written, "*The Commonweal* under Williams and Shuster was able to realize one of its earliest and most important goals—to provide a forum for some of the best contemporary thinkers on religious questions in both Europe and America."[15]

Gillis's assumption of the reins as editor coincided with a shift in Paulist leadership that directed the community toward more intellectual pursuits. Joseph McSorley, a scholar by nature and Gillis's friend and devotee by choice, was elected superior general on June 25, 1924. Like Gillis, McSorley had been mentored by Walter Elliott, who imbued him with the concepts of individual moral rigorism and personal accountability, which he in turn imposed with limited success on the Paulist community. As a scholar, McSorley fully supported Gillis's efforts to make *The Catholic World* a vehicle to reach the intellectual elite. He promoted the intellectual life as evidenced by his encouragement of capable Paulists to seek advanced degrees, the establishment of St. Peter's College,[16] and his acceptance of an additional campus ministry site at McGill University in Montreal.

Gillis wrote his first editorial in October 1922. He lauded Burke for his efforts to return the magazine to its former glory after Doyle had made it "an illustrated monthly of popular appeal." Additionally, he outlined the editorial principles under which he would operate the magazine. First, he expressed the hope to be modern in spirit and always committed to the truth. Secondly, he would not harken on some past glory in a denunciation of the present; the spirit of *The Catholic World* had always emulated the positive convictions of America and would remain so. Lastly and most important, the magazine would remain loyal to the Church and her teachings.[17]

Upon becoming editor, Gillis made some cosmetic and one major change. Within a year he abandoned the editorial "we," substituting "I" to clarify that the opinions were his and his alone. One may infer that this relieved the Paulists from any responsibility for the journal's editorial position. He also changed the printed format of the magazine with a shift to double columns which he felt were easier to read. He began to run more advertisements than his predecessors, including Paulist Press books and pamphlets, religious goods, and student summer camp programs. The length of the journal, however, remained at 144 pages per issue.

In October 1923 Gillis made the suggestion that the Paulist Press and *The Catholic World,* which had always been one entity, should be separated. He felt that independent offices would allow the Press to expand its business and, of course, allow him more autonomy. The suggestion was favorably forwarded by the consultors (of which he was one) to the delegates of the 1924 General Chapter who approved the new organization. Gillis would control the magazine and James F. Cronin would supervise the operation of the press.[18] Later Superior General Joseph McSorley assigned Gillis "exclusively to work on *The Catholic World*" and told him he was under no obligation to other activities except by his own choice.[19]

From the outset Gillis had received permission to hire an assistant editor for the magazine. He wanted John Carter Smyth for the position, "at times [when he was] not employed on missions," but the consultors felt this "inadvisable."[20] Thus, in July 1926 Father Albert A. Murray was asked to assist the editor in the business bureau of *The Catholic World*. Murray's presence was helpful, but Gillis preferred a person to serve as circulation manager for the magazine. He was disappointed that little effort had been made by the local Paulist houses to increase the journal's circulation, which formed its economic lifeline.[21] Gillis felt that a staff member dedicated solely to gaining subscriptions would remedy the problem and increase revenue for the magazine. No assignment, however, was made at this time.

Gillis's call for a circulation manager and his complaint that the community did little to promote circulation of *The Catholic World* indicated the magazine's tenuous financial status. Throughout the 1920s the journal operated in a deficit. Before separation, the Paulist Press maintained a "slender margin of profit," but this was quickly replaced by red ink once *The Catholic World* became a separate entity. In 1924 the magazine reported a $1160 deficit; between 1929–1932 it amounted to $10,805.[22] In response to fellow Paulists who were critical of the magazine's financial record, Gillis jumped to his own defense. In letters to the Superior General he reported minimal costs of operation for the magazine, much lower than *The Commonweal,* and lamented that *America* and *The Commonweal* "constantly poach upon our preserves. That is to say they attract our subscribers and our contributors."[23] The magazine's deficit operation, exacerbated by the depressed American economy, led some to call for the magazine's reduction to a quarterly. Gillis strongly rejected this idea and in response again called for a full-time circulation manager which would avoid "the chagrin and humiliation of acknowledging defeat before the public and clergy."[24] A "Committee on Finances" assigned by the 1932 General Chapter to investigate the magazine's financial status reported that little could be done to rectify the debt. In an interesting comparison, the other Paulist monthly magazine, *The Missionary,* organ of the Apostolic Mission House, reported over $12,000 in profit during this same period.[25]

As might be expected, *The Catholic World* bore the character of its editor. James Finley evaluates Gillis's mark as more distinctive and forceful than any previous editor. He directed the magazine along lines of his personal interest; national and international politics and other significant contemporary issues became the major thrust to the journal. Religious issues of the period did not attract Gillis's commentary and were, for the most part, absent from the magazine's monthly essays. Finley has also stated that the authentic Gillis was found in *The Catholic World,* where his comments were uncensored and could land with the gentleness of a pinprick or the power and force of a sledgehammer.[26] Gillis's principles, which advocated the restoration of the nineteenth-century belief in individualism, represented a particular conservative American Catholic mindset of the 1920s. His strong support of traditional Catholic moral theology and the integrity of the family, defense of the Church against persecution, both foreign and domestic, and belief in the compatibility of Catholicism and American democratic principles were positions held by the majority of Catholics. The unique aspect of Gillis's views in this period (and beyond) was his reasoning for the opinions he held, based on ideals of duty and personal responsibility. The specifics of Gillis's world view that would place him in opposition to others would not be manifest to any large extent until the presidency of Franklin Roosevelt.[27]

Gillis used a confrontative and polemical editorial style in order to put forth his personal vision and promote his agenda for American society. A well read and highly articulate man, he generally found one or more books, essays, editorials or speeches which were used as a springboard from which he dove into particular issues. Gillis held no punches, was sarcastic and comical, but seldom if ever lost control in his often biting and always clearly written editorials.[28] It appears that Gillis searched for material that could serve as grist for the mill of his ever-active mind, which continually sought to promote his message of America's duty to return to God and moral responsibility. The editorial page of *The Catholic World* would thus serve as Gillis's principal vehicle to continue the Paulist mission to non-Catholics.

As with some previous editors Gillis was able to attract quality contributors to the journal. Foreign contributors included such notables as Hilaire Belloc, G.K. Chesterton, Alphonse Lugan, and Felix Klein. A host of well-known Americans also wrote for *The Catholic World*—Theodore Maynard, John Fenlon, SS, John A. Ryan, Francis Clement Kelley, George Shuster, Michael Williams, Condé Pallen, Bishop Thomas Shahan, Anna McClure Sholl, and Agnes Repplier, as well as many leading Paulists. As editor Gillis directed the magazine toward his own views, at times referring in editorials to essays published in a particular issue which voiced his opinion. Finley claims that Gillis used the journal as his stage. His association with the likes of Belloc, Chesterton, and Ryan placed him above being a "mere editor."[29] If *The Catholic World* was his stage, then society as a whole was his audience.

From the outset Gillis blazed his own path as editor and journalist. As described most eloquently by Halsey,[30] Gillis attacked the sense of pessimism and disillusion, as symbolized by George Santayana's *Character and Opinion in the United States* (1920) and Ezra Pound's *Hugh Selwyn Mauberly* (1920),[31] which prevailed in post-World War I America. Despite his inclination to pessimism and his prophetic self-image, he opposed the postwar mood articulated by many novelists and intellectuals. Gillis expressed optimism:

> We Catholics are more hopeful for modern civilization than are they who built modern civilization. We cannot be said to be the creators of the modern system, yet we do not consider it to be altogether hopeless. We believe the world has a future....We are more modern than the moderns.[32]

The choice was simple for Gillis: "Optimism is Christianity. Pessimism is paganism."[33] He anchored his editorial comments in society's need of Christ, whose presence gave the foundation to absolute moral principles and whose absence brought chaos and eventual ruin to society. Quoting G.K. Chesterton, whom he respected greatly, he once concluded, "Confidence in the values of existence and in the intrinsic victory of virtue is not optimism but religion."[34] Optimism, as seen in Christ's presence, was to be manifest in the national conscience as it responded to its call to moral duty.

Gillis's personal pessimism and his public display of optimism exhibits what initially appears to be a contradiction. The pessimism against which Gillis wrote, however, was void of faith and hope. He possessed a dualistic world view pitting good against evil, but Gillis also possessed faith and the hope that change was possible. Thus, one must nuance the concept of pessimism in order to understand why Gillis was so critical of the pessimistic attitude of the great voices of literature and politics when a similar attitude pervaded his public message. Gillis's argument was against the hopelessness and lack of faith which he perceived in the attitude of many contemporary writers.

The variance of American Catholic opinion in the 1920s on contemporary issues is well illustrated by a comparison of editorials and essays in *The Commonweal, America,* and *The Catholic World. The Commonweal* served as "an open forum for constructive Catholic criticism and exchange"[35] and took a generally progressive stand on issues while clearly maintaining its Catholic base. One example of this stance was the journal's criticism of traditional Catholic higher education (specifically the pastoral methods of Father John O'Hara at Notre Dame) in an essay, "Insulated Catholics," written by George Shuster. In 1925 *The Commonweal* supported the right of John Scopes to teach evolution, although it never doubted that he would be convicted. Concerning prohibition the journal said there was no one Catholic opinion on the Volstead Act.[36] In communion with the prevailing Catholic opinion, Williams directed the magazine in an attack on the Mexican government for its policies which brought persecution to the Church.

America, under its editor Wilfrid Parsons, was generally conservative. The magazine fully supported Catholic education and parental rights to educate their children, especially during the period when legislation aimed at the creation of a federal department of education was many times debated in the Congress. *America* led the Catholic drive in the 1920s in criticism of the Mexican government's anticlerical policy, calling upon the United States government to take action to support the persecuted Mexican Catholics. On the issue of evolution the magazine stated, "Religion will be defended, Science advanced and Freedom safeguarded" by avoiding the two extremes and seeing a harmony between science and religion.[37]

Gillis's polemical style in *The Catholic World* left no doubt for his readers of his traditional stand on the issues of the day. He strongly promoted the need for religion to be part of education, supported Catholic education, and forcefully denounced academic freedom in higher education as a tool which generated pernicious ideas and theories in the minds of America's youth. He connected the evolution issue to education in general in stating that the concept of human evolution brought irreligion into the classroom. Like *America* and *The Commonweal,* Gillis was critical of the United States' refusal to chastise Mexico for its abuse of the Church.

Concern voiced by members of the Paulist community over the content of Gillis's editorials precipitated a request for co-editors for *The Catholic World.* The issue was initially raised in June 1927, when some members felt the Paulist community in general was committed to an anti-prohibition stance from the views expressed in the magazine. Gillis was informed the next month that Joseph Malloy, Henry Riley, and Albert Murray would be appointed as an "Advisory Board" for the journal in order to moderate the ofttimes caustic and blunt views which Gillis expressed in his editorials.[38] The assignment did not come to fruition,[39] however, and thus in the 1929 General Chapter the issue was once again raised. The Chapter proposed that the consultors also be queried when editorials involved the interests of the community. Unanimous opposition from the consultors to an editorial opinion would be referred to the Superior General for final resolution.[40] The situation remained unresolved until

1932, when the General Chapter adopted a resolution which called for a special "Board of Consultors," two in number, who "must discuss with the Editor-in-chief and pass on all articles in *The Catholic World.*" In order "to aid, not dampen" Gillis, Superior General John Harney assigned McSorley and Malloy to this board with the title "associate editors."[41]

The Preaching Platform—The Basis for Editorial Opinion— 1923–1926

James Gillis had been assigned full-time as editor of *The Catholic World,* but his position allowed him the freedom to exercise other aspects of ministry as he saw fit. He never severed his ties with preaching and public speaking, a ministry which had always been considered the chief apostolate of the Paulists. After 1922 Gillis rarely accepted invitations to give missions, but his preaching log reveals the wide breadth of his activity. He participated in Communion breakfasts, retreats, informal talks, prepared addresses, baccalaureate and graduation speeches, besides many series of talks, traveling in the process on numerous occasions from coast to coast. One can envision his demanding schedule through the following negative response to an invitation to speak:

> I am speaking for nine consecutive nights just now, and I have a great deal of writing to do for my *Catholic World* before leaving town in the middle of next week. I then have lectures in Boston, Providence and Philadelphia, almost consecutively, carrying me quite up to Lent. In Lent I have so much preaching to do that I feel it would be impossible for me to speak to you[r group].[42]

Despite the time commitment, Gillis needed to preach and voice his message of free choice and conversion in order to exercise his Paulist identity.

The impression made by a speaker in a particular address has many times led to the development of one's reputation as an orator. "False Prophets," a series of talks delivered October 21–28, 1923 at St. Paul's in New York City, was such an event for

James Martin Gillis. The lectures were syndicated in *The Catholic World* between December 1923 and July 1924 with an expanded and slightly edited version published as a book by Paulist Press in 1925. "False Prophets," understood by James Finley as the high point of Gillis's preaching career, collectively attacked the misguided ideas of several contemporary well-known personalities. According to Gillis the literary works and opinions of George Bernard Shaw, H.G. Wells, Sigmund Freud, Sir Arthur Conan Doyle, Frederick Nietzsche, and Ernst Haeckel had poisoned Christian belief, infected society with the malaise of pessimism, promoted immorality, removed ethical standards, and rejected faith and hope. "False Prophets" was Gillis's first major attack on the prosperity which he saw as a progressive illness in the body politic of America. Literary works and their creators, that promoted Godless ways and ideas, removed moral standards, and exonerated society from its duty of personal responsibility demanded such a vigorous response.

Gillis set the tone for his attack by linking paganism with immorality in his first lecture; subsequent talks were an enumeration of the errors of the promoters of this new paganism. As editor and later radio commentator and columnist, Gillis regularly attacked Shaw and Wells. He denounced Shaw's plays which, "ridicule what the human race reverences and extols what the human race abominates." He further characterized the British dramatist as a "universal iconoclast and unmitigated pessimist."[43] Gillis chastised Wells for his "vituperative contempt" for Christianity. He also felt the popular and prolific British writer wrote too much while delving into domains beyond his expertise. He used Wells' rejection of the concept of one true God to illustrate the author's ignorance.[44]

The monograph *False Prophets* attacked the godlessness of French novelist and Nobel Prize winner Anatole France (1844–1924) and Mark Twain as well. France was characterized by Gillis as one who "hates religion, but cannot leave religion alone. He denies God, but he blasphemes God. He detests and ridicules the Church, but the stamp of the Church is on his soul. He is fascinated, beguiled, charmed, hypnotized, by what he hates." Twain was called "a disillusioned misanthrope, full of contempt for human nature, and of blasphemous criticism of God."[45]

Gillis concluded this special series of lectures with a talk titled "Back to Christ or Chaos." He perceived contemporary society in a state of chaos, having lost its direction in rejecting Christ. Prosperity had removed Christ from His rightful place of prominence. Immorality and modern theories such as evolution had been substituted for God, with the consequence of moral standards becoming lost in the confusion. Society was not too puritanical; it was too loose. Gillis sought no return to a utopian time; God was just as much present in the contemporary world as any previous time. He concluded on a note of optimism which demonstrated a deep-seated value of hope,

> But though the leaders of the world have shut Christ out,
> He will enter again if they ask Him. If they do not admit
> Him, their own dire prophecies of the disintegration of civi-
> lization will be realized. It is either Christ or chaos.[46]

Gillis's polemic against intellectuals and other contemporary culture builders was shallow in its analysis. He assumed that the absence of God removed all possibility of morality in society, thus disregarding the common belief that good people of good will, regardless of their theological perspective, may possess a strong sense of morality. His rejection of godlessness in people, institutions, or ideas allowed for no possibility to discover good. Thus, in complement with his world view, Gillis placed the Church against society; Catholicism was pictured as incompatible with secular culture, a view which sharply contrasted with the belief of Paulist founder Isaac Hecker.

A second special series of lectures which helped to establish Gillis's mark as an orator was "Champions of Unbelief," delivered January–May 1925 at St. Paul's. As with "False Prophets," St. Paul's church overflowed with people who came to hear him speak; he did not disappoint them. He attacked four influential agnostics/atheists in his lectures. The philosopher Voltaire was called Mephistopheles, "a genius of the satanical sort," while Edward Gibbon and Tom Paine were chastised for their total disregard of religion. The American lawyer and politician 'Bob'

Ingersoll (1833–1899), who popularized Biblical higher criticism and championed Darwinism, was described as "hopelessly inexpert" in his attempts to use Scriptural exegesis or the philosophy of religion. Agnosticism, Gillis concluded, is inhuman in its claim that one cannot exercise the mind to solve the most basic of all questions, the meaning of life.[47]

Gillis's preaching painted a picture of the godlessness of society. With God absent, the moral absolute needed to bring order to society and restore hope was missing with the consequent loss of society's moral fiber and sense of duty. Gillis's critical oratory expressed his disapproval of American culture, which had drifted away from the Christian principles upon which it had been founded, and had gorged itself with the evil of false prosperity.

Gillis's attitude portrayed a total condemnation of unbelief despite the status of those who expressed such ideas. His view was at times anti-intellectual as he emphasized a strong Catholic ghetto mentality that "one is for us or against us." Opinions expressed which countered Gillis's world view were regularly and emphatically rejected. His anti-Protestant sentiment, earlier expressed on the mission circuit, was expanded to a rejection of all unbelievers. This attitude helps to explain the rationale behind Gillis's promotion of missions to non-Catholics in that Protestants and non-believers needed the truth of Catholicism. His opposition to non-Catholic belief, however, did not dampen his recognition and defense of the basic human rights of all people.

Radio Ministry–WLWL–1925–1932

Energetic priest editors would have been hard pressed to keep the preaching schedule of James Gillis, in view of the fact that this was a collateral ministry after his primary responsibility as editor of *The Catholic World*. Yet, in 1925 he added a third platform for his commentary as he joined the staff of WLWL, the Paulist-owned-and-operated radio station in New York.

Discussion initiated in December 1924 about the possibility of the community's entry into the new field of radio. At the

monthly consultors' meeting, in which Gillis continued to participate from his 1922 election, the Paulist League was established

> to diffuse knowledge of the Catholic Church among the
> people of the United States and Canada by the distribution
> of literature, the organizing of lectures and missions to non-
> Catholics, and such other activities as will facilitate the
> spread of the faith among those outside the fold.[48]

The latter part of this statement led to a discussion about the
establishment of a radio station at St. Paul's. Initially it was
thought that operation could be started for $25,000–35,000 with
$5,000–10,000 annually for maintenance.[49]

In February 1925 *The Catholic World* reported the foundation
of the Paulist League and announced its desire to help fund the
radio station by asking its subscribers to join the League effort.
Annual dues of one dollar were collected and placed toward the
money needed to open the station. In April 1925 the magazine
ran a full-page advertisement which solicited donations from contributors for the station. Money was received, but the estimated
start-up costs were found to be far too conservative when in March
1925 the cost was revised to $100,000 for a 5000-watt station.[50]

Paulist radio station WLWL officially went on the air on
Thursday September 24, 1925. The Paulist Choristers, under the
direction of William Finn, CSP, opened the program with
"Come Holy Spirit" and "The Star-Spangled Banner." The station then announced its motto as "For God and Country" along
the lines of the Paulist tradition.[51] Cardinal Patrick Hayes gave a
brief talk to conclude the initial broadcast. The station was
incorporated as the Universal Broadcasting Corporation with
Father James Cronin as station manager.[52]

The early years of the station were difficult but exciting. Initially programming was scheduled seven days per week in the
evenings and on Sunday afternoons. Letters were received from as
far away as England and Alaska reporting that the station was
heard. Reviews of the station's initial programming were quite
favorable, but with the formation of the Federal Radio Commission in 1927 the station was forced to regularly shift broadcast frequencies and later to share a frequency with WMCA, a commercial

enterprise, which received the bulk of the allotted air time. By the end of 1927 WLWL was reduced to fifteen hours per week of broadcast time. By 1932 things were no better as the station was forced to share its operating frequency of 1100 KHz with WPG in Atlantic City, which was granted sixteen hours per day of programming; WLWL was given only two hours per day.[53]

At the time WLWL was licensed radio was in its infancy; only seven other Catholic-owned and -operated radio stations in the United States were in operation. It was at this same time that the most famous radio priest of the day, Father Charles Coughlin, made his appearance over the air waves. A former Basilian priest and Canadian native, Coughlin was incardinated in the diocese of Detroit in 1923 when Bishop Michael Gallagher appointed him as pastor of Little Flower parish in Royal Oak, Michigan, a suburb of Detroit. Coughlin immediately discovered two significant impediments plaguing the parish—the presence of the Ku Klux Klan and a large debt incurred from the recent construction of the new parish church.

Coughlin initiated his radio ministry on October 17, 1926 in order to combat the Klan and raise money for the parish. At this time his talks were aimed at children and were mainly apologetic in defense of the faith, although at times he did attack proponents of birth control. His commanding voice and manner made him quite popular and his ministry highly successful. His popularity led in 1930 to a contract from CBS for a national radio audience. The Radio League of the Little Flower was thus established to aid fund-raising and answer correspondence which began to flood into the parish.[54]

James Gillis preceded Coughlin in his WLWL debut on October 13, 1925, less than one month after the station initiated broadcasts. His first few months on the air were as host of "Radio Question Box," a weekly program which approximated the "Question Box" of the mission circuit. Anonymous submissions of questions by mail were answered during the program. Some of the many areas covered by Gillis were: marriage, Freemasonry, use of Latin in Church services, the Bible, concept of Trinity, prohibition, separation of Church and State, and the relationship of the American Church to the Vatican. Gillis continued to host the program until late February 1926 when he severed his tie because the "questions made [his] heart sick."[55]

In his responses to the questions Gillis maintained total orthodoxy, yet was constrained by the nature and length (fifteen minutes) of the program to answer only what was asked without commentary. In hindsight it is probable that Gillis was frustrated with this program, yet he gave succinct orthodox answers to questions posed. He stated that marriage was inviolable and the center, along with children, of family life; Freemasonry was denounced because of its secrecy and anti-Catholic views. He gave a rudimentary history of the development of the Canon of Scripture, the Catholic position on Church and State relations using the ideas of John Carroll, and agreed that the Church had no formal position on the question of prohibition.[56]

On February 23, 1926 Gillis began a new program on WLWL, "Comments on Current Events." He explained his purpose:

> The newspapers, with perhaps necessary brevity, have announced the feature of our radio program as "Current Events." A more precise title would be "Comment on Current Events." For I have no intention of retailing news. WLWL is not a news bureau. I shall merely select here and there, an item or two, or perhaps sometimes three, from the daily press, and record the reaction of a mind that is interested first in religion and morality, secondly, and perhaps equally, in the general welfare of our country, and of all countries.[57]

Gillis's talks were designed for a fifteen-minute show. His words were thus more focused on the issue or question under discussion than his editorials and generally more biting in their content. In early talks he struck a cautious note on Mussolini in Italy (against a tide of Catholic support), denounced the League of Nations as ineffective and established on lies and innuendo, criticized Sinclair Lewis for his satire of American life and pessimism, and warned the United States not to disarm as it was inconceivable that other nations would follow suit.[58] Gillis's radio program served as another "pulpit" to preach his message to America.

His early radio presentations were favorably received as evidenced by extant correspondence which was overwhelmingly

positive. Letters from both Protestants and Catholics congratulated him on the new program and supported his stance on
issues; many people asked for copies of his talks. The correspondence also shows that when critical letters were received Gillis
answered the criticism without a single retraction. As he
preached during his days on the mission band, nobody was
worse than one who failed to live by his convictions. James Gillis
would never be so accused.

Radio and Editorial Commentator–1925–1932

In possession of several major public platforms from which
to comment, few items escaped the attention of James Gillis. His
commentary in the 1920s concentrated on domestic issues with a
few forays into the international scene. Gillis's public attacks on
the degradation of morality, a consequence of the false prosperity of the era which had cast out God from a position of preemi-
nence, were made and repeated time and again. He was
consistent and unwavering in his effort to return the world to the
state of idealism, the spiritual perfection, sense of duty, and message of free choice and conversion, which he had always entertained for himself and later for society as well.

The decade of the 1920s saw many American Catholics
adopt an offensive strategy, shrugging off apologetics, in their
proclamation of the Church's ideals and principles. Gillis had
anchored *The Catholic World* in the American ideal; it was the
cornerstone upon which the magazine was built and from which
it would continue to grow. He wrote, "America is a 'magnificent
experiment' not only politically but ethnically." George Shuster
and Michael Williams echoed similar feelings. Like Gillis, Shuster rarely shied from a public debate, spoke against the anti-
Catholic sentiments of the decade, and preached in *The Catholic
Spirit in America* that there were no irreconcilable differences
between Catholicism and American culture. Shuster, however,
was not polemical in his approach, possibly because of his experience in the classroom as a professor of English at the University
of Notre Dame. Williams, in an address to the Calvert Associates,
The Commonweal's parent body, proclaimed that the Church had

accepted the American state as its own, a view which echoed the theme of compatibility between Catholicism and democracy.[59] The connection of Catholicism to American ideals was a strategy aimed to push the Church more into mainstream America. Despite its numerical superiority over any other single denomination (achieved in the mid-nineteenth century) Catholics needed to break through the long-standing stereotype which placed the Church at odds with democracy. The efforts of Gillis, Shuster, Williams, and other editors of Catholic publications helped to raise the consciousness of Catholics, led to more general acceptance of the Church in the administration of Franklin Roosevelt, and culminated in American Catholicism's high tide of visibility in the 1950s.

This decade saw the continuation of earlier arguments which authors had used to demonstrate Catholic origins of the principles of democracy utilized in America's foundational documents. The 1917 thesis of Alfred O'Rahilly, which credited Robert Bellarmine as the ultimate source of Thomas Jefferson's inspiration, by way of Robert Filmer's treatise *Patriarcha,* was echoed by several authors[60] including Gillis who promoted the theory in *The Catholic World* and on WLWL.[61]

Many Protestants answered Catholicism's claim to be the legitimate source of democracy. Winfred Garrison argued that Bellarmine's ideas differed in several key points from the ideals of the framers of the Constitution, including religious tolerance and representation from the common citizen. Even some Catholics rejected the prevailing opinion such as the Capuchin friar John Lenhart, who could only say that Catholic principles were in general agreement with the principle of the Declaration of Independence. Variance in detail, however, made him conclude, "There cannot be a question of borrowing on any side."[62]

In defense of their patriotic loyalty American Catholics continued to battle the ever present menace of nativism and anti-Catholicism. Shuster saw the problem as a remnant of animus created during the period of mass immigration. Catholics needed to defend their inalienable rights granted them by the Constitution. Williams also noted the continuation of this long-standing trend but advocated an offensive posture in response, especially for the laity: "They [Catholics] should put aside all lingering restraints and inhibitions of the 'inferiority complex'."[63] Gillis fought anti-Catholic bigotry, which could "in a generation or two bring the United States to ruin." In *The Catholic World* Gillis first broached the idea of bigotry as a constitutional question, declaring that despite the law of the land, Catholics were being denied their political rights. He lamented that there appeared to be no "prospect for the removal of this notorious injustice."[64] Surprisingly, he did not worry about the Klan, which had resurfaced under Imperial Wizard Wesley Evans in the early 1920s, because he believed the organization to be in decline, characterizing it as a "curious combination of comedy and tragedy, of melodrama and burlesque, of buffoonery and villainry [*sic*]."[65]

The "roaring twenties" provided the backdrop to a major confrontation between the forces of Fundamentalism and modernity. As discussed by R. Laurence Moore, twentieth-century Fundamentalists drew clear lines between true Christianity (as they perceived it) and theological modernism, often tying themselves to beliefs in Scriptural inerrancy and Dispensational Premillennialism. In the era of World War I the movement, which "arose as a self-conscious force within already existing Protestant denominations," was more defensive than that of earlier theological conservatives. Fundamentalists equated religious behavior with American patriotism; they denounced every trend that could remotely be construed as theologically or politically liberal. One writer has referred to Fundamentalist preachers of the day, such as Carl McIntire, Gerald Winrod, and Billy James Hargis, as "Apostles of Discord." Although Fundamentalists rejected modernity, their greatest challenge, in Moore's opinion, was found in battles with other theological conservatives who were not convinced that a purge of liberals was necessary or wise.[66]

The July 1925 Scopes "monkey" trial was the one event which captured the attention of the nation in the Fundamentalist-modernity struggle. John Scopes was accused of teaching the theory of evolution in the public high school of Dayton, Tennessee. Fundamentalists, who believed Darwin's theory to be repugnant to idyllic Protestant views, found their champion in this debate in the three-time Democratic presidential nominee William Jennings

Bryan. Scopes was defended by the fledgling American Civil Liberties Union (ACLU), which obtained the services of the famous litigator Clarence Darrow. Legally the case was won by Bryan; Scopes' fine of $100 was paid by the ACLU. Ironically, Bryan died suddenly only a few days later.

James Gillis fought modernity through his characterization of it as non-religion. He claimed that the modernist mindset, with its infidelity to long-held principles as a response to the new demands of life, was a compromise rooted in intellectual dishonesty and entailed a rejection of the absolute basis for morality. Jesus, however, never compromised his convictions and thus neither should the Church. He summarized the conflict in this manner:

> Christians, Catholic and non-Catholic, must recognize, unless they are curiously blind, that the battle is on between Christianity and infidelity. Christianity may be disguised under the newly invented word "Fundamentalism" and infidelity may go masquerading under the title "Modernism," but the battle is really between religion and non-religion.[67]

Gillis fully believed that the loss of moral fiber in America was centered in the absence of the Divine; prosperity had become a false god. The divorce of religion from everyday life was the chief cause of demoralization, crime, even the domination of the state over the individual. The period was a "soft and sentimental age"; the nation needed conversion which could only be obtained through personal freedom.[68]

The loss of marriage as an institution, the rise of divorce as an acceptable option, and the presence of such alternative ideas as "companionate marriage" were signs of the degeneration of moral life in the nation. Gillis considered divorce laws "immoral" and trial marriage as a manifestation of a de-Christianized civilization. Without the perpetuation of the family, "civilization [wa]s doomed."[69] He rejected the contemporary view which promoted styles of ethics: "Right and wrong are objective and eternal....There must be no sliding scale of morality....Right is right and wrong is wrong eternally."[70] Society had become blind to proper norms through its removal of personal responsibility. In a rebuttal to comments made by

Clarence Darrow, who stated criminals were not responsible for their actions, Gillis declared, "If no [personal] responsibility, then no morality. If no morality, then no civilization."[71]

Gillis expressed the idea that the capital error of the age was the dissociation of religion from government. He saw the world fumbling along, groping in the dark, because it did not recognize the traditional teachings of Christ. According to the Paulist editor, the world was more indebted to the principles of the four Gospels than to any constitution, treaty, or declaration; until Christ and His message were brought to bear in the arbitration of international controversies and society's daily affairs, the world would remain in darkness. In an early editorial which was repeated four years later on WLWL (a practice which was common for Gillis) he wrote,

> Everybody, at least everybody who thinks, is asking, "What's wrong with the world?" Here is one thing that's wrong. Christianity is held to be an ideal, feasible in the relations of man to man, but quite unworkable in the relations of nation to nation....That is the falsehood that has broken the world, and that is frustrating the efforts of all peace conferences.[72]

For Gillis a government's dissociation from God eliminated its ability to serve its citizens and thus became a manifestation of Mr. Hyde present in society.

Gillis believed that the world's leaders and culture makers needed to be converted. The editor, who brought the fear of God into every aspect of his life, felt constrained in action by his understanding of a wrathful God and his inability to see Providence at work in the world; he felt the culture leaders needed to be constrained as well. Conversion to the belief that God must be present in every aspect of life would save the world. As alluded to previously, the principal sign of deviant prosperity which Gillis saw present in the United States was the demise of the family. His 1928 monograph, *The Catholic Church and the Home,* was only one of many media he used to hammer home his tenet that the family was foundational, the basis of all social structure; it was the sign of a vital civilization. To place the family in peril by divorce or to reject the integral nature of children in marriage by birth control was to jeopardize all society. The dissolution of marriage and the creation of its novel substitutes created a domino effect in the loss of family and eventually the demise of civilization. Gillis questioned what benefit the state could provide without the family. He wrote, "What doth it profit a state to arrange all these details [trade, debts, taxes, customs, etc.], if the home, the family, the soul of the state be lost?"[73]

Disorders in American family life in the 1920s were noted by both religious and secular groups. Jeffrey Burns, the foremost chronicler of the family crisis of the first half of the twentieth century in Catholic life, has stated of the period 1930 to 1962 in the United States, "At the head of the Catholics' list of duties was the defense and restoration of American family life." While Catholics saw the family in crisis, secular sociologists, as characterized by the opinion of the University of Chicago's Ernest W. Burgess, viewed the situation as a shift from an understanding of family unity to "personal happiness of individual members."[74]

The Catholic Church in America responded to the family crisis in theory and action. Sociologists, such as Paul Hanly Furfey, restated Church principles of family life, including the primary goal of the procreation and education of children. Several Catholic organizations acted to rescue the family. The National Catholic Rural Life Conference, organized by Edwin O'Hara in November 1923, responded most vigorously to rural America with educational programs, while the German Central Verein promoted family values against the onslaught of the modern industrial complex. The Family Life Bureau, a wing of the Social Action Department of the NCWC, founded in 1931 under the guidance of Father Edgar Schmiedeler, OSB, brought an institutional and hierarchical response to the crisis.

Birth control, an issue which touched on both the moral degradation of the nation and the family crisis, was a practice against which Gillis remained firm. His arguments were clear and consistent in his total refutation of what he at different times labeled "vice," "crime," "perversion," and, referencing Genesis 38:9, "onanism." This practice was a crude attempt to trick nature and thus was a violation of God's principles. In response to the perceived necessity to curb a burgeoning and over-popu-

lated world, Gillis often cited statistics which demonstrated that
the world could easily support more than triple its present population. Until nature proved its inability to cope with the world's
population, the argument was flawed.[75]

Gillis's final argument on birth control, a term which he
deplored for it spoke in positive terms of an unspeakable evil,
saw such a practice as racial suicide. He cited history and
claimed that the great civilizations of Greece and Rome committed suicide by their practice of birth control. While the "civilized" people of the world frustrated nature, the "barbarians"
fulfilled the (unknown to them) Biblical edict to increase and
multiply. He again used demographic statistics to show that
between three and four children per family were necessary to
maintain population at its present level. The United States at the
time averaged less than three children per family and was, thus,
in danger of repeating history. He stated, "Race suicide is at least
as immoral as warfare."[76]

Gillis applied his analysis of birth control as racial suicide to
the immigration issue which, in the opinion of many pro-birth
control advocates, needed to be restricted. Many Americans in
the 1920s believed that Americanization was ineffective, that the
"melting pot" was no longer a viable ideal. Ineffective assimilation precipitated the call for immigration restriction. Gillis
responded that if the Anglo-Saxon majority multiplied as they
should they would have nothing to fear from immigrants. For
him the problem was not immigration but rather moral degradation under the guise of birth control.[77]

Several factors contributed to a general fear of immigration
which swept the nation in the early 1920s. World War I had stimulated American nationalists to heat up the melting pot; cultural
pluralism was little in evidence before 1930. The Red Scare of
1919 heightened demands for immigration restriction resulting
in the 1921 Emergency Quota Act and the 1924 National Origins
Act (Johnson-Reed Law), which set strict quota limits for immigrants. In response to this almost rabid fear of immigrants, Gillis
suggested that all should be welcome. Poignantly, based on his
view of moral laxness in the United States, he wrote, "Do immigrants to America corrupt us, or do we corrupt them?"[78]

America's false prosperity had also raised the demon of immorality in the press and literature of the period. A favorite target of Gillis's wrath was newspaper magnate William Randolph Hearst, whom he described as "a noxious influence in America, and in the world." Gillis ridiculed Hearst for taking the money of common people, while in the process poisoning their minds and debasing their souls.[79] In more general terms he repeatedly called for decency in journalism. To increase profits, newspapers had thrown ethics to the wind, emphasized sensationalism, and published ghoulish accounts of events and half-truths which were read by many impressionable people.

Gillis attacked many of the leading columnists, playwrights, and novelists of the day as well. H. L. Mencken was criticized for his rejection of eternal verities, while his publication *The American Mercury* was ridiculed for its persistent pessimism. Sinclair Lewis' novels *Main Street* (1920), *Babbitt* (1922), *Arrowsmith* (1925), and *Elmer Gantry* (1927) were denounced for their rejection of traditional American values. Lewis himself was criticized for his uncanny desire to always portray a dark and inaccurate picture of America. Gillis wrote,

> He [Lewis] lives on the same Main Street, but he sees things that we never see, things that do not happen. He meets the same people that we meet, but he sizes them up differently, and in some inexplicable way he finds out about them things we know they cannot be guilty of. He travels on the same trains that we use, and frequents the same smoking room, but he hears—and remembers—worse stories than have ever been retailed to us, even by that much maligned fellow, the commercial traveler. In his writings he covers the same ground as Meredith Nicholson, Booth Tarkington, George Ade, William Allen White and a score of other Middle Westerners, but by some uncanny instinct he has picked more scandal in a day than they have heard in a lifetime. In consequence he gets a totally different view of life from theirs....The chief regret we Americans have over the Nobel Award to Sinclair Lewis is that [his] idea of America may possibly have been accepted as authentic by Europe. But, of course, his America is not America, it is Sinclair

Lewis' America, the America that exists in his own mean little noodle.[80]

Few of the world's best-known and most gifted writers escaped Gillis's vehement criticism. Intellectual ability or worldly credentials mattered little to the editor; the moral fiber of the nation was torn and needed repair. In a typical attack, Gillis took on Bertrand Russell, the British agnostic, philosopher, and champion of individual liberty, calling his book *Marriage and Morals,* "an almost unbelievable mental perversity":

> After much reading of modern radicals, I am inclined to award the palm of wrong-headedness to Bertrand Russell....He has abandoned or suspended his purely academic work in order to give himself wholly to what he considers the duty of uprooting the ethical ideas and moral customs that have been sacrosanct since the days of Christ. His zeal is phenomenal, his activity in a bad cause amazing. In my opinion, every book of his on ethical questions contains more potential harm than a score of nasty novels or unclean plays. For, in effect, his work tends to give a philosophical and scientific justification to what we Christians call sin.[81]

F. Scott Fitzgerald, Ernest Hemingway, and Eugene O'Neill were also targets of Gillis's caustic pen for their somber and dark portrayal of America, its people, and culture. It is ironic that Gillis could so casually criticize the sin of pessimism in others when he was fully aware of his own frequent somber mood. Yet, as suggested earlier, Gillis perceived that those whom he criticized possessed no hope for change and conversion. His belief in the possibility of good allowed him to persistently preach his message to his audience.

The rise of state power, as evidenced in postwar Europe, was a great concern to James Gillis, who regularly lamented society's loss of democratic rule which he felt had been dealt an almost mortal blow by the war. If the people were not cautious, over-centralization of the federal government would bring ruin to the individual who was to be safeguarded by a democratic state. He often quoted Abraham Lincoln's famous dictum from the Gettysburg Address, "government of the people, by the people and for the people," and proposed that if the state swallowed the individual, then government by the people was lost.[82]

One manifestation of the intrusion of the state into the purview of the individual which distressed Gillis and the Catholic community in general was the proposal to federalize the public educational system in the country.[83] Gillis, in line with Catholic tradition, maintained that the education of a child was a fundamental parental right. He also extolled parochial schools for he felt that any system of education that eliminated or ignored religion was un-American. He was wary of total academic freedom, however, as this gave open license for the promotion of pernicious ideas which circulated widely in the period.[84]

From the time of the founding of the Plymouth and Jamestown settlements Americans had always connected religion to the practical decisions of life. Nowhere is this more evident than in the question of alcohol and its use in society. Catholics and Protestants argued within their own communities, but no consensus was reached as to the correct approach to the question. The evils of drink were promoted by Catholics, as mentioned in chapter one, through the Catholic Total Abstinence Union of America and its founder, Theobald Mathew, and great champion, John Ireland. Yet, no mandate for abstinence was ever promulgated by the hierarchy. Among Protestant groups, the National Women's Christian Temperance Union, founded in Cleveland in 1874 and championed by Frances Willard, promoted total abstinence as a moral issue.

Prohibition, the state's solution to the question, was for Gillis the classic example of where government had entered into a moral issue beyond its domain with disastrous results for society. The Eighteenth Amendment to the Constitution was passed by Congress on December 1, 1917 and was ratified by the thirty-sixth state in January 1919. Legislation to enforce and define prohibition, the Volstead Act, passed over Woodrow Wilson's veto in October, making all traffic, sale, and consumption of beverages with greater than 0.5% alcohol illegal. Gillis viewed the law as unenforceable.[85] More important, as a lifetime abstainer, he felt the law was the greatest blow that had ever been given to the temperance movement. Such legislation led people who otherwise

would have been temperate to drink as a form of sport. He concluded one editorial which criticized the Volstead Act, "The passage of the law was a psychological blunder and a moral
calamity."[86] For Gillis prohibition was simply another example of
state interference in human free choice.

Gillis's views on divorce, birth control, and temperance must
be understood in the light of his understanding of free will. All
these issues involve an individual free option, but it seems that
this God-given gift could not for Gillis be universally applied. To
choose to divorce or use a form of birth control was considered by
Gillis as a rupture of America's Christian moral fiber; yet he
strongly argued against the government's abolition of drink
because it placed state power in the domain of a personal decision. The question thus arises—did Gillis believe more strongly in
the moral issue or in his rejection of creeping statism? Would
Gillis have approved of a state condemnation of divorce and birth
control? The answers are not obvious, but his personal abstinence
and disgust at drunkenness, formed in his youth, measured
against his anti-prohibition stance, suggest that the greater evil
for him was state encroachment upon the rights of the individual.
In line with the American ideal of liberty, Gillis believed that the
existential use of free will to choose rightly, to opt for God and
conversion against the world, was paramount.

In his promotion of Catholicism, Gillis continued, as in the
past, to take the offensive against Protestant critics. He professed
the infallibility of the Church; there was no need to be tolerant
of error. He often criticized the Episcopal Church leader
William Inge, Dean of St. Paul's Church in London, who regularly vilified Catholicism and its leaders, by cleverly utilizing
Inge's own sources, such as George Santayana, against him. Gillis
was also intolerant of popular evangelists, such as Billy Sunday,
whom he called a "misguided mountebank."[87]

Gillis did comment on international events though he was
preoccupied with domestic affairs. The United States emerged
from World War I in a position of relative strength compared
with other nations. Many historians have classified America's
international policy in the 1920s as isolationist, but this term
gives a false impression as the United States was politically

involved on the international scene. It is true the nation did not join the League of Nations, but the reasons for this decision had more to do with the way the body was established than its purpose.[88] The United States was, however, the catalyst behind the Four, Nine, and Five Power Treaties, which were the result of the Washington Disarmament Conference of 1921–1922. The treaties terminated the Anglo-Japanese alliance, set the China open-door policy, and established naval disarmament ratios for the dominant military powers.[89]

Gillis's antiwar stance, gained on his 1920 South American cruise, served as a shield against the pessimism of the world and immoral state of society. He belittled diplomatic solutions to war as a band-aid solution to a more severe societal problem. Disarmament would do little good if rivalries between manufacturers and merchants in different nations were not mended. The ultimate resolution to armed conflict lay with the conversion of the human spirit. He believed that Christian nations continued in warfare because they failed to apply to the relationship of states the rules which govern personal interactions. The only political solution which Gillis saw as viable in war was its total abolition. He thus supported the Kellogg-Briand Treaty, ratified by the Senate on January 15, 1929, which made war unlawful.[90]

Gillis expressed a policy of isolationism by often referring to the edict of George Washington to "mind our own business" so as to avoid entangling the nation in the affairs of others. The United States had plenty of problems at home; there was no need to take on more responsibilities which could not be maintained. Sarcastically he stated,

> As for ourselves, it would seem that we have work enough in running our own affairs. We cannot avert a coal-strike in Scranton. Do we think we could avert a war in Europe? We cannot enforce the Volstead Act. Could we enforce the Treaty of Versailles or the Pact of Locarno? Of course, as every armchair politician knows, it is much easier to run the world than to run an assembly district, or a ward.[91]

James Gillis was one of the first to speak out against Mussolini, his fascist regime in Italy, and the persecution of the

Church in Mexico. Concessions which "Il Duce" had made to Catholics, and his rejection of Bolshevism, precipitated favorable comments from many including *America's* editor Wilfrid Parsons, SJ,[92] but Gillis was critical of the Italian dictator and his fascist ideology from the outset. He considered him a potential danger to freedom, peace, and religion in his stiffling of the press and ill-timed militarism. While Mussolini's action of "restoring the crucifix" in public buildings was applauded by some, Gillis viewed the move only as a patronizing act.[93] "Il Duce" was for Gillis another manifestation of society's Mr. Hyde which needed to be exposed and converted. The persecution of the Church in Mexico and the consequent Cristero Rebellion of 1926 also attracted the attention of *The Catholic World.* As with George Shuster and especially Francis Clement Kelley,[94] who had branded the Calles government as a radical band of scoundrels who used Bolshevistic phrases as a smoke screen to justify its policy of public and private robbery,[95] so too did Gillis ridicule the barbarism in the country, labeling the Calles government "repressive." Although against military action, he felt America was remiss in its duty and condoning evil if it did not seek a diplomatic solution which would release the Church from its captivity.[96]

Affairs in the Soviet Union and other Eastern nations attracted the editor's attention. Bolshevism in Russia, in its attempt to abolish all religion and its rejection of God and individual rights, earned the Soviet government the dubious title, "the butchers of Moscow," from Gillis's pen. Sarcastically he described the "Russian Experiment": "Complete disappearance of religion, complete disappearance of the theater, complete disappearance of literature, art and music, complete disappearance of romantic love, complete disappearance of human nature. It's a great trick—if they do it."[97] He worried that diplomatic blunders of Secretary of State Henry Stimson, in the Manchurian conflict between China and Japan, could draw the United States into war, a condition which he refused to accept. The non-violent effort of Mahatma Gandhi to effect home rule in India was lauded by Gillis, who rebuked England and its Prime Minister, Ramsey MacDonald, for the policy which held the colony captive.[98]

Sursum Corda and the Great "Crash"-1928-1932

The public life of James Martin Gillis dominated his activity at this time; yet religious community affairs were integral and played a significant role in his life as a Paulist. At the 1924 General Chapter Gillis was elected as third consultor. The multiple tasks of editor and traveling preacher had, however, sapped his energy to the point that he felt he could not serve in a place of community leadership and continue his ministry as editor. Almost immediately after his election he asked newly elected Superior General Joseph McSorley for permission to resign. He cited insufficient time, health concerns, and lack of acumen in financial affairs as reasons for his withdrawal. McSorley simply responded, "not now." After several further attempts Gillis's resignation from the consultors and the Board of Directors of the Missionary Society of St. Paul was accepted in November 1925.[99] Gillis was nonetheless well-respected in the Paulist community, as evidenced by his election as a delegate to the General Chapters of 1927 and 1929.

Despite his many obligations in New York, Gillis continued to travel far and wide as a speaker; his popularity and public demand grew with time. National exposure from *The Catholic World* and WLWL made him a public figure known to a broad spectrum of Americans, both Catholic and non-Catholic. One look at his preaching log shows the intensity of his schedule, a reality which took its toll physically and most probably mentally and spiritually as well. Between January and March 1927 Gillis spoke in nine cities including New York, a swing to the northeast in Boston, Chicago, and a Lenten series at Old St. Mary's in San Francisco. Only the sudden death of his father on March 28, 1927 interrupted his schedule.[100]

After his return from Europe in the summer of 1928,[101] Gillis again expanded his public presence through acceptance of a commission to write a weekly syndicated column. Sponsored by the National Conference of Catholic Men (NCCM), *Sursum Corda*, "Lift Up Your Hearts," first appeared in October 1928. Gillis indicated that the column was to be a "comment upon the more hopeful phenomena in modern life and, when those phenomena are lacking, to make [a] deliberate search for the 'soul of goodness' in things evil." In line with this idea a subtitle was added to the column in December, "What's Right With the World."[102] In *Sursum Corda* Gillis generally addressed less controversial issues. These essays were screened by representatives at the NCWC and on occasion he was forced to revise and even resubmit his work. The column's importance as a forum that expanded the name of Gillis is clear but its ability to reveal his opinions or deeply held views is less certain. Still, these weekly essays provided an additional opportunity for him to preach his message and exercise his mission to the world.

As the decade of the 1920s continued, and now with an additional medium through which to speak, Gillis continued to comment with flair, wit, and conviction about the world about him. One is struck with the remarkable consistency in his thought. He used the same sources and arguments to promote his ideas or denounce the views of others. He was never equivocal; he spoke and wrote like a man driven, both from a standpoint of volume and breadth of interest. To support his work Gillis often read two books in a day and several in a week. He continued to promote the centrality of God as the underpinning for everything in the world, often returning to his "False Prophets" theme, "Christ or Chaos."[103]

Gillis attacked the immorality of the world, its cornerstone of God's absence, and the subsequent false prosperity which reigned. He claimed it was the imperiled state of the family through the rejection of marriage as an institution that "forced" Pius XI to publish *Casti Connubii* in 1931. He refused to bend when pressured to temper his comment. He wrote, "Compromise is always a mistake. Compromise works for a time. It is good politics. But it is bad statesmanship, and it is bad—very bad religion."[104] Gillis began regularly to comment on the immorality of contemporary theater and cinema. He claimed that the absence of censorship granted "absolute license" to the producers of theater art, and that the indecency of stage and screen was "the equivalent of libel against our country and our people."[105]

Gillis's stand on indecency and his advocacy of censorship again raises the question of the relative importance of human free will against his rejection of big government and its power to control. Censorship would necessitate government intervention into the free will of the people. Yet, he continued to maintain, with respect to other issues, that the individual was more important than the state. One can conclude that Gillis believed that men and women should be free to practice virtue, exercise human rights, and choose God; they were not free to sin. Deviations from this "right" road were criticized with a call for change. Censorship would, therefore, merely curtail one's freedom to sin. Gillis realized that any civilized society could never attain complete freedom; there would always be a need for some restrictions for the betterment of all.

The prohibition question remained a common topic for Gillis as he added new arguments to his previous critique. He began to see prohibition as a moral question where the state's manipulation of personal choice had led to greater vice and corruption. He continued to write and speak of the law's unenforceability but added the idea that lawlessness had become worse than ever because of the law. He challenged Washington to act and severely criticized President Herbert Hoover for his refusal to take a stand on the issue.[106]

Gillis's criticism of the anti-Catholic animus in the nation took a more personal direction with the presidential candidacy of New York Governor Al Smith in 1928. As before, he expressed the belief that bigotry was destructive to the fabric of American ideals and bemoaned the fact that Catholics were faced with a double standard in society—certain liberties afforded to the general population were not sanctioned for Catholics.[107] Gillis first commented upon Smith's candidacy for the 1924 Democratic presidential nomination when religious prejudice had run the New York governor's campaign aground. Now, four years later, he viewed the animus against Smith as a constitutional question. After Hoover was elected, Gillis labeled the Constitution as "pretty well shot to pieces" because religion had essentially become a test for office.[108] Although other issues pertinent to Smith were present in the 1928 campaign, it was clear to Gillis that religious bigotry had caused his defeat.[109]

The critique of state control and the promotion of the sacredness of individual free choice found added fuel and reached new heights in the later 1920s. He saw the democratic principles of America's founding fathers in danger while state absolutism, which he labeled "the fundamental evil," threatened to prevail. Quoting Hilaire Belloc, he claimed nations today were more absolute than any pagan state of past ages. Conflict between society and Catholicism was, in line with his world view, considered inevitable.[110]

Gillis continued to profess the conviction that the freedom of the individual should never be impeded by the state. It is the right of the people to determine what government should do, not the right of a governmental structure or hierarchy. He commented on the words of Pius XI, "The state must protect and promote, not absorb families and individuals and not attempt to put itself in place of them," by saying, "Now there is an *important, fundamental* and *universal* truth [Gillis emphasis]." If push came to shove in a battle between God and the State, Gillis wrote, "We shall choose God."[111]

The lawlessness which was precipitated by the nation's prohibition stance was only one aspect of a much larger problem. Gillis often referred to the work of the statistician Frederick Hoffman, who demonstrated the depth of crime present in America compared with other western nations. Respect for law could only come, he felt, through the action of the individual citizen; the government could not be blamed for the lack of personal initiative and apathy that existed. Gillis characterized the nation's crime problem as a scandal to the world, which could end the "American experiment" if not curbed.[112]

The popular optimism of the 1920s received a tragic reversal in the stock market "crash" of October 24, 1929. That day, known in United States history as "Black Thursday," over 13 million shares were sold on the exchange which precipitated a downward spiral for more than two years. The reasons for the crash are beyond the scope of this effort, but a few national statistics allow one to see the gravity of this situation, the greatest economic disaster in American history. Between 1929 and 1932 unemployment rose from 3.1 to 24%. Farm prices, which were low before the crash, fell an additional 61% and labor income dropped 42.3% in the same period.[113] The human toll was even worse as many people lost their homes, as well as their dignity and hope.

Gillis, who had preached against the false prosperity upon which the United States had fed for almost a decade, had in a prophetic sense predicted ruin for America. On January 6, 1929 he gave a lecture at St. Paul's in New York, "What Price Prosperity?" which was repeated in different locations and in other media. He stated that the nation was living an illusion, feeding off forbidden fruit which had perpetuated a "fatty degeneration" in the country. He spoke of the prosperity which America enjoyed throughout the decade, "It may be a curse. It is a disease—at least it is a danger." The danger in such prosperity was visible in two specific ways: excessive wealth many times led to selfishness; while America possessed a bounty, others starved. Secondly, economic prosperity made people jingoistic; the nation was measuring its greatness in all the wrong ways. He suggested that a better standard by which to judge the value of a nation was its degree of honesty. America had lost many of the basic values which had made it great, "justice and right and truth and honor, nobility [and] charity." Gillis saw himself as a patriot in ringing the warning bell that America was on a moral precipice and ready to fall.[114]

Gillis believed that the rejection of moral values and lack of honesty which the postwar prosperity had created had done more harm both at home and abroad than could "be undone in a generation or a century."[115] Unlike many ministers, he did not exude compassion or provide words of comfort when the crash occurred. Instead he perceived the crash as retribution for greed based upon speculation for "easy money":

> Anything is better than the exaggerated, inflated, largely fictitious prosperity of which we have been boasting. I for one grew weary of hearing that battle cry of the last presidential election, "Prosperity, Prosperity," especially when I was convinced that it was to a degree of falsehood or a delusion. So for the relief, much thanks.

With falsehood and delusion dethroned, Gillis coined his own battle cry, "Morality, Morality."[116]

Herbert Hoover–Disappointment in Leadership–1929–1932

As America began to suffer through this period of economic crisis and personal hopelessness, the Paulist community made a move to return to its ideological roots. McSorley's cerebral approach to mission and his rigidity in conformance to the common life made him unpopular as superior general. Thus in June, 1929, he became only the second Paulist leader voted out of office when John Harney polled twice as many votes as the incumbent. Harney's election gave the promoters of Paulist missions their champion. The new general attempted to restore this ministry to its previous lofty plane in Paulist life by opening new missions to rural America, a dramatic departure from Paulist tradition, but in line with 1920s Catholic evangelism.[117]

Harney's election also heralded a new direction for the Society's common life. The death of Walter Elliott in 1928 ended twenty years of his influence and opened the door to a redefinition of the Paulist lifestyle. Harney believed in a more relaxed house rule which made him a popular leader. His decision to move the community toward missions, however, had its costs. Newman Hall ministries at Columbia, Minnesota, McGill, and Toronto ended, and innovation in apostolic work was stunted. McSorley's personal rigorism was coupled with ministerial openness and the promotion of new ideas; Harney's personal openness was linked to ministerial rigidity and community stagnation. While Gillis perceived his work as that of a missionary, he clearly favored the moral rigorism and innovation of McSorley.

The return to emphasis on the mission most assuredly pleased Gillis[118] and reactivated his seemingly limitless energy which allowed him to take on another platform to preach his message of America's need to return to moral rigorism and personal accountability. In November 1930 he began his first of what would be twelve consecutive years of radio broadcasts on the recently initiated "Catholic Hour" on NBC. Conceived by Charles Dolle, executive secretary of the NCCM, the project was approved by the administrative committee of the NCWC in November 1929.[119] After calming the fears of WLWL director,

John Carter Smyth,[120] Dolle secured the permission of Cardinal Hayes to initiate the first broadcast on March 2, 1930.

Gillis was invited to speak on the program by a committee[121] headed by Father (later Archbishop of Cincinnati) Karl Alter, director of the National Catholic School of Social Service. He was the twelfth speaker in 1930 and gave a weekly series, titled "The Moral Law," which ran from November 9 to December 20. Throughout the eight weekly talks Gillis hammered away on his thesis that morality had been sacrificed to the idol of national greed. The very titles of the talks give a summary to his previously stated opinions: "Morality, Old and New," "Parental Authority and State Authority," "Crime and Warfare," "Honesty in Business and Politics."[122]

Gillis also accepted "Catholic Hour" invitations to speak during the Advent seasons of 1931 and 1932. Many of the lectures expressed similar ideas from his now multiple and varied public media "pulpits." In 1932, however, in his series "Conflicting Standards: Catholic Theology vs. Worldly Philosophy," Gillis struck two new and significant chords. He attacked jingoism in the strongest terms, labeling it "the chief enemy of peace and prosperity" and "suicide."[123] Gillis believed that no nation could call itself exclusively the people of God. Yet, the nations of the world acted independently, promoted class superiority and racial hatred, and, thereby, created nationalistic antipathy. Excessive nationalism also raised his familiar criticism of the state over the individual: "The organization has swallowed the individual body, bones, hide, hair. His identity as an independent, intelligent, responsible human being is lost."[124]

This 1932 series also allowed Gillis to speak for the first time in any consistent way about his attitude toward minorities.[125] Jews, women, and African-Americans were all defended in ways which were progressive for the day. He ridiculed the many false labels which history had attached to Jews, such as "Bolsheviks" and "Christ-killers." Though a strong advocate of traditional sex roles, he called for the improvement of women's place in society and feared that dishonor and injustice to women would lead to the collapse of contemporary civilization. Gillis's support for the cause of black Americans was based on principles of social justice. He

professed the idea that since all people come from the same God
they should be granted equal rights. He was critical of Catholics
in general for their failure to properly evangelize all people of
color.[126]

As previously mentioned, Charles Coughlin was active in
radio during this same period. Historians have focused their
attention and criticism on his addresses in the 1934 through
1939 period which have rightly been maligned for their anti-
Semitism and demagoguery. Yet, in the period 1928–1931, one
can draw many parallels between the comments of Coughlin and
Gillis. Coughlin raised a warning flag about the nation's prosperity as did his older contemporary; the spiritual depression of the
period could only be cured by a return to the principles of
Christ. Coughlin was also highly critical of what he perceived as
the loss of Lincoln's edict of government "by the people" in his
rejection of the state's oppression of the individual citizen
through excessive taxation and the seizure of private property. In
union with Gillis and most Catholics of the day, he also criticized
the League of Nations, prohibition, and the abuses of Communism which he labeled "a heresy which strikes at the root of patriotism and prosperity."[127]

Gillis was not sympathetic when the crash occurred; the
exposure of a false prosperity was a great victory for him. Of
course, like all Americans he hoped that the nation could wrest
itself from the grip of economic ruin for the betterment of its
people. All eyes looked to Washington and the Hoover administration for answers; unfortunately, few were forthcoming. At
the outset Gillis had hoped that Hoover would move the nation
away from the cry "Prosperity—Prosperity," and toward a more
realistic and for him truthful view of society, which was a truer
measure of a nation's greatness. However, Gillis soon became
disillusioned with Hoover, who was non-committal on prohibition and consistently underestimated the extent of the nation's
economic problems. Moreover, he disliked Hoover's tendency
toward statism. Quoting John A. Ryan, Gillis wrote, "President
Hoover aligns himself in effect with those who hold that the
state can do no wrong. He bids us now bow our knees before
the omnipotent state. This is neither good ethics nor good

Americanism." Hoover brought no relief to the nation, prompting Gillis to voice his frustration:

> Alas, poor President Hoover. Never since Washington have people expected more of a man elected to lead them, and never has any chief executive proved so disappointing.
>
> But one thing all good Americans desire—a leader worthy of the name, to direct us in these distressing circumstances. May heaven send us such a one.[128]

James Gillis's appointment as editor of *The Catholic World* shifted the direction of his life and ministry in ways which were immediately revealed and others which would only emerge with time. He brought his dualistic world view and identity as a Paulist preacher to what would prove to be his principal life's work. The Dr. Jekyll and Mr. Hyde perception of himself, which had been projected onto mission congregations, was immediately thrust upon the whole world in his work as editor. Through *The Catholic World* and the other "pulpits" of radio, his *Sursum Corda* column, and the lecture circuit, Gillis continued to preach about the need for conversion. Change of heart could only be found, however, in the free choice of the individual to seek and discover God; world leaders, ideologies, governments, and programs could not effect the change necessary in the individual. When James Gillis perceived that change was being imposed or its possibility jeopardized by the various institutions, peoples, and forces of society, he spoke out in an ofttimes polemical defense of his strongly-held convictions.

Gillis's work as editor provided a broader audience for his preaching ministry which was central to his Paulist identity. The 1920s was a boom time for the United States, domestically and in international influence. Gillis perceived, however, that the nation was living a false sense of prosperity that, like an overinflated balloon, would soon burst. American society had moved away from the foundational principles of individual freedom, government of, by, and for the people, and moral righteousness, which had made the nation respected by its own citizens as well as those of the whole world. As in his mission preaching he called for a restoration of nineteenth-century individualism. But the United States of Gillis's world view was rapidly evolving and he was unable to perceive or refused to accept the new more interventionist role of the state which the Wilson administration had ushered into existence. With the state and society existent in a dialectical relationship, it was impossible for one to change without affecting the other. Similarly, the move from the individual to the social, from personal liberty to social security necessitated a shift in understanding of human freedom, a move which Gillis again could not negotiate.

The economic and social prosperity which America enjoyed in the 1920s was a curse for James Gillis. As editor, columnist, lecturer, and radio personality, he denounced the prevailing national consciousness which had driven the American people away from its fundamental principles of moral responsibility and duty and given license for the government to encroach on the personal liberties of its citizens. Prosperity was a mask for darkness which imperiled society. As the nation floundered in economic depression, the American people hoped for a leader to smooth the turbulent waters; James Gillis as well longed for a savior for the nation.

CHAPTER 5

The Guardian of America— 1933–1941

The election of Franklin Delano Roosevelt as the thirty-second President of the United States brought hope to the nation after the great disappointment of Herbert Hoover. The October 1929 stock market crash and the resultant economic depression had burst the bubble of prosperity that James Gillis had campaigned against for nearly a decade. Before Roosevelt took the oath of office, the nation reached the low point of the Depression; capitalism almost failed. The Gross National Product (GNP) in March 1933 was 35% lower than October 1929; total labor income fell 42.3% during the same period.[1] Gillis, although not personally affected, was horrified, like all Americans, at the state of the nation and prayed that a savior would come[2] when Hoover was unable to make any significant strides toward economic recovery. He hailed Roosevelt's election as "another victory for the democratic system."[3]

With the bubble of prosperity burst and a new administration operating the federal government, Gillis's message of individual freedom and conversion to the world evolved into a call for reconstruction and recovery, but his mission as guardian of America remained steadfast. In his mind, the prosperity of the 1920s had worked against the basic principles upon which the greatness of the United States was based, eating away core values and in the process destroying the national economy. Gillis realized that recovery could not be effected without economic reform, a process which he fully promoted since neither the democratic principles of the country nor the precepts of Catholicism were in any way wedded to capitalism. Recovery without reform was for

123

Gillis like a sinner who received absolution without contrition. If the nation resumed its affairs as it had left them in 1929, the final state would be worse than the first.[4]

As the 1930s unfolded Gillis took to the international scene his mission to preach personal liberty, duty, conversion, and his critique of human failure to meet its moral and personal responsibilities. This was most strongly evident in his efforts as the principal Catholic champion of the non-intervention platform popular during the latter half of the decade. As the United States reformed its own house, economically and socially, it was severely threatened by a world situation which stood like a powder keg waiting for the spark that would ignite it. The devastating explosion, which seemed to many, including Gillis, to be only a matter of time, would eventually embroil the world community in its second international armed conflict in less than a full generation. The American nation and its people needed to be safeguarded; James Gillis would act as their guardian.

Franklin Delano Roosevelt and the "New Deal"–1933–1937

After World War I trends toward management, bureaucracy, and "bigness" were found in all aspects of American society. The New Deal, "a descendant of Progressive reform," was the tool used by Roosevelt to manage the "bigness" of society, which had come about through mergers and the establishment of vastly extended companies and businesses in the boom period of the 1920s. David Shannon has called the New Deal "a complex set of compromises" generated by outside pressures, which Roosevelt molded into a workable program.[5] The President believed in the full employment of the federal government in an effort to combat the Depression and to relieve those most sorely injured by it. He was thus willing to compromise and modify the traditional relationship of independence existent between government and private enterprise in the interest of the general welfare of the country. He was no opponent of capitalism, but felt that the reality of the situation necessitated bold and innovative steps which might be questionable in more normal economic conditions.

Roosevelt wasted no time in implementing his plan, viewing

his election as a mandate from the American people for immediate action. Within the first one hundred days following his March 4 inauguration the initial phase of the "New Deal," based on recovery, had been enacted as the law of the land. The Depression was attacked from three different fronts: agriculture, unemployment, and business and labor.[6]

The National Industrial Recovery Act (NIRA) of June 16, 1933 became the heart of Roosevelt's New Deal with its formation of the National Recovery Administration (NRA). Written to stimulate both business and labor, the NIRA satisfied employers' demands for government backing to trade association agreements so as to stabilize production and prevent price slashing, while giving workers wage and hours protection and the right to bargain collectively. In the hope that consumers' buying power could be raised as rapidly as prices and wages, there was attached to the act a $3.3 billion public works appropriation to "prime the pump" of the economy.[7]

The nation, enthralled that finally some significant effort had been made to stem the tide of the Depression and effect recovery, began a honeymoon with Roosevelt and his New Deal. Businesses throughout the land placed the Blue Eagle (which stated "We Do Our Part") in shop windows to show their support for the NRA; the general tone of the nation was upbeat, positive, and forward looking. Catholics as a body were equally enthusiastic about the new President and his New Deal legislation, which brought hope that the horrible downward trend of the nation for the past four years could be reversed. Catholics also rejoiced that Roosevelt had chosen two of their own for cabinet positions[8] which helped to raise the Church to its highest level to date of public recognition. Additionally, leading Catholic intellectuals of the day advocated social positions akin to that of the President, enhancing his popularity with the rank and file of the Church. The New Deal was also well received by Catholics for it was seen to be based on Catholic social teaching.[9] Catholics believed the government to be duty-bound to provide for the needs of the unemployed and other marginalized people of society. Thus, when Roosevelt launched into his campaign to curtail the power of Wall St. and to place greater regulation on the economy, his efforts were initially fully supported. The hierarchy backed the President on both personal and organizational levels. Cardinals Patrick Hayes (New York), William O'Connell (Boston) and George Mundelein (Chicago), Archbishop Edward Hanna (San Francisco), and Bishop Karl Alter (Toledo) were all in the Roosevelt camp. The best-known organizations including the National Conference of Catholic Men (NCCM), the National Conference of Catholic Women (NCCW), and the National Catholic Welfare Conference (NCWC) strongly supported the NRA.[10]

Catholic support for the policies of Roosevelt, especially the NRA and the agencies it generated, is illustrated best in the activities of John A. Ryan and Francis Haas. Ryan, labeled the "Right Reverend New Dealer" by his nemesis, Charles Coughlin, equated Roosevelt's economic policy with social justice. He served as a member of the Industrial Appeals Board of the NRA and promoted the President's New Deal through his work with the Social Action Department of the NCWC, his teaching, and writings. Broderick says, however, that Ryan's influence with the President should not be overstated; the two men met on four different occasions and corresponded a half-dozen times during their mutual tenures of service to the government.[11] The other priest, Haas, was most closely associated with Roosevelt's labor policies. The Milwaukee cleric believed in and promoted a just wage and the need for industry, labor, and the government to work in harmony and mutual cooperation. During the life of the NRA Haas served on the Labor Advisory Board and its successor the National Labor Board.[12]

The ascent of Roosevelt to the presidency and the initiation of the New Deal were observed by James Gillis from a distance. The incessant activity and demanding schedule which he continued to maintain had brought him to a Boston hospital. From January 23 to March 13, 1933 he was in traction at Robert Brigham hospital, recovering from a "spinal condition due to the slight displacement of two vertebrae."[13] There is little doubt that this physical ailment was greatly aggravated by his work ethic, which many times translated into laboring without sufficient rest for days on end. If he worked in order to run from his inner conflict, he was not successful, but only succeeded in masking a lifetime condition. His Dr. Jekyll and Mr. Hyde dualistic world view had earlier been thrust onto society; there was no escape from the reality of the world. After his release from the hospital he sailed to Europe aboard the *SS Rex* as chaplain for a Holy Year pilgrimage to Rome led by Michael Williams; he returned in early May.[14]

Like the nation in general, Gillis, at the outset, lived a honeymoon period with Roosevelt, placing almost complete trust in his efforts, a large leap of faith for the generally cautious priest editor. He initially commented favorably upon Roosevelt's activism, calling him a Trojan in his efforts to right the economic life of the nation. Consistent with his message of individual freedom, Gillis defended the President against those who saw his rapid initiation of legislation in the first hundred days as dictatorial by proclaiming him to be the free choice of the people; democracy continued to operate well.[15] His first comment about the NRA did not appear until a September 1933 *Sursum Corda* essay where he made no judgment on the program, but rather asked the nation to place its faith in the President's efforts: "I for one am ready to make an act of faith in the NRA....And I believe that if every American citizen will make that [same] act of faith, the country will be saved."[16]

The new format of the editorial section of *The Catholic World* which appeared in October 1933,[17] together with a subtle comment which questioned Roosevelt's methods in the New Deal, signaled a change in Gillis's stance with the President; the honeymoon was beginning to end. He wrote,

> He [Roosevelt] is calling not for a New Capitalism but a New Deal. I think he means not merely a new shuffle of the cards, or even a new pack, but a new game. Be that as it may, one thing is certain. The man we have now in the White House has traveled a long way from traditional Capitalism.[18]

The comment is indicative of the guardian role which Gillis felt he now played in the maintenance of America's foundational principles. One can see in Gillis's mind a fear of statism, which could evolve from what he perceived as the radical road that Roosevelt had chosen to travel. As 1933 ended, Gillis remained on the fence concerning the NRA, a characteristically unusual position for one who, as has been clearly shown, was unabashed in his criticism or support as his convictions would lead him to comment.

Over the next twenty months he wavered back and forth in a rare display of inconsistency of opinion, while calling the NRA "the burning question of the day."[19] As he had expressed earlier, Gillis believed in the famous Lincoln edict, government of, by, and for the people. The individual person was of supreme importance and should be served by the Constitution, the written will of the people, not the reverse. He wrote, "But so long as the people at large are content to have him [Roosevelt] try this one, I think that we need not scruple about the strict legality of the NRA."[20] He believed that the free will of the people was the true measure of democracy and thus for the President to accede to the public's opinion was morally sound. Gillis continued to back the NRA, because it represented the will of the majority, to the point of suggesting the Constitution be amended so that the program could continue:

> Now then either one of two things must happen: we must in the spirit of the Constitution amend or interpret the Constitution to remedy the accumulated existing evils or we shall place ourselves on the defensive in battle with those who are determined to scrap the Constitution all together.[21]

Gillis's belief in the free will of the people rightly expressed is again illustrated through his initial support of the NRA. As Jesus saw the Sabbath made for humanity and not humanity for the Sabbath, so Gillis saw the Constitution as a document to serve the people and not vice versa. Within the limits of Christian morality and in the spirit of mending the tattered moral fiber of the country, the free will of the people needed to be preserved.

The two-year New Deal experiment came to an abrupt halt as 1935 dawned. On January 6, by a vote of 6–3, the Supreme Court invalidated the Agricultural Adjustment Act (AAA) stating, "The act invades the reserved rights of the states." More important, on May 27 through *Schechter vs. the United States*, the Court declared the code structure of the NIRA unconstitutional because it wrongly delegated authority to legislate to people totally disconnected with the legislative functions of government. The Court's action stunned the nation and was quite disappointing to such Catholic backers of the administration as Ryan and Haas. In February Gillis had modified his generally supportive stand on the NRA in a statement which suggested his ever present fear of statism:

> Even the N.R.A. is only a somewhat modified repetition of the old Roman attempt to neutralize evil effects of a long-standing system of social injustice by the device of handing out governmental money to prevent revolution.[22]

In an uncharacteristic reversal of his initial stand, Gillis reacted to the loss of the NRA by calling again for national reform and the maintenance of the Constitution. He lamented the fact that economic and social reform would be stunted and worried that revolution would not wait long if conditions did not improve. However, in an apparent shift away from his full support for what he perceived to be the will of the people, he wrote of the Court's decision, "I am one of those who rejoiced at the vindication of the Constitution."[23] He now began to see the NRA as a plan of the few to crush the rights of the individual in violation of democratic principles. Thus, although Gillis shifted his stand on the NRA he was consistent in his more foundational beliefs in the need to maintain the free will of the people and his rejection of statism which jeopardized this freedom.

Catholic reaction to the demise of the NRA was swift in its call for a reinstatement of the program. Shortly after the Court passed judgment, the document "Organized Social Justice" was promulgated as a pamphlet by the Social Action Department of the NCWC. It called for an amendment to the Constitution which would empower Congress to re-establish the NRA along genuine vocational group lines. The document was largely the work of General Secretary John J. Burke and was heralded by Ryan as "the most fundamental, the most comprehensive and the most progressive publication that has come from a Catholic body since the appearance of the Bishops' Program of Social Reconstruction." It stated, "Had the NRA been permitted to continue, it could readily have developed into the kind of industrial order recommended by the Holy Father."[24] The document was signed by 131 distinguished Catholic leaders, including Ryan, Raymond McGowan, Dorothy Day, George Shuster, William Howard Bishop, Wilfrid Parsons, and John LaFarge. Gillis also signed the position paper, reversing his stance again, in promotion of a Constitutional amendment so that the will of the people, as he understood it, could be maintained. Gillis's flip-flop attitude persisted, however, as in September he referred to the NRA along with his old nemesis the League of Nations as "two object lessons of the ignorance of the learned."[25]

As we have seen, Gillis believed, in the spirit of the Declaration of Independence, that humankind had been endowed by God with the inalienable rights of life, liberty, and the pursuit of happiness. Human freedom, as restricted by Christian moral principles and the common good of society, needed to be preserved. The NRA, instituted to be a temporary measure to pull the nation from the depth of its economic plight, was judged by Gillis in a balance which weighed the free will of the people against the premises of the Constitution. It has earlier been concluded that Gillis's belief in the individual was of greater importance than his fear of how any one issue may ill-affect the nation. His changeable attitude toward the NRA also appears to be rooted in his unwavering belief in the individual. At the outset the editor felt the NRA to be an aid to the individual; later he came to believe that the program's government regulation crushed the individual. While his ideas experienced fluctuations, Gillis's missionary zeal contined to grow.

James Gillis's critical views of the New Deal were illustrative of conservative thought which feared the growing power of government in the Roosevelt administration. In August 1934 the Liberty League, a bipartisan organization that united conservative politicians and business leaders,[26] was formed to oppose the President's policies. This group compared the administration's actions to the absolute monarchies of Europe before the liberal revolutions of the eighteenth and nineteenth centuries. The League also saw similarities between "Roosevelt's America" and the totalitarian regimes that had presently formed on the European continent. In the opinion of League members the New Deal was damaging America by destroying the qualities of initiative and self-reliance which had built the nation. Government power, not that of business, was in an oppressive form; restoration of a positive attitude toward business would cure the nation's economic woes.

The New Deal was also opposed from the left by critics who felt the government needed to do more to aid the poor. Politicians such as progressives Bob and Phil La Follette and Thomas Amlie, the novelist Upton Sinclair, and the intellectuals John T. Flynn, John Dewey, Charles Beard, and Alfred Bingham formed a coalition which called for stronger government action to destroy monopolies and to form a cooperative commonwealth as a substitute for capitalism. Socialist party leader Norman Thomas also criticized Roosevelt's program, insisting that it was not socialism at all, but rather a haphazard attempt to save capitalism and a swing toward fascism.[27]

The rejection of the first or recovery New Deal led Roosevelt in 1935 to unveil a series of progressive acts aimed toward economic reform. Earlier, as was stated, the Glass-Steagall Banking Act (June 1933) had established the FDIC. In rapid succession the Works Progress Administration (WPA) under Harry Hopkins and the National Youth Administration added many to the work roles. The National Labor Relations Act (Wagner Act of 1937) created the National Labor Relations Board (NLRB), which supported trade unionism. The Social Security Act (August 1935) made provisions to bring government aid on a permanent basis to a variety of peoples in need of assistance.

In accord with these trends Gillis too called for reform, in line with his persistent theme of conversion, voicing a need for the review of capitalism while expressing his refrain over the growing power of the state at the expense of the individual. He said that the present economic and social crisis was sufficiently grave to open the eyes of even the most conservative to the injustices and incongruities that are inherent in the capitalistic system, especially the unequal distribution of wealth. Gillis preached the idea that Catholicism's ability to reform itself through the centuries could give a lesson to capitalism; the time was late and the reform required might have to be radical.[28]

Gillis's fear of growing state power began to slowly draw him away from Roosevelt's policy of recovery and reform. Throughout the world, especially in Mexico, Russia, Italy, and Germany, government power was absorbing and dominating the individual citizen. Gillis saw this same trend in America and worried about the consequences for the country. In his missionary-like drive to safeguard the nation he wrote, "I do feel some apprehension about the ever-increasing centralization of government in Washington."[29] He argued that the state, which existed solely to safeguard the basic liberties of the individual citizen, was subservient to humanity, who drew its rights directly from God.[30] For the state to deny the rights of the individual was to place itself over God. Addressing a national audience he stated, "The state that usurps the place of God and assumes the prerogatives of God must consider itself equal to God or superior to God, and this is the ultimate in sacrilege."[31]

The reservations expressed and the unspoken uncertainty which Gillis felt about Roosevelt and his policy of reform were part of a growing opposition to the administration by a number of well-known Catholics. Patrick Scanlan, editor of the Brooklyn *Tablet,* believed that the New Deal was "to provide recovery rather than to initiate vast reforms." Scanlan's major difficulty with the reform program was "its adoption of so many impractical, absurd and seemingly insane projects—most of them proposed by the so-called brains [*sic*] trust with the grand object of wasting millions of dollars."[32] *America's* gifted team of Paul Blakely and Wilfrid Parsons also began to express distrust of the President's policy; *The Commonweal* took a cautionary stance.[33]

Charles Coughlin, the best-known Catholic personality of the day, voiced the most vehement opposition to Roosevelt and his policies. Recall that Coughlin had started his radio ministry in 1926 with programs that centered on apologetics and the needs of children, with an occasional gibe at Margaret Sanger and other advocates of birth control. By the 1930s he was the most popular Catholic voice in the nation commanding an estimated ten million listeners for his weekly Sunday broadcast.[34] Coughlin was initially impressed with Roosevelt, coining the phrases, "Roosevelt or Ruin" and "The New Deal Is Christ's Deal," during his 1933 radio series. He believed that the Depression had been caused by greedy international bankers who had systematically reduced the world money supply. Rather than borrowing money, Coughlin, who believed the government's precious metals reserves were adequate to vastly increase the supply of money in circulation, proposed an economic program which promoted the revaluation of gold and the remonetization of silver.

Coughlin's honeymoon with Roosevelt's New Deal was short-lived when he realized that the President had no intention of carrying out his economic proposals. The first rift between the two men came in the spring of 1934 when Roosevelt suggested that silver holders be reported to the government in an effort to discourage silver coinage. The Radio League of the Little Flower held some reserves of silver and thus was reported, a situation which irritated Coughlin. When his monetary suggestions were not implemented, Coughlin published "Sixteen Principles of Social Justice," the creed for his new National Union for Social Justice. This manifesto sought solutions to the nation's economic woes through a combination of agrarian reforms and principles expounded in *Rerum Novarum* and *Quadragesimo Anno*.[35] Until the latter part of 1935 Coughlin remained on the fence with respect to Roosevelt, choosing to avoid any major confrontation. The final break came in November, when he declared that the principles of social justice and the New Deal were unalterably opposed; his patented phrase was altered to "Roosevelt and Ruin."[36]

Gillis was often queried about his stance on Coughlin, who had become quite controversial in and out of the Church. Unskilled in economics, he felt unqualified to render an opinion on Coughlin's monetary theories:

> All I know is that I don't know, and since I don't know I think it only wise and honest not to pretend to know. And that is why I don't venture to express an opinion one way or the other about Father Coughlin.[37]

Gillis, however, did defend Coughlin's right to voice his opinion and was critical of those who routinely berated him without sufficient knowledge to make a prudent judgment. This was especially true when people who had never read any papal encyclicals voiced opinions pro or con on Coughlin's social theory. He summarily stated, "We know too little and we talk too much."[38]

Gillis's disaffection over the Roosevelt administration

became greater as the 1936 elections drew near; the President's policies had become a Mr. Hyde of society. At the beginning of the year he entered his first public disagreement over the President's policy in a written debate with his friend John A. Ryan. Gillis severely criticized Roosevelt's New Deal program, described in his State of the Union address, for its "taking chances with the Constitution," "enormous expenditures flung recklessly here and there," and "encroachment on democracy because of startling measures to bring back prosperity." Ryan, in "An Open Letter to the Editor," responded by refuting Gillis's claims in a ringing endorsement of the administration's policy to date: "I don't see how democracy is involved. All the New Deal legislation was enacted by Congress which was elected by the people. None of it violated any person's natural rights."[39]

While battle lines were drawn on many Catholic fronts concerning the election, Gillis remained relatively neutral. Ryan, Haas, and members of the hierarchy led the Catholic charge of support, while Kenkel, Scanlan, and especially Coughlin and his National Union Party ticket[40] led the opposition. Gillis refused to choose sides, but he did emphasize that the election was the most important in his mind since that of 1860 with the domestic, social, and economic issues, and now major international crises beginning to loom large on the horizon. Gillis continued to express his concern over growing power in Washington in writing, "The question at issue in the campaign is the decline of democracy, the increase in centralization of government powers, and the possible emergence of the absolute state." He basically conceded victory to the President, but when the election became a landslide,[41] he wrote that his re-election should not be seen as a mandate to continue the policies of the previous four years, or, worse yet, to aggravate errors of the past.[42]

On February 5, 1937 President Roosevelt introduced legislation aimed toward reorganization of the judicial branch of the federal government, so it "[could] function with modern necessities." One aspect of the plan provided that for each Supreme Court justice seventy years or older who chose to remain on the bench another justice would be assigned to assist, with the Court never to exceed fifteen in number. Known in history as the

"Court Packing Plan," the move was rejected as a scheme by the President to manipulate the Court after its dissolution of the mainstays of his New Deal policy.[43]

Catholic opinion on the Court plan was mixed. Opposition, as voiced by the Brooklyn *Tablet* and *Baltimore Review* (which carried the opinion of Archbishop Michael Curley), was centered in the conviction that the Supreme Court, as the guardian of religious liberty, should be left alone. The plan was supported, however, by Ryan and Raymond McGowan of the NCWC Social Action Department, as well as *The Commonweal* and *Central Blatt and Social Justice,* "as a reasonable and sensible effort to meet demands for economic justice."[44]

Gillis, who was in Manila to address the Thirty-Third International Eucharistic Congress held February 3–7, wasted no time in denouncing Roosevelt's plan. He referred to the scheme as an attempt "to remove obstructionists in the Supreme Court and replace them with 'yes-men'"; it signified the loss of democracy. Roosevelt made every effort to manipulate Congress into urgent action, since the constitutional amendment process to reinstate the NRA would be too long and could not be controlled. Gillis saw in this attitude the mentality and actions of a dictator; the central state and its leader had grown too powerful.[45] To safeguard the nation a new direction was necessary to lead the country away from statism, with its rejection of the individual and God.

The Moral State of the Nation—1933–1941

The "roaring twenties" with its guise of "prosperity" had led to the Depression with its misery and pain; yet despite the rapid reversal the American people had not learned their lessons and were far from out of the woods of their moral dilemma. James Gillis continued his mission to preach moral responsibility and the freedom to choose God by establishing a link between the presence of God and the formation of moral standards. America could not be set on its proper path without a firm moral base. The cause of the moral dilemma continued to be the absence of God in society. Humans are inescapably linked to God; God is the greatest desire of the human heart. God, therefore, must be the anchor to all life; without God the absolute is not possible, and all becomes relative. To guard the American people Gillis preached the immediate need to seek and discover God in all aspects of society.[46] Gillis continued to carry the banner as the traditionalist voice of the nation's moral conscience.

As Gillis preached to the world his message of individual freedom and moral rigorism, so he professed the same idea in different ways to his fellow Paulists. The administration of John Harney, with its lack of emphasis on disciplined house rule and personal responsibility, did not change Gillis nor his approach to his brothers in community. Buoyed by the psychological support of McSorley, who had returned to St. Paul's in New York after a three-year "exile" in Toronto,[47] Gillis served as a community leader for the conservative and more discipline-oriented members. Harney's leadership style, which rejected "superstars" in the Society, did not, however, dampen Gillis's outspoken manner, as the General gave him free rein to operate. He wrote,

> Jot this down in your note book [sic]. Father Gillis is one of those Paulists who has carte blanche to arrange their own schedules without let or hindrance from any Superior, local or general. I never think of telling him to do this or to do that, but in case there is something that I would like to have him do I always put my request in this fashion: "will you be so kind, or so good, as to do this"; or "I'd like to have you do this."[48]

Absolute standards which promoted the eternal truth of God could not be negotiated or compromised. Relative measures were rejected by Gillis as useless, even harmful:

> When people speak of "immorality" they usually have in mind indecency, obscenity, or some other violation of holy purity. But is there not a deeper immorality—that which considers moral principle elastic, evanescent, fickle as the whims of man—or of woman....

> The deepest and most dangerous immorality of all is the immorality that thinks what was true yesterday may be false today or tomorrow....[49]

Moving from the necessity of fixed moral standards based on the natural law, Gillis returned to his earlier campaign against false prosperity by renewing his plea for personal moral responsibility. The nation had taken the concept of freedom too far, applying political freedom to morality which created licentiousness. Although the world had become more and more mechanized, humans remained as self-determined organisms and were, therefore, responsible for their personal actions. He wrote, "Nothing is so immoral as the amoral, nothing so demoralizing as to tell a man he is not responsible for his deeds, that he deserves no praise for the good, no blame for the bad." One could never say that freedom of action was lost, that circumstance forced a certain response. To safeguard the nation and its basic freedoms "required" Gillis to preach the maintenance of personal responsibility.[50]

James Gillis brought his understanding of absolute standards and an uncompromising concept of personal responsibility to the moral dilemma that continued to plague the nation. He spoke of the unholy trinity of "the world, the flesh and the devil," stating that perhaps the world was the worst enemy of the soul. He suggested that an inner journey of prayer and reflection would produce the best results in our attempts to counter the world. But his sense of realism told him that many evil temptations in contemporary society, such as theater, film, drink, and travel, needed to be avoided if they removed us from our moral responsibilities.[51]

During the 1930s Gillis spent little time revisiting old moral questions,[52] but rather launched into the more immediate questions of the day. The deplorable practice of lynching became a cause against which Gillis railed, viewing this tragedy as cowardly, a blight against our national honor, and adding to the forces which threatened the nation's moral fiber. He stated, "Lynchers must be descendants of wolves or coyotes or jackals, notoriously cowards when alone, but brave when the pack outnumbers the prey a hundred or a thousand to one."[53]

The morality of films was another important issue for the ever biting commentary of Gillis. He often referred to "the immorality of the movies," calling them "a lie" for they portrayed and promoted a lifestyle that was inconsistent with the Christian moral principles upon which the nation and its foundational documents were based.[54] He also supported the work of the Legion of Decency in its efforts to raise the moral standards of the nation and root out untruth which pervaded contemporary film.[55]

Gillis balanced a critique of the immorality of the American secular press with the responsibilities incumbent upon Catholic newspapers and journals. Moving away from his more specific harangues against William Randolph Hearst and H. L. Mencken, he criticized the press for its general tendencies to exceed decency in its display of freedom and its articulation of half-truths. He said the press was "afflicted with myopia," seeing only what was under its nose with no desire to gaze forward or any acute consciousness of what had happened previously.[56] The Catholic press, in contrast, had the responsibility to "declare the ethical aspects of contemporary events," "to throw the searchlight of eternal truth upon events that happen from day to day in the world of politics and in the social, economic and moral life of man." The Catholic press must always speak out against tyranny; editors must not be timid in what they say, but rather must declare their opinions boldly in essays and editorials. He further suggested that the Catholic editor must bring his personality and humanness to his efforts as a sign of God's presence in the work.[57]

As editor of the one of the premier American Catholic publications of the period, Gillis brought his moral beliefs to his work with *The Catholic World* which remained his principal "pulpit." Gillis "consistently maintained that *The Catholic World* was no fit instrument for running controversy,"[58] and thus he resisted the temptation to enter into written dialogue over the various issues of the day. He maintained the magazine's high literary and scholarly quality, refusing to yield to a more popular bent which may have aided the financial status of the magazine.[59] Well-known writers and scholars such as Pierre Crabites, Agnes Reppelier, Herbert Bolton, W.F.P. Stockley, John LaFarge, Peter Guilday, G.M. Godden, Paul Kiniery, Joseph Fichter, Theodore Maynard, George Shuster, John A. Ryan, and Paul Hanly Furfey contributed essays on topics ranging from "The Liturgical Art Movement" to "What's Wrong with the Sit-Down Strike."[60]

Education, a process which served to advance the whole person, mind, heart and soul, also underwent the moral scrutiny of James Gillis in the pages of *The Catholic World*. Public education needed to protect itself from the forces of moral irresponsibility and unrestrained freedom, which threatened the basic principles of the nation. For Gillis education without religion was too narrow, not sufficiently ambitious an enterprise, and "an intellectual absurdity"; in short it was "worse than no education at all" and not advantageous to America.[61]

Gillis was most distressed about the United States' system of higher education which prepared students to make money in the promotion of materialism over eternal truths. He attacked "liberal education," which in effect promulgated the doctrines of nihilism and determinism, as a "disastrous and immoral philosophy" for future generations of susceptible students. Such "education" was poison to youth and, if not checked, would ruin the country.[62] Gillis revisited his 1920s' critique of academic freedom, seeing it as license to promulgate and promote any political, social, or economic theory, regardless of moral value or content. He believed that absolute freedom in a civilized society was a fable, the logical outcome of which was intellectual and moral anarchy. People were free to choose goodness but not ideas which would lead themselves or others to ruin. In a cynical mood he stated, "O Academic Freedom, how many crimes, crimes against reason, crimes against the state, crimes against God are committed in thy name!"[63]

For some American Catholics the moral fiber of the nation was best safeguarded by the work of the faithful in carrying out the dictates of social Catholicism as articulated by the bishops. Catholic Action, the call by Pius XI for lay participation in the work of the hierarchy, reached its apex during this period through the establishment of numerous organizations and the combined efforts of people in every aspect of Catholic life. The full story of Catholic Action in the United States is beyond the scope of this book, but its Christian attitude, faithful presence, and commitment to purpose form the background to Catholicism's answer to the nation's social ills and James Gillis's personal response in his mission to bring America back to its need for dutiful action, personal responsibility, and conversion.[64]

American Catholics in all walks of life began to promote social Catholicism as a way of life rather than a new ministry in the Church. The publication of *Quadragesimo Anno* in 1931, which first coined the term "social justice," became a catalyst to the renewal of Catholic thought in its promotion of the common good above individual competing interests. The document proposed a corporatist economy based on pre-industrial guilds as an alternative to capitalism and socialism. John Ryan was a great exponent of the encyclical and used it as the basis for his idea of "economic democracy" which promoted unionization, cooperatives, and stock and profit-sharing schemes as steps to the long-range goal of a self-governing economy.[65]

In 1940 the NCWC Administrative Board issued "The Church and the Social Order," a progressive document which contained many of the principles of the New Deal and Ryan's economic democracy. The bishops used Pius XI's phrase, "to restore all things in Christ," as a means to comprehensively teach the need for Christ in all aspects of society. The document contained many similarities with *Rerum Novarum* in its teachings on a state's need to act for the public good and labor's rights to just compensation and unions.[66]

James Gillis initially dealt with the social question in generic terms, expressing sympathy, solidarity with the poor, and support for promoters of Catholic Action. He preached that it was foolish to seek answers to major national and international issues unless the glaring contradiction between super-luxury and abject poverty could be remedied. Poverty could prove a breeding ground for Communism, but voluntary economic reconstruction (as opposed to state activism) would bring moral regeneration, a condition that was necessary to safeguard the nation and return people to their sense of duty and personal responsibility.[67]

Gillis applauded the commitment shown by Catholic Action groups, especially the Catholic Worker Movement, for which he possessed a special affection,[68] but he cautioned these organizations that they must be more pro-active. He analogized Catholic

Action to a war cry whose battle was now in progress and needed to be intensified. Metaphorically he wrote, "We [Catholics] are indeed stirring in our sleep, twisting uneasily from side to side, but we are not yet awake." Gillis further challenged the clergy to "live a militant Christianity," to preach the social encyclicals, and to arouse public indignation against great wealth which preyed on the poor and the innocent.[69]

Although there was no clear consensus, this period did evoke much discussion, comment, and advocacy in the field of organized labor. In general Catholics supported the rights of labor, including the right to organize. John Ryan and Dorothy Day were two strong supporters of unionization, deploring the weakened condition of organized labor. The most avid champion, however, was Francis Haas, who considered union membership to be a sacred duty for all workers. In February 1937, John Cort, who was not satisfied with the Catholic Workers' approach to social reform for labor, led a group of five who founded the Association of Catholic Trade Unionists (ACTU). The body aimed to promote unionization, to bring Christian principles into unions, and to root out Communists from organized American labor.[70]

Gillis's views on labor were supportive of basic human rights and freedom of choice but challenged the methods used by workers to achieve their goals. He used the principles of *Rerum Novarum,* as well as references to Ryan's monographs *Distributive Justice* and *Church and State,* to call for just wages and the humane treatment of workers. Gillis, however, questioned organized labor's use of strikes: "As a matter of fact I think that the time has come when strikes should be outlawed....The strike is a very crude instrument of justice, quite as outmoded as the duel or ordeal by fire." He asked why, especially with the passage of the Wagner Act (1937), labor and capital could not solve their differences through negotiation.[71] Gillis's stance drew fire, including a reproach from Father John Cronin of St. Mary's Seminary, who chided the editor's intransigence: "We should be tolerant toward the growing pains of new unions and give them all the positive assistance to an orderly and peaceful development."[72]

James Gillis's principal activity and most significant contribution to the promotion of social Catholicism was his advocacy
of the cause for black Americans. His efforts arose, however,
from an inglorious history of the efforts of the Church to aid
blacks. Since the Civil War period, Catholics had done little to
foster evangelization or promote the social welfare of the black
community. Catholics separated themselves from the abolitionist movement for fear that it would fuel additional anti-Catholic
animus; their record to foster black vocations to religious life and
especially the clerical state was disgraceful.[73]

The black Catholic community aided its own cause by raising up leaders who took action to promote the special needs of
their people. Daniel Rudd (1854–1933) of Cincinnati, editor of
the *American Catholic Tribune,* emerged to lead the organization
and execution of five lay Black Congresses held between 1889
and 1894. Thomas Wyatt Turner, a Howard University and
Hampton Institute biology professor, in 1924 founded the Federation of Colored Catholics, which organized efforts to bring special grievances of black Catholics to the view of the Church.[74]

Gillis, as we have seen, had earlier made comments about
the injustices dealt all minorities in the United States. He
deplored race hatred, portrayed it as un-American, and linked it
directly to godlessness which reigned in society:

> I will go the full limit: if a white man discriminates against a
> black because he is black, if he cherishes race hatred he has
> no reason to complain of present conditions. If you hate the
> black, the Jew, the Italian, you had better get down on your
> knees and beg God's mercy, because in the final analysis you
> are a cause of war.[75]

Simultaneous with his other activities he began to center his
efforts on the cause of blacks, conducting his work in conjunction with the Northeastern Clergy Conference for Negro Welfare[76] and its leader, John LaFarge. Gillis described LaFarge's
work on behalf of the black community as "courageous," "informative," "persuasive," and "Catholic."[77]

Gillis was actively involved with the Clergy Conference from
its establishment in November 1933 and used it as a new plat-

form for his message to the nation. A group of concerned Catholic clergy, including several pastors and editors, gathered on several occasions in Newark, New York City, and Philadelphia in the fall of 1933 to discuss mutual concerns regarding the large and predominantly non-Catholic black population that had migrated to the urban centers of the northeastern United States. The group's first formal meeting was held on March 20, 1934 in Torresdale, Pennsylvania at the family estate of Louise D. Morrell, sister of Katharine Drexel, foundress of the Sisters of the Blessed Sacrament for Indians and Colored People.[78]

The Conference rapidly organized itself, stating its objectives and approach.[79] It was first suggested that the group could best serve its purpose if it remained a non-officially recognized body. Full sanction would require an episcopal representative at each meeting as well as hierarchical approval of all statements and proposals. Next, the Conference set forth its main objectives and planned approach to achieve them. The body's modus agendi aimed to promote conversions, social justice, negro clergy, education, race relations, and cultural development. In order to carry out these objectives the Conference members suggested the need to develop a sympathetic and enlightened clergy, to seek public means such as radio, letters, and essays to broadcast the body's message, and to promote cooperation with Catholic interracial councils, which were forming in all major urban centers of the country.[80]

Gillis dedicated himself to the work of the Conference, despite his many other pressing responsibilities, seeing the group's work as integral to the recovery of the nation's moral fiber. He suggested from the outset, as with Catholic Action, that timidity and apologetics would not help the Conference's purpose; people needed to be "shocked" into action. He heeded his own advice in a stirring speech to New York's Catholic Interracial Council:

> For in all the long history of "man's inhumanity to man" perhaps the cruelest pages are those wherein is written the record of the treatment accorded the Negro by the "dominant" race that achieved and maintained its dominance with injustice and brutality and falsehood and hypocrisy.[81]

He served as chairman of the Publicity and Literature Committee of the Conference, which encompassed approximately half of the group's business. He challenged the Conference to move beyond generic statements to more bold proclamations of full support for the education of both "white and colored in Catholic schools."[82]

With the Conference as a base of operation, Gillis launched into a full drive for black equality in the Church, using the various media at his disposal. Human inequality and segregation denied individual free choice and thus represented a new face of the darkness of society, Gillis's metaphorical Mr. Hyde. In April 1934 he was asked by the Conference members to head a subcommittee to search for ways to use radio to further the group's efforts. The selection was natural from Gillis's vast experience in that medium and he readily accepted the offer.[83] His investigation and knowledge of the radio field told him that the sensitive nature of the Conference's message would not be accepted by all and thus, after a few overtures toward the "Catholic Hour," he abandoned any thought of a national series of talks on black rights in the Church and society. He suggested that Conference members prepare talks of fifteen minutes' duration, volunteering WLWL "any night" for their broadcast.[84]

In May 1935 the "Catholic Interracial Hour" was initiated on WLWL. LaFarge was chosen to inaugurate the series with a talk "Interracial Progress." Cornelius J. Ahern, pastor of Queen of Angels Church in Newark and chairman of the Conference, was another speaker in the series. In 1936 the program featured short plays that voiced the Conference's agenda for education and increased awareness concerning prejudice, which was so commonplace in society it had become almost invisible.[85]

Gillis, with his typical missionary zeal, used his radio talks on black equality to appeal to the universal ideal of fair play and Christian tradition. In October 1935 he spoke in Augusta, Georgia:

> Unless our sympathy is universal, unless our cry for justice can be heard around the world, we are renegades from the Christian tradition of love for the underdog, and—what is more important still—we are not worthy of the noble name "Christian."

Three months later on WLWL he addressed the Scottsboro Nine case, striking out with fervor against those who had unjustly convicted and condemned the black youths, a matter of guilt by association and happenstance. Gillis felt that to make judgments based on color of skin, hair, or eyes was an unspeakable wrong:

> The Negro is my brother whether or not I prefer his complexion to my own. I would not think of discriminating against him because of the shadow on his skin any more than I would discriminate against the Scandinavian because he is blond or the Sicilian because he is a deep brunet [*sic*].[86]

Besides radio Gillis used the printed word to promulgate his message of black equality. He dedicated several essays of *Sursum Corda* calling, in a bit more subdued tone,[87] for the acceptance of blacks as equals and their evangelization by all Catholics. The ever abundant prejudice and discrimination in society created the "need for a second emancipation."[88] Gillis also promoted black equality in the pages of *The Catholic World*. Between January 1939 and December 1942 the magazine published eleven essays or editorials dealing with this issue.[89] He challenged the hierarchy to speak on the question and asked that material on blacks be added to courses on social justice being taught by Catholic leaders such as Francis Haas and Raymond McGowan.[90]

Gillis's promotion of the rights of black Catholics was notable; yet his failure to critique Church segregationist policies, from the formation of the clergy to separation in worship, demonstrates his blindness. For Gillis society was the culprit, the Mr. Hyde of his world view; the Church, full of God's presence and goodness, had no need of reform. The stark dualism of his understanding of society remained intransigent and unbending.

Guarding the International Front—1933–1937

James Gillis regularly preached that the United States should keep its own house in order before it ventured out to "solve the problems of the world." His work with social Catholicism sought to safeguard the American people and the principles upon which the republic was founded. Nevertheless, with a world society in great decay from the rise of materialism, Gillis could not blind himself to international events, especially when he perceived them as threatening the moral fiber of the United States. America might have needed a New Deal, but the world needed a whole new deck of cards.[91]

The moral state of the world was in need of repair from the philosophy of relativism, which had supplanted personal responsibility and paved the way for the rise of the absolute state and the cult of the leader. Gillis believed that nations of the world had afflicted themselves from their promotion of a double standard of honor, one for the individual and another for the corporate state. He said that the world's ills could be cured by the application of the principle of personal honor to the conduct of business and politics. A complex world required a simple answer, the return to moral responsibility. With democracy disappearing around the globe, it was incumbent on America to stand strong against the tide. Gillis applied his understanding of the world's problems and his proposed solution to several different international issues, all of which, in his mind, impinged on the United States and its salvation.[92]

In early November 1933 the new administration began formal negotiations with Maxim Litvinoff, the Soviet Commissar for Foreign Affairs, concerning the establishment of diplomatic relations between the United States and the Soviet Union, which had been severed since the Wilson administration. The move was made ostensibly by Roosevelt to increase Soviet-American trade and, thereby, invigorate the stagnant economy, and to forge a coalition between England, the United States, and the Soviet Union that could help stop the aggression of Japan against China.[93]

Catholics, who held a long tradition of opposition to the atheism practiced by the Soviet state, loosed their pens in opposition to the proposed move and the ramifications it would have for the future. Religious persecution in Russia, which had closed churches making the open practice of Christianity virtually impossible, was the principal issue of concern. The NCWC Administrative Committee declared that if recognition was afforded to the Soviets, it in no way meant that the nation sympathized with "the religious and moral institutions and teaching of the Government in question." *The Commonweal* voiced the complaint that recognition would bring the Soviets' practices of atheism and totalitarianism to greater prestige in the world. Many Catholics suggested that any recognition be linked to some concession by the Soviets that they grant greater freedom of religious practice to their citizens. Wilfrid Parsons, however, stated the common belief that the Soviets could not be trusted in anything, especially a promise of greater tolerance in religious practice.[94]

Gillis's sharply critical attitude toward recognition followed the arguments made by most Catholics. He did not believe that the economy would be stimulated by trade with Russia and wondered where the Soviets would obtain the money to buy American goods. Moreover, it was not ethically sound to do business with "a crafty, unprincipled, conscienceless, murderous group"; to enter such business would require the compromise of American principles, a condition which he had consistently rejected since the time he developed his world view. Like Parsons, Gillis did not trust the Soviets; they had no basic reason to be truthful. Surprisingly, however, when recognition was extended on November 16,[95] he made no public statement against the move.[96]

Gillis's cautious view of Mussolini and Fascism in Italy in the 1920s led to open denunciation of "Il Duce" when he invaded Ethiopia on October 3, 1935. For the editor the basic question remained: Was Mussolini, who understood himself to be a second Caesar, justified in his annexation of Ethiopia? The simple answer and plain truth was no; no nation had the right to violate the moral law. He stated, "I repeat, every nation that has annexed alien or overseas dominions will be plagued and utterly ruined by its imperialistic adventures." Gillis chided the "moral bankruptcy" of the American secular press and the Roosevelt administration for their common failure to speak out against Mussolini's policy of imperialism.[97]

Gillis's views on Mussolini and the Italo-Ethiopian war produced the first significant backlash against his commentary after almost fourteen years as editor. Gillis received many letters which accused him of being anti-Italian. His criticism of Mussolini rested squarely on the dictator's use of the state to deny human freedom, but it is probable that this argument was lost by many Italian-Americans, who perceived the editor's denunciation as an attack on a favorite son. One pastor, for example, berated the editor for his "uncalled-for attack on Italy and Mussolini" and wrote to Superior General John Harney, requesting that Gillis stop "these insidious attacks by a Catholic priest." He was also cautioned to apply his "splendid talents and beautiful style to questions paramount here at home, where you can come closer to the facts...." Frank Hall of the *NCWC News Service* was also deluged with mail critical of Gillis's *Sursum Corda* columns about "Il Duce."[98] In response Hall asked him to "shift to something less controversial" in his essays. Additionally, his opinion was not popular in Italy or with the Vatican.[99]

The "most severe strain"[100] in the generally harmonious relationship between Franklin Roosevelt and American Catholics was produced by the persecution of the Church in Mexico. The "Six-Year Plan" announced by Mexican President Plutarco Calles in 1934 pledged to amend the national constitution so as to permit only state-run schools which would teach the socialistic and anticlerical ideas upon which the Mexican Revolution was based. Religious education was to be excluded from all primary and secondary schools. Clerics were declared "professionals" and placed under the watchful eye of the government.

This state of affairs, repugnant to American Catholics, was greatly exacerbated when Josephus Daniels, the United States Ambassador, gave a speech in Mexico City on July 26, 1934 which sounded to most ears as a ringing endorsement of the planned secularization process for education in Mexico. Catholic reaction to the ill-timed statement was swift and strong. Daniels became the scapegoat in a wide-ranging diatribe by leading Catholic voices, including *The Commonweal, America,* Charles Coughlin, Francis Clement Kelley (Bishop of Oklahoma), and the NCWC, who all reacted strongly in denouncing Daniels' statement and calling for his ouster.[101] Additionally, Catholic journals called for a boycott of Mexican products, promoted an anti-tourism drive, and attacked Roosevelt, challenging him to speak out against the tyranny of the Mexican government which held the Church prisoner.[102] Pressure from the Knights of Columbus, under the guidance of Supreme Knight Martin Carmody, was credited for a July

17, 1935 statement by Roosevelt, who publicly endorsed those who were making "it clear that the American people and the Government believe in the freedom of religious worship, not only in the United States, but also in other nations."[103]

Gillis's reaction to the situation in Mexico was predictable in its vehemence, adherence to social teaching, denunciation of moral evil, and support for individual freedom. In a *Sursum Corda* essay which stretched more than double the column's normal length of six hundred words, he berated Daniels' speech and anti-Catholic attitude, and called for him to resign.

> What would you say, Mr. Daniels, if only a dozen Methodist ministers were allowed in the United States? Are you apathetic and silent when Catholic priests are persecuted and banished, though your blood would boil and your mouth open if Methodists met the same fate? Indeed it is reported that in five or six of the states of Mexico, not one church is permitted to remain open. You would not approve of that policy here at home. Do you approve of it in Mexico? What do you really mean when you say you "stand for" freedom of religion? It seems to us that you stand idly by when freedom is violated, or rather by inopportune and unqualified praise of the Calles-Rodriguez regime you stand on both sides of the fence....In a word, Mr. Daniels, why don't you be a good American in deed and not only in word? Why don't you come home, tell Mr. Roosevelt the truth and beg to be excused from your diplomatic post? [104]

Gillis did not countenance the President's non-intervention policy in Mexico, saying that moral support granted Mexico since the time of Hoover had abrogated any isolation position. He called for the removal of moral support and a lifting of the arms embargo, moves that would spell the end of the Calles regime. Anything less would be an act of apostasy toward the faith given to the nation by the founding fathers.[105] Gillis also applauded the literary efforts of Wilfrid Parsons and Francis Clement Kelley, whose books *Mexican Martyrdom* and *Blood Drenched Altars* accurately described the sad conditions present in Mexico.[106]

Although Gillis did not advocate armed intervention, his criticism of Roosevelt's failure to act in Mexico appears to be inconsistent with his staunch isolationism. When the editor's beloved institutions, the Church and the American nation, or the individual, were in jeopardy, he called for action; protection of what he considered sacred took priority in decisions pertinent to America's international involvement. International discord, perceived by Gillis to have no ramification on Church or America, was viewed in a different light and did not seem to be a candidate for his concern.

The Spanish Civil War (1936–1938), a carnage of human suffering, pitted the combined nationalist forces under the command of General Francisco Franco against forces loyal to the government (loyalists) of the Second Republic. Before the conflict began in earnest, Hitler and Mussolini had both extended assistance to Franco. Loyalists shopped in the international market for aid but were rebuffed by all except the Soviets. Thus, the war in many ways pitted Fascism against Communism.

The United States, in accord with the Neutrality Act of 1935,[107] placed an embargo on all war materials sent to Spain, thereby claiming a position of neutrality in the conflict. While most Americans supported the Spanish Loyalists,[108] Catholics, alienated by the slaughter of thousands of religious and clerics at the hands of the government and fearful of Communism,[109] were generally enthusiastic in their support for the nationalist forces under Franco. *America* and its editor Francis X. Talbot, SJ, clearly backed Franco, but *The Commonweal,* after changing its position twice, finally ended in a neutral position concerning the conflict.[110]

James Gillis was totally bewildered at the outset by the Spanish conflict. He could not fathom how a people steeped in Catholic tradition for centuries could possibly turn so savagely anticlerical and anti-Church in wanton destruction of life and property. Thus, he initially stood neutral, seeing madness on both sides of the conflict. He wrote, "If I am a genuine lover of mankind and not a bigot or partisan I must condemn one and the other impartially when they are cruel and unjust."[111] For Gillis at this point the greatest enemy was war itself and the great evil it created.

As the conflict continued, Gillis's vision began to change as he considered future prospects of a Loyalist victory. He began to berate the secular press for its inaccurate reporting of the conflict, although he did not express what the truth was. Over time Gillis became more and more anti-Communist in his stance so that by 1939 he could write, "The Communists have turned things upside down. Franco set them right side up again."[112] He began to see Communism as a vital root of all political evil.

The rise of Adolf Hitler to power in Germany in 1933 was not initially met with the backlash from the Catholic press that one might expect.[113] James Gillis, however, immediately recognized the potential problem that Hitler posed to the world, stating that society had seen nothing as ghastly for 1600 years since the reign of Julian the Apostate. The Nazi dictator stood for all the things which Gillis deplored, racial hatred, extreme nationalism, and abolition of individual thought and freedom. The editor labeled him "a menace to the peace of Europe, a tyrant, a bully, an assassin, and perhaps a maniac"; he was Mr. Hyde without mask or disguise.[114] As time passed, Gillis became much more vehement in his denunciations of Hitler due to his substitution of national religion for Christian faith and his campaign which he perceived as leading toward the destruction of civilization itself. Yet Gillis, as a man of faith, possessed hope, for history told him that so many in the past had attempted to challenge the Church and all had failed.[115]

A Policy of Non-Intervention—1937–1941

In James Gillis's overall desire to safeguard the United States from moral irresponsibility and the general malaise that had infected the world, no campaign was stronger, more passionately argued or took more of his time and attention, than his desire to keep the nation away from foreign entanglements and war. He was labeled by a contemporary in this crusade as an "integral warrior" fighting the battles for the Church in the United States "with his trenchant pen and stirring oratory."[116] As the international scene began to heat up and his campaign to meet the social needs of American Catholics progressed, Gillis began to devote the vast majority of his time, talent, energy, and certainly his public media attention to a call for America to avoid military involvement in the world. The United States could not and should not be an international police force. In his campaign Gillis often referred to the founding fathers, especially George Washington and his farewell speech to Congress, which called for the nation to avoid all outside entanglements. Gillis's crusade started early in the Roosevelt presidency, gained momentum over time, and in the end advocated a total rejection of the President and his policy.

Gillis's theme of non-intervention was initially generated from his earlier experience and observations of World War I. The carnage, death, and human suffering of World War I, about which he knew from his life experience and his earlier reading of Philip Gibbs's *Now It Can Be Told*, repulsed him and was a direct cause to his stance of non-intervention. World War I was perceived by Gillis as a great sin; keeping America out of the volatile European situation would stunt the emergence of another great evil and manifestation of Mr. Hyde. He believed that the United States had no obligation to bail out Europe from its own problems, economic or social. In doing so in the past, huge debts had been incurred which still had not been repaid to the American treasury. The United States had plenty of domestic house cleaning before it could run abroad to aid others. He also preached that involvement in one place would be like a cancer and spread rapidly to intervention everywhere; there would be no way to stop the disease which would poison the nation just when it was beginning to find economic recovery.[117] Gillis cautioned people not to be swayed by the designs of government, which procured war over the desires of the people:

> Sit tight fellow citizens. Keep your wits about you. Don't let the orators and editors bamboozle you. The only good we can do for our country and for the world is to stay right here.[118]

By 1936 Gillis was confident enough to boldly proclaim to Congress his own plan to avoid the debacle of American involvement in another war.[119]

Gillis was not alone in his isolationist position. Manfred Jonas writes of a resurgence of isolationism in America in the

1930s, principally in reaction to the activities of Germany, Italy, and Japan. Fear was rampant that another war was imminent. He states that isolationists were not obstructionists but possessed a positive view of the world and America's role in it. Transcending all bounds of geography or socio-economic levels, isolationists found their *sine qua non* in their common faith in unilateralism in foreign policy and fear of war.[120]

The high-water mark for non-intervention sentiment in the United States was reached in 1938. Gillis, who traveled to Budapest that year to address the International Eucharistic Congress, was able to experience firsthand the European situation, using it as another tool in his continuing campaign to keep America "out of harm's way." He expanded his attack on Mussolini, demonstrating the essential antagonism between Catholicism and Fascism, Nazism, and Communism.[121] Japanese aggression against China was also vigorously attacked by Gillis, who labeled it "essentially unjust and immoral, a violation of the law of nations and of the axiomatic principles of ethics." He raised the caution flag about Japan's rapid rise to power and chided the administration for its refusal to speak out so as not to jeopardize economic profit:

> Let's not fool ourselves. The Japanese have come from nothing in record time. It took the Roman Empire 760 years to get itself into compact shape. It took Great Britain some 350 or 400 years to consolidate her power. The Japanese did it in 30 years. Keep your eye on Japan.[122]

The German invasion of Poland on September 1, 1939 rekindled in Gillis his strong repugnance for war which characterized his "conversion" experience in 1920 aboard the *SS Santa Rosa*. He had long preached that the ultimate cause of war was racial hatred, but now he began to uncharacteristically promote a solution: "In the last analysis it is the Brotherhood of Man, the Communion of Saints and Sinners, the doctrine that we are all one, that will save us from war." Human carnage and economic distress were obvious results of war, but Gillis preached that "the supreme crime and tragedy of war [is] the killing of conscience." He warned that individuals and nations dare not abrogate their

responsibility in the prevention of war: "We the people are the ultimate determinant of war and peace and in the last analysis ours is
the responsibility."[123] Gillis perceived war as an immense evil that
struck at the very heart of his message of individual free choice
and conversion. War's destruction of conscience was another manifestation of the dark face of Hyde which required conversion.

Like most armed conflicts the initiation of hostilities fostered discussion of the theory of just war. Most writers claimed
that England and France were locked in a just war against Germany. Jacques Maritain, writing in *The Commonweal* in December
1939, claimed that the European conflict was a just war.[124] Gillis,
however, rejected both possibilities. England's alliance with
"satan" (Soviet Union) made a holy war inconceivable; the crite-
ria of Augustine and Aquinas for just war were, for Gillis, impossible to attain in modern society.[125]

Gillis preached against American involvement, but he was
no fool, and, with war clouds on the horizon, knew it was imperative for the United States to be prepared. Even as leader of the
non-intervention school, he realized, in the face of war and the
alien philosophies of Communism and Fascism, that the nation
needed to ready itself for every possibility. He appealed to
national pride and wrote,

> Whatever be our political opinions and our differences of
> view on the war, we are, it is to be hoped, all equally patriotic.
> All true patriots wish to see their country well defended.[126]

In 1937, despite Roosevelt's recent landslide re-election, the
mood of the nation began to show displeasure with the President's approach to the ever more complicated world situation.
This growing fear of American involvement around the globe
produced sentiment in Congress which led to the passage of a
series of three Neutrality Acts (August 31, 1935, May 1, 1937,
April 30, 1939) which tied the hands of the nation against support for belligerents. Although Roosevelt was talking tough
against other countries, many saw him as a paper lion since any
action would violate American neutrality.[127]

Gillis's crusade to guard America's ideals and people against
the impending disaster of foreign war intensified and took on a

personal character in the fall of 1939. He continued to voice concern over order in the domestic house and to challenge the President over his centralization of power,[128] but the campaign took a major shift when he began to attack the British for their past sins. In a series of editorials in *The Catholic World*, Gillis reviewed England's "history of imperialism" and its "mismanagement of certain international issues." The United States should have no qualms about denying assistance to a country whose past was clouded with incidents of land grabbing and the suppression of human rights. The oppressive situation in India, about which Gillis had earlier commented, was a perfect example of English imperialism in the world. Gillis placed the onus of responsibility for the war's cessation on England: "Will she [England] now offer to relinquish all that she has taken by force? If so the war is ended. If she will so much as say that she is prepared to discuss the matter, there will be immediately and automatically an armistice."[129]

Gillis also berated the British, as hinted at previously, for their alliance with the Soviet Union. He believed a union of the lion and the bear was morally wrong, for it gave credence to murderous activity and, thereby, shamed honor and idealism. In his typically acidic style he wrote,

> And of all the sticky, gooey hypocrisy of the last few years, it seems to me that the worst is the explanation that France and England are allying themselves with Russia to save Democracy and Christian civilization. If Democracy can be saved only with the aid of tyranny, Democracy should not be saved. The kind of religion that must be saved by alliance with atheism had better be lost.[130]

Gillis's anti-British diatribe received sustained and many times severe criticism from all fronts. *Catholic World* subscribers by the dozens wrote to denounce Gillis's opinion; many cancelled their subscriptions. One response addressed to "The Catholic World" from a twenty-one-year subscriber is illustrative,

> Your editor may be right as to Hitler's [lack of] sanity, but as a Counsel of 58 years experience I am inclined to think that his editorials in a number of your last issues furnish as

strong if not stronger evidence against him than he alleges against Hitler.[131]

Another response demonstrates the anger which Gillis's editorials had generated, "Please discontinue!—Your unjust, untrue and unwarranted attacks on England have rendered your once interesting magazine worse than useless."[132] Gillis was also reproved by British journalists and hierarchy.[133]

Gillis's criticism of England, like that of Mussolini earlier, also drew heat from Frank Hall, director of the NCWC Press Department. Hall reported to Gillis's secretary, Margaret Walsh, that a *Sursum Corda* essay, "The British Should Behave—Now," had received negative reviews from several of the sixteen Catholic newspapers which published the column. Hall carried on a running correspondence with Gillis from 1938 to 1940 on several *Sursum Corda* pieces as the editor's frustration over the course of world events was carried over to his column, subtitled "What Is Right with the World."[134]

Gillis's denunciation of the British for their history of imperialism, seeing it as a cause for the present war, appears in retrospect to be short-sighted. It is true that the British Empire was built by means of a policy which subdued many peoples, and it is equally certain that the English sought to maintain their realm. Yet, it is rash to conclude from this that Hitler would have ended hostilities if he had been ceded some of England's imperial possessions, as Gillis's comments suggest. Hitler's prosecution of the war was as much to show his might as to gain territory; it is doubtful that he would have been happy with lands merely ceded him after the onset of hostilities. Gillis's tirade against the British is best explained in the light of his perceived prophetic mission to save America from all enemies, foreign and domestic.

Although Gillis was more vehement and vocal than most, Catholic opinion, like that of most Americans, agreed with his stance on non-intervention. The hierarchy stated the official Catholic response in November 1939:

> We plead for a spirit of calm deliberation in our own nation....Our primary duty is that of preserving the strength, stability, and security of our own nation, not, indeed, in a spirit

of selfish isolation, but rather in a spirit of justice and charity to those whose welfare is our first and chief responsibility.[135]

In a series of editorials, the editor of *America,* Francis X. Talbot, clearly stood in the non-interventionist camp. In fearing that the Constitution was being usurped, he wrote, "At all events, and at all costs, the United States should keep out of the war....Every citizen should see his Government fulfills that duty."[136] Joseph Rossi, SJ, has accurately summarized the prevailing attitude: "At all costs, most Catholics in the United States wanted to see the country remain at peace."[137]

Gillis's hatred of evil and its manifestations in the European dictators Stalin, Hitler, and Mussolini, coupled with his persistent message of the need to effect conversion in the world, seems at first glance to be inconsistent with his staunch non-interventionist stance. The situation in Europe was evil in the ideologies which controlled governments and the leaders who professed them. But war, too, was a great evil, especially in its destruction of conscience and free will. Gillis's desire to avoid war was consistent with his message to shun sin, practice free choice, and discover conversion. America's chance of reform was thus preserved.

The apogee of Gillis's strident criticism of Franklin Roosevelt, the one who stood against the national belief in non-intervention, was reached in the campaign and election of 1940. Standing against intervention, Gillis summarized his ideas on the mission of the United States with the suggestion that Roosevelt should heed his words.

> This then I think is the original, genuine authentic policy of the United States of America: to keep our lamp trimmed, our light brightly burning, our house in order, to be an example for other nations: not to attempt the impossible task of guaranteeing liberty to all in the world or of rushing about like another and more deluded Don Quixote to enforce right in Europe, Asia, Africa, in all the islands and continents.

> And we shall do well to imitate his [Pius XII's] inviolable neutrality. There is no moral obligation upon our souls to join in the European war.[138]

As the 1940 election drew near, Gillis gained allies from other Catholic publications in his fight against the President. *America* declared itself against a third term for any president as early as July; *Our Sunday Visitor* feared that the Constitution had been tampered with too much in the past eight years and hinted at Roosevelt's defeat. *The Commonweal,* however, took no stand with its various officers split between Wilkie and Roosevelt.[139]

The November 1940 *Catholic World* editorial, striking with the power of a bomb blast, left no doubt where James Gillis stood on the election and the person of Franklin Roosevelt. Gillis ridiculed the President for his failures and challenged his readers to do their duty and remove him from office:

> I confess I don't understand the man. But I do think him inconsistent and unpredictable. A "dangerous," "reckless," "audacious," inconsistent, unpredictable man is no man to be three times President of the United States.
>
> To perpetuate in office a man with a mania for power who asks, obtains and holds all that he gets, and demands ever more and more would be as great a political blunder as that of Hindenburg and the Reichstag that handed over all liberties of the people to Hitler.[140]

Additionally, Gillis outlined Roosevelt's many flip-flops and somersaults in policy decisions, all of which suggested that the President should receive "his walking papers on election day."[141] Gillis's perception of evil in Roosevelt's policies had moved to a view of the President himself as evil; he became a Mr. Hyde along with other world leaders who denied human freedom.

Gillis's vociferous attack reached many more than the originally intended audience. Without his knowledge or permission, the editorial was reprinted in part by Wilkie supporters and was distributed outside many Catholic churches after Sunday Mass in an effort to sway voters away from Roosevelt. The implication was that the editorial represented an official Catholic stance on the election.

The response by the public to Gillis's editorial made the reaction to his previous fall's rebuke to Great Britain seem tame in comparison. Well over 200 extant letters reached *The Catholic*

World offices expressing sadness, amazement, and shock. Many of the letters compared Gillis with Coughlin and berated him for meddling in politics, which was not his place. Other letters repudiated his stance, calling his treatment of the President "a public scandal."[142] Even Gillis's long-time friend and fellow journalist, Michael Williams, criticized the editorial attack as politically motivated solely, without any look to the spiritual, moral, or doctrinal. Additionally, he complained, "His [Gillis's] attack on the President and his promises on behalf of Mr. Wilkie are highly inconsistent, reckless, and unpredictable in their possible dangerous consequences."[143] John Ryan, who continued his unwavering support for the President, renewed his earlier disagreement with Gillis by describing the editorial as a "discreditable performance."[144]

The great outcry to *The Catholic World's* November editorial forced Paulist Superior General Henry Stark, who had been elected in the 1940 chapter, to distance the community from Gillis's stance. Stark reprinted a section of Gillis's September 1923 editorial where he stated that in editorials he speaks for himself and not for the Paulist community or the Church. Speaking as Gillis's superior, he released the following statement:

> He [Gillis] wishes to declare emphatically that all the opinions expressed in his November [1940] editorial were purely personal opinions in accordance with this statement. Under no conditions did he expect or did he attempt to influence Catholic votes in the coming Presidential election. He expressed merely his own opinion and not the opinion or the teaching of the Catholic Church, nor the opinions of any members of the Catholic Church, clergy or laity.[145]

Adverse reaction to Gillis's stand against the President was also received as a result of his weekly *Sursum Corda* column. Frank Hall again wrote to Gillis, irritated at his "bitter assailing" of Roosevelt and reporting that many people had cancelled subscriptions of local newspapers because of his attack.[146] Gillis defended himself against the mounds of criticism, stating that he possessed no personal pique against Roosevelt, but, rather, the comments were made to save America's principles and "to free my mind and soul."[147]

Gillis's statement reveals the need he had to vent his frustration and personal anguish at the state of the nation and the world. In his personal campaign as guardian of America, Gillis had met roadblocks all along the way, but most especially in the policies of a President who was leading the nation to disaster through his escalation of America's international involvement. Roosevelt's power had continued to grow and consolidate as his presidency evolved. Gillis's great fear of statism would come closer to reality if the President was re-elected for an unprecedented third term. In his typically unabashed, but unusually harsh criticism, Gillis unleashed his emotions in a last-gasp effort to save the country from four more years of Franklin Roosevelt.

Gillis's personal crusade to safeguard America became a heated national issue as the conflict in Europe escalated, thus increasing fear of eventual United States involvement. The Committee to Defend America by Aiding the Allies and The Fight for Freedom Committee, both supporting American involvement, if not by force then at least through aid, were established in the spring of 1940 and 1941 respectively.[148] The America First Committee,[149] founded on September 4, 1940, supported non-intervention. This group advocated three principles to meet its objective: (1) to erect an impregnable home defense system, (2) to convince the public that democracy's preservation depended upon keeping out of the war, and (3) to defeat Roosevelt's foreign policy, which was leading the nation into war.[150] The heart of the Committee's support base was found in conservative Midwest business leaders. Some of the group's most notable members were Charles Lindbergh, Senator Gerald P. Nye, Philip La Follette, Lillian Gish, Chester Bowles, and General Hugh S. Johnson, former administrator of the NRA. Although not members, former Catholic labor leader Father Peter Dietz and Cardinal William O'Connell were supporters.[151]

Of no surprise to anyone, James Gillis fully supported the efforts of America First and spoke on its behalf on seven different occasions.[152] In his addresses he questioned America's motivation for contemplating war, which he felt was not to denounce Hitler but to maintain the *status quo,* thus preserving the industrial hegemony and the domination of the seas that England had for so long enjoyed. Stressing loyalty to the nation, he stated,

> Let no man say that we who are for America First are less loyal or less patriotic than those who follow a President who goes ahead on a course that leads to war without consultation with Congress and without consideration of the people. He is the best American who loves his country and its constitution more than he loves any man, even the man who happens for the time being to be chief magistrate. Under God we have loyalties to people and to President, but it is no disparagement to the President if we say that in our heart not he but the people and the nation come first.

Gillis also called on what he perceived to be a silent majority who do not want war to speak out or be guilty of "moral and mental cowardice."[153]

As Hitler's Blitzkrieg subdued the European continent during 1941, Gillis continued his personal crusade to safeguard America as best he could. He used all the media at his disposal to continue his denunciation of Roosevelt's dangerous policy with which he jeopardized the very life blood of the nation. He pictured the United States as a log drifting slowly down the Niagara River toward the Falls; the cataract was imminent and then the whirlpool.[154] Gillis also continued to warn against the sweeping powers which Roosevelt had invoked in the March passage of Lend-Lease to England and his "shoot-first" policy of September 11.[155] The President had taken matters into his own hands, centralized the government, and in the process contradicted what Gillis perceived as the will of the people. When Japan attacked Pearl Harbor on Sunday December 7 Gillis, although a realist about what was necessary, was not overjoyed with future prospects. He wrote, "Speaking for myself—[I] still [am] an advocate of non-intervention in wars that are not ours—I certainly feel no jubilation over the turn that affairs have taken."[156]

James Gillis, as his mission to America continued, became an unproclaimed guardian for the nation's principles of democracy, individual human worth, commitment to duty, and moral responsibility. He, like many Americans, was hopeful that

Franklin Roosevelt would be the leader that the nation needed to lift its people, who had been mired in the pit of economic depression. However, by 1936 reservations and doubts began to cloud the picture as creeping statism practiced by the President threatened the American principles of government. Gillis wrestled with Roosevelt's New Deal but ultimately rejected it as a program which jeopardized human freedom. When the President continued his policy of greater state intervention in the affairs of the individual, even after the invalidation of the NRA, Gillis's criticism began to take on a personal tone. Initially Gillis's dualistic world view placed the face of Mr. Hyde on the President's policy; by 1940, however, Roosevelt himself was perceived to be the personification of evil.

Gillis increasingly viewed the world as a bastion of evil. Europe, with its collection of ideologies and its cadre of dictators, was the primary target of Gillis's ofttimes vehement attacks. In an effort to root out evil and replace it with the presence of God, he relentlessly denounced Communism, Nazism, and Fascism and their respective promoters Stalin, Hitler, and Mussolini. Echoing his persistent message of free choice and conversion, Gillis preached against sin and its manifestations within society.

James Gillis's analysis of the international scene, his revulsion of World War I, and his ardent desire to keep the United States away from evil "forced" him to champion the position of non-intervention. The evil existent in the world could not be removed or changed by participation in an even greater sin. He used all means available to him, including his various public media and active voice with the American First Committee, in raising blistering attacks against Roosevelt's policy which, in Gillis's view, undermined America's foundation. The nation's failure to avoid the war would force him to again redirect to other issues his mission to America as the nation and the world entered the long dark days of a second international armed conflict in less than a full generation.

CHAPTER 6

Loss of the
American Republic—1942–1949

Pearl Harbor and the subsequent entry of the United States into a two-front global war obviously forced Gillis to refocus his isolationism. Although he was not pleased with America's presence on the international scene, he realized that it would be necessary for the nation to finish what it had begun and then return to its prewar position as an independent republic, morally concerned with world affairs, but not militarily involved. Gillis never lost his idyllic picture, which depicted the United States as an observer and supporter in the world theater, despite the fact that he could see the nation slipping more and more into the active role of an international guardian.

His perception was that the attack on the American Republic was two-pronged, coming from the outside and from within. The rise of the Soviet Union, with its closely held ideology of atheistic Communism, led the assault from the outside by threatening the security of the whole world, including the United States, which was to emerge from the war as a super-power. The attack from within was more subtle, but in the mind of Gillis no less significant. It came as a strike against truth in government, the gradual movement of United States foreign policy to one of active international participation, the continued fraying of the nation's moral fabric, and the executive policies of Presidents Roosevelt and Truman for greater centralization of government and the removal of the individual from a position of importance in the scheme of daily life. James Gillis spent the war years excoriating these perceived threats, but in the end resigned himself to the fact that the American Republic, as he understood its role and purpose, was lost.

Prosecuting the War–1942–1945

The United States entered World War II woefully unprepared and over-matched. Despite the warnings of Gillis and other advocates of preparedness, America was not ready for war, especially on two major fronts. When the war began the United States possessed a standing army of 1.6 million, a combat air force of 3000 planes and a navy with 344 capital ships.[1] This situation was quickly rectified after Pearl Harbor. Production of war materials was nothing less than phenomenal. Between 1940 and 1944 the Gross National Product (GNP) rose 125% from $88.6 billion to $198.7 billion, with the war production's share going from 2% to 40% of the whole. In 1939 American industry turned out 6000 airplanes of all types, but in 1944, 96,369 planes were produced. On the level of raw materials the production of aluminum went from 300 million tons in 1939 to 2.3 billion tons in 1944. During the war years American industry produced almost 300,000 planes, over 72,000 naval ships of all types, 86,000 tanks, and more than 8.5 million rifles and carbines.[2]

American government changed and expanded as a result of the war; Roosevelt's social agenda of the New Deal obviously became secondary to the war effort. Some of the more important bureaus established during the war were the Office of Price Administration (OPA), given the nearly impossible task of price stabilization in a war-boom economy, the War Production Board (WPB) under Donald Nelson, erected to balance the needs of the war with those of the civilian population, the Office of War Mobilization (OWM) under James Byrnes, the War Manpower Commission (WMC), the Office of Economic Stabilization (OES), and the War Labor Board (WLB), which kept the production line going by settling disputes between organized labor and capital.[3]

The effects of the war on the American economy were also very dramatic. Government spending, as would be expected, rose dramatically from slightly over $9 billion in 1940 to almost $100 billion in 1945. The government was the purchaser and controller of almost one-half of the total national output of goods and services. This condition created an equally phenomenal rise in the national debt, making the red ink of the New Deal seem insignificant. The debt rose from $43 billion in 1940 to $259 billion in 1945; inflation was 29% during the same period. On the positive side, the need for manufacturers to shift to the production of war materials and the conscription of young men for the armed forces reduced unemployment to an insignificant level, created higher wages, and promoted a more than 100% rise in the ranks of organized labor to 15 million members. Economically and militarily Richard Kirkendall has accurately summarized America's rise: "From 1942 to 1944, the United States became a global power, capable of exerting influence on events and developments in many parts of the world."[4]

Plans for the war effort, discussed in a December 1941 Washington meeting of Roosevelt and Churchill, set the European theater as first priority, with the Japanese front to be defensive. However, the objections of the military hierarchy, including Chief of Naval Operations, Ernest King, and Pacific field commanders, Chester Nimitz and Douglas MacArthur, forced Roosevelt to move offensively against the Japanese. This drive actually began at home with the massive relocation of 120,000 American men and women of Japanese heritage who lived on America's west coast. The Pearl Harbor bombing, together with isolated incidents of "reported" Japanese shellings of the California coast, raised fear in the Golden State to a fever pitch. Governor Culbert Olson, Attorney General Earl Warren, and General John L. DeWitt, commander of the Western Defense Command and the Fourth Army headquartered at the Presidio in San Francisco, convinced Roosevelt that the Japanese threat necessitated the removal of all people of Japanese heritage from close proximity to defense plants and military bases. In February 1942 the President signed an executive order which initiated the evacuation of the Japanese to camps from Arkansas to California. Known as the Japanese Exclusion Program, it has been noted as "one of the most shameful episodes in American history."[5] Surprisingly *America* voiced no real protest against the program, but only asked that the Army's actions in the operation be kept

clean. In his consistent support of minorities, Gillis said the
action was unconstitutional and asked why similar measures had
not been taken against German and Italian Americans.[6]

American Catholics quickly bedecked themselves in the
stars and stripes and took up the cause of the war. On December
22, 1941 Archbishop Edward Mooney, Chairman of the NCWC
Administrative Committee, wrote to the President pledging support:

> We, the Catholic Bishops of the United States, spiritual lead-
> ers of more than twenty million Americans, wish to assure
> you, Mr. President, that we are keenly conscious of our
> responsibilities in the hour of our nation's testing. With a
> patriotism that is guided and sustained by the Christian
> virtues of faith, hope, and charity, we will marshall [sic] the
> spiritual forces at our command to render secure our God-
> given blessings of freedom.[7]

As the impact of World War I had brought greater consolidation
and organization to the American Church in the foundation of
the NCWC and its efforts to support the war cause, so too did
World War II bring the Church to a greater self-awareness of its
need to stand with the nation. Patriotic Catholics joined the war
effort and made preparations for the sacrifices and difficulties
that war would bring. Many clerics joined the ranks of the chaplain corps,[8] with the armed services over 30% Catholic, while fraternal groups such as the Knights of Columbus and the Catholic
Daughters of America engaged in United Services Organization
(USO) activities, bond drives, and blood donation campaigns.
The Catholic effort received an unexpected boost from the
Apostolic Delegate Amleto Cicognani, who, at the prompting of
Pope Pius XII, traveled the country speaking personally with
bishops who had earlier voiced anti-Roosevelt views in order to
bring them into the fold. Archbishop Michael Curley of Baltimore, a past critic of the President, hit the keynote, "Today there
is no place for discussion between isolationists and interventionists. The die is cast—it is a matter of defense of the nation."[9]

American Catholics in general saw the war as a just enterprise pitting the righteousness of the United States against the

godlessness of Hitler's Nazi Germany. America was the "City of God" which sought to render a death blow to the spread of Fascism, Nazism, and other forms of ideology that promoted atheism as a premise of life. Leading American Catholics voiced the opinion that America's effort was just and holy. The bishops in November 1942 stated, "We of America today fight not only for human values, but also for those that are divine." Bishop Francis Clement Kelley of Oklahoma stated that there is "no question of this war of defense." Monsignor Fulton Sheen of The Catholic University of America wrote, "This war is not only a political and economic struggle, but rather a theological one."[10] *America* concurred in the belief that the United States must act but pondered the inherent problem of maintaining a right moral view in time of war. It voiced the familiar dictum, "A nation may win a war and lose its soul."[11]

Gillis only reluctantly accepted America's participation in the war. In a critical tone he wrote, "I cannot understand the wild tumult in the Capitol when the President asked Congress to declare war. An austere silence would have been more decent. They could have kept the jubilation in abeyance for the next 'Armistice Day.'"[12] Gillis's refusal to immediately support the war effort, although consistent with his belief that war was a grave evil, was costly to him. The hierarchy's proclamation of support coupled with the Paulist community's sponsorship of chaplains, compared with Gillis's reluctance to accept reality, placed him outside the mainstream with the consequent loss of part of his support structure. His conservative message, while acceptable in the prewar period, was no longer viable; James Gillis was left behind.

The isolationist attitude voiced so clearly by Gillis prompted John A. Ryan to recommend the removal of periodicals which carried material inflammatory to the war effort or the Roosevelt administration. Specifically, Ryan attacked Charles Coughlin's *Social Justice,* whose mailing privilege was eventually revoked,[13] and also criticized the Brooklyn *Tablet* and *The Catholic World.* Writing to the co-editor of *Commonweal,* Philip Burnham, Ryan stated:

The other publications [besides *Social Justice*] which are in a lesser degree interfering with the successful prosecution of the war by creating disunity need not be disturbed....For example, the *Brooklyn Tablet* mainly by its sins of omission falls into this category. Another example is the *Catholic World*. In the current issue, the "Editorial Comment" presents some thirty-four quotations from newspapers concerning the war to each of which is appended comment by the editor. Of these thirty-four comments, fourteen are untrue or unfair or consist of sniping at one of our allies. Some of the untrue statements explicitly contradict the relevant facts; the others do so by implication....The *Catholic World* diatribe will do only a limited amount of harm, owing to the meager circulation. The readers of the *Brooklyn Tablet* exceed those of the *Catholic World* by many thousands, but the silent treatment which that paper is giving the war will not do as much harm as "Editorial Comment."[14]

Interestingly Ryan's complaint makes no mention of the *Catholic Worker*, which never wavered from a position of complete pacifism, despite the cost to the movement.[15] One may infer from Ryan's action that he possessed personal pique for the position of Gillis and the editor of the *Tablet*, Patrick Scanlan, the two leading Catholic conservative voices, along with his general support for Roosevelt and the war effort.

As would be expected, America's entry into the war provided much grist for the mill of Gillis's editorials and other vehicles of public opinion. The Paulist Superior General, Henry Stark, still reeling from the adverse reaction to Gillis's November 1940 editorial critical of Roosevelt, sought to disarm the editor's vituperation before problems developed: "I write to ask the most discreet care in the preparations of your fine editorials in the *Catholic World* and your splendid column, *Sursum Corda*."[16] Stark's warning may have caused Gillis to pause and think, but it certainly did not stop his critical commentary. In a gesture of "we told you," and with an attitude of personal vindictiveness, Gillis initially wrote, "We non-interventionists called the play. It happened as we predicted. We lament the fulfillment of our prophecy."[17]

Inside Gillis most certainly must have worn a gloating smile, but his public commentary expressed a positive note to what he perceived as a bad situation. Nobody wanted war, but the reality was that the United States was again embroiled in world conflict. Thus, it was time in the editor's mind to avoid the blunders of the past, such as lack of preparedness, blind trusts (the long-time sale of scrap iron to Japan, for example), put a cap on comment, and "get down to the job—the dirty bloody job of fighting." The American people needed to throw off the cobwebs of their inactivity, spit on their hands, and roll up their sleeves; otherwise, "this country might get licked." The United States was vital to the survival of moral righteousness. In a rather unusual resignation to reality Gillis concluded his February 1942 editorial,

> The war is ours. We are now elected chief standard bearer....We have taken it over. We are not participants; we are the chief protagonists.[18]

Three months later he was still rather resigned and reserved in writing, "We went in because we had to go in. There remained no alternative but cowardice, ignominy and failure to fulfill the duty of a sovereign state."[19]

Gillis's conciliatory spirit during the first months of the war gradually changed to a more familiar position of criticism. He "entered" the war discussion in order to preserve conscience which, as he had stated earlier, was the greatest casualty of war. The editor could not support the activity of war, but he did continue to preach the need for individual freedom and conversion. The proper prosecution of the war became Gillis's new polemic. The editor attacked the administration for its poor management of the war effort. "There is bungling, incapacity, ineptitude, stupidity, jealousy, personal hatred, preoccupation with politics among those charged with the direction of our affairs." After a discussion of several leading figures, none of whom in theory possessed animosity toward Roosevelt, but who all voiced caution or complaint about America's prosecution of the war to date, Gillis concluded,

> To attempt to dismiss all this criticism with a vituperative epithet is to convict oneself of mental blindness, or of incor-

rigible stubbornness. Such criticism is made not because we love the Administration less but because we love our Country more.[20]

Gillis called for the removal of bureaucratic bungling that threatened the nation's ultimate existence. If the American Republic was to be lost on the battlefield it should not go down without its best effort:

The "We" to whom the war has not been sold, the "We" who are only ankle deep in the business of winning the war, the "We" who are losing the war, the "We" that should be blasted out of complacency, or better still removed for incompetency is that huge bureaucratic "We" at Washington and elsewhere, the "We" that is tumbling over itself, tripping itself up, getting in its own way, contradicting and stultifying itself; the "We" that is mystifying and irritating the people and that, if it does not mend its ways will soon enrage the people. That is the "We" that should be bawled out and—if damning is to be done—damned by the generals, admirals, assistant secretaries, heads of agencies and other desk-thumping administration spokesmen.[21]

Gillis believed that American self-deception extended to its choice of allies. Commenting upon the Soviet state, he foresaw any alliance with Russia as suicidal: "If we think we can co-operate with one tyranny [the Soviets] to destroy the other [the Nazis], and then drop the tyrant whose aid we accepted, we are in for a smashing disillusion."[22] While Roosevelt, Vice-President Henry Wallace, presidential advisor Harry Hopkins, along with Senator Claude Pepper of Florida and Wendell Wilkie effusively supported the USA-USSR alliance, Catholics in general supported Gillis's stance of caution. George Sirgiovanni states, "Catholics also feared that the Soviet-American alliance would blur the politico-ideological lines and confuse Americans into accepting Communism as a respectable even benign philosophy."[23] However, pragmatism prevailed.

Gillis also preached that the status quo should not be the goal of the postwar world. Society could not afford to return to 1914 or 1940; it needed reform. Unless the United States changed radically, he proclaimed, "This vast revolution will go down in history as a specimen of stupendous futility. And we shall have World War III in another generation."[24]

Gillis believed that the war had to be fought on Christian principles, no matter how great the temptation might be to lower America's moral standards. Hitler's use of rockets in his bombing of England provoked in some the desire to respond in kind, but Gillis rejected this belief, stating, "If we go in for revenge and reprisals, it will be the end of Christian civilization."[25] He invoked American idealism:

> Now that we are in we must fight with honor and chivalry. We dread indeed to think of what may happen to our American institutions of liberty and democracy while we are at war. But a far greater calamity will happen if we abandon our ethics and our religion in the attempt to reestablish civilization.[26]

Gillis's message of human freedom and the possibility for conversion "required" the United States to fight a moral war; the nation must not lose its conscience.

The war's progress became an increasingly heavy burden for the Paulist editor as he saw the ideals of the American Republic challenged and begin to slip away. The threat was the movement of the United States toward greater involvement throughout the world. America had to do its best in an ugly situation, but this did not mean placing itself at the service of the world. Gillis saw the United States falling into the trap of imperialism; the isolationist position had become *ex post facto* a heresy. He looked to the future and saw that once entangled, the United States would never again be free. Thus, he returned to his isolationist position: "Nowadays it has become customary with interventionists to say that America needs Europe as much as Europe needs America. I remain stupid and stubborn enough to doubt that theory."[27] Gillis remained unapologetic and dogmatic amidst a sea of popular support for America's emerging global role:

> An isolationist is one who has foresight enough to see that intervention—the only kind of intervention worthy of the name, full intervention—is impossible, or if possible disas-

trous. An anti-isolationist is one who either does not see
what the isolationist sees, or who sees what the isolationist
sees but hasn't the honesty to say so.[28]

Gillis's persistence in holding an isolationist position placed
him outside mainstream Catholicism as suggested by the interventionist character of the Catholic press. *The Commonweal* spoke
of the "futility of the isolationist position," linked it in opposition to social progress, and claimed that such a stance was "a real
obstacle to any plans for American leadership in the rehabilita-
tion and governance of the post-war world."[29] *America* agreed
that the isolationist stance had no place or merit in postwar society. The magazine suggested, "By turning our backs on isolation
and making a positive contribution to peace, we can avoid the
mistakes made after the first World War."[30] A rare comment that
supported a return to isolationism was voiced by Holy Cross
father Patrick Carroll, editor of *Ave Maria:*

> The *Ave Maria,* it is no secret, was opposed from the first to
> all manipulations projected to stir national feeling to play
> savior to a Europe that has always been more or less nests of
> hatred, intrigue, ambition for mastery; a continent in name,
> in fact a multitude of houses divided against one another
> and against themselves.[31]

Gillis's outrage at the ethical conduct of the war, which
allied itself with the views of Pius XII,[32] resulted principally from
the numerous reports of indiscriminate bombing that followed
the Anzio and Normandy invasions. The bombing of Rome, random bombing of German civilians in Dresden, and the fire-
bombing of Tokyo mortified the editor:

> Our moral principles are being jettisoned to save the ship of
> civilization. If we throw morality overboard we may as well
> scuttle the ship. Yet, that seems to be just what our strate-
> gists and our political authorities would have us do.[33]

America also lamented unrestricted bombing, labeling it "as
close to massacre as even the exigencies of defensive warfare
can ever admit." *The Commonweal* called the Allied bombing

operation "the murder of innocent people and the suicide of a civilization."[34] The final act of the Pacific war, the use of atomic bombs on the cities of Hiroshima and Nagasaki on August 6 and 9, 1945, precipitated a passionate outburst of anger even greater than Gillis's normal penchant for polemic. The editor believed that the bomb represented the loss of the last thread of morality in American military policy. The nation's great power and militarism had created an environment where ethics could be so manipulated and construed as to generate a case for the use of such a weapon of mass destruction. Gillis condemned the bombing as "indefensible on ethical grounds" and "the most powerful blow ever delivered against Christian civilization and the moral law." He concluded,

> But simply to relieve the pressure upon my conscience, I here and now declare that I think the use of the atomic bomb, in the circumstances [at Hiroshima and Nagasaki], was atrocious and abominable; and that civilized peoples should reprobate and anathematize the horrible deed.[35]

The Catholic press' reaction to the use of the bomb was surprisingly mixed. *America* reported the use of the bomb, but made no judgment on its morality. *The Commonweal*, at a loss as to why there was no true sense of guilt in the American populace, stated, "The name Hiroshima, the name Nagasaki are names for American guilt and shame." Dorothy Day, as would be expected from her pacifist belief, delivered a blistering attack in *Catholic Worker*. Speaking of the incinerated Japanese, she wrote, "Perhaps we will breathe their dust into our nostrils, feel them in the fog of New York on our faces, feel them in the rain on the hills of Easton."[36]

A Private War—"Catholic Hour" Dismissal—1941–1943

The European and Pacific wars dominated the front pages of the nation's papers, but for James Gillis his private war, a confrontation with the "Catholic Hour," was waged to save his personal pride. Gillis, as we recall, was a charter member of the "Catholic Hour" broadcasts, having received an invitation each year since the program's inception in 1930. In the fall of 1942 it became painfully clear to him that the annual invitation to speak would not be forthcoming. This situation precipitated a nasty conflict between Gillis and the NCCM, which eventually found its way to his Paulist superiors and to the hierarchy.

In September 1942 he wrote to NCWC General Secretary and NCCM speakers' selection chairman, Michael Ready, about the apparent snub:

> I cannot say that I had made no surmise and in the last few days word has seeped through to me that my guess was correct—that I am *persona non grata* on the Catholic Hour because of what I have written in *The Catholic World* and spoken on public platforms (before Pearl Harbor) in regard to American participation in the war, and in criticism of some of the measures and methods of the Federal Administration in its conduct of the affairs of the nation.[37]

Ready responded by saying, "Your editorial and lecture work [during the 1940 and 1941 presentations] in a special manner identified the Catholic Hour with your own personal political opinions." Furthermore, he explained that the NCCM was embarrassed to be accused of supporting a particular political opinion.[38] Gillis challenged the explanation, stating that he had made no attempt to use the "Catholic Hour" as a political platform, that he had always abided by the rules in reading his approved script, and that there was no foundation upon which the NCCM need be embarrassed about anything that he said. As to the implication that his views were anti-Roosevelt, Gillis voiced his well-developed conservative views:

> My opposition to the present administration was based upon a fear that it was abandoning fundamental principles consecrated by a century and a half of tradition. I opposed that change not as a partisan politician but as—I hope—a good American.[39]

James Gillis's typically aggressive manner would not give rest to such an affront to his character and professional status as a commentator. He wrote to Bishop John Noll, episcopal chairman of the NCCM radio program, asking whether he approved of the removal of a speaker because of comments made in other forums. Noll cautiously responded to Gillis's inquiry: "It is likely that the NCCM headquarters had more unfavorable than favorable comments on your pre-Pearl Harbor attitude." Noll also wrote to Ready, informing him of Gillis's letter and his response. Ready, in turn, wrote to Archbishop Mooney, enclosing a complete file of correspondence with Gillis on his "dismissal" from the "Catholic Hour" broadcast.[40]

Gillis's used his principal forum, *The Catholic World,* to bring his defense to the public. Earlier he had hinted to Ready about his design, "I plan to present the substance if not the text of this letter and of yours in *The Catholic World.*"[41] The November 1942 *Catholic World* editorial began with Gillis's personal defense to the perceived injustice perpetrated upon him.

> It will perhaps be of interest to readers of these editorials to know that because of opinions expressed here and similar or identical opinions spoken on the lecture platform, I have been dropped from the Catholic Hour....I still fail to understand why the kind of thing I have written in these pages or have said in public lectures unfits [sic] me to speak on a Catholic Radio program. But since the men of the Catholic Hour take a different point of view, there the matter rests, as far as they are concerned.[42]

Word of Gillis's planned editorial reached the New York chancery office, causing a flurry of activity. The Paulist Superior General, Henry Stark, was summoned by James McIntyre, auxiliary bishop of New York, to discuss the matter. McIntyre believed the editorial, "Paying the Price," to be "an attack on the NCWC & the archbishops & bishops of the conference." The bishop demanded that Stark remove the editorial, for it would give the enemies of Catholicism fuel to exploit disunity in the Church. Stark returned to the motherhouse and discussed the affair with Joseph McSorley and John Harney, two of four Paulist consultors. Harney said the editorial "should not be published as it showed lack of taste & was a personal grievance." Stark thus ordered the editorial to be struck and informed Gillis, who was in Louisville on a speaking engagement, by telegram.[43]

However, Gillis continued to plead his case. Although the November editorial was struck, a number of copies of the original were printed and sent by Gillis, without authorization, to friends and fellow journalists. He described himself in the "grip of an octopus and at that—a hybrid octopus." The extant documentation, both in response to the censured editorial and to his dismissal from the "Catholic Hour," was overwhelmingly sympathetic. The editor of *America,* Francis X. Talbot, SJ, voiced a typical response:

> You are a major victim of your convictions. For the sake of peace and unity neither you nor I can cry out loud. However, we can pray that a more courageous and intelligent attitude may supplant that of compromise and subservience.

Letters to the NCCM, in contrast to what Ready told Gillis about "being embarrassed," were overwhelmingly in favor of Gillis's talks. One woman concluded, "America and the Church need Father Gillis on the air."[44]

The real reason for Gillis's removal from the "Catholic Hour" can only be conjectured, but it appears that the affair was intentionally orchestrated by people who saw him as a threat and an embarrassment. The Paulist editor's record on the "Catholic Hour" appeared to have been good, but it was not unblemished. His Advent 1939 series, "Prophets and Kings—Great Scenes: Great Lines," required several emendations at the behest of Edward Heffron, secretary of the NCCM. Additionally, in October 1941 Ready wrote to all "Catholic Hour" speakers, requesting "that the definite religious character of the Catholic Hour be maintained during these fateful days...[and] to avoid entirely the popularly debated issues of the war."[45] It is true that one of Gillis's 1941 talks, "Total Reform or None: Economic, Political, Moral," was labeled "chiefly political and only remotely religious," but an amended and approved version of the talk was delivered on November 30. Ready, nonetheless, must have considered the talk political and, fearful of anti-Catholic comments which might arise from "suspect" patriotism, decided to act against Gillis. It is also possible that individuals within the NCCM organization or members of the hierarchy harbored animosity toward the editor that grew as Gillis's comments became more vehement while the storm clouds of war approached.[46] Gillis's failure to promptly support the war effort, in contrast to the hierarchy and his religious community, might have been an embarrassment to the NCCM and its parent body the NCWC.

Gillis also believed that there was a conspiracy to remove him. He was convinced that Ready had heard of his November 1942 editorial and had communicated this information to the New York Chancery. As to his initial removal from the "Catholic Hour," Gillis possessed his own theory:

> I am convinced that it [the one who prompted his dismissal] was one, or a few higher-ups in official ecclesiastical life, and perhaps someone in official political circles. I learned sometime ago that the White House was aware of my existence and critical of what I said. That of itself would be enough to explain what happened.[47]

Although Gillis never again spoke from the microphones of the "Catholic Hour," his radio days were far from over. Between 1944 and 1947 he conducted several series of talks, including the "Angelus Hour" for the Connecticut Broadcasting Company and "Church on the Air" for Mutual Radio. James Gillis continued to be in demand as a public speaker until the time of his death. The loss of the "Catholic Hour" forum was significant for Gillis in its representation of the removal of a major pillar of episcopal support for his work and thought.

Planning the Postwar World—1942–1946

Although the war in Europe had been raging since September 1, 1939 and the United States had yet to officially enter the conflict, plans for peace in a postwar era had already begun. During the period August 9 to 12, 1941 Franklin Roosevelt met with Winston Churchill in Argentia Bay, Newfoundland to plan war strategy. The meeting produced an eight-point document, the Atlantic Charter, of August 11, which envisioned a world of self-governing peoples who enjoyed economic prosperity and social security.[48] This document became the common pledge of a coalition of twenty-six nations, who on January 1, 1942 signed in

Washington the "Declaration by the United Nations." The document stated that all signatory parties would work in mutual cooperation toward the settlement of a common and just armistice. With eyes to the future the initial plans for the postwar world were thus laid.

The general Catholic reaction to the Charter was positive because its tenor emphasized peace. Gillis saw the document as idealistic and for that reason supported its principles, describing it as "the most exhilarating and inspiring statement on international relationships that had been issued since the Declaration of Independence." *America* declared that the Charter "remains a noble document." With an eye to the future, Joseph Rossi, SJ, states, "The Charter was seen by Catholics and others as the first common program of purposes and principles of the United Nations."[49]

As alluded to previously, Gillis was anything but pleased about the United States' presence in the war, but with its entry unavoidable it was necessary to finish the fight and then reconstruct the world. Following the lead of the American bishops, who promoted America's duty to safeguard the freedom of all peoples,[50] Gillis maintained that justice must be established as a premise to the moral victory which must encompass any military triumph. The United States must exhibit no contradiction between what we pledge to do and what the nation in fact would do. He once concluded,

> After we win a military victory, there remains the moral victory. If we are not prepared to "follow through" we never should have commenced. We are in honor bound before the world to prove that we have a conscience, and that we intend to live up to it.

If the United States could not achieve world peace by moral suasion and fair play we should "call it a day and send word to Gabriel to blow that horn."[51]

Charters, treaties, and covenants were for him so many scraps of paper unless the signatory parties backed the text with the recognition of an inviolable moral obligation to God. The world did not want to repeat its earlier mistake at Versailles which failed because God was not placed into decisions. Gillis believed that God was no adjunct in government but rather, "God is Foundation. God is Bed Rock. God is Substance."[52] He summarized the call to duty:

> Yes, search the Scriptures, you statesmen, you diplomats, you delegates to peace conferences, you post-war world planners, and you will find among a thousand other texts to your purpose this one that answers your question and solves your problem, "*Unless the Lord build the house they labor in vain that build it* [Gillis's emphasis]."[53]

God's presence in the world required the support of organized religion. For Gillis politics, diplomacy, and military might were bankrupt without the presence of religion. The postwar peace required more than the removal of dictators; it required the elimination of those ideologies which spread godlessness and led to the destruction of the moral fiber of society. He cited the need for religious principles to be foundational to the relationship of nations in any peace plan:

> Where and when have the pure principles of the Gospel been tried in international affairs? Is it not true, as Chesterton said, that "Christianity has not been tried and found wanting; it has been found difficult and left untried"? That statement, like all epigrams, must be qualified. Christianity has been tried by individuals. It made Saints or near Saints of them. It remains to try it in the next Peace Conference. It will work if we give it a chance.[54]

Peace would thus be found by promoting the family of nations within a Christian context. As a representative of organized religion, Gillis perceived his vocation to preach as salvific for the nation and the world.

Despite his support of the idealism of the prospective United Nations, Gillis considered isolationism as the only realistic principle for the postwar world. He grounded this policy on the American tradition of non-involvement in world affairs. Gillis believed that America had plenty of work to do at home before it could run around the world telling other peoples how to order and operate their lives. It was not America's role to police the world, to become a "trouble-shooter to the universe," or an imperial power. Such an attitude, as history had revealed, would ultimately lead to international conflict around the globe:

> If after the war we accept permanent responsibility for keeping peace in Europe, Asia, Africa and the Islands we shall be fighting in Europe, Asia, Africa and the Islands forever. Paradoxically, to maintain peace you have to fight, and the larger the area over which you maintain peace, the more frequently you have to fight.[55]

America would be no more successful than England had been in its role of imperial giant; internationalism would sap the strength of America:

> Our problem in the United States is how to survive. The question we must put [to] ourselves is whether we have a better chance of surviving by plunging into all the quarrels of the world or by making an attempt to stay out of them. Some of us who are said to favor "suicide" think that America and American ideal have a better chance to live if we don't try to carry the whole world on our back. That may be "isolationism," but we prefer to call it American patriotism.[56]

Such polemical writing may be perceived as a device Gillis used to delegitimate those who opposed him.

Gillis's isolationist position continued to draw fire from all sides. The Catholic press suggested that reality necessitated a new view of America's role in the world. *The Commonweal* stated that the United States had two basic options in the postwar world, imperialism or genuine cooperation among nations, with the second option being that which was truly representative of the will of the people. This "people's" peace would be maintained by a federation of nations where all shared responsibility. *America* called for a secure peace which could only become reality if the United States was willing to take moral leadership by leading the drive in search for paths of peace and security.[57] Robert Williams, a *Catholic World* subscriber, was perhaps representative of public opinion in his criticism of Gillis:

> But I am of the opinion that no more unfortunate role
> could be undertaken by a Catholic editor in a time of
> national crisis than that of a bitter critic who month after
> month can find no good in anything done by the President
> selected by votes of the American people to fill the position
> of chief executive.[58]

National defense in the postwar era prompted discussion on the concept of Universal Military Training (UMT) for American men. The idea was initially proposed by Roosevelt, but it was President Harry Truman who, in an October 1945 speech to Congress, proposed a national military force that would be composed of a small regular standing army, navy, and air corps supplemented by a force of well-trained citizens who could quickly be mobilized in time of national emergency.[59] America's Catholics on all sides rejected this proposal. The bishops said the current Selective Service Act could be extended rather than initiate new legislation. *America* declared UMT to be a "dangerous experiment," while Gillis in his polemical hyperbolic style declared the proposal "madness and a preliminary to national suicide."[60] Although Truman lobbied for UMT throughout his first term, Congress only showed minor interest when the Selective Service Act expired in 1947. When the Act was reinstated the next year, UMT lost all its supporters and the proposal was dropped.

The Communist International Threat—1942–1948

During World War II much of the hostility against the Soviet Union in the United States gave way to the crucial task of defeating Hitler and his Axis partners.[61] Americans generally felt secure that Stalin was not eager to export his revolution to western shores. In a highly publicized *Life* magazine article in March 1943, Lenin was described as "perhaps the greatest man of modern times." Russians were said to "look like Americans, dress like Americans and think like Americans"; they were "one hell of a people."[62] Soviet acceptance worldwide, as Arthur Schlesinger states, reached its zenith "toward the end of the Second [World]

War, [when] Russia gained [the] admiration and confidence of all elements in the West as never before."[63]

Catholics in general stood vigilant and wary against the Russian bear, despite being out of the mainstream view. Long before the fear of Communist subversion became what Cabell Phillips has described as a "national neurosis" in the post-war decade,[64] Catholics of the likes of James Gillis were not deferential to the Soviet ally. The editor perceived Russia as a direct threat to the integrity and lifeblood of the American system of government, the nation's way of life, and human freedom; it was a real threat to America.

Gillis consistently and forcefully rejected the Soviet advance, both ideologically and politically, on all fronts; it was the new Mr. Hyde, the darkness of his world view. The editor's attack, which aided his return to mainstream Catholic thought, was geared in such a way to show how the Soviet system was antithetical to American ideals in every conceivable way and thus posed a great threat to the nation's security and way of life. Gillis described how Communism vetoed God and warned that, "We cannot work or play, fraternize or organize with those who hold it as their prime dogma that God is a myth." The Soviet system contained no legitimate principles but rather it was laced with lies and deceit; Communists possessed no scruples and thus would employ any means to achieve their ends.[65]

Gillis called for a religious crusade against Communism:

> There is only one way of overcoming Communism. It is a religion and we must oppose it with a more powerful religion. It is a fire and we must fight it with a purer and fiercer fire. We must recapture the fire that Christ came to cast upon the earth.[66]

For the editor there was no "Red Riddle": "Everyone not of arrested mental development knows Russia is no riddle: They [sic] are building an empire and it is almost complete." The editor called for Americans to rise from their complacency and meet the challenge the Soviets presented before it became too late:

> How can we be so comfortable and confident when those
> who have sworn to destroy us are so active? Are the lessons of
> Europe lost on us? Or do we think we are somehow magically
> immune to the tragedies that have overtaken our brethren on
> another continent?[67]

Soviet expansion through the Baltic states created an intolerable situation, but Gillis viewed United States policy as one of appeasement. He said it was time for the United States to stand against the tide for fear that America too would be transformed into a Communist state. The alliance forged between the United States, England, and the Soviet Union during the war, as mentioned earlier, caused Gillis much anxiety: "This writer...has a mortal dread that during and after this war, America, the greatest stronghold and sanctuary of democracy, may become transformed into a hybrid, if not into a full-blooded Communistic State."[68] The step which would stop this possibility was the cessation of appeasement. He wrote, "Nothing brings a bully to heel so surely as to be himself bullied. In other words the way to avoid war with Russia is to stop being a fool for Russia's sake."[69] Gillis believed the Communist bogey was active within the United States as well as outside. The Soviets were making attempts to infiltrate every aspect of American life; the nation could not sleep. He surmised, "Moscow has given us abundant reason to fear Communism."[70]

American Catholic opinion as a whole stood with Gillis in his condemnation of Communism and belief that appeasement of the Soviets should cease. *America,* which declared itself "unalterably opposed to atheistic Communism," saw appeasement as a "betrayal of friends," "dangerous," and "a positive act of surrender." Too many concessions had already been made; the need was present to take a stand.[71] Michael Williams called upon President Truman to halt "the Godless totalitarian phony regime" of the Soviet State.[72]

The Commonweal, in stark contrast however, advocated a pragmatic approach:

> From a strictly realistic point of view, it must be granted that
> such claims [for boundary territories] are reasonable—if not
> moderate....Strategically, in the eyes of common sense, the
> Russian claims are not only just, they are traditional and

reflect the same foreign policy as that of the Czars....Obviously, at the present juncture the governments of Great Britain and the US cannot refuse to accede to these Russian demands, and grant their validity in principle.[73]

Gillis deplored *The Commonweal's* conciliation,

I cannot refrain from saying that I think there has not been in the history of Catholic journalism in America so unblushing an abandonment of both Catholic and American political and ethical principle.[74]

After the war had ended, the same journal experienced a complete turnabout by stating that appeasement was handing the world piecemeal to the Soviets; America had to act to stop the trend.[75]

For Gillis and many others the great test case to stop the Soviet advance was found in Poland, which had seen no peace since Hitler's invasion. The Soviet advance from the east had recaptured portions of Poland where a Soviet puppet government was established at Lublin; the true Polish government in exile in England was ignored.[76] The fate of Poland became a cause célèbre for American Catholics, who viewed that nation as representative of Christian culture. The American bishops led the charge by asking that Poland be afforded its freedom per the Atlantic Charter and urged the United States not to be silent in the wake of Soviet aggression in Eastern Europe.[77]

Gillis also saw the fate of Poland as a test case for the Atlantic Charter, but more fundamentally for American resolve to stand against the Soviets and save the nation's honor from further damage. As with moral principle the editor had no tolerance for compromise with the Soviet Union:

Christian ethics permits compromise between good and better, not between good and bad. To run out on Poland, after having sworn before the world and in the sight of high heaven that Poland was the cause of our entering the war, is not a lesser good but an evil. To profess high principle in regard to the sanctity of boundaries and to surrender that principle when the crucial case comes up is not compromise

but surrender. Surrender of principle is not a lesser good. It
is evil. With evil no compromise is permissible.[78]

When the war ended and the United States still failed to inter-
vene in Poland, he saw America dishonored before all nations.
He concluded, "The world will say we perjured ourselves."[79]

The fate of Poland drew the attention of the Catholic press
throughout the nation. *The Commonweal* was resigned to the
Yalta compromise, suggesting that the alternative would be war
with the Soviets. America hoped that the Yalta meeting of the
"big three" would save Poland. When the United States and England agreed to Stalin's policy on the Lublin government, the
magazine stated, "Let us not think that the treatment that Poland
has received in this war has been anything less than shameful."[80]

The Domestic Threat—1942–1948

The threat to the United States from the outside was readily
apparent. The Soviet Union's political and ideological views,
antithetical to the values held in the United States, made it an
enemy that was visible and one around which, as has been
demonstrated, the vast majority of American Catholics could
rally in order to save the nation. More subtle, and in the mind of
James Gillis more threatening to the nation because of its relative invisibility, was the attack perpetrated within the country.
The war years saw many of the domestic issues of earlier decades
continue to fester in society, but more important for Gillis was
the nation's loss of truth as a value and its persistent march in
foreign policy toward a course of internationalism.

Gillis argued that truth was basic to the American ideals of
freedom and moral righteousness. The editor's belief that God
was central to all aspects of life became manifest once again in a
call for the restoration of truth in society:

> No harm can come from truth. If to say so is an act of faith,
> very well. But belief in the beneficence of truth is also the
> result of experience—the experience of human life on this
> planet for thousands of years. To believe in truth is to
> believe in God. God is truth. To put one's trust in pretense

> is to trust the devil. Deceit is Satan's middle name, and by
> the way of good measure—his first and last names. A syn-
> onym for Satan is "the lie."[81]

Gillis saw untruth as dominant in society, a condition which if left unchecked would lead to moral and eventually physical dissolution of the nation.[82] He rejected all claims that truth was no longer recognizable, that one would not know the truth even if one stumbled upon it. In response to Bertrand Russell's *History of Western Philosophy* which supported this view, he wrote, "I prefer a philosophy which admits that truth exists, that we can go after it with confidence, and that we have a means of recognizing truth when we lay hold of it."[83]

Gillis applied this understanding of truth to his philosophy of government, which, as we recall, strongly advocated the role of the individual. For government to function properly it was paramount that the nation's citizens be fully and accurately informed of decisions and actions, both planned and completed. During the war years this philosophy was jeopardized by the establishment of the Office of War Information (OWI) and the Censorship Office, a creation of the War Powers Act of December 19, 1941. The OWI, established June 11, 1942 under the direction of Elmer Davis, was charged with fostering "an informal and intelligent understanding" among the American citizenry of the "aims and policies" of the nation's wartime government. The Office of Censorship, headed by Byron Price, former general manager of the Associated Press, was established in January 1942 to prevent the publication of information which might be of use to the Axis powers.[84]

Gillis believed that despite the war the American people needed to be taken into the government's confidence; it was a basic tenet of democracy. In a typically caustic tirade steeped in cynicism Gillis felt that international conditions should not change how a government dealt with its people. Truth, as the presence of God, should not be doled out in small doses at infrequent and inconsistent intervals but rather must be available to all at any time. The government served the people, not the other way around. He was highly critical of government leaders, who had a responsibility to tell the truth but continually shirked this duty. He wrote, "The truth is that the leaders of government are groping, fumbling, muddling along, procrastinating, bluffing, faking, issuing untrue statements to pacify the people." Beyond outright lies Gillis asked why the people were kept in the dark with respect to the nation's foreign policy, especially when it amounted to the abandonment of a 150-year tradition of non-interference with the affairs of others. Gillis felt the government was using truth as a convenience, to be utilized to its benefit; such a policy was totally unacceptable for it belied democratic principles.[85]

The Paulist editor laid the blame for the demise of truth and the growth of deceit in government at the feet of his demonic foe, Franklin Roosevelt.

> What America suffered from most, in the last decade or so, or to be more precise from 1933–1945, was a persistent incorrigible untruthfulness, made popular by a supreme master of the art, and imitated by his idolatrous admirers.[86]

Gillis often referred to Roosevelt's "elastic standard of veracity" preferring what might be timely or convenient for the truth. This belief achieved a semblance of validity when the secret deals that the President made at the various war meetings of the "Big Three" came to light after his death.[87]

Roosevelt's foreign policy, as American military involvement in the war grew imminent and then commenced, gradually moved the United States into a position of global involvement and influence. The aforementioned "Arsenal of Democracy" speech, promulgation of the Atlantic Charter and subsequent "Declaration by United Nations," and the "Four Freedoms" speech to Congress were early indicators of where the United States would go with its foreign policy. Although Churchill was not successful at Argentina in moving Roosevelt to overt action against the Axis, the meeting did produce the agreement that the United States and England would act as a global police force until some permanent and democratic body, not unlike the League of Nations, could be established to monitor the peace. By 1944, however, Roosevelt in his fourth inaugural address signaled a clear message of the nation's international design:

We have learned that we cannot live alone at peace—that our own well-being is dependent on the well-being of other nations far away. We have learned that we must live as men, and not as ostriches, nor as dogs in the manger. We have learned to be citizens of the world, members of the human community.[88]

Although he believed that the nation as a whole was beginning to lose its idealism, Gillis continued to wear his patriotism on his sleeve as a badge of honor, philosophy of life, and "part of [his] religion." He rejected totally the notion promoted by interventionists that the present war was the result of America's betrayal of the League of Nations, citing Europe's rejection of Wilson's "Fourteen Points" as a more fundamental cause. Additionally, he cited the Kellogg-Briand Pact, the Four and Nine Power Treaties, and the Washington Conference for Naval Disarmament as examples of where the United States had attempted peaceful measures and received no aid from its "allies." He concluded, "It's queer patriotism that reviles one's own country in the interests of nations that have played Uncle Sam for a sucker."[89] America's principles and ideals were still sound, but Gillis worried that the war and the treachery of government leaders had wounded the nation deeply: "I should hate to see my own nation lose its soul."[90]

James Gillis never believed that the mission of the United States was to save the world; yet that was the direction upon which the nation was set after the war. The international prestige and internal strength that America enjoyed would be a dangerous condition for the maintenance of the "Great American Experiment of Democracy." The weak condition of the world would cause the United States to break with its tradition; she would never be able to return. He wrote:

From now on and as long as our nation lasts, we shall be involved in all the twists and turns and tricks, the crooked maneuvers, the double crossings and the double double crossings that have been the technique of diplomacy for a thousand years. We shall now have to be as tricky, as unprincipled and as untruthful as the worst of our allies. We have sat in with them, helped concoct their schemes, taken part in their sins and crimes, and now they will not let us go.[91]

James Gillis's sister Mary with their father.

Gillis around the time he entered the Paulist seminary in 1898.

Gillis as a young priest.

PAULISTS OF GILLIS'S

Henry I. Stark

Joseph T. McSorley

Walter Elliott

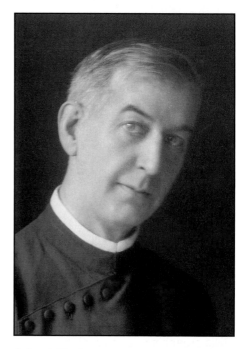

John J. Burke

Gillis in the offices of **The Catholic World** magazine

Gillis preaching during a **Catholic Hour** broadcast in the NBC Studios. Behind him are the Paulist Choristers directed by Fr. William J. Finn.

Gillis, center, poses with Francis Cardinal Spellman and Emmanuel Suarez, O.P. , Master General of the Dominican Order, following the presentation of an honorary degree from Pontifical Angelicum University in Rome. The occasion in 1951 marked Gillis's golden jubilee as a priest.

The situation was all the more distasteful to Gillis because the American people had no voice in the making of the policy which had discarded the nation's tradition. With resignation and cynicism he wrote,

> I see that we are deliberately embarked upon a course of political crime. From now on we shall emulate Britain, France, Spain, Metternich, Talleyrand, Machiavelli. We have abandoned our 150-year old tradition of political isolation. We have committed ourselves to intervention, and with intervention we have accepted the methods of interventionists.[92]

Gillis's love for America and his desire to preserve the Republic and the tradition of the founding fathers blinded him to the reality of a changing world. The United States had a long-standing tradition of non-intervention, a policy formed when the nation was small and uninfluential. The policy was good for the time, but this does not mean it was appropriate for the United States' position in 1945, where with international mobility, trade, communication, and other advances of science and technology the world had become a much smaller place. Gillis professed America's innocence in creation of the world's ills, demonized power politics in Europe, and sanctified isolationism. His refusal to see that another approach was possible, one that could still preserve the basics of life, liberty, and the pursuit of happiness, demonstrates a limiting and conservative approach to life, the rejection that America possessed the people and principle to adapt, and ultimately the denial of reality. Intransigence and maintenance of his dualistic world view stunted his personal growth and vastly restricted his ability to comment with any degree of objectivity.

The fragmented moral fabric of the nation continued, in the mind of Gillis, to deteriorate during the war and beyond. The exigencies of wartime placed additional strain on the nation's moral and social fiber. The "new freedom" which saw wives and mothers on the factory assembly lines and youth with pockets filled with money which they had never previously possessed threatened family unity in a new and dangerous way. For Gillis the war raging in Europe was only one part of a larger and

more complex conflict which threatened the nation. In a radio
address he summarized the problem:

> The battle ground is the campus, the classroom, the psycho-
> logical laboratory, the newspapers, books, magazines, the
> stage, the screen, the law courts, the divorce courts, the leg-
> islatures, State and Federal. It has been computed that we
> are fighting on 69 fronts. We must fight on 6900 fronts any-
> where, everywhere that the subversive forces of materialism,
> immoralism and irreligion are to be found.[93]

In preaching a return to God and the duty of moral righteousness, Gillis revisited many of the ethical dilemmas upon
which he had commented before the war, but with renewed vigor
due to the ever more precarious status of America's ideals and
principles. The editor continued to uphold the need for moral
absolutes while rejecting relativism, fatalism, and double ethical
standards which placed restrictions on individuals but granted
license to nations. Moral nihilism created the environment for
war; moral absolutism could save the world.[94]

The value of the family was emphasized in the new context
of the war environment. In agreement with the hierarchy and
The Commonweal, Gillis criticized the use of women in the
nation's factories, especially young mothers.[95] The editor quoted
conservative *New York Sun* syndicated columnist George Sokolsky, "Destroy the family and our civilization sinks into a swinish-
ness beyond the imagination of the most depraved."[96] Gillis
continued, as in the past, to reject divorce and birth control as
perversions of true Christian morality. America needed to
return to its duty of moral righteousness through greater self-discipline; the concept of absolute freedom as it had been practiced, from the classroom to morality, was simply not applicable
except in a world headed for destruction.[97]

Since the promulgation of the New Deal, James Gillis had
argued long and hard over the centralization of government at
the expense of individual free choice. The aforementioned war
bureaucracy created within the executive branch of the Federal
government a tangled web of agencies and bureaus. Roosevelt's
spring 1942 declaration of an "unlimited national emergency"

strengthened his ability to act decisively without the permission of Congress.[98] Gillis feared that the government monster once created would never be dismantled, suffocating the nation:

> Bureaucracy, if we permit it to live, will extend its tentacles, grasp all businesses large and small and strangle them, meanwhile darkening the waters (the governmental octopus, being a freak, is also a cuttle fish) so that no one can see what is going on.

The government itself had become the biggest business concern in the nation. Gillis proposed the principle of subsidiarity as his solution: "Democracy functions best when every state and every city, town, village, hamlet takes care of the greater part of the job of governing itself."[99]

Statism removed the concept of government by the people; it could lead to the destruction of the individual. Gillis continued to plead that the rights of individuals needed to be preserved for they were basic to the American ideal and afforded the best prospect for peace. He lamented the nation's proximity to death:

> ...I cannot bring myself to feel any joy or even satisfaction in the failure of the Great American Experiment. I think you will find that when government takes over the direction of business, of medicine, and of all other matters of interest and improvement, the government will have to go deeper and become more and more comprehensive and therefore more and more tyrannical. The time will come presently when every man will be "pushed around." As I have always understood Democracy, it is the guarantee that man shall not be pushed around. I fear that that sort of thing is now disappearing.[100]

The attack on the American Republic which emanated from within was carefully orchestrated, in the mind of Gillis, by Franklin Roosevelt. Although minor comments had been made in earlier days, the November 1940 *Catholic World* editorial discussed in chapter five was the start of a long harangue by the editor against the policies of the President which he felt were driving the country off its foundation. Gillis criticized Roosevelt for the liberties he took with the Constitution and his lack of veracity in his method of governance. He could finally admit in the spring of 1942, "To be honest, I do not like Mr. Roosevelt."[101]

Gillis was not the only commentator who criticized the President. David Lawrence, editor of *U.S. News,* Frank Kent, a columnist for the Baltimore *Sun,* Scripps-Howard newspaperman Westbrook Pegler, and Walter Lippmann were all opponents of Roosevelt. The newspaper magnate William Randolph Hearst had earlier defined the NRA as "Nonsensical, Ridiculous, Asinine interference."[102]

In the 1944 election Gillis initially was calm and collected, most probably because of all the commotion he raised four years earlier. Roosevelt's health made the selection of a vice-presidential candidate very important. Incumbent Henry Wallace was rejected by the Democratic leadership in favor of Senator Harry Truman of Missouri, a man who enjoyed good relations with the three major sections of the party, the Southern wing, the city-machine function, and the New Dealers.[103] Gillis made no mention of Truman but challenged the Republican candidate, Governor Thomas Dewey of New York, to declare himself on the question of internationalism. *The Commonweal* was highly dissatisfied with the campaign, complaining of Dewey's sniping at the President in order to attract votes and Roosevelt's plan to stand on his record.[104]

When the election drew near, however, the irrepressible and polemical opinion of the Paulist editor thundered across the pages of *The Catholic World:*

> We dare not, therefore, accept the fatalistic concept that the nation can find only one man, an indispensable man to direct us in peace, in war and in the complex post-war world. If the United States of America cannot produce out of its resources of manpower every eight years a man who can do a good job as chief executive it would perhaps be best not to prolong the agony but to admit now that the great American experiment has failed.[105]

When Roosevelt received the approbation of the electorate for the fourth time Gillis hoped that the victory would not send a message that "*carte blanche* was being given to abandon democracy." In a somber tone he vented his frustration: "But in my opinion the election was a blow, perhaps a mortal blow to democracy....Democracy is more nearly dead [in America] than it ever was before."[106] The 1944 election for Gillis was another example of the darkness of Mr. Hyde present in the world.

On April 12, 1945, while in Warm Springs, Georgia to regain his health, Franklin Delano Roosevelt died. Not totally shocked, the nation nevertheless mourned the loss of its longest-standing President. The *New York Post* on April 13 listed the President at the top of its daily list of war dead, a martyr to the cause. Wilfrid Parsons in *America* lauded the dead President saying that his important work would survive: "However much some of his fellow citizens may have disagreed with his policies, no one can question his honesty of purpose, or his whole-hearted devotion to his native land."[107] James Gillis's reaction, as might be expected, was not one of sorrow or praise. Unemotionally he wrote that while the President's "magnetism," "his charm," "his flair of doing things in a spectacular and dramatic way" would be missed, the nation would survive.[108]

In later years Gillis would not allow the dead President to rest, but rather stepped up his attack when revelations of his aforementioned "secret dealings" became public. While the nation began to "canonize" him, Gillis accused Roosevelt of being "only a magnificent fraud" in his ability to deliver on promises and "the most unprincipled politician that ever operated on the American scene." His administration was labeled "the most inglorious and most disastrous the United States has ever known" and again "our recent dictatorship."[109]

The motivation behind Gillis's vehement attacks on Franklin Roosevelt, as a person and a politician, requires some analysis. In the editor's mind Roosevelt was a powerful manifestation of Mr. Hyde, the darkness of his dualistic world view. As moral irresponsibility in the 1920s and growing statism in the 1930s were signs of the darkness of society, so in the war years (and earlier) Franklin Roosevelt was seen by Gillis as the enemy of God's righteousness. Gillis believed that Roosevelt's policies had jeopardized the very survival of the American nation. Such irresponsible action was a violation of the nation's tradition and a betrayal of the confidence of the American people who had elected him for an unprecedented four consecutive terms as chief executive. In Gillis's mind the President was the roadblock to the reform that the nation required in order to be a model to the world, a shining star—the role which Gillis advocated in keeping with the non-interventionist policy which had been American tradition for 150 years. Gillis's pique became personal when the President refused to uphold the tradition and struck out boldly on a new course which made the United States a full participant in every aspect of world affairs.

John Sheerin, CSP, expressed another opinion suggesting that Gillis's animosity was drawn from sincere intellectual conviction. At Boston Latin he had learned of the traditional concept of the American Republic and the orthodox understanding of moral integrity. Gillis was convinced in Sheerin's mind that Roosevelt "bewitched the American Republic into an imperialistic bureaucracy [in order to] police the world."[110] Sheerin's view most probably answers the primary motivation for Gillis's initiation of his criticism but it cannot answer for the personal animosity that is clearly evident in the editor's later pronouncements against Roosevelt. Gillis, like any person, could not avoid his humanity as the Mr. Hyde voice of the early diaries, now projected onto society, clearly demonstrates. His belief that America was being destroyed by the policies of Franklin Roosevelt generated anger toward the man; he grew to hate President Roosevelt and gave no apology for his stand.

The perennial clash between organized labor and employers, demonstrated throughout the twentieth century in America, was another internal source which Gillis perceived as threatening the integrity of the nation. During the war, although a no-strike pledge was made to aid the war effort,[111] some work stoppages did occur, especially in the soft coal industry where the United Mine Workers (UMW) were represented by John L. Lewis. The postwar years, however, suffered through a plethora of strikes which threatened to cripple the nation. In 1946 alone strikes cost the loss of 116 million man-days of work which shut down major industries for weeks or months at a time. Arthur McClure stated of the period, "America's problems in labor relations became as serious as in any period of its history."[112]

Several major strikes engaged the concern of the nation. In November 1945 Walter Reuther ordered 180,000 United Auto Workers (UAW) off the job; on April 1, 1946 400,000 members of the UMW hit the picket line. The UAW strike was settled in early 1946 with the union gaining an 18.5% wage increase while the UMW work stoppage ended May 21 after consultation between John L. Lewis and President Truman. The most menacing threat, however, came from railroad engineers who set a strike date for May 18. Again Truman became the mediator, going so far as to petition Congress to settle the dispute before the strike would shut down all rail service.[113]

Organized labor made great strides in the postwar era. Union membership encompassed 30% of the American work force, the greatest density of organized workers that ever existed. Nelson Lichtenstein says that the power which unions wielded was considerable. They sought a welfare state, political realignment of major parties along labor issues, a powerful voice in the management of industry, and a hand in the planning of the overall national economy.[114] The tension existent on American labor after the war was well described by CIO President Philip Murray:

> Only chaos and destruction of our industrial life will result if employers look to the war's end as an opportunity for union-breaking, wage-cutting, open-shop drive and if labor unions have to resort to widespread strikes to defend their very existence and the living standards of their members.[115]

The mid-term elections of 1946 were an unmistakable repudiation of Truman and the Democratic majority with both House and Senate returning to Republican control for the first time since Herbert Hoover. The GOP saw in its triumph a mandate to curb the power of organized labor. The Eightieth Congress, seated in January 1947, introduced several bills which sought a drastic redefinition of labor-management relations. These efforts led to the passage, over the veto of the President,[116] of the Taft-Hartley Act of 1947. The law was seen by many to favor employers in its banning of the closed shop, imposition of a sixty-day "cooling-off period" before a strike or lockout could be ordered, and its authorization of injunctions against certain union practices.

In the tradition of the papal encyclicals, *Rerum Novarum* and *Quadragesimo Anno,* most American Catholics supported organized labor, but the 1940s strike experience challenged the patience of even the most ardent union supporters. In 1942 *America* called the labor disputes "senseless and disruptive," but sided with workers over management, stating, "Although labor is not guiltless in perpetuating industrial strife, the greater blame for this senseless struggle rests squarely on management." Five years later the magazine's opinion had not changed in commenting that the Taft-Hartley Act "weakens the power of organized labor and not merely to discipline it."[117] *The Commonweal* also bemoaned the strike situation but gave its blessing to organized labor: "All of us stand to lose if management tries to wreck the present union movement."[118]

In accord with his conservative principles Gillis described labor as "intolerant, recalcitrant, unreasonable and tyrannical," while he labeled the Federal administration "cowardly and incompetent" because it refused to act against unions so as to safeguard for itself some twenty million labor votes.[119] Gillis's principal complaint was the strike's damage to the individual; a better way had to be found to settle labor disagreements:

> These strikes of ours are, especially in these crucial days, a crazy way of settling disputes. They may add up to disaster. If such industrial conflict is the only method that a highly enlightened people can think of as a means of adjudicating quarrels between labor and management we had better confess that Democracy, at least as applied to industry, is a failure....If we don't get a lucid moment ourselves and see the madness of these everlasting recurring strikes, democracy will die and dictatorship will ensue.[120]

Gillis also attacked UMW President John L. Lewis for calling strikes regardless of the public welfare. He labeled such an act "absurd—worse than absurd, it is immoral."[121]

The representative Catholic press did not like labor unrest but never wavered from its support for labor's right to use the strike. *The Commonweal* suggested that any government that denied the right to strike was "a dictatorship of the most iron sort....The right to strike is, in fact, the touchstone of genuine political democracy." *America* was a bit more conciliatory but also supported labor: "The state has no authority to take away the right to strike, but it does have the power to restrict its exercise."[122]

America—An International Power—1945–1948

From the time that the "Declaration by the United Nations" was signed by the twenty-six coalition allies on January 1, 1942, a plan was placed in action to establish a postwar organization. As the war progressed, preliminary meetings geared toward the formation of an international body for peace were held. The first conference which aimed toward the establishment of a united nations organization was held in May 1943 at Hot Springs, Virginia. The original allied coalition, which by this time had grown to forty-four members, met for two weeks to seek answers to the basic needs, such as food, clothing, and shelter, which the devastation of the war had wrought on society. In October 1943 the foreign ministers from the United States, England, and the Soviet Union met in Moscow and agreed that a postwar international body needed to be established. It was decided that a meeting of interested nations to develop the groundwork for this body should be held as soon as practicable.[123] Gillis asked whether the planned cooperative would be moral or military; he feared the latter would grow into a permanent alliance.[124]

The planned meeting of the international community took place between August 21 and October 9, 1944, when representatives from the United States, England, the Soviet Union, and China met at the sixteen-acre Dumbarton Oaks estate in Washington, D.C.[125] On October 7 a 5000-word communiqué, entitled "Proposals for the Establishment of a General International Organization," was issued. The document spoke of an international organization to maintain world peace and security, to develop friendly relations among nations, to achieve international cooperation in the solution of international economic, social, and humanitarian problems, and to establish a center for harmonizing actions of nations to achieve common ends. The Dumbarton meeting left two major issues unresolved: (1) Should a member of the permanent "Big Four" (United States, England, Soviet Union, and China) security council have the privilege of vetoing decisions to which it was a party? (2) How should membership be determined, especially in light of the Soviet Union's insistence that all sixteen of its "republics" should have independent votes?[126]

The Dumbarton Oaks conference was severely criticized by the American Catholic press and the hierarchy. It was perceived that the planned body was not truly international, but rather, because of the proposed security council, would be a forum for the superpowers to control world politics. *The Commonweal* was unusually sharp in its rejection of the Dumbarton accord:

> The whole business looks like a sweet setup for world hegemony on the part of Great Britain, Russia and the USA, with China and France playing secondary roles....This whole aspect of the scheme [the security council] has nothing whatever to commend it and obviously could lead to the worst sort of imperialism....In short the Dumbarton Oaks scheme might easily be the breeding ground for another and more terrible world war.[127]

The American bishops also worried about the proposed structure of the organization and how it could easily lead to "power politics." The hierarchy called for a more democratic group where any security council could not operate as "an instrument of imperialistic domination."[128] James Gillis, who had argued against power politics, imperialism, and their ill-effect on the individual for two decades, voiced his rejection of the proposal as drawing the nation another step closer to dissolution:

> If we once declare our determination to see to it that justice is done in all the world, and accept membership in an international court established for that purpose, we cannot wash our hands of any case without rushing, like Pontius Pilate, [into] everlasting infamy.[129]

The international community's dream of a "United Nations" organization became a reality in the spring of 1945. On

April 25 more than three hundred representatives from forty-six nations, encompassing all continents and races, met in San Francisco. At the opening session, Edward Stettinius, Secretary of State and head of the American delegation, gave the keynote and charge to the assembled international body:

> You members of this conference are to be the architects of a better world....We hold a powerful mandate from our people. They believe we will fulfill this obligation....If we do not want to die together in war, we must learn to live together in peace....Justice remains the greatest power on earth. To that tremendous power alone will we submit.[130]

In two months the assembled delegates (by the end there were fifty nations represented) pounded out a long document of 111 articles which defined the precise structure and functions of the United Nations Organization (UNO) and an International Court of Justice. A security council of five nations, the United States, England, France, the Soviet Union, and China, was incorporated into the plan. The charter was signed by the assembled delegates on June 26. President Truman addressed the final plenary session with words that echoed the sentiments of his dead predecessor:

> The Charter of the United Nations which you are signing is a solid structure upon which we can build a better world....For it is a declaration of great faith by the nations of the earth—faith that war is not inevitable, faith that peace can be maintained.[131]

In a complete reversal from its debate on the League of Nations, the Senate passed the United Nations Charter 89–2 on July 28 with less discussion than of many an appropriation bill.[132]

Catholic opinion on the UN Charter ranged from caution to total disappointment. Joseph Rossi has concluded, "Although the US Catholic Church did not advocate rejection of the UNCIO's [United Nations Conference on International Organizations] work, it did advise from the outset a drastic charter review."[133] *America* and *The Commonweal* considered the charter a noble document which provided "an admirable set of principles and

processes by which Peace with Justice may some day be achieved,"
yet stood wary of the problems that might occur because of the
power vested in the security council.[134] The hierarchy, which considered the San Francisco Charter an improvement over the Dumbarton Oaks document, was still less than satisfied, viewing the
accord as "no more than a virtual alliance of the great powers for
the maintenance of peace."[135] Before the San Francisco conference convened Gillis was hopeful that Communism might be
checked, the precepts of the Atlantic Charter adopted, and
Poland restored. By the time the conference concluded, however,
he had returned to his more common state of gloom. He wrote,
"I, for one, am profoundly disappointed in the 'blueprint' handed
to the world-builders by the architects at San Francisco."[136]

Gillis's attitude toward the United Nations grew even more
sour as the organization's work proceeded in the postwar years.
The editor believed that the world had learned nothing from the
failures and mistakes of Versailles and the war conferences of
Teheran and Yalta. Because the organization of the UNO, like
that of the League, had omitted God it fostered the spread of
Communism. Gillis was bewildered that the United States could
make efforts to ferret out Communists in business and labor
unions at home, but at the same time "pull the wool over its
eyes" in its participation with the UNO in its "protection of the
Kremlin." He caustically concluded, "The United Nations is a
fake, a fraud, a demonstrated failure."[137]

The formation of the United Nations and the American
occupation of Japan and Germany kept the United States on the
international scene. On the ideological level James Gillis never
accepted this idea, but rather he perceived the world situation in
terms of the expansion of the Soviet Union. For Gillis the United
States faced a classic dilemma: either America became international with imperialistic intent or it let the world go by default to
the Soviets. Resigned to some form of international participation, Gillis insisted that the United States had to stand up for its
moral principles, for to abandon ethical standards would only
hasten the end of the American Republic. Gillis called upon the
government to act:

The United States of America is "losing face" in all parts of the world. Fighting words are flung in our teeth and we make no reply....What's wrong at Washington?...What ails us? Is the Rooseveltian policy of appeasement still on? That policy has done us infinite harm. Must it be continued?[138]

Gillis challenged the Communist advance with his political rhetoric, but he drew the line when talk of war with the Soviets was raised. Invoking his isolationism, he said that America had always been a refuge for the afflicted of the world but the nation did not feel obliged to go to foreign lands to rescue the oppressed. The sinfulness of war could not atone for the evil of Communism. He distanced himself from any thought of armed conflict with the Soviets, stating, "Waging war with Russia would be madness and possibly suicide. It would quite probably be immoral, criminal." God was the solution to the problem, but the leaders of nations and culture builders continued to re-create the world without the Creator.[139]

United States foreign policy in the postwar era moved the nation progressively along a course of internationalism. Kirkendall claims that President Truman, in order to avoid two errors from the past—the appearance of national weakness and the refusal to get involved in international issues—guided America toward an increase in its global presence and influence. Although Gillis gave Truman high marks for his exchange of letters with Pius XII,[140] he was generally critical of the President for his indecisiveness and lack of conviction. Still, Gillis held hope that if Truman would be forthright the ideals which he as President represented and for which the country stood could be salvaged:

A President is not supposed to keep secrets from the people....If Mr. Truman, therefore, will "come clean," tell all, let Congress and the people in on his predicament and frankly ask the people to stand by him, we can help him bear the burden and—what is more important—we can save the spirit of American democracy.[141]

The predicament of which Gillis spoke, a situation which worried the whole free world, was the expansion of the Soviet Union through Eastern Europe and the Near East. After the war,

the Soviets began to pressure Turkey for control of the Dard-
anelles while claiming some of Turkish land was actually Soviet
territory. In Greece Communist influence through the rise of the
Liberation party threatened the stability of the nation. England
supported both Turkey and Greece with personnel and money in
an attempt to ward off a Communist take-over. In February 1947,
however, Prime Minister Clement Atlee informed Truman that
England was ending its aid; it simply could not afford it.

The situation in the Near East prompted President Truman
to go to Congress to ask for money to assume the financial burden abandoned by the British. His March 12 speech, which spoke
of America's responsibility to aid and support nations which
were resisting subjugation,[142] initiated what became known as the
Truman Doctrine, the first phase of a policy of containment to
halt the spread of Soviet influence. Robert Pollard states, "The
Truman Doctrine itself was designed primarily to overcome public and congressional opposition to direct U.S. involvement in
Europe, notably a comprehensive reconstruction program."[143]
Truman received from Congress $400 million for aid to Greece
and Turkey, as a goodwill sign that America would not let the
Soviet advance go unchallenged.

Catholic reaction to Truman's aid program was positive on
almost all fronts. *America* believed the United States' best interests
were served by intervention in Greece and Turkey. One editorial
read,

> Why should the United States take on itself the burden of
> world responsibility? The answer to that is easy. Our security
> depends on it. Great Britain by its own confession is unable to
> perform its former role in world politics. And the United
> States is not going to stand by while Soviet expansionism gets
> its second wind. The question to be asked is what price the
> American people are willing to pay to stop that expansionism?
> We believe the people are willing to pay the necessary price for
> the defense of their ideals and the fulfillment of their responsi-
> bilities, once the problem has been frankly laid before them.[144]

The Commonweal, which like Gillis was highly critical of Truman's
indecisive leadership at the outset, voiced caution on the Truman

Doctrine, but in the end came to realize there was really no other viable option to pursue.[145] Gillis, in an unusually resigned tone, left the question of merit of the Truman Doctrine to the American people.[146]

On June 5, 1947, Secretary of State George Marshall, in a commencement address at Harvard University, announced the second half of the administration's containment policy. Marshall, speaking in broad strokes of what was necessary to preserve freedom in Europe,[147] recommended the expenditure of $17 billion of United States money to finance a program to benefit Europe for four years. The plan, introduced to Congress in December 1947, was passed the following April. Richard Freeland believes that the public debate over the Marshall Plan (more formally known as the European Recovery Program or ERP), June 1947 to March 1948, saw a major shift in American opinion, from one of little interest in foreign affairs to one of great fear of the Soviets and with it the consequent commitment to long-term assistance to the international community.[148]

As with the Truman Doctrine, American Catholic opinion favored the Marshall Plan and its attempt to pull America away from its tradition of isolationism. *The Commonweal* believed that the ERP needed support, "simply out of fear of the Russians." *America* saw it as "a last chance short of war to stop aggression, save freedom...and win the peace." James Gillis, as with the Truman Doctrine, was sedate, only suggesting that Europeans as well as Americans had economic responsibility for the maintenance of peace in the world.[149]

The question of the establishment of a Jewish homeland within the State of Palestine created a significant problem for the international community and the fledgling United Nations Organization. Although the traditional animosity between Jews and Arabs intensified with the acceptance of the Balfour Declaration by the League of Nations in 1922,[150] the postwar period saw an even greater escalation of hostilities. The UNO met in August 1947, at the request of England, the overseer of Palestine, to fashion a plan whereby Arab and Jewish partitions within Palestine would be created. This effort proved fruitless; civil war ensued, and finally after the Zionists gained control, the British governor left Jerusalem on May 15, 1948.[151]

The situation in Palestine elicited comment from the American Catholic press. While *America* called for an implementation of the UNO-proposed solution and *The Commonweal* called for greater justice for Jews throughout the world, Gillis simply wondered why America was always the country asked to solve the world's problems. While defending the United States, the Paulist editor demonstrated once again his familiar blunt style:

> Of course there is a solution. There is always a solution. Uncle Sam is the solution. All he needs to do is to step into the most impossible solution and bring order out of chaos....We can fix it in—well let's see, we can fix it in an afternoon, as some of our admirals in the Pacific said we could settle the problem of Japan.[152]

In July 1948, following up an editorial that asked whether America was willing to go to war to secure a Jewish state, Gillis sent a letter to thirty-nine members of Congress and five presidential candidates asking the same question. The response of Thomas Dewey was representative of those received:

> I am concerned that the Palestine situation can and must be solved through the peaceful machinery of the United Nations....The United States must exercise its leadership in the United Nations to bring a just and lasting peace to Palestine and to assure continuance of the free state of Israel.[153]

Dewey's response typified the frustration which Gillis experienced with the situation in Palestine; he saw no easy solution. He opposed America's role as an international police force and did not value the work of the United Nations. In offering no workable solution Gillis continued a lifetime pattern of offering critique with no suggestions for answers.

Valedictory—1947–1948

World War II and the postwar peace process dominated the news, but James Gillis, despite his full involvement with the affairs of the war, did not stop the many activities which had made his name a household word for many families. He continued to crisscross the nation on numerous occasions, maintaining his normal yet exhausting speaking schedule. Among the many highlights of this period was his invitation to speak at the fiftieth anniversary of the founding of the Josephites. His earlier work with the Northeastern Clergy Conference for Negro Welfare and general advocacy for black Catholics made his selection quite logical.[154]

Gillis's intercommunity work continued to be visible throughout this period. He was elected as a delegate to all the general chapters of the 1940s (1940, 1943, 1946, 1949) and participated in the elections of Henry Stark (1940–1946) and James Cunningham (1946–1952) as superiors general. Gillis's contribution continued to be a voice for the traditional missionary spirit of the Paulists. In 1940, answering Stark's call for a return to urban evangelization, he suggested the appointment of a Paulist to coordinate mission schedules. In 1943 he promoted the publication of a series of pamphlets which would explain the missiology of the community, commenting that although Paulists were known as missionaries to America, their publicity was poor. In 1949 his mission approach branched out to retreats, suggesting that the community should "engage at the earliest opportunity in the work of lay retreats for Catholics and non-Catholics in houses controlled and managed by Paulist Fathers."[155]

The 1940s were also a time of personal strife and loss for the priest editor. His bouts with ill health continued throughout the war years. From November 15, 1943 to mid-January 1944 Gillis was hospitalized for surgery on a "benign hypertrophy" (swelling of an inner organ).[156] It was during this decade as well that he developed arthritis, which, according to Finley, "began to check [his] swift pace."[157] The personal losses that Gillis suffered were far greater than the deterioration of his health. In July 1942, Margaret Walsh, who had served him faithfully for twelve years as secretary in *The Catholic World* office, died suddenly while undergoing surgery. On February 19, 1944 the sting of death came home when Gillis's younger sister Katherine died in Boston.[158]

In 1947 James Gillis celebrated his silver jubilee as editor of
The Catholic World. He used the occasion to voice his understanding of ministry:

> A clergyman should not remain upon the surface of politics.
> He should dig down to the moral, bring it up, show it, and, if
> he can, bring about a union of the political and the moral.

He went on to say, "It happens to be my avocation [as a clergy-
man] to speak and write on international topics."[159] Gillis was a
preacher; it was the core of his Paulist identity. The event [his
jubilee] may have been the catalyst to his request of the Paulist
administration that an assistant be assigned to him at *The Catholic
World.* John Sheerin became Gillis's understudy with the idea that
he would succeed to the role of editor of the Paulist monthly.

Congratulatory notes on the occasion of his jubilee were
received from fellow journalists and his general readership. One
letter placed his role in perspective: "You have been the *Catholic
World* for the last twenty-five years, and the amount of good that
you have done as its head is simply incalculable." High praise was
also received from John Kennedy, priest-editor of Hartford's
Catholic Transcript, who described Gillis's editorials as "the liveli-
est, most penetrating, most forthright, and best expressed fea-
tures of contemporary journalism."[160]

James Gillis throughout his tenure had edited a sophisti-
cated magazine of high literary standards; his final seven years
continued the tradition. Well-known authors such as John Earle
Uhler, Anna McClure Sholl, Paul Hanly Furfey, Joseph Fichter,
Francis Stuart Campbell, Theodore Maynard, and Erik von
Kuehnelt-Leddihn contributed stimulating essays ranging from
theology, to science, to social and/or political thought, to fiction. The magazine, which, as demonstrated earlier, had always
run in a deficit, actually moved closer to economic solvency in
the 1940s. From an operational debt of almost $12,000 in 1940,
the red ink was eased to only $1100 in 1945.[161]

On June 28, 1948, in the privacy of his loyal staff, James
Gillis announced his retirement as editor of *The Catholic World.*[162]
His last editorial, "Valedictory," was published in September. In
announcing his retirement he gave his reason as his desire to

write a spiritual book. He admitted to his readers that he had suffered much for his convictions and strident opinions, especially with respect to President Roosevelt: "But those and other miscellaneous penalties are as a matter of course inflicted upon any man who speaks his mind. I do not complain."[163] Privately, however, the pain of his trials was revealed as he poured out his soul to a friend:

> I have not admitted the fact to many but I confess it to you that one of the reasons I resigned (beyond my desire to do some more strictly priestly work) was a kind of feeling that almost all I had written over a period of 26 years was relatively futile. The tide of public opinion in most of the years ran strongly against what I took to be the obvious truth. The recent elections confirmed my opinion in the present mood of the American people; not much good can be done by reiterated warnings that they are stampeding for the abyss.[164]

James Gillis perceived himself to be a missionary preacher who mounted "pulpits" to deliver his message of duty, moral righteousness, individual free choice, and conversion. He reflected his self-understanding in a 1946 editorial:

> As a commentator I insist upon my right—rather I recognize my duty—to tell the truth as I see it. As an American, I cry out against what I think would do damage to my country, even though in making my protest I seem to be disloyal to a friend and an ally. As a priest I remain unmoved by the fact that I am called a Fascist by Communists and [a] Communist by Fascists. Christ was hated equally by Pharisees and Sadducees who in turn hated one another. Also, He was opposed by a third group, the Herodians, "liberals" of their day, who hated both Pharisees and Sadducees. The priest, who is not above his Master, must expect sometimes to be at odds with both extremes and with the mean. Such is the lot of anyone who persists in seeing all things *sub specie aeternitatis.*[165]

Gillis closed this chapter of his life with full confidence that he had consistently promoted policies based upon his sense of morality:

So in these last lines of my last editorial, I would repeat my favorite theme: If we are to save the American Republic and Christian civilization, we must restore or establish the supremacy of the moral element in the conduct of world affairs. Looking back, I comfort my conscience with the claim that such has been my endeavor. I have used men and events, not as subjects but examples. My concern has been not with persons but with principles.[166]

James Gillis's retirement as editor of *The Catholic World* was in many ways the close of an era, for his life, the magazine, and the Paulist community. As with his silver jubilee only one year earlier, he received many letters of congratulations which form a commentary on his life and work as editor. Gillis's zeal for truth was noted by many, as was his "non-conformist stripe"; one was never in doubt as to his purpose in speaking or writing. He was further described as a "man of principle and self-discipline" who attacked evil where he found it. Gillis was not one who muffled his tone to please others but rather was, as one biographical sketch described him, a "modern Savonarola." To his faithful readers his presence would be sorely missed.[167]

During the period of World War II and the initial phases of the Cold War James Gillis continued his mission to safeguard America by preaching his message of reform through a return to individual freedom and conversion. Although his work as editor, essayist, and lecturer continued as before, America's entry into the war changed the environment of the nation and audience to whom he preached; James Gillis found himself on the outside looking in on the American Church. While the hierarchy embraced the war effort from the outset, Gillis was hesitant, which placed him at odds with mainstream Catholic thought. The Paulist editor's non-interventionist stance only shifted temporarily with a return to isolationism after the war's conclusion as seen best in his rejection of the United Nations and America's new international role. Gillis's aversion to war, which was so clearly evident from his 1920 "conversion," was transformed at this time into a call for the ethical prosecution of America's war effort. If fighting could not be avoided it remained imperative that human freedom be maintained by the preservation of conscience. Gillis spoke out in his usual vehement and polemical manner about the nation's moral violations, most especially in its use of the atomic bomb on Japan. The evil of war and its principal American prosecutor, Franklin Roosevelt, became manifestations of Mr. Hyde, the dark side of his dualistic world view.

Gillis's position within the mainstream of American Catholicism shifted during the war years. His refusal to support America's entry into the war placed him on the outside and was a direct cause to his dismissal from the "Catholic Hour." Loss of a radio "pulpit" was incidental to Gillis, but its implication that the hierarchy, which sponsored the program, had removed its support must have caused him great consternation. As priest and Paulist Gillis perceived himself as a missionary to America, but always in the context of the Church. Gillis was, however, able to place himself more in the mainstream through his rejection of Communism and its rapid spread in Eastern Europe. He was consistent with his earlier pronouncements against any ideology, leader, or institution which threatened individual human freedom and the possibility of conversion.

Gillis's retirement from the editor's chair of *The Catholic World* closed a major chapter in his life. Always a missionary, the journal had been his principal "pulpit" for twenty-six years to voice his message to the world. The style, content, and force of Gillis's editorial comment left a legacy for the magazine and the Paulist community. John Sheerin, Gillis's successor as editor, voiced opinions which many times were aligned with his predecessor's conservative agenda, but the two men possessed different personalities, approaches, and styles. Gillis's unabashed methods were drawn from his perception that the spread of evil must be curtailed; he saw himself as America's guardian. As time progressed, however, Gillis became more resigned to the fact that America had lost its identity. He never lost hope, however; he would continue to fight for reform in America and the world in new and different ways.

CHAPTER 7

A "Conservative" Retirement— 1949–1957

The United States enjoyed a wave of prosperity in the 1950s similar to that experienced after World War I. Veterans returned from the war, married, and started the "baby boomer" generation in America. Through the utilization of the GI bill benefits program,[1] enrollment at America's colleges and universities rose well beyond its highest previous level. America became a suburban community almost overnight with the construction of tract homes in planned neighborhoods on the outskirts of major metropolitan centers. Optimism was high and the economic report was favorable with inflation under control. The United States was the leader of the free world as it fought the Cold War against the expansion of Soviet influence.

Religion also enjoyed a renaissance in America in this decade. In his famous 1955 sociological analysis of American religion, *Protestant–Catholic–Jew,* Will Herberg suggested, "Religion has become a primary symbol of 'heritage' and church membership the most appropriate form of 'belonging' under contemporary American conditions."[2] He went on to suggest that Americans became more actively religious during the 1950s in response to their spiritual need created by the depersonalized contemporary society.[3]

American Catholicism in the 1950s

America's religious renewal of the postwar period aided Catholicism's rise to its apex in visibility, unity, and strength within the national community. American Catholics exhibited

210

homogeneity blending loyalty to nation and Church. "American religion's Indian summer"[4] produced many manifestations of Catholic revival. Bishop Fulton Sheen's books, such as *Peace of Soul* (1949) and the five-volume *Life Is Worth Living* (1953–1957), and his television evangelization placed the Catholic name and ideal in the living rooms of many American homes. During this period Thomas Merton's autobiography, *The Seven Storey Mountain* (1948), and his message of contemplative spirituality were introduced to American Catholics. Vocations to the priesthood and religious life swelled seminaries and convents to record levels; attendance at Catholic schools between 1949 and 1959 more than doubled from 2.6 to 5.6 million students, and the number of Catholic colleges and hospitals increased dramatically during the decade. Church attendance by Catholics was reported to be at 82%, more than fourteen points higher than the national average.[5] Hugh Nolan has captured the spirit of the times: "The Catholics of that era were a joyous group positive of their identity, proud of their church and of their priests and of their schools."[6]

Higher visibility for the Catholic hierarchy in many aspects of American life was evident. Cardinal Francis Spellman (1946–1967) was the principal national figure. His strong anti-Communist stance, active involvement with the United Nations in negotiations concerning the future of Palestine, personal friendship with Pope Pius XII, and interaction with United States Presidents from Franklin Roosevelt to Lyndon Johnson rendered him a position of influence in religion and politics. The Church possessed other national leaders in the hierarchy. Chicago's Cardinal Samuel Stritch (1939–1958), Cardinal Richard Cushing (1944–1970) in Boston, and Cardinal Edward Mooney (1937–1958) of Detroit cast large shadows in their activities within their archdioceses and in national programs.[7]

American Catholics became upwardly mobile in certain visible ways but continued to languish in intellectual endeavors and positions of power and prominence. Better education and the general economic prosperity of the period aided Catholic efforts to achieve success in business as well as the legal and medical professions. Still, John Tracy Ellis, the Church historian, in 1955 asked why a dearth of Catholic intellectual life existed in America.[8] His comments opened the floodgates to the question precipitating all sorts of answers. Despite their numbers American Catholics were still underrepresented in the decision-making positions of education, politics, and business.

The decade of the 1950s also produced a fertile environment for the revival of Catholic conservatism in the United States. As described by Patrick Allitt,[9] a conservative Catholic force was created from a coalition of anti-Communists, opponents of liberalism, and disillusioned ex-Communists. Catholic conservatives banded together and went into battle so as to challenge the specter of Communism, both foreign and domestic, and to provide an alternative response to that of the liberals which was considered too weak and lacked conviction. Capitalism received mixed reviews from the conservatives, but not so Communism, which was considered a force which could dominate the world. The revival of conservatism was deemed necessary if Christian civilization, with the United States now its chief guardian, was to be preserved. Allitt summarizes the prevailing conservative approach:

> The Catholic conservatives took a militant anti-Soviet and anti-Communist position....They understood communism as a Christian heresy, viewed the events of the cold war in religious terms, and believed themselves to be the new defenders of the heartland of Christendom, defenders of God's truth, while showing a special solicitude for the Christians of the "captive nations" behind the Iron Curtain and the "Bamboo Curtain." Many of them believed the final struggle of the world was imminent, that a third world war, heavy with theological as well as political significance, had, in effect, already begun.[10]

Catholic conservatism of the 1950s was in a sense the product of ideas generated over the previous two decades. The historian and Catholic convert Ross J. S. Hoffman promoted a conservative solution to the political and economic crises of the 1930s in his work of collected essays, *The Organic State: An Historical View of Contemporary Politics* (1939). In 1945 he founded the

[Edmund] Burke Society at Fordham University in an effort to revive "the principles, values, and traditions which are the heritage of the political and international society of Christendom." Hoffman believed that Burke's nineteenth-century writings against the French Revolution should be studied for their application to present-day America. In *The Spirit of Politics and the Future of Freedom* (1950) he summarized his belief that a Catholic-led conservative revival, in the spirit of Burke, would renew the country and guard it against the forces which threatened it, especially Communism.

Francis Graham Wilson, a political scientist and another convert to Catholicism, also articulated a conservative ideology. From teaching positions beginning in 1928, Wilson, like Hoffman, developed a conservative approach to American politics based on the writings of Burke. Many of Wilson's ideas, which emphasized the continuity of American conservatism with the Christian tradition and its consonance with natural law, were collected in a series of lectures given in 1949 and published as *The Case for Conservatism* (1951). Here he detailed five specific propositions which undergirded the conservative political disposition while making a strong case for the compatibility of Catholicism and American conservatism.[11]

A Conservative Domestic Agenda

Although he had vacated the editor's desk at *The Catholic World,* James Gillis continued his preaching ministry principally through his weekly syndicated *Sursum Corda* column. The environment of American Catholicism of the 1950s, especially the trend toward conservatism, was fertile soil indeed for the promulgation of his ever blunt and many times caustic comments. Gillis did not identify himself a conservative, but it is clear from his earlier political and social stands, which supported his world view of the battle between good and evil, that he would not have objected to such a label. He did, however, forcefully reject liberal Catholicism, chastising those on the left for their closed-minded attitude and disregard for traditional Catholic belief and practice: "In a word the liberal Catholic can only with difficulty be distinguished from the non-Catholic."[12] In one of many public debates in which Gillis entered in the 1950s, John Cogley, managing editor of *The Commonweal,* returned Gillis's salvo:

> I think it is time to complain publicly about the treatment meted out to the "liberal" Catholic—by which is usually meant any Catholic who does not agree with the *Tablet,* Father Gillis, Senator McCarthy, et al.[13]

Gillis, not to be outdone, answered Cogley by objecting to *The Commonweal's* "disservice" to him and others by their placement "in the midst of all those offensive epithets."[14]

Catholicism in general and the conservative agenda in particular found themselves on the defensive in the 1950s from a recurrence of anti-Catholicism. The principal purveyor of this animus in the public media was Paul Blanshard. In his monograph, *American Freedom and Catholic Power* (1951), Blanshard feared a total take-over of the nation by Catholics should they become a dominant plurality. Placed within the context of a master plan orchestrated by the Vatican to dominate the world, Blanshard's book professed the conviction that American education, religion, and family life would be controlled by the bishops, whom he described as, "the self-proclaimed representatives of God." Blanshard characterized Catholic opinion on Church and State, birth control, and education as "un-American attitudes."[15]

Gillis's response to the anti-Catholicism of the day centered itself in a call for the Christianization of the nation. He advocated as before the need to remove moral abuses and place God into the daily administration of politics, economics, business, labor, and entertainment.[16] He responded to Blanshard's tirade by returning to a favorite theme:

> Blanshard would have the Church not only surrender authority in the sphere of morals, but even the right to say what is moral. What the Church surrenders the state takes over. This, of course, is statism. When statism develops to that degree you have Fascism.[17]

He further derided anti-Catholics for their sniping from a distance while maintaining an outside appearance of conciliation:

If you are really Knights in shining armor and not ridiculous
Don Quixotes, you can find plenty to fight besides wind-
mills, or for that matter stone walls. But don't fight those
who are in the front line of battle contending against Communism and atheism; don't shoot at us from the rear. It isn't
good sport; it isn't good sense; it isn't good religion.[18]

The defensive stance taken by Catholic conservatives
against anti-Catholic animus of the 1950s was transformed by
Gillis into a more familiar offensive posture in critique of the
domestic agenda of Harry Truman. The President's come-from-
behind victory over Thomas Dewey was a disappointment to the
Paulist and prompted him to renew his attack in his mission to
safeguard the nation. He continued to bemoan the government's
failure to restore truth and to reform along lines more supportive of the individual.

President Truman's announcement of his "Fair Deal" policy
in his January 5, 1949 State of the Union Address set the agenda
for America's domestic policy in the early cold war years. The
President declared, "This government exists not for the benefit
of a privileged few, but for the welfare of all the people."[19] As an
extension of Roosevelt's New Deal and a modification of it, the
program aimed to enact legislation in four major areas—civil
rights, social welfare, housing, and labor.[20]

Loss of *The Catholic World* as a primary rostrum did not
inhibit Gillis's continued criticism of the Truman Administration. He perceived the "Fair Deal" as devoid of principles:

We have no philosophy, not even a policy; no continuity of
thought, no consistency of action; no concern for what we
were as a nation in the past or what we shall be in the
future....We live a hand-to-mouth existence both economically and diplomatically. We may get away with it, but to
some of us old-fashioned Americans it seems that this hand-
to-mouth policy may be our ruin.[21]

Gillis characterized Truman's policy as "political ineptitude"
and complained loudly when the administration ridiculed its
critics. More important, he smelled the smoke (but could not
locate the fire) of treason in the form of Communists in the fed-

eral government. Additionally, he sensed in Truman an attitude similar to that of Roosevelt toward the usurping of power by the executive branch of government:

> When anyone in high political position says, or thinks, or acts as if he thinks, that his power is not limited by The [sic] Constitution, or that an emergency justifies disregard of the Constitution, let the citizens beware.[22]

Gillis was not alone in the Catholic press in his critique of the Truman administration. *The Commonweal* reported, "Truman's Washington gives the impression of being more informal, slipshod and happy go lucky than any of its predecessors in recent times. It needs considerable tightening."[23]

Gillis's critique of the American government went beyond his disapproval of the ideas of President Truman. As in the past, he hammered home his disgust with policies which would lead the nation to the demise of its status as a republic and substitute an empire in its place:

> To be honest with ourselves, we have so far departed from the original idea of the American Republic that we have become something essentially different from what the fathers had in mind. To talk, as some do, about our present form of government as being a legitimate evolution of the government of 1789 is to talk nonsense. A true development retains the essential characteristics of the original. We are no more like a Republic as conceived by the founders than a hippopotamus is like a horse.[24]

Gillis possessed no patience and felt no mercy toward those who refused to admit their errors:

> If Western Civilization is to succumb to the Oriental despotism of the Soviets, it will perish because of the blunders of presidents, premiers, politicians, diplomats, "statesmen." They all make mistakes but they seldom confess them.[25]

The deterioration of the nation's moral fiber, which he had perceived since the "false prosperity" of the 1920s, reappeared in the post-World War II period. Political depravity became his new internal enemy which if left unchecked would bring havoc and dissolution to the American government. According to Gillis, government needed to return to its basic purposes rooted in Gospel values:

> In all my public utterances the constant theme has been the imperative need of morality in the political as in the domestic sphere. We cannot save our country—not to say the world—by waging war or political maneuvering. The first condition of national or international salvation is truthfulness, honesty, sincerity.[26]

Gillis professed that the government's failure to keep the people informed about its decisions had threatened human freedom by usurping the common citizen's right to rule. Untruth had betrayed the American people and corrupted government to the point that Gillis placed it as the top priority of the Eisenhower administration which assumed control in January 1953:

> So here is what one citizen, from among the 150 million, takes to be the primary concern of the President of the United States. He must see that political corruption is cut down to a minimum and if possible destroyed altogether....That's the first job of the new President. He must purify the moral atmosphere of the Capital of the nation.[27]

Gillis's war against Mr. Hyde, whose manifestation of darkness varied over the decades, continued to rage in the battle between truth and the lie. "God is Truth. Satan is The Lie. Let's have the courage and the faith to oppose the lie with the truth, and see which will win."[28] Once again he was poised to exorcise the demons from politics.

Armed with the truth, Gillis continued to offer his rather trite solution of a return to God in order to solve the world's ills. He viewed the "monstrous-hybrid" Christo-paganism as the root cause to the evils in the world. In order to defeat the various forms of relativism which had been created by this monster, the world needed "the perennial philosophy and indeed the perennial religion" which possessed the conviction that God's Spirit was necessary for the redemption of the world. The human need for God was deep-seated; to take advantage of what was natural was totally logical.[29]

The ever-growing power of the state became for Gillis a grave danger, which threatened individual freedom, both in the United States and the world community. Statism was manifest most visibly in the power of the executive branch and the office of the President, which had exceeded its limits and transgressed the law and spirit of the Constitution, thereby jeopardizing the nation's republican status. Gillis refuted those who criticized his stance as un-American:

> We are the best Americans of all. We are the champions of the rights of the individual and of a number of individuals grouped in a society. We do not intend to permit the State to crush us, smother us, destroy us. If that is not good patriotic Americanism I should like to know why not.[30]

He wondered why the American government, in violation of its political tradition, made efforts to take away from its citizens the very rights for which the allied nations had fought in two world wars:

> What has happened to the first two-thirds of Abraham Lincoln's description of the American Republic, "government of the people, by the people and for the people"? Nowadays we have government for the people (presumably) but not of the people and certainly not by the people. Ours has become a government by the President, the State Department, the Federal Bureaus, and even the Supreme Court which has no constitutional right to govern at all. The people are alterably flattered and scolded but not really consulted and still less obeyed. Lip service to the people is given on occasion but only when it serves some political purpose.[31]

Gillis's anti-statism campaign reached greater heights in the 1950s as a result of the publication of Clarence Manion's book, *The Key to Peace.* Manion, Dean of the Notre Dame School of Law, expressed the belief that traditional Americanism offered the only valid formula for the achievement of human brotherhood. Bishop John O'Hara of Buffalo (formerly President of the

University of Notre Dame and later Cardinal Archbishop of Philadelphia) believed that Manion's thesis was true and wrote the book's publisher, The Heritage Foundation, requesting that a copy be sent to every member of the hierarchy. This was done with a very positive response received from bishops across the country. O'Hara wrote to Gillis, expressed his appreciation of the book, and asked the Paulist to comment himself. Gillis described the monograph as "the wisest, most penetrating and most profound treatise on Statism in a small volume."[32]

Gillis's approval of the book was criticized by members of the Catholic press, precipitating a war of words in the late winter of 1951. George Higgins in his "Yardstick" column wrote, "Fr. Gillis happens to think that Manion's book is 'colossal—in a small way.' I happen to think it's superficial—in a big way." He claimed the book was "likely to do a lot of harm," particularly to free nations, in its promotion of an "exaggerated 'Americanism' and its all too conspicuous contempt for 'Europeanism' whatever that may be."[33] The former editor of *America,* Wilfrid Parsons, SJ, also criticized Manion's effort as "wholly individualistic" and "only too apt to play into the hands of those, in and out of the Church, who would whittle away [a] most fundamental part of Catholic social teaching." In writing to Gillis, Parsons explained that political scientists had denounced the book and described any support that came from the hierarchy as "irrelevant" for the bishops were "innocents in political science."[34]

Gillis's conservative domestic agenda included a renewed attack on organized labor which paralleled his immediate post-war comments. The pendulum of the labor-capital struggle in his mind had swung too far to the side of unions with devastating results for the common good. The strike continued to be used by labor as a club to hold hostage innocent citizens who were ill-affected by such work stoppages. He quoted Archbishop Richard Cushing:

> If the workman has inalienable rights, he has duties. His attitude toward his employer should be one of good will and co-operation without malice, hatred, or unreasonable conflict. He should sincerely offer an honest day's work for an honest day's pay.[35]

Gillis attacked George Higgins for his strident advocacy which kept unions and their leaders blameless in labor disputes. The Paulist in turn was criticized for his equally one-sided opinion which placed all blame at the feet of organized labor.[36]

Gillis's belief that labor had grown too powerful was echoed in his call for tighter control on academic freedom, which became another heated debate in the 1950s. Russell Kirk and William F. Buckley, Jr. described academic freedom as liberty required for researchers to pursue their convictions and theories in private, wherever they might lead, but it did not entitle them as teachers to promulgate whatever they happened to consider true. Rather, teachers were to defend the traditional wisdom of society and transmit established truths to those students in their charge until such time as new theories gained intellectual acceptance.[37]

Buckley's monograph *God and Man at Yale: The Superstitions of "Academic Freedom"* (1951), which criticized the University's lax attitude toward material presented in the classroom, pushed the academic freedom debate into the public forum. Gillis supported Buckley's "attack upon collectivism and atheism," judging it as "a superlatively fine piece of work."[38] *America* responded by taking issue with the author's thesis and challenging many of the specific precepts of the book. Gillis felt *America's* attitude was a "distinct disservice" as it misrepresented Buckley's ideas and placed him outside the mainstream of opinion.[39] In one of his last published essays the Paulist connected academic freedom with his overall call for moral standards and a return to truth:

> In the name of learning, the professors are destroying learning. They are providing a race of agnostics or even numerous skeptics. They teach that there is no such thing as truth, pure and simple. There is your truth and my truth and the other fellow's truth. No truth is permanent....There is no norm of truth, no standard.[40]

The Specter of Communism

As the Cold War intensified and the United States continued to promote George Kennan's containment policy, as manifest in the ERP, American fear of Communism grew. After a somewhat conciliatory attitude in the immediate postwar years the public's perception of the Soviet Union and American Communists grew increasingly negative. Many Americans believed that a conspiracy existed which aimed to entangle the United States in a web of Communist subversion. Several organizations, such as the American Legion and Daughters of the American Revolution, as well as the Hearst and McCormick newspaper chains, served as voluntary watch dogs to keep the Communist ideology from spreading any further. The House Committee on Un-American Activities (HCUAC), whose power had been clipped during the war, roared back to prominence in an aggressive way. Belief in the "Red Menace" was rampant in America; the HCUAC served as the great exorcist.[41] The celebrated case of Alger Hiss and his eventual conviction on perjury charges fueled the fire of America's fear.[42]

Catholics maintained their fear of Communism, as mentioned previously, throughout the war years. While Gillis and other Catholic writers continued to raise fears of Communism's potential to destroy the American way of life, it was Cardinal Francis Spellman who was the recognized Church leader in the anti-Communist fight. As early as 1946 he declared that "Communism is un-American" and promised that he would engage in "no conspiracy of silence" on the subject.[43]

President Truman, in an effort to stem the tide of Communist infiltration into American government, established a loyalty program for government workers. On November 25, 1946 the President, by executive order, created a Temporary Commission on Employee Loyalty. This was followed in March 1947 with a permanent Federal Employee Loyalty Program which created a Loyalty Review Board to coordinate and provide impartial overview of the plan. Athan Theoharis has written that the purpose of the program "was absolute security: the operational premise was preventative, not corrective—i.e., to avert any possible...threat of subversion."[44]

The concern of the American people in the 1950s lay primarily with the spread of Communism in the United States. Arthur Schlesinger, in his 1949 book *The Vital Center,* spoke of the power and growth of domestic Communism:

> There can be no serious question that an underground
> Communist apparatus attempted during the late thirties and
> during the war to penetrate the United States Government,
> to influence the formation of policy and even to collect intel-
> ligence for the Soviet Union.[45]

The American Communist Party (CPUSA), which grew more
active and numerous during the Cold War, existed to support the
Soviet Union and to promote the establishment of Communism
in the United States.

James Gillis understood Communism to be a conspiracy, a
manifestation of Mr. Hyde, which the American people had to
recognize and contain: "America en masse had better awake to a
realization of the danger and come immediately to a determination to deal with Communism vigorously and with no semblance
of coddling."[46] He could not understand how people could, now
more than thirty years after the Bolshevik Revolution, be so
blind and gullible to the methods, tactics, and possible ramifications of Communism. This ideology of atheism needed to be
rooted out from American society as did those who attacked the
efforts of anti-Communists. The ultimate solution, however, for
Gillis was not to be found in war but in perseverance, vigilance,
and patience. The Soviet state with time would "hang herself,"
collapse, and be replaced by God:

> With the Soviet lie will pass the Soviet tyranny. Other lies
> will spring up and other tyrannies. They come and go,
> appear and disappear. Only the Truth comes and stays,
> appears and does not disappear. For truth and God—let us
> repeat—are One and the Same.[47]

Not since the "Red Scare" of 1919 and the subsequent
purge of Attorney General A. Mitchell Palmer had the American
people witnessed a campaign as virulent and incessant as that of
the four-year effort of Senator Joseph McCarthy to expose Communists in the United States government. McCarthy, a Marine
war veteran and former judge, was elected by the voters of Wisconsin in 1946 to fill the seat vacated by Robert LaFolette.
McCarthy's campaign to expose Communists in the American

government was initiated when he addressed the Republican Women's Club of Wheeling, West Virginia on February 9, 1950:

> While I cannot take the time to name all the men in the State Department who have been named as members of the Communist Party and members of a spy ring, I have in my hand a list of 205 that were made known to the Secretary of State as being members of the Communist party and who nevertheless are still working and shaping policy of the State Department.[48]

McCarthy's accusations placed in motion an emotional and heated campaign, laced with charges and counter-charges, which captured the attention of all Americans. The environment which would promote such a campaign existed in America. Truman's more forceful policy against the Soviets and the intensification of the Cold War helped set the stage. Additionally, McCarthy's views were consistent with Cold War rhetoric and, most important, his timing was perfect. Coming on the heels of the convictions of Alger Hiss and Ethel and Julius Rosenberg, the conquest of China by Mao Tse-tung, and the explosion of the Soviet Union's first atomic bomb (1949), and with the Korean War to begin in five months, the United States was primed to root out subversion.[49] McCarthy's "uncanny ability to hypnotize and ravish the press by means of sensational charges" added to his effectiveness and attraction.[50]

McCarthy's initial charges, which centered about Professor Owen Lattimore of Johns Hopkins University, were investigated by a special committee chaired by Senator Millard Tydings of Maryland that met in March 1950. The committee, which published its report in July, found no evidence to support the Senator's claims and labeled him "a fraud." McCarthy would not be deterred: "Let me assure you that regardless of how high-pitched becomes the squeaking and screaming of left-wing bleeding-heart, phony liberals, this battle is going to go on."[51]

The Senator's supporters, "the ring around McCarthy," consisted of conservative intellectuals, including William F. Buckley, Jr., John T. Flynn, and William Schlamm. These men were not blind to the Senator's faults, but they considered them trivial when compared with liberal critics who defended known traitors and blindly rushed to the defense of each of McCarthy's targets. Flynn expressed a prevailing attitude, "There is no mystery about Joe McCarthy. He just doesn't like Communists....What is so peculiar about this point of view that it should call for an explanation."[52] McCarthy was also supported by George Sokolsky, William Randolph Hearst, and the Texas oil men Clint Murchison, Hugh Roy, and H.L. Hunt. While Hearst and Sokolsky supported McCarthy's stand against Communism, the Texas oil tycoons were more concerned about the expansion of government and the intellectual community which were "trying to ruin the American system." McCarthy's attacks on the Fair Deal gained the oil men's support.[53]

At the outset McCarthy's opponents were not numerous, at least any who possessed the courage to voice their opinion. McCarthy's biographer Richard Rovere states, "The truth is that everyone in the Senate, or just about everyone, was scared stiff of him. Everyone there believed that McCarthy had the power to destroy those who opposed him, and the evidence was not lacking."[54] When Millard Tydings lost his 1950 re-election bid (following his committee's negative report) he was thought to be a casualty of McCarthy's power and influence. Richard Fried draws a similar conclusion labeling the Senate opposition as never greater than "a corporal's guard." However, he states, "Very few Democratic conservatives believed his [McCarthy's] charges, and fewer still had any respect for him." Still, their lack of respect and disbelief seldom translated into open opposition.[55]

McCarthy's campaign became a source of great debate within the Church as well as American society in general.[56] Although McCarthy himself never associated his crusade with the Catholic Church, many outsiders nonetheless drew the connection. The truth was that Catholics, like the rest of the nation, were split in their opinions on the Senator. Most people approved of the goal of the removal of Communists from the government, but the method used was suspect. Polls showed that Catholic support for McCarthy ran between 7–9% above the national average, with New York and Massachusetts the most favorable. Of those prominent Catholics who voiced an opinion most offered support.[57] None, however, offered the support and visibility provided by Cardinal Francis Spellman in New York, who when queried about the Senator replied,

> There are three things I will say about Senator McCarthy. He was a Marine, and having been with the Marines myself, the fact that a man was a Marine places him very high in my book as regards patriotism. He is against Communism and he has done and is doing something about it. He is making America aware of the danger of Communism. He has been elected Senator from his native State, and no one is better known than by his neighbors. I am willing to accept the verdict of the citizens of Wisconsin concerning Senator McCarthy.[58]

Strong and vocal Catholic opposition to McCarthy did exist. Bernard Sheil, auxiliary bishop of Chicago, was the only member of the hierarchy to criticize the Senator, but his one voice was loud and reached great distances. He described McCarthy's style as "a monstrous perversion of morality" which justified "lies, calumny, the absence of charity and calculated deceit" in an effort to combat Communism. George Higgins contended that the belief that a majority of Catholics were behind McCarthy was "a falsehood pure and simple."[59]

The main attack against McCarthy and his campaign came from *America* and *The Commonweal.* In April 1950 *America* perceived a need to seek out Communists, even though McCarthy's "charges are pretty irresponsible." However, when McCarthy attacked Democratic presidential candidate Adlai Stevenson at the height of the 1952 campaign, accusing him of association with Alger Hiss, *America*'s editor Robert Hartnett, SJ, became incensed. He vehemently attacked McCarthy, labeling his accusation a "cheap stunt" and a "tissue of innuendoes."[60] *The Commonweal* opposed McCarthy consistently from the outset. As early as March 1950 the magazine described the Senator's methods as "shooting at political records and personal reputations like a drunken sailor attacking the rotary ducks at Coney Island." Eighteen months later the attack was more pointed and severe:

> There no longer seems to be any excuse for intelligent
> Americans, especially journalists, to nurture any illusions
> about the Senator. The record of his reckless accusations,
> his evasive and half truths, his shaky methods, his contempt
> for the processes of law and for the safeguards of civil rights
> is no secret.

In September 1952 McCarthy's method was labeled "the technique of the Big Lie."[61]

Gillis fully supported Joseph McCarthy's campaign, echoing
his conservative political slant and deep anti-Communism. He
observed the McCarthy crusade with a blind eye, seeing only a
campaign against Communism, but apparently unable or unwill-
ing to believe that the Senator's methods were worthy of criticism. Gillis's support for McCarthy, who was hated by many
Americans, stands in sharp contrast to the Paulist's rejection of
Franklin Roosevelt, who as time passed became increasingly
revered among the American people. In response to *The Commonweal's* rebuke of the Senator he wrote, "I have not detected the
vicious things which his enemies call 'McCarthyism.'" Gillis
believed McCarthy to be a defender of the nation and spoke out
against those who rendered epithets against anti-Communists:
"Why [are opponents] so hostile and so vituperative toward those
who are trying to rid the government of other lurking traitors?"[62]

As McCarthy's crusade became more involved and accusations were issued against Adlai Stevenson and George Marshall,
Gillis continued to play the apologist in his support for the Senator. In the Paulist's opinion all concerned Americans should
scrutinize the attitudes of candidates for public office as
McCarthy had investigated Stevenson's relationship with Hiss.
He saw the Senator as one who dug up the moles of Communist
traitors who lay underground and at times dormant awaiting an
appropriate time to poison the country with the Soviet ideology.
In mutual correspondence Gillis congratulated McCarthy "upon
the vigor and the success of your campaign" while the Senator
expressed his gratitude for the priest's moral support and
encouragement.[63] Gillis berated McCarthy's accusers including
the CBS news journalist Edward R. Murrow, who was labeled
"partial and biased in his critique of McCarthy."[64]

Reaction to Gillis's unwavering support for the Senator's campaign ran the full spectrum. Father Philip Conneally, SJ, supported Gillis's opinion over that of Robert Hartnett when the aforementioned *America* debate was at its height. Another writer was chagrined at Gillis's stance: "I fail to see anything amusing in your sponsorship of McCarthy at all."[65] John Cogley debated with Gillis in the pages of *The Commonweal,* exchanging gibes on the tactics used by the Senator.[66]

McCarthy's favor began to wane in the spring of 1954,[67] but Gillis's support only grew greater. In reference to James Burnham's *The Web of Subversion–Underground Networks in the U.S. Government*[68] (1954) Gillis continued to emphasize the specter of Communism and to overlook entirely McCarthy's method of accusation and innuendo without documentary evidence. He wrote, "The simple fact is, of course, that McCarthy cannot ruin the United States of America, but Communism can." Blindly Gillis wrote that the attacks on McCarthy "remain undocumented" while failing to see that the Senator's campaign was unverifiable and a violation of human rights.[69] The Paulist's refusal to examine the facts is clearly evident in a written response to an opponent:

> For myself I do not know of any statement made by Senator McCarthy in regard to the Communist menace that cannot be supported by abundant information. I think you will find it difficult to quote any statement of his behind which there is not substantial evidence and I also think you will find it difficult to name an innocent person whom he has maligned.[70]

The infamous Army hearings[71] produced no tangible results but they did lead to the appointment on August 2 of a Senate select committee, chaired by Arthur Watkins, to investigate McCarthy and make recommendations. Although the committee recommended censure, Gillis was not to be deterred in his personal judgment: "'Good news for America' shouted the *Daily Worker,* when the Watkins news broke. That is to say good news for the Communists, bad news for America." On December 2, 1954 the Senate voted 67–22 to condemn McCarthy (a lesser punishment) based on the Watkins' Committee report. Gillis lamented the action, but *The Commonweal* voiced its approval:

> Senator McCarthy has accomplished his own destruction as a major force in American politics. He now seems safely placed where he should always have been—in isolation from all moderate and responsible forces in American life. And here we will be happy to leave him—a footnote, at most, to the history our country has to make in the years ahead.[72]

Gillis's unfailing support for McCarthy illustrates his fear of Communism, blindness to reality, and inability to evolve his thought. It is clear that for Gillis, the ideology of Communism, its leaders, and institutions represented a satanic evil and were manifestations of Mr. Hyde in the world. Communism's compromise of human freedom and the loss of possible conversion could not be tolerated by the Paulist; yet he refused to perceive the harm that McCarthy's methods produced. The world was not simply black and white, good and evil; the necessity to look beyond the immediate was something Gillis never understood. The world view which he carried simply could not answer all situations.

The Critique of American Internationalism

The 1950s provided many new issues for America's foreign policy and a renewed opportunity for James Gillis to critique its direction when he saw that justice and right were sacrificed to expediency or national advantage. He questioned the Truman administration's "resist aggression everywhere" creed stating that it was a front for a "wage war everywhere" platform. America should use common sense, caution, and "look before we leap" into the international scene. Through a policy of appeasement, "Uncle Sam has become Uncle Sap," which proved that "we [Americans] are rank amateurs at internationalism."[73]

Gillis expressed no significant change from his earlier critique of America's foreign policy agenda but rather simply adapted his views to the issues of the day. He described war as "barbarism," "outmoded as an instrument of political policy," and "national suicide." It was wrong to commit a crime to promote

Christian civilization; war brought no answers.[74] He also returned to his isolationist stance, especially when the mood of the nation looked for answers to the world's ills along American lines of thought.[75] Using the familiar adage "We told you so," Gillis professed the belief that Americans were reviving the isolationist stance because it favored moral solutions over those of politics or war.[76]

The isolationist question was the focus of another public debate between Gillis and *The Commonweal*. The managing editor, James O'Gara, wrote that the Catholic isolationist in America, however sincere, was a double danger. Such a position threatened the safety and security of the United States and seriously compromised the Church by giving the impression, intended or not, that the isolationist position represented the Catholic point of view. The magazine criticized Gillis for using the Pope's 1950 Christmas[77] message as supportive evidence for his isolationist stance. America's refusal to aid Europe would lead to great suffering. The Paulist responded by stating that American involvement might lead to war and thus, "not the lessening but the enormous increase of human suffering."[78]

The United States' commitment to the freedom and safety of Europe, after the fashion of the Truman Doctrine and Marshall Plan, was made firmer through the North Atlantic Treaty. President Truman first announced America's desire for a pact with Europe in his January 20, 1949 inaugural address. Catalysts for such a treaty were found in the unhindered consolidation of the Soviet bloc in Europe, the total frustration of the United States in trying to negotiate with Russia, especially at the United Nations, and the Brussels pact of March 17, 1948 by which the Western European nations pledged "all military assistance in their power" to any of them that might be the object of an armed attack in Europe. Objections to the negotiation of this treaty included fear that such a treaty would undermine and perhaps destroy the United Nations, and concern that monies earmarked for the ERP would be diverted to a military-aid program which would be the result of the proposed treaty. Despite the objections the pact was formally promulgated on April 4 and approved by the Senate, 82–13, on July 21.[79]

Catholic reaction to the treaty was generally positive. *The Commonweal* described the pact as "one component of a constructive policy pursuing peace through concomitant economic and military strength" and a step toward "the self-preservation and perfection of our free institutions." Predictably, Gillis did not approve of the treaty, although his comments were unusually terse and less biting in critiquing the French government: "No matter how they [the French] go, we must go with them. That's the meaning of NATO. That is what we have let ourselves in for."[80]

Gillis also continued to voice his objection to the United Nations. He believed that the UN had been constructed on the flawed premises of God's absence and the idea that good and wicked people could work together for the "political and moral betterment of the world," a notion which he labeled "criminal absurdity." Moreover, the UN threatened human freedom by its imposition of policy on member nations. The only solution was to scrap the body and form another, based on the proper premises.[81]

The Korean conflict (1950–1953) was the dominant concern of American foreign policy during the first half of the 1950s. The June 25, 1950 invasion of the South by forces of the Democratic People's Republic of Korea prompted President Truman to call for UN action. The Security Council met and hastily drew up a resolution calling for immediate cessation of all hostilities. When the fighting continued the Council met again and on June 27 passed a second resolution recommending that the "Members of the United Nation[s] furnish such assistance to the Republic of Korea as may be necessary to repel the armed attack and to restore international peace and security in the area."[82] Truman ordered United States air and sea forces to Korea and, in a separate move, instructed the Seventh Fleet to steam toward Formosa to prevent any attack on the nationalist Chinese. On July 7 the Security Council requested the United States to designate a commander for UN forces; Truman appointed General Douglas MacArthur.

America's entry into the Korean conflict was deemed necessary to stem the tide of Communist expansion. The June 25 attack struck against the basic presuppositions of the nation's containment policy and thus it was perceived to be incumbent on the United States to repulse Soviet-backed aggression. Additionally, in order to hold together the Western powers, the United States was obligated to respond as a proponent of freedom in line with the NATO agreement.[83]

Catholic opinion in general also favored America's entry into the conflict. *The Commonweal* spoke of America's "resisting aggression [as being] in our own interest." If Korea was not defended it would encourage Soviet sorties against other weak nations adjacent to the Communist heartland. *America* also voiced its approval of the United States' efforts to save Korea, stating that military action was the only course open.[84] Gillis, in contrast, challenged the constitutionality of America's entry into the conflict (Truman ordered forces to Korea without Congressional approval) and rejected the nation's need to fight the world's battles:

> We, the United States of America, have in this bold declaration of our President, assumed the leadership of the world. More than that. We are not only the leader of the nations; we are their champion. Their cause is our cause, their battle is our battle. We will fight for any nation, large or small, great or once great, in all Europe, or Asia, or Africa, or South America, or here on our own continent.[85]

Gillis's rejection of American involvement in Korea was consistent with his staunch military isolationism and rejection of war, but it conflicted with his stand against Communism. It is true that Gillis believed that Communism would die by its own hand, but his apparent inability to even recognize the presence of Soviet aggression in Korea and speak against it is significant. The explanation must lie in Gillis's more basic objective of saving America from all forces, foreign and domestic. Communism at arm's length, as seen in Eastern Europe and China or Korea, was of little concern to the Paulist, but when it threatened to corrupt the American government he was one of the first to jump to action and support those, such as McCarthy, who acted to save the nation. Along with the Paulists' founder Isaac Hecker, James Gillis's belief in America as the "City on the Hill" never wavered.

On April 10, 1951 Truman, after several months of being rebuffed by MacArthur, removed the UN commander,[86] a move which generated a storm of protest and raised significant issues concerning the prosecution of the conflict. MacArthur's belief that the war must be expanded in order to drive Chinese Communists from the field of battle contrasted sharply with the administration's policy of limited war and led to the General's insubordination. As David Halberstam has commented, "He [MacArthur] thought of himself as a sovereign power in the pacific....Essentially he believed himself above the authority of his commander-in-chief."[87] Although Truman's decision led to much criticism from the American people, some could see no alternative to the action taken. MacArthur returned to cheering crowds across the nation, was given a hero's ticker-tape parade in New York, and addressed a joint session of Congress. A Gallup poll reported that 54% of Americans favored the General's proposals, but only 30% were willing to risk all-out war with China.[88] *The Commonweal*, however, which had heretofore been less than complimentary to Truman in his decision-making, commented,

> But certainly his [Truman's] decision was for the common good; it was, we believe, the only decision he could have taken in the interests of discharging his responsibility to the country and to all those throughout the world who look to us now for a reasonable example of leadership.[89]

Gillis, although he spoke very highly of MacArthur, was only concerned about the dissension which the conflict generated in Americans.[90]

The Truman-MacArthur controversy raised the question of the prosecution of war on a limited basis. Truman believed MacArthur's plans would lead to full-scale war with Russia, since the Soviets backed the efforts of the Communist North Koreans. In order to prevent World War III, the President opted for a limited war:

> I believe that we must try to limit the war to Korea for three vital reasons: to make sure that the precious lives of our fighting men are not wasted; to see that the security of our country and the free world is not needlessly jeopardized; and to prevent a third world war.[91]

The historian John Spanier has accurately summarized the dilemma in which Truman found himself in Korea:

> The Administration was compelled to fight a limited war to preserve its total-war policy; it was forced to respond by less than total means to a Soviet satellite in order to prevent the disintegration of a policy predicated upon massive retaliation as the principal means of deterring or winning a total war with the Soviet Union.[92]

James Gillis disapproved of America's efforts in Korea on all fronts. As mentioned previously, he questioned the United States' reason for entering the war. He demanded to know what the nation's ultimate goal was in prosecuting the conflict and feared that, in the end, it would be discovered to be all to no purpose. Gillis was more adamant in his rejection of limited war, calling it "the most illogical and indefensible as well as most curious [form of] war in which America or any other nation has ever engaged." He further declared, "The present plan is outrageous....The American citizen who tolerates it is delinquent in his duty." War would always be a grave evil for James Gillis.[93]

Although the war was fought for three years, a near stalemate was reached as early as July 1951. At that time negotiations toward an armistice were begun, but an agreement was not reached until July 27, 1953 at Panmunjom. Gillis ridiculed the armistice, labeling it "surrender" and a betrayal of America's purpose of prosecuting the war:

> We went into Korea to settle a dispute by means of warfare. We pulled out explaining (after three years and 116,500 casualties) that the dispute is to be settled not by military but by political means. Innocent, ignorant, guileless Americans![94]

In rejecting the armistice one might sense that Gillis was again inconsistent since he was so ardent in his opposition to American involvement in Korea from the outset. As with Poland before, Gillis believed that America's honor was being besmirched in the nation's failure to carry out its commitments. Preservation of the American ideal remained paramount.

The Catholic press generally accepted the armistice and

America's reasons for prosecuting the war. *The Commonweal* considered the war "a worthy cause" and the armistice "a practical expression of the realities of war." *America* wrapped itself in the flag, finding little patience with those who spoke of the purposelessness of the war:

> Our soldiers fought in a just and noble cause. They achieved the great purpose which led this nation, amid the applause of free men everywhere, to resist the armed spread of Red barbarism.

Even John Sheerin at *The Catholic World* saw America's effort in Korea as salvific for the nation's soul.[95]

Retirement, Celebration, and Death

When James Gillis announced his retirement as editor of *The Catholic World* in September 1948 he gave as his reason the desire to write a spiritual book. Actually, Gillis, in his usual prolific style, published four books after he left the journal; three contained original material on "spiritual" themes and a fourth *On Almost Everything* (1955) was a collection of seventy *Sursum Corda* columns. He was asked by Image Books to produce an autobiography but he declined.[96] Gillis's books, which received positive reviews, were spiritual in topic and theme, but the message proclaimed was the familiar battle between the forces of good and evil. The issues which had dominated Gillis's writings for more than three decades were found, sometimes subtly tucked away and on other occasions openly proclaimed, within the pages of these monographs.

Gillis dedicated his first publication in retirement, *So Near Is God* (1953), to his Paulist mentor, Walter Elliott, "whose conferences on religious life were the inspiration of my youth, and, after all these years, the model for what appears in these pages."[97] Gillis summarized his ideas on society, government, and morals by placing them in the spiritual context that all is from God, all is of God, and all must return to God. In a self-revelatory initial reflection "Know Thyself," Gillis, using Augustine as an example, said that many look for God on the outside and never find

Him, because God is discovered within the human heart.[98] One wonders if the author spent his life searching for God without success. The book described the presence of God in opposition to sin, with prayer as the means by which the human bridges the gap between the two.

Gillis could not, however, leave his world of comment and thus connected what he knew best with his investigation of the spiritual. In various reflections he described the need for moral responsibility, forcefully rejected political compromise, which fostered godlessness, and internationalism, and promoted the need for truth, categorizing it as the most basic catechetical effort of the Church.[99]

This Mysterious Human Nature, published in 1956, might well be described as volume II of his earlier work. Divided into five sections of reflections, the essays were described by one reviewer "as gems of clear, incisive, penetrating thinking."[100] The fifth section "Christianity: The Touchstone," subtitled "Essays in Practical Ethics," summarized many earlier views with reflections on "The Individual and the Organization," "Communism: Academic and Actual," "Academic Freedom," and "Tell the Truth: Save the World." Building on his ideas presented in *So Near Is God,* he commented on the promotion of patriotism and rejection of relativism, war, and the United Nations.

This second book encapsulated the essence of Gillis's realization of the "Jekyll and Hyde" that existed in every person and that led to the battle of good against evil in society:

> There in a word is the heart of the paradox, the center and core of the anomaly of man. Heaven and hell are in the heart. God and Satan are tearing at each other....The heart and soul of man is a battleground of Titans, supernatural Titans. And what is worse—if anything can be worse than the conflict of God and Satan—is that man is at odds with himself as to which side he shall take. Sometimes loyal, he stands with God; sometimes treacherous he finds himself fighting or following the fight on the side of Satan. Alternately, or even simultaneously, he is good and bad, saint, sinner, animal, angel, hero, coward, slave, soldier, victim and victor,

winning, losing, pathetic, tragic, but in the end let us hope, triumphant—this is man![101]

Gillis's last work, *My Last Book,* is a collection of what he described as "thoughts," "opinions," "musings." Written during his recovery from a stroke suffered on Palm Sunday 1956, Gillis most probably reflected on his own life and mortality in writing about the cross and suffering: "The primary purpose of pain is purification. If it fail of that purpose it is largely wasted, and the man who wastes it has missed a God-given opportunity of spiritual advance."[102] Gillis's spirituality united him with the cross of Christ in expiation of his past sins.

Despite the effects of deteriorating arthritis, spinal pain, and the difficulties that come with advanced years, James Gillis lived an active retirement. He did not travel as extensively as before but continued to lecture in the New York–Philadelphia–Boston triangle with occasional visits to the Midwest and in June 1955 a final trip to California. During this period he spoke on numerous occasions for the Catholic Total Abstinence Union of America, including the keynote speech at the group's 79th annual convention held in Brooklyn in August 1951.[103] He continued as well with his correspondence with such well-known conservatives as the journalists Westbrook Pegler, Patrick Scanlan, and William F. Buckley, Jr., the theologian and historian Henri Daniel-Rops, and his life-long friend Joseph Gibbons, who had become a monsignor.

At home at St. Paul's Church in New York, Gillis at times presented a lighter side to his personality. He many times wrote limericks and other quips and sent them to friends and opponents alike. Once when the priest next door played his phonograph too loudly, Gillis slipped this note under the door:

> I've a big, noisy neighbor named Ryan
> His conduct is sometimes quite tryin'
> He plays records galore
> With a blare and a roar
> I could moider da guy—I ain't lyin'![104]

Retirement is a time for celebration and James Gillis was feted on several occasions. On December 16, 1951 he was honored with a special Mass and banquet to celebrate his fiftieth anniversary of ordination five days early. He was surrounded by his friends and relatives; Cardinal Spellman celebrated the Mass and Joseph McSorley preached the sermon. McSorley's tribute concluded, "Well done, James Gillis, loyal American, apostolic Catholic, zealous disciple of St. Paul, holy priest—well done, well done!"[105] After the speeches and testimonies, the highlight of the day was Gillis's reception of an honorary Doctorate in Sacred Theology (S.T.D.) from the Dominican College, the Angelicum, in Rome, the first American so honored.[106]

In January 1955 Gillis reached another milestone when he wrote his last *Sursum Corda* column and bade farewell to the world of Catholic journalism. Gillis had informed Frank Hall of the NCWC News Service of his decision the previous December.[107] Hall asked Gillis to reconsider but in the end accepted the decision, expressing gratitude for over twenty-six years of service and 1369 consecutive articles:

> Throughout the years, your columns have been one of the best things we have had in our Feature Service—independent, fearless, always interesting and well written so that the reader enjoys himself while being instructed.[108]

Gillis's final essay, "Farewell to This Column," explained that he wanted more time to write, rejected the idea that he was retiring due to recent battles lost (McCarthy), and thanked his well-wishers and the NCWC for the opportunity to express his ideas.[109]

Gillis's retirement generated salutes, congratulatory letters, and notes of praise from bishops, fellow priests, journalists, and hundreds of his faithful readers. John A. O'Brien of Notre Dame spoke for many in his description of Gillis:

> A bold warrior, he did not hesitate to unsheathe his sword for unpopular causes when convinced of their truth or righteousness. Scorning cant and the mere weight of popular opinion, he struck out manfully for what he believed was right.[110]

Gillis was also lauded for his patriotism by the Protestant newsletter, *One Man's Opinion,* which labeled him a man of unusual foresight and courage. [He] is an American to stand with the founding fathers themselves in his love for the principles of our Declaration of Independence, for our Constitution, and for the freedom, opportunities, and responsibilities which combine to form "the American way of life."[111]

Gillis's termination of his weekly column provided the opportunity for Archbishop Richard Cushing to announce on January 10, 1955 a national fundraising drive to build an information center on Park St. beside Boston Common in honor of Gillis. In praising the Paulist's accomplishments, Cushing stated,

> I am interested in perpetuating the name of this great man of God who has been an inspiration to many priests, myself among them, and to countless readers of his column, Sursum Corda....

> I know of no better way of perpetuating the unique contributions that Father Gillis has made to the Church of this country than to call the proposed new Center, "The Father Gillis Catholic Center."[112]

Thomas Sheridan and Paulist William McDonald headed a national capital drive to raise $1.2 million for the project. The cornerstone of the facility was laid on November 4, 1956. Gillis, who was gaunt and unsteady, traveled from New York for the event, where Cushing again applauded him as a "fearless exponent of Catholic truth and philosophy" and "an inconvertible force of logic and inspiration."[113]

The Park St. ceremony would prove to be his final public appearance. He had never fully recovered from his earlier stroke, even though he had managed to write *My Last Book* and make the Boston trip. On February 28, 1957 he suffered a heart attack and died in Roosevelt Hospital without returning home on March 14. Due to renovation of St. Paul the Apostle Church, his funeral was held on March 18 at St. Patrick's Cathedral. Cardinal Spellman presided and Vincent Holden, CSP, preached the funeral oration. He described Gillis as

...a hero of the first magnitude, a champion of the Church in the first lines of battle, in the pulpit, in the lecture hall, the market place, in the press and on the radio. Using to the best possible advantage the extraordinary talents God had given him, a brilliant mind, a rich and powerful voice, a superb literary ability, he worked tirelessly for the Church and the salvation of the country he loved.[114]

As with his retirement two years earlier, tributes to Gillis and his work were published by many Catholic journalists and other prominent Church members. Friends lauded his faithfulness to duty; opponents, such as John Cogley, buried their hatchets in praise of one of the leading American Catholic journalists of the century. One description published more than a year after his death, however, captured James Gillis fully, the gallant commentator and the anxious pursuer of God:

This was the paradox that was Father Gillis: fearless and uncompromising, belligerent and ruthlessly frank when error (as he saw it) had to be exposed, yet he was himself subject to indecision and doubt and self-accusation which accounted for the low estimate he held himself in God's eyes, a humility that hid itself well even from the searching eyes of his greatest admirers.[115]

Despite his retirement as editor of *The Catholic World*, the 1950s was a fertile environment for James Gillis to exercise his role as a preacher, giving voice to his conservative message which called for a return to duty, moral righteousness, individual freedom, and conversion. This period produced several events which provided grist for the mill of Gillis's probing mind and his sharp pen. Communism, especially on the domestic front, continued to be for him a grave evil which manifests in society the Mr. Hyde of his world view. In his role as guardian of America, he supported all measures and people which aimed to rid the nation of Communism. In this vein Gillis fully supported the polemical campaign of Joseph McCarthy, despite the Senator's violations of human freedom, his brash and unchecked tactics, and his refusal to seek the truth. Gillis's unreserved support for McCarthy best illustrates his blindness to reality. Gillis would

not allow his perception of the nation and its values to be undermined at any price.

The Korean War was the other major concern for Gillis in
the 1950s. The fire of his past revulsion of war was rekindled in
this United Nations police action. Gillis believed America's
involvement to be another example of how the nation had lost its
way in becoming an international police force. As was evident
throughout his career, Gillis could not perceive or refused to
accept that time and events had changed the world and America's role in it. Certainly Gillis did not enjoy the spread of Communism into South Korea, but as he preached during World War
II, the great evil of war was not the solution to the darkness of
Mr. Hyde. James Gillis in his role as preacher continually voiced
opinions to safeguard the nation and its foundational principles.

Active people of mind and body never fully retire and so it
was with Gillis. Almost until the end of his life he continued to
write essays and books which applied his conservative message to
the many issues of the day, and those which he entertained for
more than thirty years as one of America's leading Catholic journalists. Formed by influences which created in him a dualistic
world view, pitting good against evil, Gillis projected his private
struggle onto society in his role as priest, missionary, and journalist. James Gillis persistently battled forces of darkness to preserve individual human freedom and safeguard the nation of his
birth. His memory would be preserved.

Epilogue

Put on the armor of God so that you may be able to stand firm
against the tactics of the devil. Our battle is not against human
forces but against the principalities and powers, the rulers of
this world of darkness, the evil spirits in regions above. You
must put on the armor of God if you are to resist on the evil
day; do all that your duty requires, and hold your ground.
Stand fast, with the truth as the belt around your waist, justice
as your breastplate, and zeal to propagate the gospel of peace
as your footgear. In all circumstances hold faith up before you
as your shield; it will help you extinguish the fiery darts of the
evil one. Take the helmet of salvation and the sword of the
spirit, the word of God. (Ephesians 6:11–17)

This exhortation to the Christian community at Ephesus can be
applied to any person or group at any time. Such is the timeless-
ness of the word of God. But these words when applied to James
Gillis provide a template or blueprint for his life, both the professional role, the Dr. Jekyll, as editor, writer, and speaker, and
the private man of turmoil, his Mr. Hyde.

Gillis saw himself as a champion for the cause of moral
righteousness and absolutism against the forces of darkness
which manifested themselves in various ways. The war continued
throughout his life with battles waged on numerous fronts, all
prosecuted to protect the American Christian way of life which
was instilled in him from childhood. Gillis believed that truth
should enwrap all decisions and be the basis for all policies; it
was the belt which bound the world to God. Justice and freedom
for the individual, who was constantly in jeopardy of absorption
by the organization, was the foundation from which he built his
argument against statism. Zeal was apparent in every aspect of

241

his life; he attacked all tasks with a degree of fervor that bordered on obsession. His activity, which at times in the 1930s found him speaking on two weekly radio programs, writing editorials and columns, and traveling the lecture circuit, makes an industrious worker today appear as a moderate activist.

James Gillis's faith was manifest in his fear of God; it was his shield and protector. His views were at some points out of touch with time and reason, as in his inability to grasp that two world wars had changed America's role and his refusal to recognize the outrageous tactics of Joseph McCarthy's anti-Communist crusade. Additionally, Gillis possessed a rigid attitude of absolutism, rejected relativism, and outwardly offered little compassion, peace or forgiveness to opponents. Yet, his uncompromising method demonstrated that his ideas and opinions were held as convictions of faith; he stood his ground and never backed down. Gillis believed with complete sincerity that not only were his opinions correct, but that failure to reform along his recommended line would be disastrous and possibly fatal for the nation. His belief in America's democratic principles that originated with the founding fathers never wavered. With the fear of God as his shield Gillis fended off the forces of darkness which imperiled America while he attacked perceived wrongdoing or faulty ideas, using the pen and fiery oratory as his swords.

Gillis understood himself to be an Irish-American Catholic; he was proud to wear such a badge of identity. Influenced by his father and a puritan New England ethic, Gillis came to the Paulists and later to the nation as a man steeped in the nineteenth-century theology of absolute certitude, based upon the neo-scholastic synthesis, which became manifest in a dualistic world view pitting good against evil. This was applied to his professional life and became the foundation upon which the American Church would experience and judge him.

Gillis's message was well received by those who held similar views, but it is clear that his mission to safeguard the American ideal, as he perceived it, and to call the nation to repentance was a failure. Gillis realized this when he retired from *The Catholic World;* it was a catalyst to his action. He felt in many ways his voice had gone unheard and unheeded. The America of Gillis's world view changed over time and he was not able to adjust. His work as editor was highly informative and for many readers entertaining; yet there is no accurate measure that indicates that it transformed people's lives. Gillis's contribution, therefore, must be found in his courageous stand against any person, ideology, or program which jeopardized his sense of the integrity or future of the United States and its Christian principles of democracy. His vision was not complex or ambiguous; in a polemical manner he voiced clear arguments and proposed a return to God as the solution to society's ills. James Gillis can be faulted for his inability to grow, but he must be admired for his commitment to truth and dedication to purpose. He was a major figure in twentieth-century American Catholic journalism.

Gillis was a spiritual man, but not in a way readily recognizable by his contemporaries or people today. John Selner has pictured Gillis's spiritual life as one of asceticism:

> If you could characterize the spiritual life of Father Gillis by any one expression, you might use the word "discipline." There was the discipline of mind, discipline put upon him by the requirements of faith, the discipline of steadiness, constancy and consistency, but above all, the discipline of the cross and self-abnegation.[1]

Gillis's life of discipline was most manifest as a countervailing voice of true conviction, symbolic of a certain mindset and way of life. James Gillis's place in American Catholic history will be maintained from his extant record, but it is his strength of belief and unqualified devotion to purpose which will continue to serve as an example of faithfulness in ministry for future generations.

Notes

INTRODUCTION

1. Katherine Crofton, review of *James Gillis, Paulist* by James Finley, in *Catholic World* 188 (December 1958): 251–52. Crofton, who was Gillis's administrative assistant for the majority of his tenure as editor, was very critical of Finley's account, considering his opinions on various aspects of Gillis's life, including his abstinence from alcohol, as too harsh and an inaccurate portrait.

2. Clinton Rossiter, *Conservatism in America* (New York: Alfred A. Knopf, 1955), 21–26, 31, 55, 49, 179, 187–89. The conservatism outlined by Rossiter has been updated by Patrick Allitt. Using the writings of Ross J.S. Hoffman and Francis Graham Wilson as examples of Catholics who served as precursors to the thought of the 1950s, Allitt describes the conservative characteristics of the Cold War era: (1) strongly anti-Communist, (2) uncertainty over the capitalist order in the United States. Many Catholic conservatives championed a regulated capitalist economy, finding it consonant with Church teaching and enriching for the population as a whole. See Patrick Allitt, *Catholic Intellectuals & Conservative Politics in America 1950–1985* (Ithaca, New York: Cornell University Press, 1993), 59–82.

3. William M. Halsey, *The Survival of American Innocence–Catholicism in an Era of Disillusionment 1920–1940* (Notre Dame: University of Notre Dame Press, 1980), 2.

4. Besides James Finley's biography, Gillis's public record as editor of *The Catholic World* and his conservative voice have been noted by many contemporary historians. Representative Catholic historians include: James Hennesey, SJ, *American Catholics–A History of the Roman Catholic Community in the United States* (New York: Oxford University Press, 1981), 235, 253, 269–71, 275, 282, 294; David J. O'Brien, *American Catholics and Social Reform–The New Deal Years* (New York: Oxford University Press, 1968), 58–60, 64, 80–81, 87,

91–92; Donald F. Crosby, SJ, *God, Church and Flag–Senator Joseph R. McCarthy and the Catholic Church 1950–1957* (Chapel Hill: University of North Carolina Press, 1978), 9, 37, 67, 150, 178; George Q. Flynn, *American Catholics and the Roosevelt Presidency, 1932–1936* (Lexington: University of Kentucky Press, 1968), 101–02, 129, 131, 154, 176, 205–06, 235; Flynn, *Roosevelt and Romanism: Catholics and American Diplomacy, 1937–1945* (Westport, Connecticut: Greenwood Press, 1976), 64–70, 79–81, 139–41, 143, 151, 153, 215–16. Secular historians have also described Gillis's views, noting his opinions on international issues, especially Communism. Representative authors include: John Diggins, *Mussolini and Fascism: The View from America* (Princeton, New Jersey: Princeton University Press, 1972), 187–90, 300–01; George A. Sirgiovanni, *An Undercurrent of Suspicion: Anti-Communism in America During World War II* (New Brunswick, New Jersey: Transaction Publishers, 1990), 27, 36, 147, 156–57, 190.

5. James Gillis, *This Mysterious Human Nature* (New York: Charles Scribner's Sons, 1956), 7.

6. James Gillis, Retreat Notes 1903, Gillis Papers, Paulist Fathers Archives (hereafter PFA).

7. Adolphe Tanquerey, *The Spiritual Life–A Treatise on Ascetical and Mystical Theology.* trans. Herman Branderis (Paris: Desclée & Co., 1930), 1–6, 18. Tanquerey calls ascetical theology "spiritual science," the art of perfection and mystical theology. Its goal is to lead souls to Christian perfection. He writes, "Ascetical theology is a part of the Christian Life. In truth, it is its most noble part, for its purpose is to make us perfect Christians." He states further that the study of ascetical theology is "necessary for the priest" and "useful for the faithful."

8. Joseph Chinnici, OFM, *Living Stones–The History and Structure of Catholic Spiritual Life in the United States* (New York: Macmillan Publishing Company, 1989), 135–71. Chinnici uses the term "fractured inheritance" to describe the split between idealism and reality in American Catholicism in the period 1900–1930.

1. TOWARD THE PRIESTHOOD–1876–1901

1. Lawrence J. McCaffrey, "Irish Textures in American Catholicism," *Catholic Historical Review* 78(1) (January 1992): 2.

2. There are many monographs, collected works, and essays which outline in detail the anti-Catholic animus of nineteenth-century America. Among the best sources are: Ray Allen Billington, *The Protestant Crusade, 1800–1860: A Study of the Origins of American Nativism* (New

York: Rinehart & Company, 1952); Gustavus Myers, *History of Bigotry in the United States* (New York: Random House, 1943); James J. Kenneally, "The Burning of the Ursuline Convent: A Different View," *Records of the American Catholic Historical Society of Philadelphia* (Hereafter *Records*) 90 (1979): 15–22; Michael Feldberg, *The Philadelphia Riots of 1844: A Study of Ethnic Conflict* (Westport, Connecticut: Greenwood Press, 1975); James F. Connelly, *The Visit of Archbishop Gaetano Bedini to the United States of America (June 1853–February 1854)* (Rome: Gregorian University Press, 1960); Mark J. Hurley, *The Unholy Ghost: Anti-Catholicism in the American Experience* (Huntington, Indiana: Our Sunday Visitor, 1992).

3. The best complete history of the Northern Know Nothing Party is: Tyler Anbinder, *Nativism & Slavery: The Northern Know Nothings & the Politics of the 1850s* (New York: Oxford University Press, 1992). Know-Nothing party members took an oath "that they would not vote or give influence for any [person] for any office...unless he be an American-born citizen, in favor of Americans ruling Americans nor if he be a Roman Catholic."

4. Two notable late nineteenth-century incidents illustrate the ways in which many German Catholics in America resisted assimilation to American Catholic ways. In 1886 Peter Abbelen, a priest from Milwaukee, wrote his "Memorial" which asked for greater clarification of the status of German national parishes in the United States. Later in 1891 the St. Raphael's Verein, headed by General Secretary Peter Paul Cahensly, generated its "Lucerne Memorial" which made very specific requests of the Vatican to stop "leakage" of German Catholics in America to Protestantism. Both memorials were rejected almost unanimously by the American hierarchy. These documents raised resentment within the Church among the various nationalities that now called the United States home. See Colman J. Barry, OSB, *The Catholic Church and German Americans* (Milwaukee: Bruce Publishing Company, 1953), 44–85 and Philip Gleason, *The Conservative Reformers: German-American Catholics and the Social Order* (Notre Dame, Indiana: University of Notre Dame Press, 1968), 131–82.

5. The best source for a detailed history of the American Protective Association (APA) is Donald L. Kinzer, *An Episode in Anti-Catholicism: The American Protective Association* (Seattle: University of Washington Press, 1964). Its period of influence was short, 1887–1896, but quite virulent. Like the Know-Nothings, the APA sought to elimi-

nate Catholics from public office, but worked within the two-party system. Their efforts achieved limited success.

6. Patrick W. Carey, "American Catholic Romanticism, 1830–1888," *Catholic Historical Review* 74 (October 1988): 594; Chinnici, *Living Stones,* 91–133. Chinnici argues that Hecker, John Keane, and Walter Elliott promoted a theological view which corresponded to their political ideas. A positive anthropology which emphasized God's immanence in the person and the nation was the result.

7. Donna Merwick, *Boston Priests, 1848–1910* (Cambridge, Massachusetts: Harvard University Press, 1973), 10, 69. See also Robert H. Lord, John E. Sexton, and Edward T. Harrington, *History of the Archdiocese of Boston in the Various Stages of Its Development, 1604–1943,* Volume III (New York: Sheed & Ward, 1944), 56–238, which discusses the middle years of Bishop Williams' administration of the Boston archdiocese.

8. Ibid., 3, 60, 61; Merwick, *Boston Priests,* says immigration numbers in Boston went from an annual influx of 4,534 in 1866 to 70,164 in 1907. See also James O'Toole, "Prelates and Politicos: Catholics and Politics in Massachusetts, 1900–1970," in *Catholic Boston: Studies in Religion and Community 1870–1970,* eds. Robert E. Sullivan and James O'Toole (Boston: Roman Catholic Archdiocese of Boston, 1985), 16.

9. Merwick, *Boston Priests,* 34.

10. Ibid., 123, 125. See also Dennis P. Ryan, *Beyond the Ballot Box: A Social History of the Boston Irish, 1845–1917* (Amherst: University of Massachusetts Press, 1983), 57–76. Ryan describes a Brahmin intellectual tradition present in Boston which necessitated a Catholic response through parochial education. Such competition was more evident in Boston than other urban centers.

11. Merwick, *Boston Priests,* 116.

12. The spirit of *Romanità* was most evident in O'Connell. Before his rise to power in Boston he had been the rector of the North American College in Rome and Bishop of Portland, Maine (1900–1906). James Gillis emulated O'Connell's strict orthodoxy and commented favorably about the Cardinal. The best biography of O'Connell is: James O'Toole, *Militant and Triumphant: William Henry O'Connell and the Catholic Church in Boston, 1859–1944* (Notre Dame, Indiana: University of Notre Dame Press, 1992). See also Douglas Slawson, "'The Boston Tragedy and Comedy': The Near Repudiation of Cardinal O'Connell," *Catholic Historical Review* 77(4) (October 1991): 616–43.

13. James F. Finley, CSP, *James Gillis, Paulist* (Garden City, New York: Hanover House, 1958), 22–23.

14. Colleen McDannell, "Catholic Domesticity 1860–1960," in *American Catholic Women: A Historical Exploration,* ed. Karen Kennelly, CSJ (New York: Macmillan Publishing Company, 1989), 50–65. McDannell stresses the role of the woman in the immigrant Irish home. The woman's role as a peacemaker and the one who held things together was critical. Religious expression through the maintenance of a typically Catholic home was expected of all women.

15. Finley, *James Gillis,* 20–38. Finley interviewed Mary and John Gillis for his biography of their brother James Martin. The tape recordings of these conversations are no longer extant. With respect to parochial education during Gillis's childhood, the 1884 Third Plenary Council of Baltimore had mandated that all parishes build a school, if not already supporting one. Parochial education was considered necessary to keep Catholic youth away from Protestant influences which were promoted by the public school system, championed in the nineteenth century by Horace Mann. Despite the Baltimore mandate, schools could not be built fast enough to meet the need of the burgeoning Catholic population. Financial constraints were also a limitation to the spread of Catholic education.

16. James F. Finley, CSP, interview by author, April 6, 1994, Oak Ridge, New Jersey. Father Finley lived with Gillis for ten years. He related many incidents that speak of Gillis's possession of wit and a sense of humor. Also the Paulist Fathers' Archives at St. Paul's College in Washington, D.C. possesses a file in a box marked "Gillis Biographical Information" in which is listed a series of limericks, short jokes, and witty sayings penned by Gillis.

17. James Gillis, "Editorial Comment," *Catholic World* 155 (May 1942): 130. Gillis once stated that his father "influenced my character and my thinking habits more than any other man, cleric or lay." Members of the Gillis family have also related the great influence of James Gillis, Sr. on the family, and especially on James Martin Gillis. Mary Doherty to author, July 5, 1994; Anonymous Gillis Family Member to author, June 6, 1994.

18. Robert E. Sullivan, "Beneficial Relations: Toward a Social History of the Diocesan Priests of Boston, 1875–1944," in *Catholic Boston,* eds. Sullivan and O'Toole, 210. There were insufficient parochial schools for the Catholic population.

19. Pauline Holmes, *A Tercentary History of the Boston Public Latin School 1635–1935* (Cambridge, Massachusetts: Harvard University Press,

1935), 107, 293. Gillis later stated how Merrill gave the students "what was to all intents and purposes a sermon, just as full of religion as if it came from the pulpit." See James Gillis, WLWL Talks, November 15, 1926, Gillis Papers, PFA.

20. Merwick, *Boston Priests,* 99, 100.

21. Finley, interview, April 7, 1994. Finley stated, "James Gillis epitomized the 'proper Bostonian.'" Gillis himself later commented on his love of Boston culture: "You see we were particularly patriotic in Boston; we were proud of possessing Faneuil Hall, 'The Cradle of Liberty,' the Old North Church, Bunker Hill and a dozen other vivid reminders of the Revolution." See James Gillis, WLWL Talks, December 13, 1934, Gillis Papers, PFA.

22. O'Toole, *Militant and Triumphant,* 13–14; attendance records for St. Charles College, Archives Sulpician Fathers (hereafter ASF). Records show that many students from Boston attended St. Charles, both before and after the establishment of St. John's. There is no record, however, that Fr. O'Brien went to St. Charles.

23. James Gillis, Diary, n.d. (September) 1895, Gillis Papers, PFA.

24. Ibid.

25 Ibid.

26. Gillis's stance on alcohol was not uncommon among Catholics of his day. The Catholic Total Abstinence Union of America and the great temperance crusader Father Theobald Mathew were active in the mid-nineteenth century. In the 1890s several leading Catholics, most noticeably Archbishop John Ireland and Bishop John Keane, promoted the total abstinence cause. The story of the Catholic Total Abstinence Union of America, founded at Philadelphia in February 1872, is told in: Sr. Joan Bland, *Hibernian Crusade: The Story of the Catholic Total Abstinence Union of America* (Washington, D.C.: The Catholic University of America Press, 1951). An excellent recent synopsis of the Catholic temperance movement in the United States is given in Paul Robichaud, CSP, "Catholic Total Abstinence," unpublished manuscript.

27. Merwick, *Boston Priests,* 98; Finley, *James Gillis,* 34, 179. Finley, Interview, April 6, 1994.

28. James Gillis, Diary, April 29, 1896, November 10, 1895, April 24, 1896, Gillis Papers, PFA. The only extant incident at St. Charles where Gillis drank at all was once when a lingering illness necessitated in his mind a "sweat" to promote his recovery. Thus, he took "strong drink" and retired in hopes he would feel better. There is also "some evidence" that Gillis took an abstinence pledge as a

seventeen-year-old student at Boston Latin School. See Finley, *James Gillis*, 33.

29. The history of the Society of Saint Sulpice in the United States is completely described in: Christopher J. Kauffman, *Tradition and Transformation in Catholic Culture: The Priests of Saint Sulpice in the United States from 1791 to the Present* (New York: Macmillan Publishing Company, 1988). For details about the foundation of St. Charles see pages 122–26.

30. James Gillis, Diary, November 12, 1895, Gillis Papers, PFA. Gillis's reflection was especially poignant on this day as it was his nineteenth birthday, a day for reflection as his quest for personal understanding continued. Gillis, in both his private and public writings, exhibited a general existential pattern of self-reliance and initiative leading to a dualistic world view. His faith presented itself in his hope that God's presence was always a possibility.

31. Kauffman, *Tradition and Transformation*, 143.

32. James Gillis, Diary, October 21, 1895, Gillis Paper, PFA.

33. Ibid., January 21, 1896, January 30, 1896, April 28, 1896. The "summa" was an award granted to any student who achieved an aggregate average score of 93 in all academic subjects. Gillis not only wanted the distinction of the summa, but if more than one student reached this plateau, he desired the highest average. Excellence was non-negotiable for Gillis as a student at St. Charles.

34. Ibid., November 5, 1895.

35. Ibid., January 5, 1896. Gillis believed the American environment provided the best opportunity for Catholicism to prosper and grow. Yet his world view, which argued for national reform, placed the Church and State at odds with each other.

36. Ibid., May 14, 1896.

37. Finley, *James Gillis*, 193–95.

38. James Gillis, Diary, June 18, 1896, Gillis Papers, PFA.

39. Quoted in Finley, *James Gillis*, 194.

40. Ibid., 34–35.

41. The early history of St. John's is told in John E. Sexton amd Arthur J. Riley, *History of Saint John's Seminary, Brighton* (Boston: Roman Catholic Archbishop of Boston, 1945).

42. Kauffman, *Tradition and Transformation*, 169–70, 176. See also R. Scott Appleby, *"Church and Age Unite!": The Modernist Impulse in American Catholicism* (Notre Dame, Indiana: University of Notre Dame Press, 1992), 94–100.

43. Kauffman, *Tradition and Transformation,* 179, 189–90; Joseph M. White, *The Diocesan Seminary in the United States: A History from the 1780s to the Present* (Notre Dame, Indiana: University of Notre Dame Press, 1989), 170, 231.

44. Kauffman, *Tradition and Transformation,* 199–200.

45. Sullivan, "Beneficial Relations," 217, 219–21.

46. Finley, *James Gillis,* 74.

47. James Gillis, Diary, September 23, 1896, October 7, 1896, October 20, 1896, February 14, 1897, Gillis Paper, PFA.

48. Kauffman, *Tradition and Transformation,* 207. After his time at St. John's, Gigot joined the faculty of The Catholic University of America. For more information on Gigot see: Appleby, *"Church and Age Unite!",* 101–06, 134–42 and Gerald P. Fogarty, S.J., *American Catholic Biblical Scholarship: A History from the Early Republic to Vatican II* (San Francisco: Harper & Row, Publishers, 1989), 122–30, 194–96.

49. James Gillis, Diary, September 16, 1896, Gillis Papers, PFA.

50. Ibid., September 23, 1896, September 28, 1896, October 23–24, 1896. Gillis described Gigot, "He is very earnest and eager to excel in all things that he does." Gillis often played tennis with Gigot, both as partners and opponents.

51. Ibid., January 13, 1897, May 21, 1897.

52. Ibid., December 16, 1896, December 18, 1896, December 31, 1896, January 15, 1897.

53. Ibid., May 24, 1897.

54 Ibid.

55. Ibid. Gillis's youthful opinion of the Sulpicians was in great contrast to that of his mature years. In a funeral oration for his friend the Sulpician Father John Fenlon he stated, "No one who has had the privilege of sitting under the Sulpician Fathers in college or seminary; no one who has lived for years under the one roof with them and has observed them at close range, and indeed (after the manner of students) with almost a microscopic scrutiny, can fail to admit that they are the supreme example of the inconspicuous, unobtrusive virtues [of] simplicity, humility, self-effacement." See James Gillis, "Not in Eulogy," *Voice* 21(1) (October 1943): 7, ASF.

56. William Laurence Sullivan, *Under Orders: The Autobiography of William Laurence Sullivan* (New York: Richard R. Smith, 1944), 51–52.

57. No comprehensive history of the Paulist community has been completed. Several books and monographs exist, however, about Hecker, his life, and spirituality. See Vincent F. Holden, *The Yankee*

Paul: Isaac Thomas Hecker (Milwaukee: Bruce Publishing Company, 1958); Joseph McSorley, *Father Hecker and His Friends* (St. Louis: B. Herder Book Company, 1952); David O'Brien, *Isaac Hecker: An American Catholic* (New York: Paulist Press, 1992); John Farina, *An American Experience of God: The Spirituality of Isaac Hecker* (New York: Paulist Press, 1981); John Farina, ed., *Hecker Studies: Essays on the Thought of Isaac Hecker* (New York: Paulist Press, 1983). A popular book on the formation, work and charism of the Paulist community is James Gillis, *The Paulists* (New York: The Macmillan Company, 1932).

58. Thomas J. Jonas, *The Divided Mind: American-Catholic Evangelists in the 1890s* (New York: Garland Publishing Company, 1988), 46–47, 79–80; see also O'Brien, *Isaac Hecker,* 97.

59. Paul Robichaud, CSP, Memorandum "The Apostolic Mission House: September 1902 to September 1940," November 26, 1991, PFA.

60. Elliott was influenced by Hecker, but also by George Deshon, who served as his formation director. Deshon, a West Point graduate and engineer, had a different view from Hecker's on many aspects of the community and certain theological principles. Although Elliott may have carried the mantle of the founder, it is not fully clear that the understanding he took forward was that of Hecker, but rather a combination of Hecker and Deshon.

61. Jonas, *Divided Mind,* 76, 79.

62. Quoted in David J. O'Brien, "An Evangelical Imperative: Isaac Hecker, Catholicism and Modern Society," in *Hecker Studies,* ed. Farina, 106.

63. Farina, *American Experience of God,* 96–97, 115, 177.

64. A good summary of the characteristics of Hecker's thought and its influence on the American Church is found in Margaret Mary Reher, *Catholic Intellectual Life in America* (New York: Macmillan Publishing Company, 1989), 45–60.

65. James Gillis, Diary, September 30, 1897, September 27, 1897, February 11, 1898, Gillis Papers, PFA.

66. Ibid., November 12, 1897.

67. Ibid., April 18, 1898, May 30, 1898, June 4, 1898.

68. Ibid., August 14, 1898, August 16, 1898.

69. Ibid., August 16, 1898.

70. St. Thomas Student Handbook 1890–1906, September 11, 1896 PFA. Gillis was one of eight who entered the Paulist formation program that day.

71. Several fine monographs exist which describe the history of The Catholic University of America. For detailed information on the foundation of the University see: John Tracy Ellis, *The Formative Years of The Catholic University of America* (Washington, D.C.: American Catholic Historical Association, 1946). For details on the early years of the University see: Patrick Henry Ahern, *The Catholic University of America 1887–1896: The Rectorship of John J. Keane* (Washington, D.C.: The Catholic University of America Press, 1948); Peter Hogan, SSJ, *The Catholic University of America, 1896–1903: The Rectorship of Thomas J. Conaty* (Washington, D.C.: The Catholic University of America Press, 1949) and Colman J. Barry, OSB, *The Catholic University of America, 1903–1909: The Rectorship of Denis J. O'Connell* (Washington, D.C.: The Catholic University of America Press, 1950). An overview history of the University is found in C. Joseph Nuesse, *The Catholic University of America: A Centennial History* (Washington, D.C.: The Catholic University of America Press, 1990).

72. Ahern, *Catholic University–Keane*, 33; Barry, *Catholic University–O'Connell*, 121. Today St. Paul's College is located at the same site adjacent to the National Conference of Catholic Bishops on Fourth Street Northeast in Washington, D.C.

73. The St. Thomas Student Handbooks fully describe the daily life in the seminary. When Gillis arrived in Washington he found a familiar face as his director. Peter O'Callaghan was assigned in late August as the new novice master and professor of dogma. Michael Smith was the house superior and taught moral theology. William Simmons rounded out the staff as professor of philosophy. At this time Paulist students were considered "novices" for the entire duration of their priestly formation. The community did not sponsor a formal novitiate year program. When students were properly prepared for minor orders they were received into the community and ordained sub-deacons followed by the diaconate. Paulist formation was well rounded and emphasized an integration of the spiritual and intellectual life with periods of social and physical recreation.

74. St. Thomas Student Handbook 1890–1906, September 13, 1898, PFA.

75. Paulist Constitution 1899, Chapter 3, PFA.

76. Ibid., Chapter 2, Chapter 3.

77. Gillis, *Paulists*, 47. Gillis wrote that the primary and essential purpose of the Paulists is "the pursuit of spiritual perfection."

78. James Gillis, Diary, October 7, 1898, November 9, 1898, Gillis

Papers, PFA. Pope Leo XIII in *Aeterni Patris* (1879) ordered Thomism to be the philosophy used in seminary training.

79. The classic work on reform movements in America is: Richard Hofstadter, *The Age of Reform: From Bryan to F.D.R.* (New York: Alfred A. Knopf, 1955). More recent scholarship focuses on cooperatives and away from Hofstadter's thesis that depressed economic conditions were the catalyst for the rise of the movement. See: Lawrence Goodwyn, *Democratic Promise: The Populist Moment in America* (New York: Oxford University Press, 1976) and Robert C. McMath, Jr., *American Populism: A Social History, 1877–1898* (New York: Hill and Wang, 1993). Many of the planks of the Populist's (People's Party) 1892 and 1896 platforms, such as a graduated income tax, popular election of senators, and an eight-hour work day, were later adopted through legislation.

80. The War was important to the American Church in a negative way of which few in the nation probably were aware. A leading American prelate John Ireland, Archbishop of St. Paul, had been asked by the Vatican to negotiate a peace between Spain and the United States before hostilities began. Ireland's failure to effect a settlement may have played some role in Leo XIII's action on the Americanism issue which was in hot debate in Europe and which would have a major impact on the Paulist community. Detailed accounts of the failure of Ireland's mission of peace are given in: John Offner, "Washington Mission: Archbishop Ireland on the Eve of the Spanish-American War," *Catholic Historical Review* 73 (October 1987): 562–75 and John T. Farrell, "Archbishop Ireland and Manifest Destiny," *Catholic Historical Review* 33 (October 1947): 269–301. Farrell comments that Ireland's failure during the high point of the Americanism crisis produced repercussions.

81. James Gillis, Diary, February 21, 1898, Gillis Papers, PFA.

82. Ibid., December 31, 1896.

83. Gillis was not the only Brighton product present at St. Thomas. In fact, as described by Paul Robichaud, a Boston-Washington connection existed which resulted in several vocations for the Paulists. As mentioned previously Peter O'Callaghan found the Paulists by this route. More significant at the time was the presence of William Laurence Sullivan, who was one year senior to Gillis. He considered Sullivan a friend and mentions him on numerous occasions in his diaries and later in retreat notes. Although Sullivan does not mention Gillis in his autobiography (he fails to mention any of his Paulist contemporaries at St. Thomas), the close association

between these two men would lead to various questions later in their respective careers which would take completely different paths, in practice and theology. See Paul G. Robichaud, CSP, "Modernist Ghosts in the Hall of St. Thomas: The Paulists in Washington, D.C., 1902–1907," *Journal of Paulist Studies* 1 (1992): 44.

84. James Gillis, Diary, November 1, 1898, December 2, 1898, Gillis Papers, PFA. Gillis stated about his new role and responsibilities, "I must hold myself strictly to task in the future in these matters." Finley, Interview, April 6, 1994. Father Finley feels that Elliott was a great influence in the development of Gillis's ethics of personal conduct.

85. Pope Leo XIII, "*Testem Benevolentiae,*" in *Documents of American Catholic History* Vol. II, ed. John Tracy Ellis (Wilmington, Delaware: Michael Glazier, 1987), 538.

86. Many outstanding monographs, books and essays exist on the subject of Americanism. A sampling of the literature is: Thomas T. McAvoy, CSC, *The Great Crisis in American Catholic History, 1895–1900* (Chicago: Henry Regnery Company, 1957); Gerald P. Fogarty, SJ, *The Vatican and the Americanist Crisis: Denis J. O'Connell, American Agent in Rome, 1885–1903* (Rome: Gregorian University Press, 1974); Robert Emmett Curran, SJ, *Michael Augustine Corrigan and the Shaping of Conservative Catholicism in America, 1878–1902* (New York: Arno Press, 1978); Margaret Mary Reher, "Pope Leo XIII and 'Americanism'," *Theological Studies* 34 (1973): 679–89; Gerald Fogarty, "The Catholic Hierarchy in the United States Between the Third Plenary Council and the Condemnation of Americanism," *U.S. Catholic Historian* 11 (3) (Summer 1993): 19–35; Thomas E. Wangler, "Americanist Beliefs and Papal Orthodoxy: 1884–1889," *U.S. Catholic Historian* 11(3) (Summer 1993): 37–51; Margaret Mary Reher, "The Church and the Kingdom of God in America: The Ecclesiology of the Americanists" (Ph.D. diss., Fordham University, 1972).

87. Hennesey, *American Catholics,* 202.

88. The Paulist Superior General George Deshon had earlier asked Archbishop Corrigan to speak out against Charles Maignen and his book. Corrigan, however, refused the request. After the publication of *Testem,* Deshon directed *The Catholic World* to publish a pamphlet which stated that in time all Father Hecker's statements would be proven to be orthodox. Corrigan admonished Deshon for his efforts. See Curran, *Michael Augustine Corrigan,* 491–99.

89. James Gillis, Diary, February 23, 1899, Gillis Papers, PFA.

90. Curran, *Michael Augustine Corrigan,* 490–92.

91. In response to *Testem* Cardinal Gibbons wrote, "This doctrine, which I deliberately call extravagant and absurd, this Americanism as it has been called, has nothing in common with the views, aspirations, doctrine and conduct of Americans. I do not think in the whole country could be found a single bishop or priest or even a well-instructed layman who had ever put forward such extravagances. No, that is not, has never been and will never be our Americanism." See John Tracy Ellis, *The Life of James Cardinal Gibbons Archbishop of Baltimore 1834–1921* Volume II (Milwaukee: The Bruce Publishing Company, 1952), 71. John Ireland agreed with his progressive colleague in his comment: "It is the enemies of the Church in America and the faithless interpreters of the faith who 'imagine' that there exists or that some desire to establish in the United States a Church differing in one iota from the Holy and Universal Church...." See Marvin R. O'Connell, *John Ireland and the American Catholic Church* (St. Paul: Minnesota Historical Society Press, 1988), 463–64.

92. James Gillis, Foreword to *Americanism: A Phantom Heresy* by Abbé Felix Klein (Atchison, Kansas: Aquin BookShop, 1950), iii. Earlier in 1932 Gillis wrote, "If 'Americanism,' therefore, be understood to involve any slightest degree of disloyalty to the Church or any diminution of the Faith, there is not and there has not been any 'Americanism' in the lives or teachings of the Paulists." See Gillis, *Paulists,* 11. Gillis made similar statements throughout his public career. It must be noted that Gillis's natural reaction to defend the Paulists does not mean that Americanism did not exist. Recent scholarship has shown that the ideas condemned by Leo XIII in *Testem* were present in the writings and thought of contemporary Church leaders. See: Reher, "Pope Leo XIII and 'Americanism',": 679–89 and David P. Killen, "Americanism Revisited: John Spalding and *Testem Benevolentiae,*" *Harvard Theological Review* 66 (1973): 413–54.

93. "Pastoral Letter of 1884," in *Pastoral Letters of the United States Catholic Bishops* Vol. I., ed. Hugh J. Nolan (Washington, D.C.: National Conference of Catholic Bishops, United States Catholic Conference, 1984), #15, 215–16.

94. John J. Keane, "Loyalty to Rome and Country," *The American Catholic Quarterly Review* 15 (July 1890): 515.

95. John Ireland, "Catholicism and Americanism," appendix to *Catholic Principles of Politics,* by John A. Ryan and Francis J. Boland, CSC (New York: The Macmillan Company, 1940): 347.

96. James A. McFaul, "Catholic and American Citizenship," *North American Review* 171(September 1900): 321–22; Henry D. Sedgwick, "The United States and Rome," *Atlantic Monthly* 84 (October 1899): 447; William Barry, "The Troubles of a Catholic Democracy," *Contemporary Review* 76 (July 1899): 84. These are representative comments of a significant corpus of essays written at the turn of the century on this topic.

97. One example of Gillis's opinion which demonstrates a close connection between Catholicism and America was heard in a 1935 radio broadcast: "In all her long career of nineteen centuries the Catholic Church has never taken root in a more congenial soil or breathed a more favorable atmosphere than the soul and atmosphere of this youngest and freest of nations—America." James Gillis, "The Church and Democracy," "Catholic Hour" Broadcast, June 9, 1935, Gillis Papers, PFA.

98. James Gillis, Diary, May 5, 1899, May 4, 1899, Gillis Papers, PFA.

99. James Gillis, Retreat Notes 1899, Gillis Papers, PFA.

100. Ibid.

101. Ibid.

102. Walter Elliott to Sr. Camper, February 27, 1901, Elliott Papers, PFA.

103. Angelyn Dries, OSF, "Walter Elliott's Foundations for Evangelization," *Journal of Paulist Studies* 1 (1992): 7–9. Dries points out how often Elliott mentions St. Francis de Sales in his various published works. His confessional style followed that of the seventeenth-century French saint.

104. Walter Elliott, *A Retreat for Priests* (Washington, D.C.: The Apostolic Mission House, 1924), 168, 170; Elliott, *The Spiritual Life* (New York: Paulist Press, 1914), 132–33.

105. James Gillis, Meditation Books, November 18, 1900, Gillis Papers, PFA.

106. Ibid., December 14, 1901.

107. It is noteworthy that Gillis quoted Manning, an Englishman, and did not mention Cardinal Gibbons, who also wrote on the priesthood. Gibbons' monographs *The Faith of Our Fathers* (1876) and *Our Christian Heritage* (1889) were widely circulated and read by Catholic clergy. Section XXIX of *The Faith of Our Fathers* deals directly with the priesthood.

108. St. Thomas Handbook, 1890–1906, December 21, 1901, PFA.

109. James Gillis, Diary, December 21, 1901, Gillis Papers, PFA.

2. THE YOUNG PAULIST—1902–1910

1. James Gillis, "Editorial Comment," *Catholic World* 127 (May 1928): 332; John S. Kennedy, "Father Gillis's Fifty Years," *Catholic World* 174 (December 1951): 167. Gillis described Shahan, "He was a dear friend and such a prodigy of learning, commanding endless and diverse information, stimulating intellectual curiosity and a love of scholarship in anyone who worked with him." Although Gillis's academic record at The Catholic University is not available, University bulletins and catalogues show a variety of courses offered including hermeneutics, authorship of the Fourth Gospel, dogmatic questions, and moral questions from the *Summa Theologica*.
2. Finley, *James Gillis,* 68.
3. James M. Gillis, CSP, "The Christian Agape," *Catholic University of America Bulletin* 9(4) (October 1903): 467, 505.
4. A full discussion of Modernism in Europe is found in: Lester R. Kurtz, *The Politics of Heresy: The Modernist Crisis in Roman Catholicism* (Berkeley: University of Califiornia Press, 1986).
5. St. Thomas College Student Handbook 1890–1906, September 15, 1903, PFA.
6. Robichaud, "Modernist Ghosts," 44–48. William Walsh, Thomas Healey, and William Laurence Sullivan ultimately left the Paulists, but not until Searle had completed his term of office.
7. James Gillis, Diary, September 1, 1905, Gillis Papers; Paulist Mission Chronicles, Summer 1905, PFA.
8. James Gillis, Preaching Log, December 1901–March 1904, Gillis Papers, PFA.
9. James Gillis, Diary, September 1, 1905, Gillis Papers, PFA.
10. Gillis's extant retreat notes describe a tortured figure who sought "conversion" (he never fully defines what he means) so as to find interior peace. This personal transformation was never successfully completed.
11. James Gillis, Retreat Notes, August 1903, Gillis Papers, PFA.
12. Ibid.
13. James Gillis, Meditation Books, n.d. 1902, Gillis Papers, PFA.
14. James Gillis, Retreat Notes, August 27, 1902, Gillis Papers, PFA.
15. Ibid., August 25, 1902.
16. Ibid., August 21, 1902; August 25, 1902.
17. Stanley Ayling, *John Wesley* (Cleveland: William Collins Publishers, Inc., 1979), 306. Many monographs and books exist which describe the eighteenth-century "Great Awakening" and the beginnings of

Christian revivalism in the United States. See: Nathan O. Hatch and Harry S. Stout, eds., *Jonathan Edwards and the American Experience* (New York: Oxford University Press, 1988); Maximin Piette, *John Wesley and the Evolution of Protestantism* (New York: Sheed & Ward, 1937); John B. Boles, *The Great Revival 1787–1805* (Lexington: University of Kentucky Press, 1972); Timothy Smith, *Revivalism and Social Reform in Mid-Nineteenth Century America* (Nashville: Abingdon Press, 1957).

18. Jay P. Dolan, *Catholic Revivalism: The American Experience 1830–1890* (Notre Dame, Indiana: University of Notre Dame Press, 1978), xvi.
19. Ibid., 23–24, 185–204, 161.
20. Ibid., 111.
21. Ibid., 25–56; Jonas, *Divided Mind*, 87–88.
22. Quoted in Walter Elliott, CSP, *A Manual of Missions* (Washington, D.C.: The Apostolic Mission House, 1922), 145.
23. Farina, *American Experience of God*, 124.
24. James McVann, CSP, "The Beginnings of the Paulist Apostolate to Non-Catholics." Uncompleted STL diss., The Catholic University of America, 1932, Section II, Chapter IV, p. 1, McVann Papers, PFA.
25. Dries, "Walter Elliott's Foundations," 7–8; Jonas, *Divided Mind*, 198–200. A complete analysis of Walter Elliott's spirituality is given in Angelyn Dries, OSF, "The Whole Way into the Wilderness: The Foreign Mission Impulse of the American Catholic Church, 1893–1925" (Ph.D. diss., The Graduate Theological Union, Berkeley, 1990).
26. Jonas, *Divided Mind*, 171–206. This progressive thought was canonized with the publication of the following Vatican II documents: Decree on Ecumenism, Declaration on the Relationship of the Church to Non-Christian Religions, and the Declaration on Religious Freedom.
27. Elliott, *Manual of Missions*, 10.
28. McVann, "Beginnings of the Paulist Apostolate," Section II, Chapter V, p. 4, McVann Papers, PFA.
29. Bertrand L. Conway, CSP, *The Question Box* (New York: Paulist Press, 1929), v.
30. Elliott, *Manual of Missions*, 84–97, 171–96.
31. Ibid., 47.
32. St. Thomas College Student Handbook 1890–1906, March 12, 1904, PFA.
33. James Gillis, Retreat Notes, 1904, Gillis Papers, PFA. He wrote, "I

know of no one personally, nor can I think of any kind of sinner generically who is more near in danger of hell than I am....I confess before God that it is true."

34. Quoted in James Gillis, Retreat Notes, 1904, Gillis Papers, PFA.

35. Ibid.

36. When Gillis arrived Peter O'Callaghan, the one who had persuaded him to enter the community and who served as his first novice master, was pastor of the parish and superior of the mission band. O'Callaghan had come to Chicago the previous year when the Paulists opened Old St. Mary's. Gillis also shared the rectory with Elias Younan, the first Paulist he had ever met, the missionary who had gone to St. Charles in the fall of 1896.

37. James Gillis, Diary, December 11–18, 1904, Gillis Papers, PFA. Gillis does report the enthusiasm which he received but tempers it with comments on the "ungrateful" attitude of the people toward Father Dan Riordan, the pastor. Gillis says that Riordan returned the parish to financial solvency after Augustine Tolton, the first black Josephite priest, had economically ruined the parish. He refers to the parishioners as "impressionable poor people." Stephen Ochs in *Desegregating the Altar: The Josephites and the Struggle for Black Priests, 1871–1960* (Baton Rouge: Louisiana State University Press, 1990), 94–95 makes no mention of Tolton's financial mismanagement at St. Monica's. Rather he says the Josephite was removed for health reasons. Gillis's comments contrast sharply with his strident advocacy later in life for black Americans.

38. James Gillis, Diary, November 5, 1904, November 7, 1904, Gillis Papers, PFA. Gillis did not define a "whiskey punch," but a strong alcoholic jolt to the system is indicated.

39. Ibid., November 20–30, 1904.

40. Ibid., January 15, 1905.

41. Ibid., June 11, 1905.

42. James Gillis, Retreat Notes, June 1906, PFA.

43. Finley, *James Gillis*, 85.

44. James Gillis, Diary, September 1, 1905, Gillis Papers, PFA.

45. James Gillis, Retreat Notes, 1905, Gillis Papers, PFA.

46. James Gillis, Diary, September 1, 1905, Gillis Papers, PFA.

47. Ibid., October 8–15, 1905.

48. Ibid., October 29–November 26, 1905.

49 Ibid., May 7–14, 1906.

50. Ibid., June 1906.

51. James Gillis, Sermon, "The Church," November 1, 1904, Gillis Papers, PFA.

52. Ibid., "Be Not Wise in Your Own Conceits," 1905.

53. Ibid., "Temptation," June 1907.

54. Ibid., "New Year's Day," January 1, 1906.

55. Martin Marty, *The Irony of It All–1893–1919* (Chicago: University of Chicago Press, 1986), 183–84.

56. Quoted in Aaron I. Abell, *American Catholicism and Social Action: A Search for Social Justice 1865–1950* (Garden City, New York: Hanover House, 1960), 146.

57. Ibid.

58. St. Thomas College Student Handbook 1906–1911, June 11 and June 12, 1907; Consultor Meeting Minutes, June 22, 1907; St. Thomas Student Handbook 1906–1911, July 20, 1907, PFA.

59. Michael V. Gannon, "Before and After Modernism: The Intellectual Isolation of the American Priest," in *The Catholic Priest in the United States: Historical Investigation,* ed. John Tracy Ellis (Collegeville, Minnesota: St. John's University Press, 1971), 350. Gannon argues that Catholic intellectual pursuit did not regain life until the onset of Catholic action in the 1930s.

60. Appleby, *"Church and Age Unite!"* Appleby's monograph is the first full treatment of modernists in the American Church. The case of William Laurence Sullivan, CSP is fully described.

61. The *New York Review,* edited by James Driscoll, at St. Joseph's Seminary (Dunwoodie), was the most progressive American Catholic publication of its day. During its short life (1905–1908), it published the leading modernists and other progressive thinkers. The full history of the *Review* is found in: Michael DeVito, *The New York Review (1905–1908)* (New York: United States Catholic Historical Society, 1977).

62. Finley, interview, April 7, 1994.

63. Charles G. Herbermann, Edward A. Pace, Condé B. Pallen, Thomas J. Shahan, John J. Wynne, SJ, eds., *The Catholic Encyclopedia* (New York: Robert Appleton Company, 1907), s.v. "Bible Societies," by James Gillis. Gillis attacked Bible Societies for their violation of Catholic principles, such as their promotion of the idea that the Bible alone is sufficient for religious knowledge and their support for the concept of the validity of one's private interpretation of Scripture.

64. James Gillis, Retreat Notes, 1915 "Sincerity and Truth," and "Fearless Facing of Truth," Gillis Papers, PFA.

65. Ibid.

66. James Gillis, Retreat Notes, 1909, "Faith," Gillis Papers, PFA. Gillis's disappointment in the condemnation of Modernism and the promotion of neo-scholasticism must have prompted this outburst.

67. Robichaud, "Modernist Ghosts," 48. Finley, interview, April 7, 1994. Father Finley concurs with this statement.

68. James Gillis, Retreat Notes, 1915, "Sincerity and Truth," Gillis Papers, PFA.

69. James Gillis always understood himself as priest and although he had negotiated the major portion of his inner struggle with perfection, he still considered the sacerdotal life as *"noblesse oblige."* Gillis on numerous occasions, as late as 1924, wrote of G[eorge] T[yrrell] and Willy [William Laurence] Sullivan as men who could have been productive members of the Church if they had only been allowed to speak out. In an academic atmosphere Gillis privately supported Modernism. See Gillis Retreat Notes 1907, 1911, 1915, 1924, Gillis Papers, PFA.

70. St. Thomas College Student Handbook 1906–1911, September 16, 1907; James Gillis Preaching Log, September 17, 1907, Gillis Papers, PFA.

71. Finley, *James Gillis,* 92.

72. James Gillis, *The Paulists,* 66–67; Gillis Sermons, "Reception of the Habit," May 1, 1908 and May 26, 1909, Gillis Papers, PFA.

73. James Gillis, Diary, September 13, 1908, Gillis Papers, PFA.

74. Ibid., September 19, 1908.

75. General Chapter Log, 1904–1914, PFA. The Chapter met discontinuously from June 29 to July 31, 1909. From the outset a question existed as to the validity of the election for the New York mission band delegates. In June, 1909 John Harney was approached by a delegation led by Gillis and Bertrand Conway, who promised him a seat as a delegate at the chapter if he would agree to vote for John Hughes as superior general and Walter Elliott as first consultor. Gillis supported Elliott's effort to unseat Searle, who was considered too weak to deal with the diverse problems present in the Society. Harney, who supported Hughes but had reservations about Elliott, was shaken by the offer and reported it to Searle. The General, in turn, suspended the chapter for almost a month to allow an investigation to be completed and delegates to be elected without coercion. At the chapter the Gillis-Conway ticket was elected

with Hughes as general and Elliott, Thomas Daly, and John J. Burke as the consultors.

76. James Gillis, Preaching Log, August 9, 1909, Gillis Papers, PFA.
77. Finley, interview, April 7, 1994.
78. Ibid., "Perfection," 1909.

3. MISSIONARY TO AMERICA—1911–1922

1. Sydney E. Ahlstrom, *A Religious History of the American People* (New Haven: Yale University Press, 1972), 798. Strong was also an active voice in the anti-Catholic movement. He worried about the flood of Catholic immigrants into the country and questioned the double loyalty of Catholics in America. He stated, "Manifestly there is an irreconcilable difference between papal principles and the fundamental principles of our free institutions." Quoted in Edwin Scott Gaustad, *A Religious History of America* (San Francisco: Harper & Row, Publishers, 1990), 193–94.

2. Rauschenbusch's monographs *Christianity and the Social Crisis* (1907), *Christianizing the Social Order* (1912) and *A Theology for the Social Gospel* (1917) formed a synthesis of the social message of the prophets, the teachings of Jesus, and a plan for present reform and future possibilities. This message, which spanned the old and the new, the traditional and the progressive, forced society to see the horrors of the present situation and to seek their solutions.

3. Sean Dennis Cashman, *America in the Age of Titans: The Progressive Era and World War I* (New York: New York University Press, 1988), 1–5.

4. Arthur Stanley Link and Richard L. McCormick, *Progressivism* (Arlington Heights, Illinois: Harlan Davidson, Inc., 1983), 2.

5. Corruption in Tammany Hall is described in Jerome Mushkay, *Tammany: The Evolution of a Political Machine 1789–1865* (Syracuse: University of Syracuse Press, 1971) and Charles Henry Parkhurst, *Our Fight with Tammany* (New York: Arno Press, 1970). San Francisco's political machine of the Progressive Era is detailed in Walton Bean, *Boss Ruef's San Francisco: The Story of the Union Labor Party, Big Business and the Graft Prosecutions* (Berkeley: University of California Press, 1952).

6. Many other Catholic social programs were started at this time. Peter Dietz established his Militia of Christ for Social Justice in 1910 and followed it with the foundation of the Social Service Commission. In this same year the National Conference of

Catholic Charities (NCCC) was organized. This agency served to unify and promote the efforts of smaller Catholic charities that worked to foster justice. Other organizations in the period were The School for Social Studies, 1912, organized at Fordham University as part of Terence Shealy's retreat movement, and the Eunomic League, established in 1913, which gathered college graduates and professionals to discuss and scientifically examine social problems. The Catholic Colonization Society, formed in 1911 under the leadership of Archbishops John J. Glennon of St. Louis and Sebastian Messmer of Milwaukee, served as a source of information, gave direction, and assisted in the protection of Catholic settlers.

7. James Gillis, Retreat Notes, 1910, Gillis Papers, PFA.

8. Ibid.

9. Finley, *James Gillis*, 3.

10. Paul Robichaud, CSP, "The Very Reverend Superior General," *Paulist History* 4(1) (May 1994), 17–18.

11. James Gillis, Retreat Notes, 1921, Gillis Papers, PFA.

12. Jonas, *The Divided Mind*, 263.

13. Ibid., 135.

14. James Gillis, Retreat Notes, 1921, "The Priest's Sanctity," Gillis Papers, PFA.

15. St. Mary's was the home parish of Richard Burtsell, member of the *accademia* and friend of Father Edward McGlynn. Between 1886 and 1892 McGlynn conducted a running battle with his ordinary, Archbishop Michael Corrigan. McGlynn supported the "single tax" theory of Henry George. Corrigan told McGlynn to withdraw his support and later excommunicated the priest when he failed to comply. McGlynn was eventually reinstated by Archbishop Francesco Satolli, the first apostolic delegate in the United States, in December 1892. This struggle was seen as a victory for the progressives in the "Americanist" debate of the period. The best summary of the McGlynn-Corrigan conflict is found in Curran, *Michael Augustine Corrigan*, 168–394.

16. James Gillis, Preaching Log, October 2–December 18, 1910, Gillis Papers, PFA.

17. Ibid., March 5–19, 1911.

18. Ibid., January 1914. The three Paulists each chose a different section of the state in which to conduct their respective missions. Gillis began his tour in Fayetteville, which became for him "an oasis in a desert of bigotry and inhospitality." He then traveled to the rural communities of Bentonville and Rogers. He preached wherever he

could gain permission. Although the Arkansas tour was not successful, Gillis was not discouraged but, after a short respite, continued his regular mission schedule.

19. James Gillis, Sermon, "Opening to a Non-Catholic Mission," n.d., Gillis Papers, PFA.

20. Ibid., "Confession," n.d., "Judgment," n.d., "Sin," n.d.

21. Ibid., "Anti-Christ Scandal-Giver," n.d.

22. Ibid., "Zeal," n.d.

23. Ibid., "World, Flesh, Devil," n.d., "True Spirit of Inquiry," n.d.

24. Ibid., "True Spirit of Inquiry," n.d.

25. Ibid., "Divinity of Christ," n.d.

26. Ibid., "Character of Christ," n.d.

27. Ibid., "Ordination Sermon," n.d.

28. Christopher J. Kauffman, *Faith and Fraternalism: The History of the Knights of Columbus 1882–1982* (New York: Harper & Row, Publishers, 1982), 178–80; Debra Campbell, "A Catholic Salvation Army: David Goldstein, Pioneer Lay Evangelist," *Church History* 52 (September 1983): 323.

29. Lyle Dorsett, *Billy Sunday and the Redemption of Urban America* (Grand Rapids, Michigan: William B. Eerdmans Publishing Company, 1991), 113.

30. While Gillis was on the west coast he traveled and continued to preach, despite the advice of doctors. In Seattle he addressed a Columbus Day celebration hosted by the combined council of Knights of Columbus of Seattle. His topic was the "Catholic Church and Ally Principles." This is one of the few extant references to comments made by Gillis about the war raging in Europe. By this date the United States had entered the fray and thus most probably, considering the audience, Gillis's comments supported America's war effort. An earlier reference gives a different slant to his opinion on the war. In 1915 he wrote, "The battles of the jungle [the mission apostolate] are peace compared with this hideous European war—the war of the most highly civilized peoples that ever have [been] seen—That's the worst." The work of the Knights of Columbus during the war is fully described in Kauffman, *Faith and Fraternalism*, 190–227. See also Gillis, Retreat Notes, 1915, Gillis Papers, PFA.

31. General Chapter Notes 1919, PFA.

32. Ibid., June 25, 1919.

33. James Towey to Thomas Burke, July 17, 1919, Superior General Papers, PFA. See Paul Robichaud, "The Very Reverend Superior 1858–1978," *Paulist History* 4(1) (May 1994): 17–18, for additional details.

34. Joseph McSorley to Thomas Burke, August 20, 1919, Superior General Papers, PFA.

35. James Gillis to Thomas Burke, August 22, 1919, Superior General Papers, PFA.

36. Thomas Burke to Edward Mullaly, September 9, 1919; John Smyth to Thomas Burke, October 3, 1919; Peter Moran to Thomas Burke, September n.d., 1919, Superior General Papers, PFA. Extant correspondence shows that shortly after Burke appointed Gillis to publish mission assignments, some complaints against the latter's decisions were made by John Carter Smyth and Peter Moran. No serious animosities seem to have lingered.

37. James Gillis to Thomas Burke, July 22, 1919, Superior General Papers, PFA.

38. In the spring of 1917 Gillis, Conway, and fellow Paulist David Kennedy offered twelve two-week catechetical courses aimed toward non-Catholics. In September the Catholic Unity League, later reorganized as the Catholic Truth Society, was established. Its purpose was to finance lecture courses to non-Catholics in poor parishes, distribute free books and pamphlets to inquiring non-Catholics, and provide a lending library for Catholics. From the outset the group received the approbation of Cardinal Farley (and later Hayes) and Paulist Superior General John Hughes. Gillis's association was only part-time and began in 1919. See pamphlet "Catholic Unity League," 1917, Catholic Unity League Papers, PFA.

39. James Gillis to Thomas Burke, July 22, 1919, Superior General Papers, PFA.

40. The Knights of Columbus set up recreational facilities in the United States and Europe for use by American service personnel. This massive project was supported by both Church and government officials.

41. Douglas J. Slawson, *The Foundation and First Decade of the National Catholic Welfare Council* (Washington, D.C.: The Catholic University of America Press, 1992), 26–44. Slawson gives the most complete story of the formation of the NCWC. For a more detailed look at the involvement of Father Burke see: John B. Sheerin, *Never Look Back: The Career and Concerns of John J. Burke* (New York: Paulist Press,

1975), 36–55. The most complete history of the War Council's work is given in Michael Williams, *American Catholics in the War: National Catholic War Council 1917–1921* (New York: The Macmillan Company, 1921). The endeavors of all churches to aid the war cause is presented in John F. Piper, Jr., *The American Churches in World War I* (Athens, Ohio: Ohio University Press, 1985).

42. Joseph M. McShane, SJ, *"Sufficiently Radical": Catholicism, Progressivism, and the Bishops' Program of 1919* (Washington, D.C.: The Catholic University of America Press, 1986), 136–89. This monograph gives the complete history of the genesis of the 1919 NCWC document.

43. Quoted in Sirgiovanni, *An Undercurrent of Suspicion*, 21. The most complete analysis of this short but intense period in American history is found in Robert K. Murray, *Red Scare: A Study in National Hysteria 1919–1920* (Minneapolis: University of Minnesota, 1955).

44. Martin E. Marty, *The Noise of Conflict 1919–1941* (Chicago: University of Chicago Press, 1991), 59–79.

45. James Gillis to Thomas Burke, July 7, 1919, November 6, 1919, November 7, 1919, Gillis Papers, PFA.

46. James Gillis, *SS Santa Rosa* Log, June 23, 1920; Gillis to Thomas Burke, July 17, 1920, Gillis Papers, PFA.

47. Finley, *James Gillis*, 113.

48. James Gillis, *SS Santa Rosa* Log, June 27, 1920, Gillis Papers, PFA.

49. Philip Gibbs, *Now It Can Be Told* (New York: Harper & Brothers Publishers, 1920), vii.

50. Bishop John Cantwell of Los Angeles did not actually give the Paulists administration of this parish until 1928.

51. James Gillis, Preaching Log, November 27, 1921–December 18, 1921, Gillis Papers, PFA.

52. Ibid., January 1922.

53. Joseph Malloy to Thomas Burke, April 26, 1922, Superior General Papers, PFA.

54. General Chapter Notes 1922, PFA.

55. The 1922 chapter was important for the Paulists in other ways. Burke reinitiated the process started by Augustine Hewit to achieve Roman approbation of the Society. The Church of Santa Susana in Rome was obtained by the Paulists in 1922, a procurator general was assigned, and a new constitution was adopted in 1923. Later, Burke established a Paulist novitiate to formalize the first stages of Paulist religious formation and conform to Roman directives.

4. "WHAT PRICE PROSPERITY?"—1923–1932

1. David A. Shannon, *Between the Wars: America 1919–1941* (Boston: Houghton Mifflin Company, 1965), 93–95. By 1918 all states had established some requirements for youth attendance at schools. Not until 1960, however, did all fifty states require attendance to age sixteen.

2. Alan Dawley, *Struggles for Justice: Social Responsibility and the Liberal State* (Cambridge: Harvard University Press, 1991), 5.

3. James Gillis, "Creedless Christianity," *The Missionary* 42(12) (December 1928): 431–35.

4. James Gillis to Thomas Burke, July 20, 1922, Superior General Papers, PFA.

5. John J. Burke, CSP, "The Catholic World," *Catholic World* 101 (April 1915): 8; McVann, "The Beginnings of the Paulist Apostolate," Chapter V, p. 5, McVann Papers, PFA. See also O'Brien, *Isaac Hecker*, 200–01. Hecker's brother George financed the magazine, John R.G. Hassard, formerly of the New York *Tribune,* served as managing editor, and Lawrence Kehoe handled the business side of the journal. Hecker attempted to avoid internal Church controversy in the magazine, but he did respond to anti-Catholicism. O'Brien states, "The *Catholic World* fit less into Hecker's plan of direct evangelization than into his effort to awaken priests and laity to more zealous and intelligent concern for their own religion."

6. The Catholic press was born in nineteenth-century America in a spirit of apology to defend doctrine and to answer calumnies. Charleston, South Carolina's first Catholic prelate John England founded the *United States Catholic Miscellany* in 1822 with this understanding. The immigrant nature of American Catholicism in the nineteenth century was also a major catalyst to the foundation of newspapers and periodicals. Boston's *Pilot,* was originally titled *The Irish and Catholic Sentinel* and served as the organ for the immigrant Irish Catholics of the city. The Catholic press of this period has been characterized as "swashbuckling" in its boisterous and at times daring essays and editorials. This approach became "subdued and reserved, if not completely docile," after the publication of *Testem Benevolentiae* in 1899 and *Pascendi Dominici Gregis* in 1907. See John G. Deedy, "The Catholic Press," in *The Religious Press in America*, ed. Martin E. Marty (New York: Holt, Rinehart and Winston, 1963), 71.

7. For all practical purposes, Hewit had been the official editor of *The Catholic World* since approximately 1870. During Hecker's trips to

Europe for Vatican I and later for an extended period to regain his health the journal was placed in Hewit's hands. Even upon Hecker's return Hewit was the mainstay of the magazine.

8. William L. Lucey, SJ, "Catholic Magazines: 1865–1880," *Records* 63(1): 25; Sheerin, *Never Look Back,* 22.

9. Sheerin, *Never Look Back,* 31–32.

10. Gillis's conservative stance was in opposition to liberal intellectuals, who found a haven in New York City and Columbia University. American liberalism has been labeled "a surrogate socialism" in that it fought the evils of industrial capitalism. See Gary Gerstle, "The Protean Character of American Liberalism," *The American Historical Review* 99(4) (October 1994): 1045, 1048–49.

11. Halsey, *The Survival of American Innocence,* 64.

12. Deedy, "The Catholic Press," 88.

13. Martin J. Bredeck, *Imperfect Apostles: The Commonweal and the American Catholic Laity 1924–1976* (New York: Garland Publishing, Inc., 1988), 5.

14. The complete story of *The Commonweal* from 1924 to 1974 is told in Rodger Van Allen, *The Commonweal and American Catholicism: The Magazine, The Movement, The Meaning* (Philadelphia: Fortress Press, 1974).

15. Thomas E. Blantz, CSC, *George N. Shuster: On the Side of Truth* (Notre Dame, Indiana: University of Notre Dame Press, 1993), 63.

16. St. Peter's was a two-year college (juniorate) which operated between 1927 and 1968, and served as a feeder school for St. Paul's College in Washington.

17. James Gillis, "Editorial Comment," *Catholic World* 116 (October 1922): 137–40.

18. Consultor Minutes, October 6, 1923; General Chapter 1924, Summary Paper of Superior General Joseph McSorley to "Fathers" [Superiors], PFA.

19. Joseph McSorley to Henry F. Ridley, CSP, September 9, 1925, Superior General Papers, PFA.

20. Consultor Minutes, March 11, 1924, PFA. The minutes do not give any indication why Smyth's appointment was considered "inadvisable."

21. Joseph McSorley to James Gillis, July 17, 1926; James Gillis to Joseph McSorley, October 31, 1928, Superior General Papers, PFA.

22. General Chapter Minutes, 1917; Consultor Minutes, January 13, 1925; General Chapter Minutes, 1932, PFA.

23. James Gillis to Joseph McSorley, February 10, 1927, October 31, 1928, Superior General Papers, PFA.

24. Ibid., October 31, 1928. Gillis reported that $10,000 in annual paid subscriptions would make the magazine profitable. The magazine's continual deficit operation shows that this goal was not achieved.

25. Financial Statement 1928, Superior General Papers, PFA. The $12,000 profit was reported between January 1, 1927 and December 31, 1928. The Apostolic Mission House also reported a profit of more than $24,500 for calendar year 1927.

26. Finley, interview, April 7, 1994; A.J. Nevins, "The Catholic Press in the United States," in *Twentieth Century Catholicism: A Periodic Supplement to the Twentieth Century Encyclopedia of Catholicism,* ed. Lancelot Sheppard (New York: Hawthorn Books, 1966), 34.

27. Gillis's traditional stands on moral values, the right of parents to educate their children, rejection of anti-Catholic animus, and promotion of the compatibility of Catholicism and American democracy were held by the leading Catholic voices of the day.

28. Gillis was critical and his opinion was clear, but he was civil and professional in his writing. He valued the right of others to state different views, but he believed that some ideas were clearly wrong and should not be promulgated to an easily impressionable American people.

29. Finley, interview, April 6, 1994.

30. Halsey, *The Survival of American Innocence,* 1–84. Halsey says that after World War I, "[American] Catholics attempted to construct a world impervious to the disruptions of modernity and determined to preserve the receding boundaries of American innocence." Catholics set out to defend the promises of American idealism which were threatened by various forms of irrationalism: probability in scientific thought, the subconscious in psychology, skepticism in literature, and relativism in law and morality. This defense was centered in neo-scholasticism, a philosophy in which James Gillis was educated and which he promoted. He called neo-scholasticism the philosophy of common sense and "the stone that was rejected by the builders." See James Gillis, "Limits of Logic," *Catholic World* 118 (November 1923): 146 and Gillis, "Wanted: A Guide, Philosopher and Friend," *Catholic World* 125 (June 1927): 369. Halsey goes further and shows how Catholics turned their isolation from the prevailing disillusionment of society into unexpected opportunities. The Catholic retreat before World War I was thus transformed into Catholic action, resurgence, and awakening. Halsey cites historians

Sydney Ahlstrom and Robert Handy who described the period after the war as "post-Protestant America." It was the time for Catholics to take the initiative and become more assertive.

31. Santayana viewed the war as a puberty rite which transformed the world from innocence to experience, from callousness to tragedy. Pound wrote of the catastrophic waste which the war had created, a condition which had bled the younger generation dry and returned the nation to the corruption of earlier days.

32. James Gillis, "Editorial Comment," *Catholic World* 116 (October 1922): 142–43.

33. Ibid., 116 (November 1922): 282.

34. Ibid., 283.

35. Van Allen, *The Commonweal,* 17.

36. Ibid., 14–32.

37. "Editorial Opinion," *America* 33 (July 1925): 352.

38. Joseph McSorley to James Gillis, July 20, 1927, Superior General Papers, PFA.

39. General Chapter Notes, 1927 and 1929, PFA. There is no extant documentation as to why the Advisory Board, after being appointed, was not actually constituted.

40. General Chapter Notes 1929, PFA.

41. General Chapter Notes 1932; John Harney to James Gillis, July 4, 1932; Harney to Joseph Malloy, July 4, 1932, Superior General Papers, PFA. There is no indication, however, that these "associate editors" had any influence on the content of *The Catholic World* or its editorial slant. The journal remained under the control of Gillis for his entire tenure as editor. Harney's action was most likely a means to demonstrate his belief that the community needed no "superstars," but rather functioned better when all members worked for common goals.

42. James Gillis to Lawrence Rose, February 4, 1925, Engagements 1922–1925, Gillis Papers, PFA.

43. James Gillis, *False Prophets* (New York: Paulist Press, 1925), 5, 9.

44. Ibid., 20–44.

45. Ibid., 150, 143. Richard Reed in his essay "James M. Gillis, C.S.P. Editor," in *Contemporary Catholic Authors* (November 1940) gave a rousing endorsement to Gillis's book: "*False Prophets* should be a *vade mecum* for every informed Catholic and for every intelligent Christian who meet people who have been so attracted by the honeysuckle of such doctrine that they have not examined it closely enough to discover it is intertwined with poisoning."

46. Gillis, *False Prophets,* 201.
47. James Gillis, "Voltaire," *Catholic World* 120 (February 1925): 577–88; "Edward Gibbon," *Catholic World* 120 (March 1925): 775–77; "Tom Paine," *Catholic World* 121 (April 1925): 57; "'Bob' Ingersoll," *Catholic World* 121 (May 1925): 218; "To Believe or Not to Believe," *Catholic World* 121 (June 1925): 374.
48. Consultor Minutes, December 16, 1924, PFA.
49. Ibid.
50 Ibid., March 17, 1925.
51. It is probable that the use of the Star-Spangled Banner on the opening program did more than show the Paulist tradition. It also demonstrated anew Catholicism's commitment to national principles in the wake of the June 1, 1925 Supreme Court decision which had invalidated the Oregon School Law of mandatory public education for children 8–16 years of age.
52. James Gillis, "Editorial Comment," *Catholic World* 122 (October 1925): 119; Consultor Minutes, November 3, 1925, PFA.
53. Finley, *James Gillis,* 120–21; WLWL Correspondence, n.d. 1932, PFA. The extant sources do not give specifics on why WLWL was forced to shift frequencies. Its religious programming and noncommercial status may have been factors, although this is only conjecture.
54. Charles J. Tull, *Father Coughlin and the New Deal* (Syracuse: Syracuse University Press, 1965), 1–22; Alan Brinkley, *Voices of Protest: Huey Long, Father Coughlin and the Great Depression* (New York: Vintage Books, 1983), 90–92.
55. James Gillis, WLWL Talks "Radio Question Box," October 1925–February 1926, PFA; Gillis, "Editorial Comment," *Catholic World* 125 (June 1927): 407.
56. James Gillis, WLWL Talks, November 3, 1925, November 10, 1925, November 17, 1925, Gillis Papers, PFA.
57. Ibid., February 23, 1926.
58. Ibid., March 2, 1926, March 9, 1926, April 20, 1926, July 20, 1926.
59. James Gillis, "Editorial Comment," *Catholic World* 125 (July 1927): 553; Blantz, *George N. Shuster,* 78, 30–31; George N. Shuster, *The Catholic Spirit in America* (New York: Dial Press, 1927), 103; Michael Williams, "The Present Position of Catholics in the United States" (New York: Calvert Publishing Co., 1928), 47.
60. John Rager, *Democracy and Bellarmine* (Shelbyville, Indiana: Quality Print, Inc., 1926), Moorhouse F.X. Millar, *Unpopular Essays in the Philosophy of History* (New York: Fordham University Press, 1928),

Sylvester McNamara, *American Democracy and Catholic Doctrine* (Brooklyn: International Catholic Truth Society, 1924), and Frederick Kinsman, *Americanism and Catholicism* (New York: Longman, Green, and Co., 1924) were representative authors of the period who supported O'Rahilly's thesis.

61. James Gillis, "Editorial Comment,"*Catholic World* 117 (May 1923): 253–55; Gillis, WLWL Talks, July 6, 1926, Gillis Papers, PFA.

62. Winfred Ernest Garrison, *Catholicism and the American Mind* (Chicago: Willett, Clark & Colby, 1928), 169–70; John M. Lenhart, OFM, Cap., "Genesis of the Political Principles of the American Declaration of Independence," *Central Blatt and Social Justice* 24–25 (September and October 1932): 155–56, 191–94.

63. Shuster, *Catholic Spirit in America*, 108–10; Michael Williams, *Catholicism and the Modern Mind* (New York: Dial Press, 1928), 125.

64. James Gillis, WLWL Talks, December 6, 1926, PFA; Gillis, "Editorial Comment," *Catholic World* 118 (March 1924): 835.

65. James Gillis, "The Ku-Klux Klan," *Catholic World* 116 (January 1923): 433.

66. R. Laurence Moore, *Religious Outsiders and the Making of Americans* (New York: Oxford University Press, 1986), 150–72.

67. James Gillis, "Editorial Comment," *Catholic World* 118 (February 1924): 697.

68. James Gillis, *The Catholic Church and the Home* (New York: The Macmillan Company, 1928), 73.

69. James Gillis, "Editorial Comment," *Catholic World* 118 (February 1924): 695; 126 (February 1928): 689–91; Gillis, *Catholic Church and the Home*, 24.

70. Gillis, *Catholic Church and the Home*, 37.

71. James Gillis, WLWL Talks, January 3, 1928, Gillis Papers, PFA. Gillis's belief that America's moral fibre was being torn was echoed by historian William E. Leuchtenburg, *The Perils of Prosperity 1914–32* (Chicago: University of Chicago Press, 1958), 78. He writes, "The nation [during the period 1914–32] had lost its fear of the wrath of God. It no longer had the same reverence for the old mores, and it was determined to free itself from the harsh imperatives of religious asceticism." In general he calls the 1920s a period of "assault on traditional standards" in America.

72. James Gillis, "Editorial Comment," *Catholic World* 117 (October 1923): 117–18; Gillis, WLWL Talks, December 20, 1927, PFA.

73. Gillis, *Catholic Church and the Home*, 64.

74. Jeffrey M. Burns, *American Catholics and the Family Crisis 1930–1962* (New York: Garland Publishing, Inc., 1988), 5, 12–21.

75. Gillis, *Catholic Church and the Home*, 77–93.

76. James Gillis, "Editorial Comment," *Catholic World* 119 (April 1924): 123.

77. Ibid., 118 (December 1923): 399–406.

78. Ibid., 122 (November 1925): 259–60.

79. Ibid., 122 (October 1925): 117–18; Gillis, WLWL Talks, December 6, 1927, Gillis Papers, PFA.

80. James Gillis, "Editorial Comment," *Catholic World* 132 (January 1931): 488.

81. Ibid., 130 (November 1929): 226. Russell was known for his rejection of the proofs of God, disdain for theology, promotion of non-religious humanism, and polemics against Christian religious bodies.

82. James Gillis, WLWL Talks, May 25, 1926, July 20, 1926, October 10, 1926, October 11, 1926 and January 10, 1927, Gillis Papers, PFA; Gillis, "A Theistic Basis of Morality," *Religious Education* 27(6) (June 1932): 507, 510.

83. The 1920s was a period where American Catholics fought long and hard to safeguard their right to educate their children. Two major drives, one by the federal government and the other by religious bigots of the Scottish-Rite Masons and the Ku-Klux Klan, aimed, in the minds of Catholics, to take away this right. Throughout the decade a series of bills was introduced into Congress to create a federal department of education. Led by its General Secretary John J. Burke, CSP, the NCWC opposed each federal initiative. The complete story of this effort is given in Douglas Slawson, "The Attitudes and Activities of American Catholics Regarding the Proposals to Establish a Federal Department of Education Between World War I and the Great Depression" (Ph.D. diss., The Catholic University of America, 1981). The other battle for American Catholics and education was fought on different fronts over the same issue—the desire by some to make public education mandatory. The principal case, and the one which decided the issue in favor of private education, was the Oregon School Case of 1922. Led by the Masons and Klan, an initiative was passed by Oregon's voters in November 1922 which required all children from ages 8–16 to attend public schools. The law was immediately challenged by the Church. The NCWC again led the fight which resulted in the law's rejection by the United States Supreme Court in June 1925. Several good essays describe the events of this case. The most recent is Thomas J. Shelley, "The

Oregon School Case and the National Catholic Welfare Conference," *Catholic Historical Review* 75 (July 1989): 439–57. In both cases the Church argued, not from a religious point of view, but from the inherent right of parents to choose for their children.

84. James Gillis, "Editorial Comment," *Catholic World* 116 (November 1922): 286; 122 (December 1925): 404–06. Gillis's views on academic freedom were more fully outlined in later years. See chapters 5, 6, and 7 for more details.

85. Ibid., 123 (April 1926): 112–18; 123 (May 1926): 263–64. Gillis's view was widely held by leading Catholic voices. John A. Ryan, who initially backed the legislation, withdrew his support when he saw that the initiative was ineffective and even detrimental. See Francis L. Broderick, *Right Reverend New Dealer: John A. Ryan* (New York: The Macmillan Company, 1963), 165–85.

86. James Gillis, "Editorial Comment," *Catholic World* 123 (April 1926): 112–18.

87. Ibid., 119 (June 1924): 409; 117 (July 1923): 541; 116 (March 1923): 833; 120 (October 1924): 114.

88. Many Americans, including most American Catholics, felt the United States had a better chance of avoiding war in its rejection of the League of Nations. The treachery, lies, and innuendo which was part and parcel to the formation of the League did not sit well with Americans. Gillis expressed these same concerns on many occasions. See Shannon, *America Between the Wars,* 7–15.

89. J. Leonard Bates, *The United States 1898–1928* (New York: McGraw-Hill Book Company, 1976), 296.

90. James Gillis, WLWL Talks, October 9, 1928, May 18, 1926, Gillis Papers, PFA; Gillis, "Editorial Comment," *Catholic World* 117 (August 1923): 686. This treaty was signed by over 40 nations in an attempt to legislate war out of existence.

91. James Gillis, WLWL Talk, March 16, 1926, Gillis Papers, PFA.

92. Wilfrid Parsons, SJ, *The Pope and Italy* (New York: The American Press, 1929), 1. Parsons said Mussolini was due honor "for his determination to see it [the Lateran Treaty] through."

93. James Gillis, "Editorial Comment," *Catholic World* 122 (March 1926): 838–40; 117 (May 1923): 261–62. Gillis said that the Pope was the only person in Italy who possessed the courage to speak out against Mussolini. See also William Barry Smith, "The Attitude of American Catholics Towards Italian Fascism Between the Two World Wars" (Ph.D. diss., The Catholic University of America, 1969), 85. Barry writes, "*Catholic World* seems to have taken

the most decisive stand against Italian Fascism from the very beginning."

94. Francis Clement Kelley, founder of the Catholic Church Extension Society (1905), was involved in the problems in Mexico from 1914 when he had served as a representative of exiled Mexican bishops to President Woodrow Wilson. In the 1920s and beyond Kelley denounced the Calles' government in numerous articles. His 1935 monograph *Blood Drenched Altars* was written to arouse American support for action in Mexico. His biographer calls him Mexico's "Guardian Angel." See James P. Gaffey, *Francis Clement Kelley & The American Catholic Dream*, Volume II (Bensonville, Illinois: The Heritage Foundation, Inc., 1980), 3–103.

95. Shuster, *Catholic Spirit in America*, 281.

96. James Gillis, WLWL Talks, February 23, 1926, PFA; Gillis, "Editorial Comment," *Catholic World* 123 (September 1926): 836–43.

97. James Gillis, *Sursum Corda* #86, "The Biggest Experiment of All," June 16, 1930, Gillis Papers, PFA.

98. James Gillis, *Sursum Corda* , "The Soviet Idea of Fair Play," December 23, 1929, Gillis Papers; WLWL Talks, October 15, 1931, May 8, 1930, PFA.

99. General Chapter Notes 1924; James Gillis Preaching Log, October 27, 1924, Gillis Papers; Gillis to McSorley, October 19, 1925; McSorley to Gillis, November 3, 1925, Superior General Papers, PFA. Gillis remained as a board member of the Society of St. Paul of New Jersey and the Universal Broadcasting Corporation which was the parent body for WLWL. In retrospect, it seems clear that Gillis's reasons for resigning the consultor position had more to do with his inability or lack of desire to serve than overwork since he continued to add more responsibilities to his already heavy slate of public activities.

100. James Gillis, Preaching Log, January 9–March 27, 1927, Gillis Papers; Joseph McSorley to Paulist Community, April 23, 1927, Superior General Papers, PFA. Gillis's father died from injuries incurred in an automobile accident.

101. Gillis's incessant activity and intensity caused another one of his many breakdowns of health. In May 1928 he left on the *Leviathan* for Europe and the baths at Karlsbad. He spent six weeks there in an effort to regain his health after another outbreak of his painful psoriasis. See James Gillis, Preaching Log, May 5, 1928, Gillis Papers; Gillis to McSorley, June 10, 1928, Superior General Papers, PFA.

102. James Gillis, Preaching Log, November 12, 1928, Gillis Papers; Gillis, *Sursum Corda* #1, "What's Right with the World," October 22, 1928, Gillis Papers, PFA.

103. James Gillis, *Sursum Corda* #161, "It Always Did Clear Off," November 23, 1931; #37, "O Ye of Little Faith!", July 8, 1929; WLWL Talk, May 26, 1932, Gillis Papers, PFA; Gillis, "Editorial Comment," *Catholic World* 135 (September 1932): 742.

104. James Gillis, "Why the Encyclical on Christian Marriage," *Catholic Action* 14 (July 1932): 5–6; WLWL Talk, January 8, 1931, Gillis Papers, PFA.

105. James Gillis, *Sursum Corda* #53, "The Censorship in Boston," October 28, 1929; WLWL Talk, January 15, 1929, Gillis Papers, PFA.

106. Gillis claimed that a conservative estimate of 30,000 speakeasies in New York City alone paid an equally conservative amount of $100 weekly as protection money in order to operate free of the law. Taken nationally the amount of capital wasted in such activity was immoral. Gillis was also angered that Congress talked "dry" yet lived "wet." Such hypocrisy, combined with Hoover's refusal to take a stand, led to many comments by Gillis. See James Gillis, "Editorial Comment," *Catholic World* 133 (April 1931): 104; WLWL Talk, January 9, 1930, Gillis Papers; Pamphlet "Prohibition—Speak, Mr. Hoover!" (New York: Paulist Press, 1930), PFA.

107. James Gillis, *Sursum Corda* #41, "The Beast That Refuses to Return to the Jungle," August 5, 1929; "Editorial Comment," *Catholic World* 130 (February 1930): 746.

108. James Gillis, "Editorial Comment," *Catholic World* 128 (December 1928): 358.

109. Smith was not liked for reasons other than his Catholicism. He represented the immigrant voice against the Yankee spirit and was seen as a big city slicker against common rural people. Most important, Smith openly advocated a "wet" policy and criticized the prohibition standard. Gillis claimed that it was Smith's honesty, as well as the prevailing religious bigotry, which led to his defeat.

110. James Gillis, WLWL Talks, February 27, 1930, October 8, 1931 October 22, 1931, PFA.

111. James Gillis, WLWL Talks, January 23, 1930, October 22, 1931; *Sursum Corda* #66, "The State Above God?", January 27, 1930, Gillis Papers, PFA.

112. James Gillis, *Sursum Corda* #160, "Rights and Responsibilities,"

November 16, 1931; Gillis, WLWL Talk, November 6, 1930, Gillis Papers, PFA.

113. Shannon, *Between the Wars*, 109–11.

114. James Gillis, Sermon, "What Price Prosperity?", January 6, 1929, Gillis Papers, PFA; "Editorial Comment," *Catholic World* 128 (February 1929): 617.

115. James Gillis, *Sursum Corda* #31, "Europe Looks at America," May 27, 1929, Gillis Papers, PFA.

116. James Gillis, WLWL Talks, November 28, 1929, December 5, 1929, Gillis Papers, PFA.

117. The 1920s was a period when the Catholic mission to rural America began in earnest. The National Catholic Rural Life Conference was established in 1923 through the efforts of Edwin O'Hara and William Howard Bishop. O'Hara was also responsible for initiating the Confraternity of Christian Doctrine in rural areas. Lay evangelism through the efforts of people like David Goldstein and Martha Moore Avery became popular as well. See Timothy Michael Dolan, *"Some Seed Fell on Good Ground": The Life of Edwin V. O'Hara* (Washington, D.C.: The Catholic University of America Press, 1992), Christopher J. Kauffman, *Mission to Rural America: The Story of W. Howard Bishop, Founder of Glenmary* (New York: Paulist Press, 1991), and Debra Campbell, "A Catholic Salvation Army: David Goldstein, Pioneer Lay Evangelist," *Church History* 52 (September 1983): 322–32, as examples of works which describe this period, its people, and the mission to rural America.

118. In an uncharacteristic move, Gillis, at the 1929 General Chapter, asked to be removed as chairman of the Committee on Missions "because of the pressure of his work." General Chapter Notes, 1929, PFA.

119. Annual Report of the NCWC Administrative Committee Chairman, November 1930, pp. 6–7, Archives, The Catholic University of America (hereafter ACUA).

120. Smyth was upset about "The Catholic Hour" usurping the purpose and ministry of WLWL. Dolle was able to have John J. Burke, NCWC General Secretary, intercede for him and calm Smyth's fears. See Charles Dolle to J.F. Burke, September 21, 1929, Catholic Hour Correspondence, ACUA.

121. Members of the committee were: Very Rev. Edward Fitzgerald, OP, of Catholic University, Rev. Thomas Chetwood, SJ, of Georgetown University, Rev. John K. Cartwright of St. Patrick's Parish in Washington, D.C., Revs. George Johnson and John A.

Ryan of the NCWC and Rev. Joseph Malloy, CSP, of the Apostolic Mission House in Washington. See Karl Alter to J.J. Burke, March 13, 1930, NCWC General Secretary Papers, ACUA.

122. James Gillis, *The Ten Commandments* (New York: Paulist Press, 1931). Gillis's 1930 "Catholic Hour" talks were edited and collected in this book.

123. James Gillis, "Catholic Hour" Broadcast, "Citizens and Aliens," November 13, 1932.

124. Ibid., "The Individual and the Organization," December 11, 1932.

125. Earlier extant material does exist where Gillis gave his view on America's racial issue. For example in 1930 he stated, "Race hatreds are artificial, and have to be artificially stimulated." James Gillis, Sermon, April 13, 1930, Gillis Papers, PFA.

126. James Gillis, "Catholic Hour" Broadcast, "White Man & Black," November 20, 1932; Sermon to Catholic Students Mission Crusade, October 12, 1932, PFA.

127. Charles E. Coughlin, "Christ or Chaos" and "Internationalism," in *Father Coughlin's Radio Sermons, October 1930–April 1931 Complete* (Baltimore: Knox and O'Leary, 1931), 100, 131; Coughlin, "The Secret Is Out," in *Father Coughlin's Radio Discourses, 1931–1932* (Royal Oak, Michigan: The Radio League of the Little Flower, 1932), 174.

128. James Gillis, "Editorial Comment," *Catholic World* 129 (June 1929): 360; 134 (December 1931): 363.

5. THE GUARDIAN OF AMERICA—1933–1941

1. Shannon, *Between the Wars,* 109. The misery of the Depression is described in: Anthony J. Badger, *The New Deal: The Depression Years, 1933–40* (New York: Hill and Wang, 1989).

2. See chapter 4, note 128. For Gillis and many others Roosevelt was an answer to prayer.

3. James Gillis, *Sursum Corda* #234, "Have We a Dictator?", April 17, 1933, Gillis Papers, PFA.

4. James Gillis, "Editorial Comment," *Catholic World* 138 (October 1933): 6. Gillis wrote, "We [Catholicism] are not wedded to it. We owe it no special loyalty....If capitalism reforms, we shall give it another trial. But the reform must be radical."

5. Shannon, *Between the Wars,* 149.

6. The Agricultural Adjustment Act (AAA) of May 13, 1933, the first branch of the three-pronged attack, aimed to establish a better

balance between the prices of agricultural products (which had dropped so significantly and in the process bankrupted many farmers) and industrial products so as to bring them into the same ratio as existed in the period 1909–1914. The legislation did raise farm prices, but the renewed prosperity of farmers eventually forced sharecroppers off the land with a consequent loss of livelihood. Unemployment was attacked by the establishment of the Federal Emergency Relief Administration and the Public Works Administration (PWA) which both produced numerous government jobs. Initially, however, in order to free capital for use in the economy the Emergency Banking Act was passed by Congress on March 9, which was followed by the more "reform"-minded legislation of the Glass-Steagall Banking Act in June 1933, which established the Federal Deposit Insurance Corporation (FDIC) to insure funds and restore consumer confidence.

7. General Hugh S. Johnson, administrator of the NRA, worked with committees representing each industry. Fair codes of practice within the industry, which were desired by capital, were worked out as well as setting labor standards which in many cases eliminated sweat shops and child labor. Before the codes were negotiated Johnson asked the nation to accept an interim blanket code which set work standards of 35–40 hours per week, a minimum pay of 30–40 cents per hour, and the elimination of child labor.

8. Roosevelt appointed James Farley (New York) as Postmaster General and Thomas Walsh (Montana) as Attorney General.

9. Roosevelt had effectively quoted from the two foundational social encyclicals, *Rerum Novarum* (1891) and *Quadragesimo Anno* (1931), in his campaign speeches, which misled many into thinking that the New Deal was based on the Church's social teaching. Roosevelt was a shrewd politician and courted the Catholic vote throughout his administration. David O'Brien has correctly stated, "The New Deal was essentially a political procedure seeking simultaneously to satisfy the frantic demands of savagely conflicting interests and to reestablish a workable economic order." See O'Brien, *American Catholics and Social Reform*, 234.

10. Several authors have fully discussed the support given by the Church to the initial efforts of Roosevelt. See O'Brien, *American Catholics and Social Reform*, 47–69; Flynn, *American Catholics and the Roosevelt Presidency*, 36–60, 78–102; Abell, *American Catholicism and Social Action*, 230–40. It should be noted that not all Catholics supported the New Deal, even in this early stage. Al Smith and Frederick Kenkel, editor

of the Central Verein's *Central Blatt and Social Justice,* for example, saw Roosevelt's policy as socialism.

11. Broderick, *Right Reverend New Dealer,* 211–43.

12. Thomas Blantz, CSC., *A Priest in Public Service: Francis J. Haas* (Notre Dame, Indiana: The University of Notre Dame Press, 1982), 66–88.

13. WLWL File, January 26, 1933, Gillis Papers, PFA.

14. James Gillis, Preaching Log, January–March 1933, Gillis Papers; T.L. O'Neil to John Harney, April 11, 1933, Superior General Papers, PFA.

15. James Gillis, *Sursum Corda* #234, "Have We a Dictator?", April 17, 1933, Gillis Papers, PFA.

16. Ibid., #255, "What of the NRA?", September 11, 1933.

17. Beginning with the October 1933 issue of *The Catholic World,* the editorial section of the magazine was placed first, rather than toward the back where it had always previously been situated. Additionally, the editorials received titles. Whether this shift of format was intended to highlight Gillis's editorials, sensing that they were a major draw for subscriptions, or to show his personal control of the magazine is not clear. It is certain, however, that the decision to make the format shift was his. Since October 1922 *The Catholic World* was James Gillis.

18. James Gillis, "Editorial Comment," *Catholic World* 138 (October 1933): 3.

19. James Gillis, WLWL Talk, September 20, 1934, Gillis Papers, PFA.

20. James Gillis, "Editorial Comment," *The Catholic World* 139 (April 1934): 6.

21. James Gillis, WLWL Talk, September 20, 1934, Gillis Papers, PFA.

22. James Gillis, *Sursum Corda* #330, "Live and Learn," February 18, 1935, Gillis Papers, PFA.

23. James Gillis, "Editorial Comment," *Catholic World* 141 (July 1935): 387–88.

24. Abell, *American Catholicism and Social Action,* 251; "Organized Social Justice," in *American Catholic Thought on Social Questions,* ed. Aaron I. Abell (New York: The Bobbs-Merrill Company, Inc., 1968), 386.

25. James Gillis, "Editorial Comment," *Catholic World* 141 (September 1935): 648.

26. Famous personalities in the Liberty League included Al Smith, John J. Raskob, James Beck, John W. Davis, and business leaders Alfred Sloan and William Knudsen of General Motors, J. Howard

Pew of Sun Oil Company, and Sewell Avery of Montgomery Ward. The complete history of the Liberty League is told in George Wolfskill, *The Revolt of the Conservatives: A History of the Liberty League, 1934–1940* (Boston: Houghton Mifflin, 1962).

27. Richard S. Kirkendall, *The United States 1929–1945: Years of Crisis and Change* (New York: McGraw-Hill Book Company, 1974), 55–67. A complete analysis of Roosevelt's foes during the New Deal period is found in George Wolfskill and John A. Hudson, *All But the People: Franklin D. Roosevelt and His Critics, 1933–1939* (New York: Macmillan, 1969).

28. James Gillis, "Starve or Steal?", *The Mother of Sorrows* (June 1936): 12; Gillis, "Editorial Comment," *Catholic World* 138 (October 1933): 3; 138 (December 1933): 260–61; Flynn, *American Catholics and the Roosevelt Presidency,* 30, 32. Gillis repeated his arguments often and interlaced them with the common theme that democracy did not need capitalism to survive.

29. James Gillis, "Editorial Comment," *Catholic World* 139 (July 1934): 391; Gillis, WLWL Talk, April 26, 1934, Gillis Papers, PFA.

30. James Gillis, "Catholic Hour" Broadcast, "Life, Liberty and the Pursuit of Happiness," November 20, 1938, Gillis Papers, PFA.

31. Ibid., "Hegelianism: The State as God," November 24, 1935.

32. O'Brien, *American Catholics and Social Reform,* 60. Also see: Patrick J. McNamara, "A Study of the Editorial Policy of the Brooklyn *Tablet* Under Patrick F. Scanlan, 1917–1968" (M.A. thesis, St. John's University, New York, 1994), 45–87.

33. O'Brien, *American Catholics and Social Reform,* 58–60, 155–60; Blantz, *George Shuster,* 80. Initially both Blakely and Parsons supported Roosevelt's New Deal in line with the majority of Catholics. Blakely feared that federal authority was reducing the states to dependency on Washington and was destroying the traditional American form of government. Parsons saw the New Deal as a transition move, a pause between laissez-faire and some form of collectivism. He, like Blakely, feared greater federal control. *The Commonweal* was more conciliatory in its opinion, seeing much of the New Deal as partial implementation of the precepts of *Quadragesimo Anno.*

34. Brinkley, *Voices of Protest,* 119–23; Tull, *Father Coughlin,* 75–100.

35. Tull, *Father Coughlin,* 59–103. The "Sixteen Principles" emphasized the living wage, right of private property, government control of money, right of labor to organize, and the priority of human rights over property rights.

36. Ibid., 102–03.

37. James Gillis, "Editorial Comment," *Catholic World* 138 (March 1934): 647.

38. Ibid.

39. Ibid., 142 (February 1936): 515; John A. Ryan, "An Open Letter to the Editor," *Catholic World* 143 (April 1936): 23.

40. Coughlin on June 19, 1936 announced his support for the Union Party with Representative William Lemke of North Dakota as its candidate for President and former Massachusetts Attorney General Thomas O'Brien for Vice President. Although Coughlin vigorously campaigned for the ticket, the party failed to muster one million popular votes or carry any state in what proved to be a Roosevelt landslide.

41. Roosevelt's victory was the most lopsided since the election of James Monroe in 1820. He carried every state save Maine and Vermont, with a plurality of nearly eleven million votes.

42. James Gillis, "Editorial Comment," *Catholic World* 144 (December 1936): 265. Gillis as discussed above believed in the necessity of reform, but he was still wary of Roosevelt's method. He wrote, "I am in the position of one who is eager for social and economic reform, but a little bit—to tell the truth a little bit more than a little bit— uneasy about the Rooseveltian method of accomplishing reform."

43. A good summary of the Court packing case, for Roosevelt and his enemies, is given in Wolfskill and Hudson, *All But the People*, 259–64.

44. James J. Kenneally, "Catholicism and the Supreme Court Reorganization Proposal of 1937," *Journal of Church and State* 25(3) (Autumn 1983): 470–75.

45. James Gillis, "Editorial Comment," *Catholic World* 145 (May 1937): 130, 134–36.

46. James Gillis, "Catholic Hour" Broadcast, "Jesus to Pilate," December 31, 1939; Gillis, *Sursum Corda* #471, "Einstein and Ethics," November 1, 1937, Gillis Papers, PFA.

47. McSorley was assigned by Harney as superior of the Toronto house in 1929 after the chapter. McSorley wanted to succeed Elliott Ross at the Columbia Newman Center, but was removed from New York (most probably) to dampen his influence.

48. John Harney to James Towey, October 15, 1934, Superior General Papers, PFA. Harney indicates further in his letter that this was his general approach to leadership: "Father Gillis is not the only one whom I treat in this fashion. It is my way of dealing with all the

brethren, as a rule, though occasionally, especially in making appointments and assignments, I may speak as one having authority."

49. James Gillis, "Catholic Hour" Broadcast, "The Fifth Freedom: From the Mass Mind," November 16, 1941, Gillis Papers, PFA.

50 James Gillis, *Sursum Corda* #331, "The Glands Theory of Crime," February 25, 1935; Gillis, "Catholic Hour" Broadcast, "Freedom of Conscience," May 26, 1935, Gillis Papers, PFA. Gillis often criticized the work of Clarence Darrow, who often represented clients with a defense centered on the idea that the accused was not responsible for his actions.

51. James Gillis, Speech to National Conference of Women's Retreat Movement, July 4, 1937, Gillis Papers, PFA.

52. Gillis did, however, continue his diatribe against birth control, using the principal argument that such a practice was racial suicide. The passage of the 21st Amendment, abrogating prohibition and the Volstead Act, prompted him to ask for government regulation of the sale and licensing of liquor. He also continued to promote temperance and voluntary total abstinence. See Gillis, *Sursum Corda* #240, "Will They Wake Up?", May 29, 1933; #600, "Voila L'Ennemi," June 17, 1940; WLWL Broadcast, December 21, 1933, Gillis Papers, PFA.

53. James Gillis, *Sursum Corda* #445, "How [to] Suppress Lynching?" May 3, 1937; Gillis, WLWL Talk, April 15, 1937, Gillis Papers, PFA.

54. James Gillis, *Sursum Corda* #278, "Immoral Movies: Exhibit A," February 19, 1934, Gillis Papers, PFA.

55. Through the efforts of Bishop John Cantwell of Los Angeles, the Legion of Decency was formed in November 1933 to monitor films and to pressure motion picture makers into producing films of better quality and greater moral integrity. An episcopal committee, chaired by John T. McNicholas of Cincinnati, supervised the Legion's operations, which were so highly successful that in June 1934 Hollywood producers, who felt the loss of revenues from the absence of Catholics at films, petitioned the bishops and asked for direction. Within two years all United States dioceses had a chapter of the Legion, which evaluated movies and published results for the faithful. The complete story of the Legion is told in James M. Skinner, *The Cross and the Cinema: The Legion of Decency and the National Catholic Office of Motion Pictures, 1933–1970* (Westport, Connecticut: Praeger Publications, 1993). See also John T. McNicholas, "The Episcopal Committee and the Problem of Evil Motion Pictures," *The Ecclesiastical Review* 91(2) (August 1934): 113–19 and

Hugh C. Boyle, "The Legion of Decency: A Permanent Campaign," *The Ecclesiastical Review* 91(4) (October 1934): 367–70.

56. James Gillis, "Editorial Comment," *Catholic World* 144 (March 1937): 645–50; 143 (July 1936): 390; Gillis, Catholic Hour Broadcast, "Free Thought, Free Speech, Free Press," May 19, 1935, Gillis Papers, PFA.

57 James Gillis, *Sursum Corda* #464, "Primary Function of the Catholic Press," September 13, 1937; Gillis, "Ethics in the Reading Content of Catholic Magazines," Speech to the Catholic Press Association, May 21, 1931; "Plea for a More Personal Journalism," Speech to the Catholic Press Association, May 24, 1935; Gillis Papers, PFA.

58. James Gillis to Evelyn Richmond, March 4, 1936, *Catholic World* Papers, PFA.

59. *The Catholic World* continued throughout the 1930s to run in the red. Annual deficits for the magazine during the period 1933 to 1940 ranged from $13,839.22 in 1933 to $11,821.95 in 1940. General Chapter Notes (Financial Reports), 1934, 1937, and 1940, PFA.

60. Gillis possessed a faithful staff who aided but never impeded the editor's efforts. Katherine Crofton, who from her letters seemed to idolize Gillis, served as his editorial assistant, running the office and answering correspondence in his absence which was frequent due to his many outside speaking engagements. Margaret Walsh was his secretary. Fellow Paulists Joseph McSorley and Joseph Malloy served as associate editors. Since McSorley and Malloy are never found in correspondence it is uncertain exactly what their role was. Their assignment by the 1932 General Chapter may have been more to appease community members who thought Gillis required some restraints than to give him help with the physical task of editing the magazine.

61. James Gillis, "Without Religion No University," *Catholic World* 153 (July 1941): 462, 465–67; Gillis, "Editorial Comment," *Catholic World* 140 (December 1934): 259; Gillis, Sermon, "Dedication of St. Madeline's Church and School," n.d., Gillis Papers, PFA.

62. James Gillis, WLWL Talk, October 18, 1934; Gillis, "A Philosophy of Life," Lecture to Wisconsin Catholic Club Women's Conference, May 11, 1933, Gillis Papers, PFA.

63. James Gillis, *Sursum Corda* #627, "Pity Poor President Butler," October 28, 1940; Gillis, WLWL Talk, March 26, 1936; Gillis, Catholic Hour Broadcast, "Academic Freedom," June 2, 1935; Gillis, WLWL Talk, November 7, 1935, Gillis Papers, PFA.

64. The story of Catholic Action in the United States is long and is painted with the sweat, tears and faith of many, only a few of whom history well remembers. In brief summary the better known movements and principals were: The National Conference of Catholic Women (NCCW) and the National Conference of Catholic Men (NCCM) under the NCWC worked directly under the hierarchy. The Liturgical Movement, fostered most notably by Dom Virgil Michel, OSB, fostered the concept of the Mystical Body of Christ which brought the laity into greater participation in the celebration of the Eucharist. *Orates Fratres* (1926) (presently *Worship*) was the Movement's major organ. The Young Christian Workers (YCW or Jocists) fostered a means of Christian formation through the living of ordinary life. Its threefold purpose was the formation of youth, service, and representation. Its method for action was "Observe, Judge, Act." The Catholic Family Movement (CFM), headed by Pat and Patty Crowley, was started in 1943 and aimed at adult education and service. The Cana Movement (1943) was a program of retreats for couples. The Grail Movement (1944) promoted worldwide spiritual renewal for women in the Church. Alternate forms of Catholic Action were the Catholic Worker Movement, headed by Dorothy Day and Peter Maurin, and Friendship House, founded by Baroness Catherine de Hueck-Doherty. The Catholic Worker (May 1, 1933) had a threefold approach of round-table discussions, houses of hospitality, and farming communes. Friendship House (Harlem 1938) supported the black community with services and education. Numerous resources describe Catholic Action and the other efforts of social Catholicism during this period. A good summary of the movements and their context within American Catholicism is Debra Campbell, "The Heyday of Catholic Action and the Lay Apostolate, 1929–1959," in *Transforming Parish Ministry: The Changing Roles of Catholic Clergy, Laity, and Women Religious,* ed. Jay P. Dolan (New York: Crossroad, 1989), 222–52. Numerous essays and books exist on individual movements and peoples. For example see Debra Campbell, "Part-time Female Evangelists of the Thirties and Forties: The Rosary College Catholic Evidence Guild," *U.S. Catholic Historian* 5(3–4) (1986): 371–83.
65. David O'Brien, *Public Catholicism* (New York: Macmillan, 1989), 170. O'Brien says that Ryan's "Economic Democracy" became the centerpiece of official Catholic social teaching.
66. "Statement of the Archbishops and Bishops of the Administrative Board, NCWC, on the Church and Social Order," in *Our Bishops*

Speak, ed. Raphael Huber (Milwaukee: The Bruce Publishing Company, 1952), 324–43.

67. James Gillis, *Sursum Corda* #388, "The King in the Slums," March 30, 1936; Gillis, Catholic Hour Broadcast, "The Attitude of the Church Toward Economic Experiments," December 9, 1934, Gillis Papers, PFA.

68. David Gordon to Douglas Woodruff, April 12, 1939, Superior General Papers, PFA. Gillis knew Dorothy Day and was a regular visitor at the Mott St. house of hospitality. Gordon wrote, "Father Gillis is the principal clerical supporter in this country of the lady Dorothy Day." Day in turn lauded Gillis, "We [at the Catholic Worker] are grateful to you for your generosity and grateful too for all the writing and saying [*sic*] all over the country. I have seen the effects of your work on my west coast trip. You are truly a pillar [of] strength." Dorothy Day to Gillis, July 1, 1942, Gillis Papers, PFA.

69. James Gillis, "Editorial Comment," *Catholic World* 139 (August 1934): 515; "Father Gillis Urges Active Faith," *The Voice* 14(9) (June 1937): 6; Gillis, "Editorial Comment," *Catholic World* 137 (April 1933): 103.

70. O'Brien, *American Catholics and Social Reform,* 110–19; Blantz, *Francis Haas,* 47–65; John C. Cort, "The Association of Catholic Trade Unionists and the Auto Workers," *U.S. Catholic Historian* 9(4) (Fall 1990): 335–51.

71. James Gillis, WLWL Talks, January 29, 1931, March 5, 1936, Gillis Papers, PFA; Gillis, "Editorial Comment," *Catholic World* 145 (July 1937): 385–89. Recall that the Wagner Act had mandated the formation of the NLRB, which supported trade unions.

72. John Cronin, SS, to Gillis, July 1, 1937, Gillis Papers, PFA.

73. The attitude of Catholics toward slavery and abolition found its justification in Scripture (Paul's Letter to Philemon, for example) which does not condemn domestic slavery. Additionally, Catholics also based their opinion on material reasons including the fear of losing what position they had attained in American society and economic considerations. The classic text which describes this situation is Madeline Hooke Rice, *American Catholic Opinion in the Slavery Controversy* (New York: Columbia University Press, 1944). For a more detailed look at the Catholic attitude toward the abolitionist movement see Gilbert Osofsky, "Abolitionists, Irish Immigrants and the Dilemma of Romantic Nationalism," *American Historical Review* 80 (October 1975): 889–912; Douglas C. Riach, "Daniel O'Connell and American Anti-Slavery," *Irish Historical*

Studies 20 (March 1976): 3–25; Walter G. Sharrow, "John Hughes and a Catholic Response to Slavery in Antebellum America," *Journal of Negro History* 57 (July 1972): 254–69. The sad story of the efforts to promote black vocations to the priesthood is told in Ochs, *Desegregating the Altar.*

74. Cyprian Davis, OSB, *The History of Black Catholics in the United States* (New York: Crossroad, 1990). Davis gives the most complete history of black Catholics in America. For details on the various black lay organizations of the first half of the twentieth century see pages 238–54. On Daniel Rudd see Joseph H. Lackner, S.M., "Dan A. Rudd. Editor of the *American Catholic Tribune,* from Bardstown to Cincinnati," *Catholic Historical Review* 80(2) (April 1994): 258–81.

75. James Gillis, "Christian Thinking Is Way to Peace," *Catholic Mind* 36 (March 8, 1932): 89.

76. The best complete history of the Conference is found in Teresa Hruzd, "The Northeast Clergy Conference for Negro Welfare, 1933–1944" (M.A. thesis, University of Maryland, College Park, 1990). The Conference operated between 1933–1944, only dissolving when the war mentality of the nation turned hearts and minds to issues other than social justice for blacks.

77. James Gillis, review of *Interracial Justice,* by John LaFarge, SJ, in *Catholic World* 145 (June 1937): 370–71.

78. Founding members included LaFarge, Gillis, John J. Burke, CSP, Joseph Corrigan, rector of Overbrook Seminary in Philadelphia, Cardinal John Dougherty of Philadelphia, Archbishops John Floersh (Louisville) and John McNicholas (Cincinnati), Bishops Thomas Malloy of Brooklyn, Wilfrid Parsons, SJ, and Louis Pastorelli, SSJ, Superior General of the Josephites.

79. The Conference's stated aims were: (1) To bring to clergy and religious a better understanding of the Negro apostolate, (2) to arouse in the clergy a general interest in the spiritual welfare of the Negro, to give or provide a periodic sympathetic attitude toward those who work in this ministry, to give an understanding of problems which beset the Negro. The work of the Conference was not to decide controversial issues. See Meeting Minutes, Northeastern Clergy Conference for Negro Welfare, John LaFarge Papers, Archives Georgetown University (hereafter AGU); *Our Province* 5(12) (1937): 8–9, Archives Josephite Fathers (hereafter AJF).

80. Thomas J. Harte, *Catholic Organizations Promoting Negro-White Relations in the United States* (Washington, D.C.: The Catholic University of America Press, 1947), 137–39; Meeting Minutes of Northeastern

Clergy Conference for Negro Welfare, March 20, 1934, LaFarge Papers, AGU; *Our Province* 5(12) 1937: 8–9, AJF.

81. James Gillis, Speech to Catholic Interracial Council of New York, May 20, 1934, CIC New York Papers, ACUA.

82. Hruzd, "Northeast Clergy Conference," 37–38; Meeting Minutes of Northeastern Clergy Conference on Negro Welfare, October 12, 1935, LaFarge Papers, AGU. Gillis said that statements which condemned such practices as lynching were not sufficiently bold since this practice was already universally condemned by right-thinking people. In order for people to take note the Conference had to speak louder and more forcefully than the general public.

83. Meeting Minutes of the Northeastern Clergy Conference for Negro Welfare, April 11, 1934, LaFarge Papers, AGU.

84. Ibid., May 9, 1934, December 11, 1934, October 12, 1935. John Harney, CSP Press Release, March 17, 1934, WLWL Correspondence; James Gillis, WLWL Talk, March 22, 1934; Gillis, *Sursum Corda* #286, "Independent Catholic Radio," April 16, 1934, Gillis Papers; General Chapter Notes 1934, PFA. Gillis's presumption of the availiability of WLWL for the promulgation of the Conference's message is somewhat suspect because of the precarious status of the station. As related earlier, WLWL maintained a running battle with federal commissions, which resulted in reducing the station's allotted broadcast time. The financial status of the station was another problem; it had always operated in the red and the community's resources to make up the shortfall were overstretched.

85. *Our Colored Missions* 21(5) (May 1935): 66, AJF; John Lafarge, Speech "Interracial Progress," LaFarge Correspondence; Meeting Minutes of Northeastern Clergy Conference for Negro Welfare, May 6, 1936, LaFarge Papers, AGU. WLWL's financial burden on the Paulists eventually forced an agreement with CBS in December 1935 where the network rented the station and allotted WLWL thirty minutes each evening with ninety minutes on Sunday. In March 1937 the Paulists sold WLWL to Arde Bulova, the wrist watch tycoon, for $275,000. In the station's final broadcast, June 16, 1937, Gillis sadly stated, "To me it is pain—to you I believe it is at least a matter of regret."

86. James Gillis, Radio Talks, October 13, 1935, April 24, 1938; WLWL Talk, January 30, 1936; Gillis Papers, PFA. The basic facts of the Scottsboro case are as follows: In July 1931 two white women, avowed prostitutes, were allegedly raped by nine black youths aboard a freight car that all had "hopped" near Scottsboro,

Alabama. Several trials, all of which ended in conviction and the punishment of death, were finally overturned.

87. It must be remembered that Gillis wrote for the NCCM in his column; his was not the final say on approval. Thus, his tone was less caustic and condemnatory.

88. James Gillis, *Sursum Corda* #394, "The Catholic and the Negro," May 11, 1936; #498, "Waking Up to the Negro Problem," May 9, 1938, Gillis Papers, PFA.

89. As a note of comparison *America* during the same period published twenty-five essays or editorials on the black issue through the influence of John Lafarge.

90. Meeting Minutes of the Northeastern Clergy Conference for Negro Welfare, February 1, 1938, LaFarge Papers, AGU.

91. James Gillis, "Editorial Comment," *Catholic World* 137 (August 1933): 609–14; Gillis, WLWL Talks, October 11, 1933, September 27, 1934, Gillis Papers, PFA.

92. James Gillis, "Editorial Comment," *Catholic World* 141 (April 1935): 9. An excellent chronology and analysis of American foreign policy at this time is: Robert Dallek, *Franklin D. Roosevelt and American Foreign Policy, 1932–1945* (New York: Oxford University Press, 1979).

93. Leo V. Kanawada, Jr. *Franklin D. Roosevelt's Diplomacy and American Catholics, Italians and Jews* (Ann Arbor, Michigan: UMI Research Press, 1982), 4.

94. Ibid., 8–9; Flynn, *American Catholics and Social Reform,* 123–49; Blantz, *George Shuster,* 84; Wilfrid Parsons, SJ, "An Open Letter to M. Litvinov," *America* 50 (November 4, 1933): 107–08.

95. Recognition was given with the proviso that the Soviets would soften their stand against public worship. This condition was placed in the agreement as a result of Catholic pressure on Roosevelt. See Kanawada, *Roosevelt's Diplomacy,* 3.

96. There are no extant sources where Gillis expressed any reaction to America's recognition of the Soviet Union. His public silence is unusual, but certainly does not mean that he approved of the move.

97. James Gillis, *Sursum Corda* #378, "War a Matter of Morals," January 20, 1936; Gillis WLWL Talk, October 31, 1935, Gillis Papers, PFA; Gillis, "Editorial Comment," *Catholic World* 142 (November 1935): 136–37; 143 (May 1936): 138; Diggins, *Mussolini and Fascism,* 300–01. Diggins suggests that *The Catholic World* was the only Catholic periodical to take an uncompromising stance critical of Italy in the Italo-Ethiopan War.

98. Charles Brodrick to Gillis, January 25, 1936, Gillis Correspondence; Joseph Trivisonno to John Harney, May 27, 1936, Superior General Papers; Frank Hall to Gillis, January 24, 1936, *Sursum Corda* Correspondence, PFA.

99. In May 1936 Paulist Superior General John Harney was informed that the Italian consulate in New York had placed the Paulist Fathers "and particularly Gillis" under observation. In July Harney was told that a representative for the Secretary of the Sacred Congregation of Extraordinary Ecclesiastical Affairs had contacted the Paulists in Rome upset about Gillis's May *Catholic World* editorial and May 7 WLWL talk, both of which attacked Mussolini. See Gillis to Katherine Crofton, May 11, 1936; Thomas O'Neill to Harney, June 19, 1936, Harney to Gillis, July 2, 1936, Superior General Papers, PFA.

100. Flynn, *American Catholics and Roosevelt,* 150.

101. Kanawada, *Roosevelt's Diplomacy,* 23; Flynn, *American Catholics and Roosevelt,* 32–36, 170–72. The NCWC issued two separate statements on the crisis. "Anti-Christian Tyranny in Mexico" (November 1934) called for an end to United States indifference. "Government's Silence on Mexico" (May 1935) called on the President to be consistent in his defense of the principles of freedom of conscience, religious worship, and education. America could not be blind to the removal of these freedoms in Mexico. See Huber, *Our Bishops Speak,* 205–09, 307–09.

102. E. David Cronon, "American Catholics and Mexican Anti-Clericalism," *Mississippi Valley Historical Review* 45 (1958–1959): 206. See also: Douglas Slawson, "The National Catholic Welfare Conference and the Mexican Church-State Conflict of the Mid-1930's: A Case of *déjà vu,*" *Catholic Historical Review* 80 (January 1994): 58–96.

103. Kanawada, *Roosevelt's Diplomacy,* 30–35; Kauffman, *Faith and Fraternalism,* 306. The full story of the Knights' campaign in Mexico is given by Kauffman in pages 287–314.

104. James Gillis, *Sursum Corda* #317, "What Say Mr. Daniels?", November 19, 1934, Gillis Papers, PFA.

105. James Gillis, WLWL Talk, November 1, 1934, Gillis Papers, PFA; Gillis, "Editorial Comment," *Catholic World* 142 (March 1936): 643–44.

106. James Gillis, WLWL Talk, May 14, 1936; Gillis, *Sursum Corda* #342, "The Bishop Has a Name for It," May 13, 1935, Gillis Papers, PFA.

107. The Neutrality Act stated that once a world conflict was "recognized" as such by the President, an embargo was then placed on war materials to all belligerents in the particular struggle. Thus shortly after the onset of hostilities in Spain, Roosevelt "recognized" the war with the consequent result of the imposition of the embargo.

108. Allen Guttmann, *The Wound in the Heart: America and the Spanish Civil War* (New York: The Free Press of Glencoe, 1962), 3. Guttmann states, "The Loyalist government was supported because it was thought to be legal, constitutional, republican, [and] liberal democratic."

109. Robert L. Frank, "Prelude to Cold War: American Catholics and Communism," *Journal of Church and State* 34(1) (Spring 1992): 48. Frank writes, "In their unceasing attacks on the 'communist' nature of the Loyalist government in Spain, Catholics viewed themselves as the lone defenders of those human rights that constitute the essence of democracy."

110. *The Commonweal* shifted its position on the Spanish conflict several times. Initially the managing editor, George Shuster, felt it was impossible to support Franco and his Fascist beliefs. An April 1937 editorial promulgating this stance received rapid criticism from many Catholic sources, including Talbot at *America*. Michael Williams, who feared financial ruin for the magazine (which at this time was not economically sound), shifted the journal's position in a series of open letters that supported Franco. Shuster, who could not support the new policy, left the magazine. Still later in 1938, growing opposition to Williams' stand led the magazine's officers to initiate a second coup. Williams was removed as editor and the magazine took a neutral position. Considered soft on Communism by some, *The Commonweal's* neutral position was criticized by Coughlin, John T. McNicholas, and Michael Ready, NCWC General Secretary. See David J. Valaik, "American Catholic Dissenters and the Spanish Civil War," *Catholic Historical Review* 53 (January 1968): 537–55 and Blantz, *George Shuster*, 84–88.

111. James Gillis, "Editorial Comment," *Catholic World* 145 (June 1937): 261.

112. James Gillis, *Sursum Corda* #460, "The Catholic Press Shows the Way," August 16, 1937; #549, "There Are No Accidents," May 1, 1939, Gillis Papers, PFA.

113. Frederick Wentz, "American Catholic Periodicals React to Nazism," *Church History* 31 (1962): 401–06. Wentz states, "The

attitude [of Catholics toward the Nazis] was one of complacency compared with Protestant thinking and compared with the Catholic response to other foreign affairs."

114. James Gillis, WLWL Talks, November 23, 1933, September 27, 1934, Gillis Papers, PFA.

115. James Gillis, "Editorial Comment," *Catholic World* 139 (May 1934): 129–32; Gillis, WLWL Talk, December 5, 1935, Gillis Papers, PFA.

116. "Father Gillis Urges Active Faith," *The Voice* 14(9) (June 1937): 5, ASF.

117. James Gillis, *Sursum Corda* #249, "Wisdom Where You Don't Expect It," July 31, 1933; Gillis, WLWL Talk, February 22, 1934, Gillis Papers, PFA.

118. James Gillis, *Sursum Corda* #420, "We're Out: Let Us Stay Out," November 9, 1936, Gillis Papers, PFA.

119. Gillis gave the following five-point plan: (1) Forbid the sale of arms and munitions by Americans to any warring nation, (2) send no food or goods to nations at war, (3) forbid Americans to travel or to remain in countries at war, (4) forbid loans or credits by Americans to warring nations, (5) if war comes, let an income tax on war profits be so high that no one will profit from the conflict. See Gillis, *Sursum Corda* #427, "How Not to Go to War," December 28, 1936, Gillis Papers, PFA.

120. Manfred Jonas, *Isolationism in America 1935–1941* (Ithaca, New York: Cornell University Press, 1966), 21–24.

121. Ibid., 148 (October 1938): 1–6. In an interesting contrast Charles Coughlin during this same period corresponded with "Il Duce," supporting the dictator's policies fully. The priest wanted to complete some type of formal agreement, but Mussolini was cautioned to stand clear lest any such pact look bad in the eyes of Americans. See Philip V. Cannistraro and Theodore P. Kovaleff, "Father Coughlin and Mussolini: Impossible Allies," *Journal of Church and State* 13 (1971): 427–43.

122. James Gillis, *Sursum Corda* #443, "Japan: Phenomenon: Portent?", April 19, 1937; #472, "Fancy Talk About Morals," November 8, 1937, Gillis Papers, PFA; Gillis, "Editorial Comment," *Catholic World* 150 (March 1940): 647–48. Japan was a great trading partner with the United States. Gillis realized that the scrap iron purchased would probably be made into instruments of war.

123. James Gillis, "The Brotherhood of Man," Radio Talk, April 24, 1938; Gillis, *Sursum Corda* #282, "Conscience and War," March

19, 1934; #313, "Aren't We All Responsible for War?", October 22, 1934, Gillis Papers, PFA. It should be noted that Gillis, unlike his friend Dorothy Day, did not believe in Christian pacifism. He wrote, "In the last analysis not peace but war, not law and order but anarchy would be the outcome of extreme pacifism." See Gillis, "Editorial Comment," *Catholic World* 139 (July 1934): 389.

124. Jacques Maritain, "Just War," *The Commonweal* 31 (December 22, 1939): 199–200.

125. James Gillis, "Editorial Comment," *Catholic World* 150 (February 1940): 513–21; 150 (March 1940): 645–46.

126. James Gillis, *Sursum Corda* #659, "The Heat of Defense," June 9, 1941, Gillis Papers, PFA.

127. James Gillis, "Editorial Comment," *Catholic World* 146 (December 1937): 257–60. Gillis referred to Roosevelt's tough talk against Japanese aggression in China.

128. James Gillis, *Sursum Corda* #545, "None of Our Business," March 27, 1939; "Editorial Comment," *America* 61 (July 29, 1939): 373.

129. James Gillis, "Editorial Comment," *Catholic World* 147 (April 1938): 4; 150 (October 1939): 6; 150 (November 1939): 135; 150 (December 1939): 258; 153 (April 1941): 4.

130. Ibid., 149 (July 1939): 391–92.

131. L.G. McPhillips to "The Catholic World," Gillis Correspondence, January 2, 1940, PFA.

132. Joseph Menendez to K. Crofton, January 2, 1940, Gillis Correspondence, PFA. Menendez was *Catholic World's* business manager. He wrote to Crofton to inform her of the cancellations and included this quote as an example of the opinion of those angered by the editorials.

133. "Neutrals and Truth About War," *Tablet* (London) 174 (December 2, 1939): 631–32. Douglas Woodruff, editor of London's *Tablet*, said that Gillis "over-reaches himself" in efforts to show the dubious nature of the war and English involvement. Cardinal Arthur Hinsley, Archbishop of Westminster, also criticized Gillis for his stand on neutrality. See Gillis to Hinsley, January 2, 1940, Gillis Correspondence, PFA.

134. Frank Hall to Margaret Walsh, October 4, 1940, *Sursum Corda* Correspondence, Gillis Papers, PFA. Two theories exist in the literature as to why Gillis harbored such a grudge against the British. Arnold Lunn suggested in 1941 that Gillis's attitude was latent Irish animosity toward England. Martin Cyril D'Arcy, SJ, the British priest and philosopher, relates a story of how when Gillis

was leading a group of American Catholics on a tour of England, he was asked to speak at a banquet. Gillis's talk was eloquent and spoke of ties between English and American Catholics. Hilaire Belloc in response said, "The first thing one's got to remember is that there's no more relation between the American Catholic and English Catholic [Churches] than there is between the Laplander and the Hottentot." Gillis was greatly offended and swore from that date he would never again have anything to do with England or English Catholics. D'Arcy says Gillis's animosity toward England stemmed from this incident. See Arnold Lunn, "A Letter from Arnold Lunn," *Catholic World* 153 (June 1941): 330-33 and William S. Abell, ed., *Laughter and Love of Friends: Reminiscences of the Distinguished English Priest and Philosopher Martin Cyril D'Arcy, SJ* (Westminster, Maryland: Christian Classics, Inc., 1991), 115-17. D'Arcy's opinion is inconsistent with Gillis's statements later in life, as he continued to applaud the works of several British writers including G.K. Chesterton and Hilaire Belloc. Gillis's defense of the individual and the right of limited human freedom, which he viewed as in jeopardy because of Britain's international policies, is a better explanation of this critical outburst.

135. "Statement of the Hierarchy of the United States Regarding Peace and War", November 16, 1939, in *Our Bishops Speak*, ed. Huber, 226.

136. "Our Attitude Toward Europe's War," Editorial Opinion, *America* 61 (September 16, 1939): 540-41.

137. Joseph Rossi, SJ, *American Catholics and the Formation of the United Nations* (Washington, D.C.: University Press of America, 1993), 7.

138. James Gillis, Sermon, Labor Day Field Mass, September 2, 1940.

139. "Editorial Comment," *America* 63 (July 27, 1940): 422; Edward Skillin, Jr., "The Catholic Press and the Election," *The Commonweal* 33 (November 1, 1940): 52; "Editorial Comment," *The Commonweal* 33 (November 1, 1940): 43.

140. James Gillis, "Editorial Comment," *Catholic World* 152 (November 1940): 132, 138.

141. Ibid., 130.

142. Charles Fielding to Gillis, October 22, 1940; Thomas Harney to Gillis, October 23, 1940, Gillis Correspondence, PFA.

143. Michael Williams, "Views and Reviews," *The Commonweal* 33 (November 1, 1940): 53-54.

144. John S. Ryan to Edward J. Dempsey, November 23, 1940, Ryan Papers, ACUA.

145. Henry Stark, CSP, "Statement Released Pertinent to November 1940 Gillis Editorial in *The Catholic World*," October 31, 1940, Gillis Correspondence, PFA.

146. Frank Hall to Gillis, November 23, 1940; Hall to Gillis, November 29, 1940, *Sursum Corda* Correspondence, Gillis Papers, PFA.

147. James Gillis to Frank Hall, December 3, 1940, *Sursum Corda* Correspondence, Gillis Papers, PFA; Gillis, "Editorial Comment," *Catholic World* 152 (December 1940): 257.

148. The Committee to Defend America by Aiding the Allies took a stance akin to Roosevelt's including support of the March 1941 Lend-Lease agreement with England. It became an unofficial public relations group for the President. Among its prominent Catholic members were John A. Ryan, George Shuster, and Michael Williams. The Fight for Freedom Committee, with Senator Carter Glass of Virginia as honorary chairman and Episcopal bishop of Southern Ohio Henry W. Hobson as chairman, favored American participation in the war as a full belligerent against the Axis.

149. The full history of this organization is told in Wayne Cole, *America First* (Madison: University of Wisconsin Press, 1953).

150. Ibid., 15–16.

151. Ibid., 72–77, vii–viii; Peter Dietz to Gillis, May 23, 1941; James Gillis to Cardinal William O'Connell, May 24, 1941, Gillis Correspondence, PFA.

152. James Gillis, Preaching Log, 1941, Gillis Papers, PFA. The log reports Gillis spoke on the following dates at America First rallies: April 29, New Haven; May 23, New York; September 22, Brooklyn; October 17, Rockville Center, New York; October 23, Springfield, Massachusetts; October 27, Baltimore; October 29, Cleveland.

153. James Gillis, "See Life Steadily and See It Whole," *New York Daily News*, May 6, 1941, America First File; Gillis, Speech America First Rally, September 22, 1941, Gillis Papers, PFA.

154. James Gillis, "Editorial Comment," *Catholic World*, 152 (January 1941): 390–95.

155. Lend-Lease allowed the United States to aid any nation resisting aggression by the sale of munitions or other war stuffs. The policy was basically cash and carry, but when credit was awarded, the English were crowding American ports for goods with payment to be a matter of future negotiation. The "shoot first" policy allowed

American vessels to shoot first at Axis ships if deemed necessary for their safety and preservation.

156. James Gillis, "Editorial Comment," 154 (January 1942): 389.

6. LOSS OF THE AMERICAN REPUBLIC—1942–1949

1. Cabell Phillips, *The 1940s: Decade of Triumph and Trouble* (New York: Macmillan Co., Inc., 1975), 67, 68. America's lack of preparedness for war is explainable on one level by Roosevelt's firm resolve to retain peace. On December 29, 1940, the President, surrounded by his Secretary of State Cordell Hull and Hollywood personalities Clark Gable and Carole Lombard, gave his famous "Arsenal of Democracy" fire side chat, where he continued to state his public penchant that America must aid the Allies in order to avoid military involvement in Europe. "This is not a fireside chat," the President began, "it is a talk on national security." One week later on January 6, 1941 Roosevelt went before Congress to report on the annual State of the Union. He again voiced American concern for peace by articulating a dream of "Four Freedoms" for all peace-loving peoples. For people "everywhere in the world," he called for "freedom of speech and expression...freedom for every person to worship God...freedom from want...[and] freedom from fear [to the end] that no nation anywhere will be in a position to commit an act of aggression against any neighbor." The speech stirred the hearts of Americans and gave them pride that their President believed in the furtherance of the American dream for all people. In typical fashion Gillis was not impressed with the President's words. He gave Roosevelt high marks in the popular appeal of his fireside chat, saying that he spoke "sonorously and with beautiful prose rhythm" and that, "the speech was a superb piece of forensic presentation." However, Gillis believed that he saw through the veneer of the President's rhetoric and voiced a more realistic look, one with the much less altruistic value of preparing the people for war. He wrote that the President's purpose was "to prepare one hundred and thirty million Americans for the Next Step. I fear it achieved that purpose." See James Mac-Gregor Burns, *Roosevelt: The Soldier of Fortune* (New York: Harcourt Brace and Jovanovich, Inc., 1970), 34–35; James Gillis, "Editorial Comment," *Catholic World* 152 (February 1941): 519.

2. Phillips, *The 1940s*, 140, 170.

3. Kirkendall, *The United States 1929–1945*, 209–10; Phillips, *The 1940s*, 80–85.
4. Kirkendall, *The United States 1929–45*, 209–11, 232; Gerald D. Nash, *The Great Depression and World War II: Organizing America, 1933–1945* (New York: St. Martin's Press, 1979), 134–40.
5. Kirkendall, *The United States 1929–1945*, 197–99, 223–24; Phillips, *The 1940s*, 107.
6. Editorial Comment, "West Coast Japanese," *America* 67 (October 3, 1942): 715–16; James Gillis, "Editorial Comment," *Catholic World* 155 (May 1942): 133.
7. "Letter of Most Rev. Edward Mooney, Chairman Executive Board, NCWC to Hon. Franklin D. Roosevelt, President, USA Pledging Support in the National Crisis of World War II," December 22, 1941, in *Our Bishops Speak*, ed. Huber, 350–51.
8. Paulist Superior General Henry Stark approved the requests of twenty-two members of the Society to enter the armed services as chaplains, proportionally the largest single contribution of any diocese or religious order.
9. Quoted in Flynn, *Roosevelt and Romanism*, 185.
10. Quoted Ibid., 190–93.
11. Editorial Comment, "Charity for All," *America* 67 (June 27, 1942): 323.
12. James Gillis, "Editorial Comment," *Catholic World* 154 (January 1942): 389.
13. In April 1942 Attorney General Francis Biddle asked Postmaster General Frank Walker to invoke the Espionage Act of 1917 and revoke the second-class mailing privileges of *Social Justice* on grounds that the paper was inflammatory to the war effort and "presumably reached persons in the armed forces and those subject to induction and enlistment." The removal of the magazine from circulation was the catalyst which precipitated action by Archbishop Edward Mooney, who silenced Coughlin on May 1. Mooney did not support Coughlin as had Michael Gallagher, but he walked a fine line in censuring the priest in that many still liked Coughlin and the fact that the Constitution provided for such freedom of expression. The postal department's action with Coughlin's organ gave Mooney the precedent he needed to act. See Tull, *Father Coughlin*, 234–37 and Brinkley, *Voices of Protest*, 267–68.
14. John A. Ryan to Philip Burnham, March 30, 1942, Ryan Papers, ACUA.
15. The pacifist stance that *Catholic Worker* took during the war was

very costly in loss of support on at least two fronts. The paper during the war years lost 100,000 in circulation and thirty houses of hospitality closed (from internal disputes as much as the lack of need with unemployment almost nil) so that by January 1945 only ten remained in operation. See Mel Piehl, *Breaking Bread: The Catholic Worker and the Origins of Catholic Radicalism in America* (Philadelphia: Temple University Press, 1982), 196–98.

16. Henry Stark to Gillis, December 9, 1941, Gillis Papers, PFA.
17. James Gillis, "Editorial Comment," *Catholic World* 154 (March 1942): 653.
18. Ibid., 154 (February 1942): 519–20.
19. Ibid., 155 (May 1942): 135.
20. Ibid., 156 (October 1942): 6, 7–11.
21. Ibid., 156 (November 1942): 136.
22. Ibid., 154 (March 1942): 647.
23. Sirgiovanni, *An Undercurrent of Suspicion,* 147.
24. James Gillis, "Editorial Comment," *Catholic World* 155 (June 1942): 258. Gillis referred to the world's leaders as "bandits" who promoted the ideology, "nothing above the state, nothing beyond the state, nothing outside the state." Such an attitude which ignored the presence of God was abhorrent to the editor and was causal to the present war. See Gillis, "God in Government," Pamphlet, 1943, in John O'Brien Papers, AUND.
25. James Gillis, *Sursum Corda* #823, "Robots, Reprisals, Revenge?", July 24, 1944, Gillis Papers, PFA.
26. Quoted in Finley, *James Gillis,* 166.
27. James Gillis, "Editorial Comment," *Catholic World* 155 (September 1942): 644; 155 (July 1942): 385–89; 159 (August 1944): 389.
28. Ibid., 162 (January 1946): 299.
29. Editorial Comment, "The Spirit of Isolationism," *The Commonweal* 41 (November 10, 1944): 92; "Peace of Isolationism," 37 (January 29, 1943): 364; "What of the Future?" 38 (July 30, 1943): 360.
30. Editorial Comment, "Economy and International Obligations," *America* 76 (March 8, 1947): 624.
31. "Editorial Comment," *Ave Maria* 65(2) (January 11, 1947): 38.
32. In his editorials Gillis often mentioned Pius XII's aversion to war, human suffering, and the hope that the war would be waged in a moral manner—on the battlefield and not in cities full of innocent civilians.
33. James Gillis, *Sursum Corda* #859, "No Ethics in War?", April 2, 1945, Gillis Papers, PFA.

34. Editorial Comment, "Precautions and Bombing," *America* 71 (May 27, 1944): 210; Editorial Comment, "Area Bombing," *The Commonweal* 39 (March 17, 1944): 532.

35. James Gillis, *Sursum Corda* #879, "Lesson of the Atomic Bomb," August 20, 1945, Gillis Papers, PFA; Gillis, "Editorial Comment," *Catholic World* 161 (September 1945): 449–50.

36. Editorial Comment, "Atomic Bomb," *The Commonweal* 42 (August 31, 1945): 468; "Horror and Shame," 42 (August 24, 1945): 443–44; quoted in Flynn, *Roosevelt and Romanism*, 209.

37. James Gillis to Michael Ready, September 8, 1942, Catholic Hour Correspondence, Gillis Papers, PFA.

38. Michael Ready to Gillis, September 17, 1942, Catholic Hour Correspondence, Gillis Papers, PFA.

39. Gillis to Michael Ready, September 25, 1942, Catholic Hour Correspondence, Gillis Papers, PFA.

40. James Gillis to John Noll, September 29, 1942; Noll to Gillis, October 2, 1942; Noll to Michael Ready, October 2, 1942; Ready to Edward Mooney, October 7, 1942, NCWC General Secretary Papers, ACUA.

41. Gillis to Michael Ready, September 25, 1942, Catholic Hour Correspondence, Gillis Papers, PFA.

42. James Gillis, "Editorial Comment" (Not Used), November 1942, Superior General Papers, PFA.

43. Henry Stark, "In Re Father Gillis," October 23, 1942, Superior General Papers, PFA. One wonders whether Harney's comments were based as much on his rejection of Gillis and those who advocated strict house discipline as it was his belief that the editorial was inappropriate and/or hurtful to the Paulist community.

44. James Gillis to John Dunne, October 27, 1942; Francis X. Talbot, SJ, to Gillis, November 9, 1942; Grace Welch to Secretary of NCCM, December 26, 1942, Catholic Hour Correspondence, Gillis Papers, PFA.

45. Edward J. Heffron to Gillis, November 22, 1939; November 29, 1939; December 7, 1939; Gillis to Heffron, December 9, 1939; Michael Ready to Gillis, October 17, 1941, Catholic Hour Correspondence, Gillis Papers, PFA.

46. Edward J. Heffron to Gillis, November 21, 1941, Catholic Hour Correspondence, Gillis Papers, PFA. Extant correspondence received in reaction to Catholic Hour broadcasts is available in the Gillis Papers, PFA and the Catholic Hour Files of the NCCM, ACUA. There is no indication from these sources that complaints against Gillis's 1941

talks were received. It is interesting to note as well that NBC received over 100 phone complaints over an address given by Fulton Sheen, who along with Gillis was an extremely popular Catholic Hour speaker. The talk, "More Barnacles on the Ship of Democracy," delivered on January 24, 1943, was considered "untimely and undesirable in times of war." Yet, there was no move to remove Sheen from his Catholic Hour broadcast post. See Max Jordan to Edward Heffron, January 25, 1943 and Heffron to Michael Ready, January 25, 1943, NCWC General Secretary Papers, ACUA.

47. James Gillis to Joseph Lamb (Supreme Secretary of the Knights of Columbus), January 15, 1943; Gillis to Arthur Keefe, December 9, 1942, Catholic Hour Correspondence, Gillis Papers, PFA.

48. Some of the more important points to the Charter were: (1) countries would seek no aggrandizement, territorial or other, (2) no national boundaries would be altered without the freely expressed wishes of the peoples concerned, (3) right of peoples to choose their own form of government must be preserved, (4) following the war a peace would be secured which would assure the people of all lands that they could live in freedom from fear and want. See Burns, *Roosevelt,* 130–31.

49. James Gillis, *Sursum Corda* #860, "Idealism, Realism, Which," April 9, 1945, Gillis Papers, PFA; Editorial Comment, "The Atlantic Charter," *America* 69 (April 28, 1943): 575; Rossi, *American Catholics and the United Nations,* 10. The complete chronicle of American Catholicism's attitudes and actions relative to the formation of the United Nations is given in Rossi's work.

50. The bishops stated, "It is our solemn responsibility, in the reconstruction, to use our full influence in safeguarding the freedoms of all people. This, we are convinced, is the only way to an enduring peace." See "Statement of the Administrative Committee, NCWC, April 15, 1945, in *Our Bishops Speak,* ed. Huber, 359.

51. James Gillis, Radio Address, July 2, 1944, Gillis Papers, PFA, reprinted as "Victory Beyond Victory," *Catholic World* 159 (August 1944): 450; Gillis, *Sursum Corda* #924, "A Nation's Conscience," July 1, 1946, Gillis Papers, PFA; Gillis, "Editorial Comment," *Catholic World* 158 (January 1944): 328.

52. James Gillis, "God in Government" Pamphlet, John O'Brien Papers, AUND.

53. James Gillis, Radio Address, "Religion," September 24, 1944, Gillis Papers, PFA.

54. James Gillis, *Sursum Corda* #788, "Bull's Eye for G.B.S.," November 22, 1943, Gillis Papers, PFA.

55. James Gillis, "Editorial Comment," *Catholic World* 156 (March 1943): 647.

56. Ibid., 159 (April 1944): 5; 165 (April 1947): 6–7.

57. Editorial Comment, "Foreign Policy: the Choice," *The Commonweal* 39 (October 29, 1943): 28; "Role of the New Big Three," 40 (June 2, 1944): 147; "Alliance or Federation," 38 (October 8, 1943): 600; Editorial Comment, "Peace at a Price," *America* 71 (August 5, 1944): 454; "Our Moral Leadership," 75 (June 29, 1946): 275.

58. Robert Williams to James Gillis, October 3, 1942, Gillis Papers, PFA.

59. Louis W. Koenig, *The Truman Administration: Its Principles and Practice* (New York: New York University Press, 1956): 223.

60. "Resolution of the Hierarchy of the United States on Compulsory Military Training," November 17, 1944, in *Our Bishops Speak,* ed. Huber, 234; Editorial Comment, "A Citizen Army," *America* 72 (January 13, 1945): 291; James Gillis, "Editorial Comment," *Catholic World* 166 (March 1947): 487.

61. It must be noted, however, that the Special U.S. House Committee for the Investigation of Un-American Activities, better known as the Dies Committee after its right-wing chairman, Representative Martin Dies of Texas, was active from 1938 to 1944. This committee, which was a forum aimed to root out Communists in government, gained a reputation for witch-hunting. One of the best histories of the Dies Committee is found in August Raymond Ogden, FSC, *The Dies Committee: A Study of the Special House Committee for the Investigation of Un-American Activities 1938–1944* (Washington, D.C.: The Catholic University of America Press, 1945).

62. Quoted in Sirgiovanni, *An Undercurrent of Suspicion,* 5.

63. Arthur M. Schlesinger, Jr., *The Vital Center: The Politics of Freedom* (Boston: Houghton Mifflin Company, 1949), 92.

64. Phillips, *The 1940s,* 361. Phillips says that in the period 1945–1955 the American people became obsessed with the idea of the evil aegis of the Kremlin "boring from within" to destroy the American way of life. The Communists' aim was not so much revolution as dissolution—the steady relentless erosion of America's moral and civic fiber to the point that a Communist state could arise from the ashes of the debris.

65. James Gillis, *Sursum Corda* #887, "Degenerating into Religion,"

October 15, 1945; #995, "Communist Concern for the Constitution!", October 11, 1947, Gillis Papers, PFA.

66. Ibid., #927, "Communism a Crusade," July 22, 1946.
67. Ibid., #890, "Only 12,000 Communists Present," November 5, 1945.
68. James Gillis, "Editorial Comment," *Catholic World* 155 (August 1942): 520.
69. Ibid., 164 (November 1946): 104.
70. Ibid., 157 (May 1943): 119. Although Gillis rejected liberalism and Protestantism, he would have agreed with Liberal Protestantism which "likened Communism to the anti-Christ stalking the world." See Kenneth D. Wald, "The Religious Dimension of American Communism," *Journal of Church and State* 36(3) (Summer 1994): 491.
71. Editorial Opinion, "Russian Policy," *America* 75 (September 7, 1946): 556; "Red Saber-Rattling," 75 (August 31, 1946): 527.
72. Michael Williams, "An Open Letter to the President of the United States," Released July 5, 1945, Gillis Papers, PFA.
73. Editorial Comment, "The Rub," *The Commonweal* 36 (June 12, 1942): 172.
74. James Gillis, "Editorial Comment," *Catholic World* 155 (August 1942): 520.
75. Editorial Comment, "The Washington Sphinx," *The Commonweal* 43 (March 15, 1946): 540–41.
76. At Yalta in February 1945 Churchill and Roosevelt proposed an interim government for Poland with representatives from the exiled government and the Lublin group sharing control until free elections could be held. Stalin vetoed this plan but did allow a slight modification where Poles outside the puppet Lublin regime were contracted to aid the government with free elections.
77. "Between War and Peace," Statement of the American Catholic Hierarchy, November 18, 1945, in *Our Bishops Speak*, ed. Huber, 128.
78. James Gillis, "Editorial Comment," *Catholic World* 160 (February 1945): 393.
79. James Gillis, *Sursum Corda* #1007, "Lest We Forget," February 2, 1948.
80. Editorial Comment, "Yalta and Poland," *The Commonweal* 41 (March 2, 1945): 483; Editorial Comment, "Lublin," *America* 71 (January 20, 1945): 310–11; "Poland," 72 (February 24, 1945): 411.
81. James Gillis, *Sursum Corda* #1003, "The Success of Failure," January 5, 1948, Gillis Papers, PFA.

82. James Gillis, "Editorial Comment," *Catholic World* 162 (December 1945): 201.

83. James Gillis, *Sursum Corda* #897, "Cancel to Zero," December 24, 1945, Gillis Papers, PFA.

84. Phillips, *The 1940s,* 94–100.

85. James Gillis, "Editorial Comment," *Catholic World* 166 (February 1948): 394; 166 (November 1947): 104–05; 164 (December 1946): 201–02; 162 (March 1946): 486; 167 (June 1948): 200; 163 (April 1946): 7; Gillis, *Sursum Corda* #992, "Have We a Foreign Policy?", September 20, 1947, Gillis Papers, PFA.

86. James Gillis, "Editorial Comment," *Catholic World* 165 (June 1947): 195.

87. After Roosevelt's death it was revealed that he had made secret deals and promises with the Chinese, the Zionists, Arabs, Czechoslovakia, and the Baltic nations that were never kept. See John T. Flynn, *The Roosevelt Myth* (New York: The Devin-Adair Company, 1948), 417–19.

88. Quoted in Phillips, *The 1940s,* 198–204, 226.

89. James Gillis, "Editorial Comment," *Catholic World* 155 (May 1942): 136; 155 (September 1942): 648.

90. Ibid., 157 (September 1943): 569.

91. Ibid., 163 (June 1946): 198–99.

92. Ibid., 167 (July 1948): 290.

93. James Gillis, "Make it a Crusade," Radio Address, March 14, 1943, Gillis Papers, PFA.

94. Ibid., #856, "John D. Once Again," May 12, 1945; #901 "Old, Simple, True," January 21, 1946; Gillis "Man—Freedom of Will," Radio Address, December 30, 1945, Gillis Papers, PFA.

95. James Gillis, *Sursum Corda* #725, "A Highly Important Utterance," September 14, 1942, Gillis Papers, PFA; "Hierarchy of the United States Statement on Victory and Peace," November 14, 1942, in *Our Bishops Speak,* ed. Huber, 112; Editorial Comment, "Women and the War Effort," *The Commonweal* 36 (May 29, 1942): 125.

96. James Gillis, "Why I Like Sokolsky," *Sign* 24(5) (December 1944): 247.

97. James Gillis, *Sursum Corda* #996, "Not All Funny," October 18, 1947, Gillis Papers, PFA.

98. Roosevelt used executive orders more freely than any previous president. During the first four years of his administration he issued 1486 orders with the effect of law. Before this time the greatest number of executive orders issued in a similar time period

was 166. See James Gillis, *Sursum Corda* #1236, "The Republic Remains," June 21, 1952, Gillis Papers, PFA.

99. James Gillis, "Editorial Comment," *Catholic World* 160 (March 1945): 483–88.

100. James Gillis to S.A. Gillen, December 1, 1948, *Sursum Corda* Correspondence, Gillis Papers, PFA.

101. James Gillis, "Editorial Comment," *Catholic World* 154 (February 1942): 519; 155 (May 1942): 133.

102. Wolfskill and Hudson, *All But the People*, 174–75.

103. Kirkendall, *The United States 1929–1945*, 246–47.

104. James Gillis, "Editorial Comment," *Catholic World* 159 (April 1944): 1–9; Editorial Comment, "The Harangue Is On," *The Commonweal* 40 (October 6, 1944): 579–80; 40 (July 7, 1944): 268.

105. James Gillis, "Editorial Comment," *Catholic World* 159 (September 1944): 483.

106. Ibid., 160 (December 1944): 193–194.

107. Wilfrid Parsons, SJ, "Franklin D. Roosevelt: A Look at the Record," *America* 73 (April 28, 1945): 68–69; "Comment on the Week," *America* 73 (April 21, 1945): 45.

108. James Gillis, *Sursum Corda* #863, "The Government Still Lives," April 30, 1945, Gillis Papers, PFA.

109. James Gillis, "Editorial Comment," *Catholic World* 165 (June 1947): 201–02; 167 (May 1948): 101; 167 (June 1948): 199; 167 (September 1948): 488. The influence of Roosevelt on future presidents was immense. It was because of Roosevelt's administration that Harry Truman, Dwight Eisenhower, and Lyndon Johnson came to prominence. John Kennedy was introduced to the Washington scene through his father who had served in the Roosevelt administration as ambassador to England. The influence of Roosevelt is fully analyzed in: William E. Leuchtenburg, *In the Shadow of FDR: From Harry Truman to Ronald Reagan* (Ithaca, New York: Cornell University Press, 1983).

110. John Sheerin, "Editorial Comment," *Catholic World* 168 (October 1948): 3.

111. Within two weeks after Pearl Harbor a large delegation of leaders of organized labor and industry assembled in Washington. They agreed, under the impetus of the national emergency, to a pledge of no strikes and no lockouts during the duration of the war. The pledge was valuable as a national testament but it could not solve all the problems that would materialize. The War Labor Board working with the Office of Price Administration attempted to

maintain wages and cost of living on equal footing during the war years in an effort to minimize tensions that would lead to strikes. See Phillips, *The 1940s*, 91–92.

112. Phillips, *The 1940s*, 278–79; Eric F. Goldman, *The Crucial Decade–and After: America 1945–1960* (New York: Alfred A. Knopf, 1966), 21–24; Arthur F. McClure, *The Truman Administration and the Problem of Postwar Labor, 1945–1948* (Rutherford, New Jersey: Fairleigh Dickinson University Press, 1969), 11.

113. Phillips, *The 1940s*, 283–89. While Truman was addressing Congress asking for the most drastic anti-strike law ever enacted, the railroad engineers settled the dispute.

114. Nelson Lichtenstein, "Labor in the Truman Era: Origins of the 'Private Welfare State,'" in *The Truman Presidency*, ed. Michael Lacey (Cambridge: Cambridge University Press, 1989), 130–31.

115. Quoted in Ibid., 134.

116. Truman vetoed the Taft-Hartley bill, stating, "I am convinced it is a bad bill. It is bad for labor, bad for management, and bad for the country." See Koenig, *The Truman Administration*, 242.

117. Editorial Comment, "Industrial Peace," *America* 67 (September 12, 1942): 631; "The Taft Bill," 77 (May 24, 1947): 203.

118. Editorial Comment, "Strike Prospect," *The Commonweal* 43 (February 1, 1946): 396.

119. James Gillis, "Editorial Comment," *Catholic World* 167 (May 1948): 106.

120. James Gillis, *Sursum Corda* #1053, "Strikes Are a Luxury," December 27, 1948, Gillis Papers, PFA.

121. James Gillis, "Editorial Comment," *Catholic World* 164 (January 1947): 295. One area of common ground for most all Catholic periodicals was their dislike of the tactics of the principal labor leaders, especially John L. Lewis and Philip Murray. Gillis felt these men had too much power, while *The Commonweal* expressed the opinion that Lewis abused the privilege and power that he had been given in order to represent labor.

122. Editorial Comment, "The Strike Wave," *The Commonweal* 42 (October 5, 1945): 588; Editorial Comment, "The Right to Strike," *America* 76 (December 7, 1946): 259.

123. Phillips, *The 1940s*, 210; Kirkendall, *The United States 1929–1945*, 260.

124. James Gillis, "Editorial Comment," *Catholic World* 158 (November 1943): 120.

125. Because of protocol difficulties the Chinese and Russians could

not participate in the proceedings together. A second series of sessions was held where the Chinese attended and the Russians abstained. See Phillips, *The 1940s,* 220.

126. Phillips, *The 1940s,* 219–21.

127. Editorial Comment, "Organizing the World," *The Commonweal* 40 (October 6, 1944): 581.

128. "The Hierarchy of the United States, Statement on International Order," November 16, 1944, in *Our Bishops Speak,* ed. Huber, 123. In its "Statement on World Peace" of April 15, 1945 the bishops again voiced their fear that the proposed United Nations would become "an alliance of Great Powers." See Huber, 355–56.

129. James Gillis, "Justice," Radio Address, September 10, 1944, Gillis Papers, PFA.

130. Quoted in Phillips, *The 1940s,* 227.

131. Ibid., 229.

132. Kirkendall, *The United States 1929–1945,* 276–77; Goldman, *The Crucial Decade,* 31.

133. Rossi, *American Catholics and the United Nations,* 24.

134. Editorial Comment, "San Francisco Round-Up," *America* 73 (June 23, 1945): 235; Editorial Comment, "What Was Done at San Francisco," *The Commonweal* 42 (July 20, 1945): 323–24.

135. "Hierarchy of the United States—Between War and Peace," November 18, 1945, in *Our Bishops Speak,* ed. Huber, 128. American Catholics were represented at the San Francisco Conference. Under pressure from various national organizations, Stettinius sent invitations to forty-two groups to send consultants to the conference. Catholics were represented by Dr. Richard Pattee of the NCWC and Thomas H. Mahony, a Boston lawyer, who represented the Catholic Association for International Peace (CAIP). Joseph Rossi suggests that the CAIP and the specific work of Father Edward Conway, SJ, who traveled the country speaking on behalf of the CAIP and NCWC, were responsible for the shift of the American hierarchy from its initial position of opposition to the decree of Dumbarton Oaks to one of acceptance, albeit with reservations, of the San Francisco accord. See Rossi, *American Catholics and the United Nations,* 11, 20, 27–38, 61.

136. James Gillis, "Editorial Comment," *Catholic World* 161 (April 1945): 1–7; 161 (August 1945): 370.

137. Ibid., 165 (September 1947): 483; 166 (October 1947): 5; 166 (November 1947): 103.

138. Ibid., 166 (October 1947): 7; 165 (July 1947): 293; 166 (November 1947): 101–02.

139. Ibid., 167 (August 1948): 392; James Gillis, Sermon, March 8, 1948, Gillis Papers, PFA.

140. James Gillis, *Sursum Corda* #988, "Two Magnificent Utterances," August 23, 1947, Gillis Papers, PFA. Truman and Pius XII exchanged letters discussing what was necessary for the survival of civilization. Truman wrote the Pope, "I desire to do everything in my power to support and contribute to a concert of all forces striving for a moral world." Gillis congratulated the President saying, "But never has any president written or spoken more eloquently than Mr. Truman of the essentially religious character of our national government."

141. James Gillis, "Editorial Comment," *Catholic World* 165 (June 1947): 201.

142. Phillips, *The 1940s*, 309. Truman stated, "I believe that it must be the policy of the United States to support free peoples who are resisting attempted subjugation by armed minorities or by outside pressures. I believe that we must assist free peoples to work out their own destinies in their own way. I believe our help should be primarily through economic and financial aid which is essential to economic stability and orderly political processes. The world is not static, and the status quo is not sacred. But we cannot allow changes in the status quo in violation of the charter of the United Nations by such methods as coercion or by such subterfuges as political infiltration."

143. Robert A. Pollard, "The National Security State Reconsidered: Truman and Economic Containment, 1945–1950," in *The Truman Presidency*, ed. Lacey, 214.

144. Editorial Comment, "Crisis in Foreign Policy," *America* 76 (March 22, 1947): 678.

145. Editorial Comment, "The State of the Union," *The Commonweal* 45 (January 17, 1947): 339. The magazine stated of Truman, "Like most of his previous speeches and messages to Congress, it [the State of the Union Address] reflects a man whose heart is in the right place but who has little ability to strike the sparks required for true leadership under a republican form of government." With respect to the Truman Doctrine *The Commonweal* came to agree that it provided a possibility for good: "It now begins to be within the range of legitimate hope that we shall get a fairly decent implementation of something which could just as easily

have turned out badly." See Editorial Comment, "The Truman Doctrine," *The Commonweal* 46 (April 18, 1947): 3.

146. James Gillis, *Sursum Corda* #962, "It's Up to Us," March 24, 1947, Gillis Papers, PFA.

147. Phillips, *The 1940s*, 312. Marshall stated in his address, "The remedy lies in breaking the vicious circle and restoring the confidence of the European people in the economic future of their own countries and of Europe as a whole....The United States should do whatever it is able to do to assist in the return of normal economic health in the world, without which there can be no political stability and no assured peace."

148. Richard M. Freeland, *The Truman Doctrine and the Origins of McCarthyism: Foreign Policy, Domestic Politics, and Internal Security 1946–1948* (New York: Alfred A. Knopf, 1972), 6. The best recent analysis on the Marshall Plan and its genesis is: Wilson Miscamble, CSC, *George F. Kennan and the Making of American Foreign Policy, 1947–1950* (Princeton: Princeton University Press, 1992).

149. Editorial Comment, "The Stage Is Set," *The Commonweal* 46 (October 3, 1947): 587; Editorial Comment, "Debate Over ERP," *America* 78 (January 24, 1948): 454; James Gillis, *Sursum Corda* #985, "'We' Take the Rap," August 2, 1947, Gillis Papers, PFA.

150. The Balfour Declaration committed Britain to a promise to support the establishment of a national home for the Jews. Jewish immigration to Palestine was initiated under this policy, creating greater tension between Arabs and Jews and resulting in numerous outbreaks of violence.

151. The story of the foundation of the State of Israel is beyond the scope of this work, but the British exodus in May 1948 was only the beginning of a bloody war which was won by the Zionists.

152. Editorial Comment, "Palestine Solution," *America* 78 (December 13, 1947): 286; Editorial Comment, "Palestine," *The Commonweal* 47 (December 12, 1947): 219; James Gillis, "Editorial Comment," *Catholic World* 164 (March 1947): 489.

153. Statement of Governor Thomas Dewey, June 1, 1948, Gillis Papers, PFA.

154. Apparently Gillis's sermon on the occasion of the Josephite anniversary was not well received. His comments were oriented toward a well-educated white congregation while the Baltimore

Cathedral was filled with black Catholics served by the Josephites. Peter Hogan, SSJ, interview with the author, May 16, 1994.

155. General Chapter Notes 1949, PFA. Gillis's missionary spirit throughout his journalistic career was recognized by John McGinn, CSP, who commented at the 1949 chapter, "Father Gillis did not cease to be a missionary when he became editor of *The Catholic World.*"

156. The extant sources do not give any details on Gillis's illness nor the success of the surgery. His return to active ministry seems to indicate that he was returned to health.

157. Alice Walsh to Clara Muxen, November 18, 1943, Gillis Papers, PFA; Finley, *James Gillis*, 232.

158. James Gillis, *Sursum Corda* #715, "Salt of the Earth," July 6, 1942; Alice Walsh to Hugh Gibson, February 24, 1944, Gillis Papers, PFA; Finley, *James Gillis*, 202.

159. James Gillis, *Sursum Corda* #987, "Clergy Keep Out?", August 16, 1947, Gillis Papers, PFA.

160. Thomas Coakley to Gillis, February 12, 1947, Gillis Papers, PFA; John S. Kennedy, "We Ought to Pay Him Honor," *The Catholic Transcript* 49(34) (January 9, 1947): 4.

161. General Chapter Notes, Financial Reports 1943 and 1946, PFA.

162. Katherine Crofton, review of *James Gillis, Paulist*, by James F. Finley, CSP, in *Catholic World* 188 (December 1958): 252. Crofton said the staff referred to that day as "Black Monday."

163. James Gillis, "Editorial Comment," *Catholic World* 167 (September 1948): 487.

164. James Gillis to Naomi McGarry, November 23, 1948, Gillis Papers, PFA.

165. James Gillis, "Editorial Comment," *Catholic World* 163 (April 1946): 9.

166. Ibid., 167 (September 1948): 490.

167. Frank Hall to Gillis, September 21, 1948, Catholic News Service Files, *Sursum Corda* Papers, ACUA; Editorial Comment, "Father Gillis Valedictory," *America* 79 (September 18, 1948): 528; John Selner, SS, "Truth and Consequence," *The Voice* 26 (November 1948): 20, (ASF); John Sheerin, "Editorial Comment," *Catholic World* 168 (October 1948): 2; Matthew Hoehn, OSB, ed., "Reverend James Martin Gillis, CSP, 1876-," in *Catholic Authors: Contemporary Biographical Sketches 1930-1947* (Newark, New Jersey: St. Mary's Abbey, 1948), 269.

7. A "CONSERVATIVE" RETIREMENT—1949–1957

1. The Servicemen's Readjustment Act of 1944 paid tuition, incidental educational fees, and provided a monthly stipend for living expenses.

2. Will Herberg, *Protestant–Catholic–Jew* (Revised Edition) (Garden City, New York: Doubleday & Company, Inc., 1960), 57.

3. A survey conducted in 1955 reported that 95% of Americans identified themselves with one of the three major religious divisions of Protestant (67%), Catholic (23%) or Jewish (5%). In 1950 57% of the American population were members of a Church; in 1958 membership rose to 63% and all-time high in the nation's history. Church attendance itself was also high at 68% where in 1944 it was reported at 58%. See Ibid., 46–48.

4. James Hennesey, SJ, *American Catholics–A History of the Roman Catholic Community in the United States* (New York: Oxford University Press, 1981), 284.

5. Ibid., 296; Herberg, *Protestant–Catholic–Jew,* 48.

6. Quoted in Hennesey, 287.

7. Stritch was active in the NCWC Department of Catholic Action and served as Chancellor of the Catholic Church Extension Society. He supported America's role in international affairs such as the UN and the Marshall Plan. Cushing, labeled in *Current Biographies* 1952 as "the most pervasive social force in Boston," championed ecumenism and social liberalism. Mooney was known in his role as chairman of the NCWC administrative committee (1936–1939 and 1941–1945), his support of labor, especially the CIO, and the rescue of his archdiocese from threatening financial collapse.

8. John Tracy Ellis, "American Catholics and the Intellectual Life," *Thought* 30 (1955): 351–88. George Shuster in 1925 and Robert Hutchins in 1937 had written about the absence of Catholic intellectual life in America, but it was Ellis's essay, which was originally given as a paper in May 1955 at a meeting of the Catholic Commission on Intellectual and Cultural Affairs, that initiated a storm of oral and printed responses and consequent plans of action.

9. Allitt, *Catholic Intellectuals and Conservative Politics,* 17–48.

10. Ibid., 81–82.

11. Wilson's five points were: (1) History has an intelligible pattern; it is a not a series of unrelated events. (2) Human nature is imperfect and corruptible. (3) There is a moral order in the universe from

which canons or principles of political judgment may be derived. (4) Government must be closely circumscribed. (5) Private property is the foundation of civilization. With regard to the consonance of Catholicism with American conservatism he wrote that both groups shared disdain for the French and Russian revolutions, yet supported the American revolution. Both bodies as well accepted representative government and justified rebellion against tyranny. See Allitt, *Catholic Conservatives,* 58–60 and Francis Graham Wilson, *The Case for Conservatism* (Seattle: University of Washington Press, 1951), 1–24, 49–74.

12. James Gillis to Westbrook Pegler, February 1, 1955, Gillis Correspondence; Gillis, *Sursum Corda* #1313, "The 'Liberal' Catholic," December 14, 1953, Gillis Papers, PFA.

13. John Cogley, "Anathema Sit," *The Commonweal* 59 (February 26, 1954): 516.

14. James Gillis, "Letter to the Editor," *The Commonweal* 59 (March 19, 1954): 601. Along with *The Commonweal* Catholic liberal thought was prominent in *Cross Currents, Jubilee,* and *America.*

15. Paul Blanshard, *American Freedom and Catholic Power* (Boston: The Beacon Press), 1951), 47, 52, 266–88.

16. James Gillis, "No Time for Dissension," *Catholic World* 172 (December 1950): 172.

17. James Gillis, *Sursum Corda* #1079, "Blanshard the Fascist," October 17, 1949, Gillis Papers, PFA.

18. James Gillis, "Open Letter to Anti-Catholic Agitators," *Catholic World* 170 (March 1950): 412.

19. Quoted in Koenig, *Truman Administration,* 93.

20. In civil rights the Fair Deal aimed to eradicate political, economic, and to some extent social discrimination against blacks, establish the Fair Employment Practices Commission (FEPC), and eliminate the poll tax and "Jim Crow" segregation tactics. The social welfare agenda advocated a program of national health insurance and an increase in federal loans for homes. In the realm of labor there was a call for repeal of the Taft-Hartley Act and the raising of the minimum wage from forty to seventy-five cents per hour.

21. James Gillis, *Sursum Corda* #1104, "Hand to Mouth Policy," December 5, 1949, Gillis Papers, PFA.

22. Ibid., #1196, "No Bellyaching?", September 10, 1951; #1232, "Read History," May 24, 1952.

23. Editorial Comment "Weakness or Strength," *The Commonweal* 52 (September 22, 1950): 571.

24. James Gillis, *Sursum Corda* #1233, "New Kind of Empire," May 31, 1952.

25. Ibid., #1188, "Diplomatic Blunders," July 16, 1951.

26. Ibid., #1312, "American and Catholic," December 7, 1953.

27. Ibid., #1264, "That Mandate Again," January 4, 1953.

28. Ibid., #1297, "Clear Your Mind of Can't," August 24, 1953.

29. James Gillis, "The Crisis: Atheism: Christo-Paganism," *Catholic World* 168 (December 1948): 193–99; Gillis, *Sursum Corda* #1333, "It May Not Be Too Late," May 3, 1954, Gillis Papers, PFA.

30. James Gillis, *Sursum Corda* #1136, "Closing in On the Church," July 17, 1950, Gillis Papers, PFA.

31. Ibid., #1132, "The People's Foreign Policy," June 19, 1950.

32. John O'Hara to James Gillis, December 21, 1950, Manion Affair File; Gillis, *Sursum Corda* #1164, "An Important Little Book," February 2, 1951, Gillis Papers, PFA.

33. George Higgins, "Yardstick," *Michigan Catholic,* February 8, 1951, clipping in Catholic Total Abstinence Union of America file, Gillis Papers, PFA.

34. Wilfrid Parsons, SJ, review of *The Key to Peace* by Clarence Manion, in *America* 84 (March 24, 1951): 728; Parsons to Gillis, May 3, 1951, Catholic Total Abstinence Union of America File, Gillis Papers, PFA. Gillis responded in personal correspondence against Higgins calling him a "special pleader" and one who professed the belief that "the welfare state can do no wrong." See Gillis to George Morrell, March 20, 1951 and Gillis to Arthur Conrad, March 6, 1951, Gillis Papers, PFA.

35. James Gillis, *Sursum Corda* #1224, "A Word to Organized Labor," March 30, 1952.

36. James Gillis to Arthur Conrad, March 6, 1951, Catholic Total Abstinence Union of America File; Joseph P. Conlon to "Editor of the Catholic Review," January 11, 1949, Gillis Papers, PFA.

37. Russell Kirk, *Academic Freedom: An Essay in Definition* (Chicago: Henry Regnery Company, 1955), 1; William F. Buckley, Jr., *God and Man at Yale: The Superstitions of "Academic Freedom"* (Chicago: Henry Regnery Press, 1951), 1–10.

38. James Gillis to William F. Buckley, Sr., November 16, 1952; Gillis, *Sursum Corda* #1230, "Once Again: Academic Freedom," May 10, 1952, Gillis Papers, PFA.

39. James Gillis, "Fr. Gillis on *America,*" *America* 87 (May 24, 1952): 219–20.

40. James Gillis, "Catholics and Intellectuals," *Catholic World* 183 (June 1956): 171.

41. Sirgiovanni, *Undercurrent of Suspicion*, 15; Phillips, *The 1940s*, 362–65.

42. Alger Hiss, who had clerked for Supreme Court Justice Oliver Wendell Holmes and later served in the State Department and assisted with the organization of the San Francisco United Nations Conference, was in August 1948 accused by ex-Communist and now *Time* magazine editor Whittaker Chambers in testimony before the HCUAC of Communist activities. Hiss denied the charges but the case continued to be pushed by first-term Congressman Richard Nixon. Eventually in January 1950, in his second trial, Hiss was convicted of perjury, fined $10,000, and sentenced to five years in prison. See Phillips, *The 1940s*, 368–77 and O'Neill, *American High*, 151–52.

43. Quoted in Hennesey, *American Catholics*, 289.

44. Athan Theoharis, "The Escalation of the Loyalty Program," in *Politics and Policies of the Truman Administration*, ed. Barton J. Bernstein (Chicago: Quadrangle Books, 1972), 242. The loyalty program provided for: (1) the investigation of applicants for posts in the executive branch and (2) removal of disloyal employees. Investigation of individual cases was mainly the responsibility of the Civil Service Commission. Removal was made the responsibility of the head of each department, assisted by loyalty boards of not less than three representatives of that department. Between 1947 and 1956 the program was responsible for 2700 dismissals and 12,000 resignations. See O'Neill, *American High*, 162.

45. Schlesinger, *The Vital Center*, 128.

46. James Gillis, *Sursum Corda* #1349, "An Extraordinary Gathering," August 23, 1954, Gillis Papers, PFA.

47. Ibid., #1081, "Let Russia Destroy Herself," September 4, 1949; #1161, "Truth Will Prevail," January 8, 1951.

48. Quoted in David Halberstam, *The Fifties* (New York: Fawcett Columbine, 1993), 50.

49. Athan Theoharis, "The Rhetoric of Politics," in *Politics and Policies*, ed. Bernstein, 200–02; Freeland, *Truman Doctrine*, 4.

50. David Caute, *The Great Fear: The Anti-Communist Purge Under Truman and Eisenhower* (New York: Simon and Schuster, 1978), 106.

51. Quoted in Ibid., 48.

52. Quoted in David M. Oshinsky, *A Conspiracy So Immense–The World of Joe McCarthy* (New York: The Free Press, 1983), 308.

53. Ibid., 302–03.
54. Richard H. Rovere, *Senator Joe McCarthy* (New York: Harcourt, Brace and Company, 1982), 35.
55. Richard M. Fried, *Men Against McCarthy* (New York: Columbia University Press, 1976), 182–84. There does not seem to have been any noticeable individuals or group in the Senate which approved of McCarthy. See Oshinsky, *A Conspiracy So Immense*, 214–15.
56. The complete history of American Catholicism and Senator McCarthy is told in: Donald F. Crosby, SJ, *God, Church and Flag–Senator Joseph R. McCarthy and the Catholic Church 1950–1957* (Chapel Hill: University of North Carolina Press, 1978).
57. Patrick Scanlan at the Brooklyn *Tablet* and Patrick Carroll, CSC, at *Ave Maria* were staunch McCarthy defenders. William F. Buckley, Jr. and L. Brent Bozell's book *McCarthy and His Enemies: The Record and Its Meaning* has been described by Patrick Allitt as "the only defense of McCarthyism that was even partially intellectually plausible." See Allitt, *Catholic Conservatives*, 22.
58. Robert I. Gannon, SJ, *The Cardinal Spellman Story* (Garden City, New York: Doubleday & Company, Inc., 1962), 348.
59. Quoted in Hennesey, *American Catholics*, 293; Vincent P. DeSantis, "American Catholics and McCarthyism," *Catholic Historical Review* 51(1) (April 1965): 21. See also Philip A. Grant, Jr., "Bishop Bernard Sheil's Condemnation of Senator Joseph R. McCarthy," *Records* 97(1986): 43–49 and Steven Avella, *This Confident Church: Catholic Leadership and Life in Chicago, 1940–1965* (Notre Dame, Indiana: University of Notre Dame Press, 1992), 143–45. Avella writes, "McCarthy's accusations reawakened the old social reformer in Sheil." Additionally, it should be noted that Spellman's support for the senator raised Sheil's interest since the two prelates were old foes.
60. Robert Hartnett, SJ, "Pattern of GOP Victory," *America* 88 (November 22, 1952): 208–09; Hartnett, "*Daily Worker* on Stevenson," *America* 88 (December 13, 1952): 301–02. As time passed Hartnett's attacks on McCarthy grew to the point that his crusade became a controversy for the magazine and for the Jesuits. In June 1954 the Jesuit Superior General Jan B. Janssens ordered *America* to avoid discussion of "merely secular or political matters." Ultimately in September 1955 Hartnett retired as editor, although much speculation existed that he was forced out. See Crosby, *God, Church and Flag*, 98–101, 178–84 and Hennesey, *American Catholics*, 294.
61. Editorial Comment, "And I'll Tell You No Lies," *The Commonweal*

51 (March 31, 1950): 646; "The McCarthy Question," 55 (October 26, 1951): 54; "Victory for McCarthy," 56 (September 26, 1952): 600.

62. James Gillis, "Letter to the Editor," *The Commonweal* 53 (January 19, 1951): 373; Gillis, *Sursum Corda* #1219, "President Truman and Senator McCarthy," February 24, 1952, Gillis Papers, PFA.

63. Joseph McCarthy to James Gillis, April 17, 1953; Gillis to McCarthy, April 21, 1953, McCarthy to Gillis, June 30, 1954, Gillis Papers, PFA.

64. James Gillis, *Sursum Corda* #1332, "Caught in the Act," April 26, 1954, Gillis Papers, PFA.

65. James Gillis to Philip Conneally, SJ, June 23, 1952; Thomas M. Jennings to Gillis, January 19, 1954, Gillis Papers, PFA.

66. John Cogley, "A Matter of Escape," *The Commonweal* 56 (September 19, 1952): 574; James Gillis, "Letter to the Editor," *The Commonweal* 57 (October 24, 1952): 64–65; Cogley to Gillis, September 18, 1952, Gillis Papers, PFA.

67. The spring of 1954 became the time of Armageddon for Joseph McCarthy and his anti-Communist crusade. The election of the Republican Dwight Eisenhower to the Presidency in 1952 had, as mentioned previously, led to McCarthy's appointment as chairman of the Senate Committee on Government Operations, but with the GOP in command of the government, the need for McCarthy's antics to gain party notoriety passed. Thus, a more hostile environment existed when the Senator's special subcommittee began to investigate the Army. Between April 22 and June 17, 1954 the Washington drama, where both McCarthy's accusations against the Army and the Army's counter-charges against the Senator were debated, was played out on national television.

68. Burnham's book, along the lines of the McCarthy campaign and Gillis's rhetoric, suggested that a conspiracy existed in the U.S. government to shield Communists from detection.

69. James Gillis, *Sursum Corda* #1337, "'Shameful' Group in Washington," May 31, 1954; #1320, "Communism and Intellectual Curiosity," February 1, 1954, Gillis Papers, PFA.

70. James Gillis to Virginia Furlong, April 15, 1954, Gillis Paper, PFA.

71. In the spring of 1954 McCarthy and the Department of the Army met in congressional hearings where charges and countercharges were leveled by each party against the other. This was another effort by the Senator to expose perceived Communists in the government.

72. James Gillis, *Sursum Corda* #1357, "Senator McCarthy's Latest Trial," October 18, 1954; #1364, "It Is Not Really McCarthy," December 6, 1954; Editorial Comment, "The Decline of McCarthy," *The Commonweal* 61 (December 24, 1954): 325. Gillis noted in his final appraisal of the McCarthy campaign that the Senate had never in the past worried about its manners or methods. McCarthy's condemnation for Gillis was more evidence that the conspiracy of Communism had penetrated to the very roots of the American government and was now manifest in opposition to one who fought diligently and faithfully to rid the nation of the Soviet ideology.

73. James Gillis, *Sursum Corda* #1154, "Resist Aggression Everywhere?", November 20, 1950; #1321, "Why Not Common Sense," February 8, 1954; #1207, "Look Before You Leap," November 26, 1951; #1198, "The Tito Question," September 24, 1951, Gillis Papers, PFA.

74. Ibid., #1138, "French Hierarchy and the A-Bomb," July 31, 1950; #1141, "Not Traitors But Patriots," August 21, 1950; #1192, "Obsessed by Politics," August 13, 1951; #1171, "The Pacifists Have Something," March 19, 1951.

75. Norman A. Graebner, *The New Isolationism* (New York: The Ronald Press Company, 1956), v–vii. Graebner's thesis is that American foreign policy between 1950 and 1955 was dominated by heirs of the old tradition of isolationism. Characteristics of American invincibility, moralism, and utopianism led people in positions of power to deal with the world by applying American solutions, thus creating a purely internal solution. Graebner believed that Americans felt superior to other peoples and nations of the same period.

76. James Gillis, *Sursum Corda* #1125, "Told You So," May 1, 1950; #1112, "Isolationism Reviving," January 30, 1950, Gillis Papers, PFA.

77. Pius XII stated in his 1950 Christmas message, in answer to an accusation from Communists that he wanted war, "Sift the twelve troubled years of our pontificate; weigh every word that our lips have uttered, every sentence our pen has written; you will find in them only appeals for peace." *The Commonweal* stated that Gillis's use of this statement as evidence to prove that the Pope believed in military isolationism was simply wrong.

78. James O'Gara, "The Catholic Isolationist," in *Catholicism in America* (New York: Harcourt, Brace and Company, 1954), 112, 120–21; Editorial Comment "The Pope Isolationist?", *The Commonweal* 53

(February 9, 1951): 435; James Gillis to "Editor of *The Commonweal*," February 12, 1951, Gillis Papers, PFA.

79. The North Atlantic Treaty committed the United States and eleven other signatories: (1) to maintain and develop, by means of continuous and effective self-help and mutual aid, their individual and collective capacity to resist attack, (2) to consult together in the event of a threat to the territorial integrity, independence, or security of any of the parties, (3) to consider an armed attack on any one of the parties in the North Atlantic area as an attack against them all, and (4) to assist the party so attacked by taking forthwith, individually and in concert with other parties, such action as each party should deem necessary, including the use of armed force, to restore the security of the North Atlantic area. See Koenig, *Truman*, 282; Alonzo L. Hamby, *Beyond the New Deal: Harry S. Truman and American Liberalism* (New York: Columbia University Press, 1973), 357–59.

80. Editorial Comment "North Atlantic Treaty," *The Commonweal* 49 (April 1, 1949): 603–04; James Gillis, *Sursum Corda* #1266, "Disunion in France," January 18, 1953, Gillis Papers, PFA.

81. James Gillis, *Sursum Corda* #1365, "Apropos of Andrei Y. Vishinsky," December 13, 1954; #1310, "'Sniping' at the UN," November 23, 1953; #1298, "Is the U.N. God?", August 27, 1953; #1268, "The U.N. a Failure?", February 1, 1953; #1334, "Don't They Believe in the U.N.," May 3, 1954, Gillis Papers, PFA; Gillis, "They Don't See the Church," *Catholic World* 175 (April 1952): 8.

82. Quoted in Koenig, *Truman*, 339.

83. John W. Spanier, *The Truman-MacArthur Controversy and the Korean War* (New York: W.W. Norton & Company, Inc., 1965), 257–59. Spanier writes, "The Korean War was a necessary war: to teach the Soviet leaders that aggression would not pay; to hold together the Western alliance; and to preserve the military basis of containment."

84. Editorial Opinion "The Threat of 'Little Wars'," *The Commonweal* 52 (August 4, 1950): 403; "Taking a Stand," 52 (July 7, 1950): 307; Editorial Comment, "Korea—Turning Point," *America* 83 (July 8, 1950): 370.

85. James Gillis, *Sursum Corda* #1134, "At Last An Answer," July 3, 1950.

86. Truman stated in his order of dismissal, "It is with the deepest personal regret that I find myself compelled to take this action. General MacArthur is one of our greatest military commanders. But

the course of world peace is more important than any individual." See Koenig, *Truman*, 354.

87. Halberstam, *The Fifties*, 69.

88. O'Neill, *American High*, 132.

89. Editorial Comment "In the Public Interest," *The Commonweal* 54 (April 20, 1951): 27–28.

90. James Gillis, *Sursum Corda* #1178, "We'd Better Hang Together," May 7, 1951.

91. Quoted in Koenig, *Truman*, 353–54.

92. Spanier, *Truman and MacArthur*, 259.

93. James Gillis, *Sursum Corda* #1201, "What About Korea?", October 15, 1951; #1237, "The War Not Phony but 'Funny'," June 28, 1952; #1255, "Intolerable Situation in Korea," November 2, 1952; #1286, "The Truth About Korea," June 8, 1953, Gillis Papers, PFA.

94. Ibid., #1290, "Moral Debacle at Korea," July 6, 1953.

95. Editorial Comment "Peace in Korea," *The Commonweal* 58 (August 7, 1953): 432–33; Editorial Comment "Truce in Korea," *America* 89 (August 8, 1953): 453; John Sheerin, Editorial Comment "Truman Saves Korea," *Catholic World* 171 (August 1950): 321.

96. John J. Delaney to James Gillis, February 23, 1955, Gillis Papers, PFA.

97. James Gillis, *So Near Is God* (New York: Charles Scribner's Sons, 1953), dedication.

98. Ibid., 3–9.

99. Ibid., 91–99.

100. Gerald Buck, review of *This Mysterious Human Nature* by James Gillis, In *Spiritual Life* 3(4) (December 1957): 304.

101. James Gillis, *This Mysterious Human Nature* (New York: Charles Scribner's Sons, 1956), 7.

102. James Gillis, *My Last Book* (New York: P.J. Kenedy & Sons, 1957), 68.

103. John Keough to James Gillis, June 29, 1951; Keough to Gillis, August 27, 1951, Gillis Papers, PFA.

104. Finley, *James Gillis*, 211.

105. *Paulist News* 12(1) (January 1952): 5, PFA.

106. The Paulist Superior General James Cunningham had requested the honor, which was granted by Pope Pius XII. Dominican Master-General Emmanuel Suarez was present for the degree's conferral. This marked the last of seven honorary degrees which

Gillis had received in his life: Litt. D., College of Mt. Saint Vincent, New York, 1934; Ph.D., Fordham University, New York, 1935; Ph.D., St. Francis College, 1935, Brooklyn; Ph.D, St. Benedict's College, Atchison, Kansas, 1940; Ph.D., Boston College, 1941; L.L.D., University of Detroit, 1940. List found in "Personal History," Gillis Papers, PFA.

107. James Gillis to Frank Hall, December 12, 1954, Gillis Papers, PFA.

108. Frank Hall to James Gillis, December 14, 1954, Gillis Paper, PFA.

109. James Gillis, *Sursum Corda* #1369, "Farewell to This Column," January 10, 1955, Gillis Paper, PFA.

110. John A. O'Brien, "Father Gillis—Fisher of Men," *Catholic News*, January 29, 1955, Clipping found in Gillis Paper, PFA.

111. "This Month We Salute," *One Man's Opinion* 1(5) (November 1956), back cover, found in Gillis Papers, PFA.

112. Pamphlet "Father Gillis Catholic Center," Park St. File, Gillis Papers; *Paulist News* 15(2) (February 1955): 2, PFA.

113. *Paulist News* 16(11) (December 1956): 1; Richard Cushing "Address at Cornerstone Ceremony," Park St. File, Gillis Papers, PFA; *NCWC News Service* November 21, 1955, NCWC News Service Files, ACUA.

114. *Paulist News* 17(4) (April 1957), Special Insert, PFA.

115. Raymond Tartre, review of *James Gillis–Paulist*, by James Finley, in *Emmanuel* 64 (12) (December 1958): 526.

EPILOGUE

1. John Selner, "Father James Gillis, C.S.P.," *The American Ecclesiastical Review* 137 (July 1957): 31.

Bibliography

Primary Sources

ARCHIVAL SOURCES

Paulist Fathers Archives (PFA) Washington, D.C.

Papers of James Martin Gillis, CSP, Walter Elliott, CSP, Superior General Correspondence, WLWL Papers, General Chapter Meeting Minutes, Consultor Meeting Minutes, Papers of James McVann, CSP, *Paulist News*.

Archives The Catholic University of America (ACUA), Washington, D.C.

Papers of National Conference of Catholic Men (NCCM) (Catholic Hour), NCWC General Secretary Papers (John J. Burke and Michael Ready), Catholic Interracial Council (CIC) of New York Papers, John A. Ryan Papers, Francis Haas Papers, NCWC Administrative Committee Meeting Minutes.

Archives Georgetown University (AGU), Washington, D.C.

John LaFarge, SJ Papers (Northeastern Clergy Conference on Negro Welfare), Wilfrid Parsons, SJ Papers (Correspondence).

Archives University of Notre Dame (AUND), South Bend, Indiana.

Patrick Joseph Carroll, CSC Papers, John O'Brien Papers, Sheed and Ward Papers, John Noll Papers.

Archives Sulpician Fathers (ASF), Baltimore, Maryland.

The Voice Collection, Papers of John Fenlon, SS.

Archives Josephite Fathers (AJF), Baltimore, Maryland.

John Gillard Papers, Catholic Intrerracial Council Papers.

BOOKS AND ARTICLES

Coughlin, Charles E. *"Am I an Anti-Semite?" 9 Addresses on Various "isms," Answering the Question.* Detroit: Cordon Printing Company, 1939.

———. *Eight Lectures on Labor, Capital and Justice.* Royal Oak, Michigan: The Radio League of the Little Flower, 1934.

———. *Father Coughlin's Radio Discourses, 1931–1932.* Royal Oak, Michigan: The Radio League of the Little Flower, 1932.

———. *Father Coughlin's Radio Sermons, October 1930–April 1931, Complete.* Baltimore: Knox and O'Leary, 1931.

———. *The New Deal in Money.* Royal Oak, Michigan: The Radio League of the Little Flower, 1933.

———. *A Series of Lectures on Social Justice, 1935–1936.* Royal Oak, Michigan: The Radio League of the Little Flower, 1936.

———. *Why Leave Our Own? 13 Addresses on Christianity and Americanism.* Royal Oak, Michigan: The Radio League of the Little Flower, 1939.

Finley, James F., Paulist Priest. Interview by Author, April 5–7, 1994, Oak Ridge, New Jersey.

Gillis, James M., CSP. "'Americanism': Fifty Years Later." *Catholic World* 169 (July 1949): 246–53.

———. "To Believe Or Not To Believe." *Catholic World* 121 (June 1925): 374–83.

———. "'Bob' Ingersoll." *Catholic World* 121 (May 1925): 216–26.

———. *The Catholic Church and the Home.* New York: The Macmillan Company, 1928.

———. "The Catholic Editor Today." *Catholic World* 165 (July 1947): 347–53.

———. "The Catholic Press." *Messeneger of the Sacred Heart* 42(4) (April 1927): 259–63.

———. "Catholics and Intellectuals." *Catholic World* 183 (June 1956): 166–72.

———. "The Christian Agape." *Catholic University of America Bulletin* 9(4) (October 1903), 465–508.

———. "Christian Thinking Is Way to Peace." *Catholic Mind* 36 (March 8, 1932): 88–90.

———. *Christianity and Civilization.* New York: Paulist Press, 1932.

———. "The Church and State in Higher Education." *Christian Education* 19(3) (February 1936): 170–75.

———. "Coueism and Catholicism." *Catholic World* 116 (March 1923): 790–803.

———. "Creedless Christianity." *The Missionary* 42(12) (December 1928): 431–35.

———. "The Crime of Cain." *Journal of Negro Life* 12(6) (June 1934): 175, 185.

———. "The Crisis: Atheism: Christo-Paganism." *Catholic World* 168 (December 1948): 193–99.

———. "Edward Gibbon." *Catholic World* 120 (March 1925): 772–85.

———. "The Eucharist—The International Bond of Charity." *Catholic World* 147 (July 6, 1938): 477–81.

———. *False Prophets.* New York: Paulist Press, 1925.

———. "Father Hecker and His Friends." *American Benedictine Review* 4(1953): 47–64.

———. "God in the Law." *Catholic World* 166 (November 1947): 157–160.

———. "Hints of Immortality." *Catholic World* 123 (April 1926): 84–91.

———. "How the Church Regards Sinners." *Spiritual Life* 3(1) (March 1957): 27–31.

——. "In Defense of Democracy." *The Sign* 15(1) (August 1935): 12–13.

——. "Insobriety: A Danger to the American Republic." *Tablet* (Brooklyn) (August 11, 1951): 10.

——. Review of *Interracial Justice*, by John Lafarge. *Catholic World* 145 (June 1937): 370–71.

——. "Journalism and Literature." *Catholic World* 165 (April 1947): 66–69.

——. "The Ku-Klux Klan." *Catholic World* 116 (January 1923): 433–43.

——. "A Letter and a Reply." *Catholic World* 171 (June 1950): 214–15.

——. "Limits of Logic." *Catholic World* 118 (November 1923): 145–52.

——. "Loud and Bold." *Catholic World* 155 (August 1942): 605–08.

——. "Mrs. Eddy, A Creative Intellect." *Catholic World* 116 (November 1922): 189–97.

——. *My Last Book*. New York: P.J. Kenedy & Sons, 1957.

——. "No Time for Dissension." *Catholic World* 172 (December 1950): 166–72.

——. "Not Past, or Present, But Future." *The Homiletic and Pastoral Review* 50(1) (October 1949): 26–31.

——. *On Almost Everything*. New York: Dodd, Mead & Company, 1955.

——. "One Father of All." *Interracial Review* 7(7) (July 1934): 88–89.

——. "Open Letter to Anti-Catholic Agitators." *Catholic World* 170 (March 1950): 406–12.

——. "Patron of Catholic Writers." *Catholic World* 117 (April 1923): 84–89.

——. *The Paulists*. New York: The Macmillan Company, 1932.

——. "Psychiatry or Prayer?" *Catholic World* 176 (March 1953): 406–10.

——. "Quid Timidi Estis?" *The Missionary Unions of the Clergy Bulletin* (September 1939): 22–27.

——. "The Radio and Religion." "The Ball and Cross," *Catholic World* 146 (October 1937): 88–93.

——. "Random Thoughts on the Story of Philosophy." *Catholic World* 124 (December 1926): 370–79.

——. *So Near Is God*. New York: Charles Scribner's Sons, 1953.

——. "Starve or Steal?" *The Mother of Sorrows* (June 1936): 9–14.

——. *The Ten Commandments*. New York: Paulist Press, 1931.

——. "A Theistic Basis of Morality." *Religious Education* 27(6) (June 1932): 505–10.

——. "They Don't See the Church." *Catholic World* 175 (April 1952): 6–11.

——. *This Mysterious Human Nature*. New York: Charles Scribner's Sons, 1956.

——. "Tom Paine." *Catholic World* 121 (April 1925): 48–58.

——. "Victory Beyond Victory." *Catholic World* 159 (August 1944): 447–50.

——. "Voltaire." *Catholic World* 120 (February 1925): 577–88.

——. "Wanted: A Guide, Philosopher and Friend." *Catholic World* 125 (June 1927): 360–69.

——. "What Russia Is Doing to Us." *Catholic World* 163 (September 1946): 540–45.

——. "White and Black." *The African Missionary* (June 1936): 130–31.

——. "Why I Like Sokolsky." *Sign* 24(5) (December 1944): 245–47.

——. "Why the Encyclical on Christian Marriage." *Catholic Action* 14 (July 1932): 5–6, 12.

——. "Without Religion No University." *Catholic World* 153 (July 1941): 462–67.

Herbermann, Charles, Edward Pace, Conde Pallen, Thomas Shahan, and John Wynne, SJ, eds. *The Catholic Encyclopedia.* New York: Robert Appleton Company, 1907. S.v. "Bible Studies," by James Gillis.

Hogan, Peter, SSJ, Josephite Priest. Interview by author, May 16, 1994, Baltimore, Maryland.

Secondary Sources

Abell, Aaron I., ed. *American Catholic Thought on Social Questions.* New York: The Bobbs-Merrill Company, Inc., 1968.

——. *American Catholicism and Social Action: A Search for Social Justice 1865–1950.* Garden City, New York: Hanover House, 1960.

Abell, William S., ed. *Laughter and the Love of Friends: Reminiscences of the Distinguished English Priest and Philosopher Martin Cyril D'Arcy, S.J.* Westminster, Maryland: Christian Classics, Inc., 1991.

Adler, Selig. *The Isolationist Impulse: Its Twentieth-Century Reaction.* London: Abelard-Schuman, 1957.

Ahern, Patrick Henry. *The Catholic University of America 1887–1896: The Rectorship of John J. Keane.* Washington, D.C.: The Catholic University of America Press, 1948.

Ahlstrom, Sydney E. *A Religious History of the American People.* New Haven: Yale University Press, 1972.

Allen, Frederick Lewis. *Only Yesterday: An Informal History of the Nineteen-Twenties.* New York: Harper & Brothers Publishers, 1931.

Allitt, Patrick. "American Catholics and the New Conservatism of the 1950s." *U.S. Catholic Historian* 7(1) (Winter 1988): 15–37.

——. *Catholic Intellectuals and Conservative Politics in America 1950–1985.* Ithaca, New York: Cornell University Press, 1993.

Anbinder, Tyler. *Nativism & Slavery: The Northern Know Nothings & the Politics of the 1850s.* New York: Oxford University Press, 1992.

Appleby, R. Scott. *"Church and Age Unite!" The Modernist Impulse in American Catholicism.* Notre Dame, Indiana: University of Notre Dame Press, 1992.

Avella, Steven M. *This Confident Church: Catholic Leadership and Life in Chicago, 1940–1965.* Notre Dame, Indiana: University of Notre Dame Press, 1992.

Ayling, Stanley. *John Wesley.* Cleveland: William Collins Publishers, Inc., 1979.

Badger, Anthony J. *The New Deal: The Depression Years, 1933–40.* New York: Hill and Wang, 1989.

Baritz, Loren, ed. *The Culture of the Twenties.* Indianapolis: The Bobbs-Merrill Company, 1970.

Barrett, Patricia, RSCJ. Review of *My Last Book*, by James Gillis. In *America* 100 (November 1, 1958): 139.

Barry, Colman J., OSB. *The Catholic Church and German Americans.* Milwaukee: Bruce Publishing Company, 1953.

——. *The Catholic University of America, 1903–1909: The Rectorship of Denis J. O'Connell.* Washington, D.C.: The Catholic University of America Press, 1950.

Barry, William. "The Troubles of a Catholic Democracy." *Contemporary Review* 76 (July 1899): 70–86.

Bates, J. Leonard. *The United States 1898–1928.* New York: McGraw-Hill Book Company, 1976.

Belloc, Hilaire. *The Catholic Church and History.* New York: The Macmillan Company, 1926.

——. *Essays of a Catholic.* London: Sheed and Ward, 1931.

Bernstein, Barton J., ed. *Politics and Policies of the Truman Administration.* Chicago: Quadrangle Books, 1972.

Betten, Neil B. *Catholic Activism and the Industrial Worker.* Gainesville: University Presses of Florida, 1976.

——. "Catholic Periodicals in Response to Two Divergent Decades." *Journalism Quarterly* 47 (1970): 303–08.

Billington, Monroe L. "Roosevelt, the New Deal, and the Clergy." *Mid-America* 54 (1972): 20–33.

Blanchard, Paul. *American Freedom and Catholic Power*. Boston: The Beacon Press, 1951.

Blantz, Thomas E., CSC. "George N. Shuster and American Catholic Intellectual Life." In *Studies in Catholic History*, eds. Nelson H. Minnich, Robert B. Eno, SS and Robert F. Trisco, 345–65. Wilmington, Delaware: Michael Glazier, 1985.

——. *George N. Shuster: On the Side of Truth*. Notre Dame, Indiana: University of Notre Dame Press, 1993.

——. *A Priest in Public Service: Francis J. Haas and the New Deal*. Notre Dame, Indiana: University of Notre Dame Press, 1982.

Bode, Carl. *The American Lyceum: Town Meeting of the Mind*. New York: Oxford University Press, 1956.

Boyle, Hugh C. "The Legion of Decency A Permanent Campaign." *The Ecclesiastical Review* 91(4) (October 1934): 367–70.

Braeman, John, Robert H. Bremmer and Everett Walters, eds. *Change and Continuity in Twentieth Century America*. Columbus: Ohio State University Press, 1964.

Bredeck, Martin J. *Imperfect Apostles: The Commonweal and the American Catholic Laity, 1924–1976*. New York: Garland Publishing, Inc., 1988.

Brinkley, Alan, "The Problem of American Conservatism." *American Historical Review* 99 (2) (April 1994): 409–29.

——. *Voices of Protest–Huey Long, Father Coughlin and the Great Depression*. New York: Vintage Books, 1983.

Broderick, Francis L. "The Encyclicals and Social Action: Is John A. Ryan Typical?" *Catholic Historical Review* 55 (April 1969): 1–6.

——. *Right Reverend New Dealer–John A. Ryan*. New York: The Macmillan Company, 1963.

Brown, Thomas N. *Irish-American Nationalism 1870–1890*. Philadelphia: J.B. Lippincott Company, 1966.

Bryce, James. *The American Commonwealth*. New York: Macmillan, 1910.

Buchholz, Sr. M. Dominica. "A Bio-Bibliography of Reverend James Martin Gillis, CSP." M.A. thesis, The Catholic University of America, 1958.

Buck, Gerald. Review of *This Mysterious Human Nature*, by James Gillis. In *Spiritual Life* 3 (4) (December 1957): 304–05.

Buckley, William F. Jr. *God and Man at Yale: The Superstitions of "Academic Freedom."* Chicago: Henry Regnery Company, 1951.

—— and L. Brent Bozell. *McCarthy and His Enemies: The Record and Its Meaning*. Chicago: Henry Regnery Company, 1954.

Buenker, John D., John C. Burnham, and Robert M. Crunden. *Progressivism*. Cambridge, Massachusetts: Schenkman Books, Inc., 1977.

Burke, John J. "Father Hecker and Present Problems." *Catholic World* 110 (January 1920), 564–75.

Burke, Robert E. and Richard Lowitt. *The New Era and the New Deal 1920–1940*. Arlington Heights, Illinois: Harlan Davidson, Inc., 1981.

Burnham, James. *The Web of Subversion–Underground Networks in the U.S. Government*. New York: The John Day Company, 1954.

Burns, James MacGregor. *Roosevelt: The Soldier of Fortune*. New York: Harcourt Brace and Jovanovich, Inc., 1970.

Burns, Jeffrey M. *American Catholics and the Family Crisis 1930–1962*. New York: Garland Publishing, Inc., 1988.

"The Call for a Legion of Decency." *The Sign* 13 (12) (July 1934): 708.

Campbell, Debra. "A Catholic Salvation Army: David Goldstein, Pioneer Lay Evangelist." *Church History* 52 (September 1983): 322–32.

——. "The Heyday of Catholic Action and the Lay Apostolate, 1929–1959." In *Transforming Parish Ministries: The Changing Roles of Catholic Clergy, Laity, and Women Religious*, ed. Jay Dolan, 222–52. New York: Crossroad, 1989.

Cannistraro, Philip V. and Theodore P. Kovaleff. "Father Coughlin and Mussolini: Impossible Allies." *Journal of Church and State* 13 (1971): 427–43.

Carey, Patrick W. "American Catholic Romanticism, 1830–1888". *Catholic Historical Review* 74 (4) (October 1988): 590–606.

Carr, Robert K. *The House Committee on Un-American Activities 1945–1950.* Ithaca, New York: Cornell University Press, 1952.

Carter, Paul A. *The Twenties in America.* New York: Thomas Y. Crowell Company, 1975.

Cashman, Sean Dennis. *America in the Age of the Titans: The Progressive Era and World War I.* New York: New York University Press, 1988.

"A Catholic Interracial Meeting". *America* 51 (June 2, 1934): 170.

Catholicism in America, A Series of Articles from The Commonweal. New York: Harcourt, Brace and Company, 1953.

Caute, David. *The Great Fear: The Anti-Communist Purge Under Truman and Eisenhower.* New York: Simon and Schuster, 1978.

Cecil, Lord Hugh. *Nationalism and Catholicism.* London: Macmillan, 1919.

Chinnici, Joseph, OFM. *Living Stones–The History and Structure of Catholic Spiritual Life in the United States.* New York: Macmillan Publishing Company, 1989.

Cogley, John. "Anathema Sit." *The Commonweal* 59 (February 26, 1954): 516.

———. "Farewell to Father Gillis." *The Commonweal* 66 (April 5, 1957): 13.

———. "A Matter of Escape." *The Commonweal* 56 (September 19, 1952): 574.

Cogley, John and Rodger Van Allen. *Catholic America.* Kansas City, Missouri: Sheed & Ward, 1986.

Cohalan, Florence D. Review of *This Mysterious Human Nature*, by James Gillis. In *The Catholic World* 185 (June 1957): 233–34.

Cole, Wayne. *America First*. Madison, Wisconsin: University of Wisconsin Press, 1953.

——. *Roosevelt & the Isolationists 1932–45*. Lincoln: University of Nebrasksa Press, 1983.

Conway, Bertrand L. CSP. *The Question Box*. New York: Paulist Press, 1929.

Costello, Gerald M. *Without Fear of Favor–George Higgins on the Record*. Mystic, Connecticut: Twenty-Third Publications, 1984.

Crofton, Katherine. Review of *James Gillis–Paulist*, by James F. Finley CSP. In *The Catholic World* 188 (December 1958): 251–52.

Cronon, E. David. "American Catholics and Mexican Anti-Clericalism." *Mississippi Valley Historical Review* 45 (1958–1959): 201–30.

Crosby, Donald F., SJ. "Boston's Catholics and the Spanish Civil War: 1936–1939." *New England Quarterly* 44 (1971): 82–100.

——. *God, Church and Flag–Senator Joseph R. McCarthy and the Catholic Church 1950–1957*. Chapel Hill: University of North Carolina Press, 1978.

Cross, Robert D. *The Emergence of Liberal Catholicism in America*. Cambridge, Massachusetts: Harvard University Press, 1968.

Curran, Robert Emmett. *Michael Augustine Corrigan and the Shaping of Conservative Catholicism in America, 1878–1902*. New York: Arno Press, 1978.

Dallek, Robert. *Franklin D. Roosevelt and American Foreign Policy, 1932–1945*. New York: Oxford University Press, 1979.

Davis, Cyprian, OSB. *The History of Black Catholics in the United States*. New York: Crossroad, 1990.

Dawley, Alan. *Struggles for Justice: Social Responsibility and the Liberal State*. Cambridge: Harvard University Press, 1991.

Deedy, John G. "The Catholic Press." In *The Religious Press in America*, ed. Martin E. Marty, 57–95. New York: Holt, Rinehart and Winston, 1963.

DeSantis, Vincent P. "American Catholics and McCarthyism." *Catholic Historical Review* 51(1) (April 1965): 1–30.

DeSaulniers, Lawrence B. *The Response in American Catholic Periodicals to the Crisis of the Great Depression, 1930–1935.* Washington, D.C.: University Press of America, 1984.

DeVito, Michael J. *The New York Review.* New York: United States Catholic Historical Society, 1977.

Diggins, John P. *Mussolini and Fascism: The View from America.* Princeton, New Jersey: Princeton University Press, 1972.

Divine, Robert A. *Roosevelt and World War II.* Baltimore: Johns Hopkins Press, 1969.

Dohen, Dorothy. *Nationalism and American Catholicism.* New York: Sheed and Ward, 1967.

Dolan, Jay P. *The American Catholic Experience: A History from Colonial Times to the Present.* Garden City, New York: Doubleday & Company, Inc., 1985.

——. *Catholic Revivalism: The American Experience 1830–1890.* Notre Dame, Indiana: University of Notre Dame Press, 1978.

Dolan, Timothy Michael. *"Some Seed Fell on Good Ground": The Life of Edwin V. O'Hara.* Washington, D.C.: The Catholic University of America Press, 1992.

Dorsett, Lyle W. *Billy Sunday and the Redemption of Urban America.* Grand Rapids, Michigan: Wiliam B. Eerdmans Publishing Company, 1991.

Doyle, Thomas F. "Catholicism and the Negro." *Catholic World* 152 (October 1940): 10–20.

Dries, Angelyn, OSF. "Walter Elliott's Foundations for Evangelization." *Journal of Paulist Studies* 1 (1992): 7–16.

Droze, Wilmon H., George Wolfskill and William E. Leuchtenburg. *Essays on the New Deal.* Austin: University of Texas Press, 1969.

Ebner, Michael H. and Eugene M. Tobin, eds. *The Age of Reform: New Perspectives on the Progressive Era.* Port Washington, New York: Kennikat Press, 1977.

Elliott, Walter, CSP. *A Manual of Missions.* Washington, D.C.: The Apostolic Mission House, 1922.

———. "The Diocesan Clergy and Missions to Non-Catholics." *American Ecclesiastical Review* 11 (September 1894), 226–36.

———. "Experiences of A Missionary." *Catholic World* 58 (November 1893): 264–74.

———. "Experiences of A Missionary." *Catholic World* 58 (December 1893): 389–402.

———. "Experiences of A Missionary." *Catholic World* 58 (January 1894): 578–86.

———. "Experiences of A Missionary." *Catholic World* 59 (April 1894): 107–19.

———. "Experiences of A Missionary." *Catholic World* 59 (September 1894): 824–34.

———. *The Life of Father Hecker.* New York: Columbus Press, 1894.

———. *Mission Sermons.* Washington, D.C.: The Apostolic Mission House, 1926.

———. *Non-Catholic Missions.* New York: The Catholic Book Exchange, 1895.

———. "Our Centenary: A Glance into the Future." *Catholic World* 50 (November 1889): 239–49.

———. *Parish Sermons on Moral and Spiritual Subjects.* New York: Paulist Press, 1913.

———. *A Retreat For Priests.* Washington, D.C.: The Apostolic Mission House, 1924.

———. *The Spiritual Life.* New York: Paulist Press, 1914.

Ellis, John Tracy. *American Catholics and the Intellectual Life*. Chicago: Heritage Foundation, 1956.

——. *Documents of American Catholic History,* Vol. II. Wilmington, Delaware: Michael Glazier, 1987.

——. *The Life of James Cardinal Gibbons, Archbishop of Baltimore 1834-1921*. Westminster, Maryland: Christian Classics, Inc., 1987.

Ellsberg, Robert, ed. *By Little and By Little: The Selected Writings of Dorothy Day*. New York: Alfred A. Knopf, 1984.

Fallows, Marjorie R. *Irish Americans: Identity and Assimilation*. Englewood Cliffs, New Jersey: Prentice-Hall, 1979.

Farina, John. *An American Experience of God–The Spirituality of Isaac Hecker*. New York: Paulist Press, 1981.

——, ed. *Hecker Studies: Essays on the Thought of Isaac Hecker*. New York: Paulist Press, 1983.

Farrell, James. "Thomas Fitzsimmons, Signer of the Constitution." *Records of the American Catholic Historical Society of Philadelphia* 39(3) (1928), 175-224.

"Father Gillis Urges Active Faith." *The Voice* 14(9) (June 1937): 5-6, 18.

"Father Gillis and the U.N." *Catholic Mind* 52 (February 1954): 73.

"Father Hecker and America." *Missionary* 1 (March 1896): 5.

Faulkner, Harold U. *From Versailles to the New Deal: A Chronicle of the Harding-Coolidge-Hoover Era*. New Haven: Yale University Press, 1950.

Findlay, James F. Jr. *Dwight L. Moody: American Evangelist 1837-1899*. Chicago: The University of Chicago Press, 1969.

Finley, James F. *James Gillis–Paulist*. Garden City, New York: Hanover House, 1958.

Finley, Mary Joan. "Rev. James Gillis Discusses Youth and Foreign Affairs." *Salvator* (March 1938): 3.

Fisher, James Terence. *The Catholic Counterculture in America 1933-1962*. Chapel Hill: University of North Carolina Press, 1989.

Flynn, George Q. *American Catholics & the Roosevelt Presidency 1932–1936*. Lexington: University of Kentucky Press, 1968.

——. *Roosevelt and Romanism: Catholics and American Diplomacy, 1937–1945*. Westport, Connecticut: Greenwood Press, 1976.

Flynn, John T. *The Roosevelt Myth*. New York: The Devin-Adair Company, 1948.

Fogarty, Gerald P., SJ. *American Catholic Biblical Scholarship: A History from the Early Republic to Vatican II*. San Francisco: Harper & Row, Publishers, 1989.

——. *Denis J. O'Connell–American Agent in Rome 1885–1893*. Miscellanea Historia Pontificae, Vol. 36. Rome: Universita Gregoriani Editrice, 1974.

——, ed. *Patterns of Episcopal Leadership*. New York: Macmillan Publishing Company, 1989.

——. *The Vatican and the American Hierarchy from 1870 to 1965*. Collegeville, Minnesota: The Liturgical Press, 1985.

Foik, Paul J., CSC. *Pioneer Catholic Journalism*. New York: The United States Catholic Historical Society, 1930.

Frank, Robert L. "Prelude to Cold War: American Catholicism and Communism." *Journal of Church and State* 34 (1) (Spring 1992): 39–56.

Frater Edmund, O.C.D. Review of *My Last Book*, by James Gillis. In *Spiritual Life* 4 (4) (December 1958): 362.

"A Free and Responsible Press." Chicago: The University of Chicago Press, 1947.

Freeland, Richard M. *The Truman Doctrine and the Origins of McCarthyism: Foreign Policy, Domestic Politics, and Internal Society, 1946–1948*. New York: Alfred A. Knopf, 1972.

Freidel, Frank, ed. *The New Deal and the American People*. Englewood Cliffs, New Jersey: Prentice-Hall, Inc., 1964.

Fried, Richard M. *Men Against McCarthy*. New York: Columbia University Press, 1976.

Furey, Francis T. "Roman Catholics and the American Revolution." *Catholic World* 65 (July 1897): 495–505.

Furfey, Paul Hanly. "Curse of Nationalism." *Catholic World* 156 (March 1943): 652–57.

Gaffey, James P. *Francis Clement Kelley & the American Catholic Dream.* Two Volumes. Bensonville, Illinois: The Heritage Foundation, Inc., 1980.

Gannon, Michael V. "Before and After Modernism: The Intellectual Isolation of the American Priest." In *The Catholic Priest in the United States: Historical Investigations,* ed. John Tracy Ellis, 293–383. Collegeville, Minnesota: St. John's University Press, 1971.

Gannon, Robert I., SJ. *The Cardinal Spellman Story.* Garden City, New York: Doubleday & Company, Inc., 1962.

Garrison, Winfred Ernest. *Catholicism and the American Mind.* Chicago: Willett, Clark & Colby, 1928.

Gaustad, Edwin Scott. *A Religious History of America.* San Francisco: Harper & Row, Publishers, 1990.

Geaney, John J. "The Contemporary Press Reaction to Reverend Charles E. Coughlin 1926–1936." M.A. thesis, The Catholic University of America, 1964.

Gerstle, Gary. "The Protean Character of American Liberalism." *The American Historical Review* 99(4) (October 1994): 1043–73.

Gibbons, Cardinal James. "Catholic Christianity." *North American Review* 173 (July 1901), 78–90.

———. *Our Christian Heritage.* Baltimore: John Murphy Company, 1889.

———. *The Faith of Our Fathers.* Baltimore: John Murphy Company, 1876.

———. *Retrospect of Fifty Years, Vol I.* Baltimore: John Murphy and Co., 1916.

Gibbs, Philip. *Now It Can Be Told.* New York: Harper & Brothers Publishers, 1920.

Gillard, John T., SSJ. *Colored Catholics in the United States*. Baltimore: The Josephite Press, 1941.

Gleason, Philip. "American Identity and Americanization." In *Harvard Encyclopedia of American Ethnic Groups*, ed. Stephen Thernstrom, 31–58. Cambridge, Massachusetts: Harvard University Press, 1980.

——. *The Conservative Reformers: German-American Catholics and the Social Order*. Notre Dame, Indiana: University of Notre Dame Press, 1968.

——. *Keeping the Faith: American Catholicism Past and Present*. Notre Dame, Indiana: University of Notre Dame Press, 1987.

——. "In Search of Unity: American Catholic Thought, 1920–1960." *Catholic Historical Review* 65 (1979): 185–205.

Goldman, Eric F. *The Crucial Decade–And After: America 1945–1960*. New York: Alfred A. Knopf, 1966.

Graebner, Norman A. *The New Isolationism*. New York: The Ronald Press Company, 1956.

Greene, Michael J. "The Catholic Press in America." In *Catholics/U.S.A.: Perspectives and Social Change*, eds. William T. Liu and Nathaniel J. Pallone, 227–53. New York: John Wesley & Sons, Inc., 1970.

Gribbin, Raymond. Review of *On Almost Everything*, by James Gillis. In *Priest* 12 (4) (April 1956): 348–49.

Griffin, James F. "What Did You Say?" *The Catholic World* 177 (July 1953): 264–67.

Griffin, William D. *A Portrait of the Irish in America*. New York: Charles Scribner's Sons, 1981.

Guttmann, Allen. *The Wound in the Heart: America and the Spanish Civil War*. New York: The Free Press of Glencoe, 1962.

Halberstam, David. *The Fifties*. New York: Fawcett Columbine, 1993.

Halsey, William M. *The Survival of American Innocence: Catholicism in an Era of Disillusionment, 1920–1940*. Notre Dame, Indiana: University of Notre Dame Press, 1980.

Hamby, Alonzo L. *Beyond the New Deal: Harry S. Truman and American Liberalism*. New York: Columbia University Press, 1973.

Handlin, Oscar. *Boston's Immigrants 1790–1865–A Study in Acculturation*. Cambridge, Massachusetts: Harvard University Press, 1941.

Handy, Robert T. "The American Religious Depression, 1925–1935." *Church History* 29 (1960): 3–16.

Hanna, Mary T. *Catholics and American Politics*. Cambridge: Harvard University Press, 1979.

Harte, Thomas J. *Catholic Organizations Promoting Negro-White Race Relations in the United States*. Washington, D.C.: The Catholic University of America Press, 1947.

Hayes, Carlton J.H. *Essays of Nationalism*. New York: Macmillan, 1926.

Healy, John J., SJ. Review of *So Near Is God*, by James Gillis. In *America* 89 (August 22, 1953): 504.

Hennesey, James, SJ. *American Catholics–A History of the Roman Catholic Community in the United States*. New York: Oxford University Press, 1981.

———. *Catholics in the Promised Land of Saints*. Marquette, Wisconsin: University of Marquette Press, 1981.

Herberg, Will. *Protestant–Catholic–Jew*. Garden City, New York: Doubleday & Company, Inc., 1960.

Higgins, George G. (with William Bole). *Organized Labor and the Church: Reflections of a "Labor Priest."* New York: Paulist Press, 1993.

Higham, John. *Send These to Me–Immigrants in Urban America*. Baltimore: Johns Hopkins University Press, 1984.

———. *Strangers in the Land*. New Brunswick, New Jersey: Rutgers University Press, 1955.

Hoehn, Matthew, OSB, ed. *Catholic Authors: Contemporary Biographical Sketches 1930–1947*. Newark, New Jersey: St. Mary's Abbey, 1948.

Hoffman, Ross J.S. "The American Republic and Western Christendom." *Historical Records and Studies* 35 (1946): 3–17.

——. *Restoration.* New York: Sheed and Ward, 1934.

——. *The Spirit of Politics and the Future of Freedom.* Milwaukee: The Bruce Publishing Company, 1950.

——. *Tradition and Progress.* Milwaukee: The Bruce Publishing Company, 1938.

——. *The Will to Freedom.* New York: Sheed and Ward, 1935.

Hofstader, Richard. *The Age of Reform: From Bryan to F.D.R.* New York: Alfred A. Knopf, 1955.

Hogan, Peter, SSJ. *The Catholic University of America, 1896–1903: The Rectorship of Thomas J. Conaty.* Washington, D.C. The Catholic University of America Press, 1949.

"Hold to the Constitution!" *America* 53 (July 13, 1935): 314.

Holden, Vincent F. *The Yankee Paul: Isaac Thomas Hecker.* Milwaukee: Bruce Publishing Company, 1958.

Holmes, Pauline. *A Tercentary History of the Boston Public Latin School 1635–1935.* Cambridge, Massachusetts: Harvard University Press, 1935.

Hruzd, Teresa. "The Northeast Clergy Conference for Negro Welfare." M.A. thesis, University of Maryland, College Park, 1990.

Huber, Raphael M., ed. *Our Bishops Speak.* Milwaukee: The Bruce Publishing Company, 1952.

Hunt, Gaillard. "The Virginia Declaration of Rights and Cardinal Bellarmine." *Catholic Historical Review* 3 (October 1917): 276–89.

Husslein, Joseph, SJ. "Democracy a 'Popish' Innovation." *America* 21 (July 5, 1919): 338–40.

Jonas, Manfred. *Isolationism in America 1935–1941.* Ithaca, New York: Cornell University Press, 1966.

Jonas, Thomas J. *The Divided Mind: American–Catholic Evangelists in the 1890s.* New York: Garland Publishing, Inc., 1988.

Jones, Joseph M. *The Fifteen Weeks.* New York: The Viking Press, 1955.

Kanawada, Leo V. Jr. *Franklin D. Roosevelt's Diplomacy and American Catholics, Italians and Jews*. Ann Arbor, Michigan: UMI Research Press, 1982.

Kane, Paula M. *Separatism and Subculture: Boston Catholicism, 1900–1920*. Chapel Hill: The University of North Carolina Press, 1994.

Kauffman, Christopher J. *Faith and Fraternalism: The History of the Knights of Columbus 1882–1982*. New York: Harper & Row Publishers, 1982.

——. *Tradition and Transformation in Catholic Culture*. New York: Macmillan Publishing Company, 1988.

Keane, John J. "Loyalty to Rome and Country." *The American Catholic Quarterly Review* 15 (July 1890): 509–28.

Keller, Morton, ed. *The New Deal–What Was It?* New York: Holt, Rinehart and Winston, 1963.

Kenneally, James J. "Catholicism and the Supreme Court Reorganization Proposal of 1937." *Journal of Church and State* 25 (3) (Autumn 1983): 469–89.

Kennedy, John S. "Father Gillis's Fifty Years." *The Catholic World* 174 (December 1951): 166–72.

——. "Religion for Everyone." Review of *So Near Is God*, by James Gillis. In *Catholic World* 177 (June 1953): 176–81.

——. Review of *On Almost Everything*, by James Gillis. In *Catholic World* 182 (December 1955): 232.

——. "We Cannot Answer It." *The Catholic Transcript* 45 (28) (December 3, 1942): 4.

——. "We Ought to Pay Him Honor." *The Catholic Transcript* 49 (34) (January 9, 1947): 4.

Kennelly, Karen, CSJ, ed. *American Catholic Women: A Historical Exploration*. New York: Macmillan Publishing Company, 1989.

Kerby, John B. *Black Catholics in the Roosevelt Era: Liberalism and Race*. Knoxville: University of Tennessee Press, 1980.

Kinsman, Frederick Joseph. *Americanism and Catholicism*. New York: Longman, Green and Co., 1924.

Kirk, Russell. *Academic Freedom: An Essay in Definition* Chicago: Henry Regnery Company, 1955.

Kirkendall, Richard S. *The United States 1929–1945: Years of Crisis and Change*. New York: McGraw-Hill Book Company, 1974.

Klein, Felix. *Americanism: A Phantom Heresy*. Atchinson, Kansas: Aquin Book Shop, 1950.

Kloppenberg, James T. *Uncertain Victory: Social Democracy and Progressivism in European and American Thought, 1870–1920*. New York: Oxford University Press, 1986.

Koenig, Louis W. *The Truman Administration: Its Principles and Practice*. New York: New York University Press, 1956.

Lacey, Michael J., ed. *The Truman Presidency*. Cambridge: Cambridge University Press, 1989.

Lafarge, John, SJ. "The Interracial Apostolate." *America* 53 (June 8, 1935): 198–200.

———. *Interracial Justice: A Study of the Catholic Doctrine of Race Relations*. New York: America Press, 1937.

———. *The Manner Is Ordinary*. New York: Harcourt, Brace and Company, 1954.

———. "Publicizing Negro Welfare." *The Interracial Review* 9 (6) (May 1936): 88–89.

Lane, James W. "The Negro and American Democracy." *Catholic World* 156 (October 1942): 172–77.

Lears, T. J. Jackson. *No Place of Grace: Antimodernism and the Transformation of American Culture, 1880–1920*. New York: Pantheon Books, 1981.

Lenhart, John M., OFM, Cap. "Genesis of the Political Principles of the American Declaration of Independence." *Central Blatt and Social Justice* 24–25 (September and October 1932): 155–56, 191–94.

Leuchtenburg, William E. *In the Shadow of FDR: From Harry Truman to Ronald Reagan*. Ithaca, New York: Cornell University Press, 1983.

——. *The Perils of Prosperity, 1914–32*. Chicago: University of Chicago Press, 1958.

Link, Arthur Stanley and Richard L. McCormick. *Progressivism*. Arlington Heights, Illinois, Harlan Davidson, Inc., 1983.

Lord, Robert H., John E. Sexton, and Edward T. Harrington. *History of the Archdiocese of Boston on Various Stages of Its Development, 1604–1943*. Three Volumes. New York: Sheed & Ward, 1944.

Lucey, William L., SJ. "Catholic Magazines: 1865–1880." *Records of the Americam Catholic Historical Society of Philadelphia* 63 (1) (March 1952): 21–36.

——. "Catholic Magazines: 1880–1890." *Records of the American Catholic Historical Society of Philadelphia* 63 (2) (June 1952): 65–109.

——. "Catholic Magazines: 1890–1893." *Records of the American Catholic Historical Society of Philadelphia* 63 (3) (September 1952): 133–56.

——. "Catholic Magazines: 1894–1900." *Records of the American Catholic Historical Society of Philadelphia* 63 (4) (December 1952): 197–223.

Lunn, Arnold. "A Letter fron Arnold Lunn." *Catholic World* 153 (June 1941): 330–33.

MacIver, Robert M. *Academic Freedom in Our Time*. New York: Columbia University Press, 1955.

Malone, Thomas H. "Catholic Citizens and Constitutional Rights." *North American Review* 171 (October 1900): 594–99.

Manion, Clarence. *The Key to Peace*. Chicago: The Heritage Foundation, Inc., 1951.

Manning, Cardinal Henry Edward. *The Eternal Priesthood*. Philadelphia: The Peter Reilly Company, 1944.

Manton, Joseph, C.SS.R. "He Carved on Granite." *The Catholic World* 185 (May 1957): 82–84.

Maritain, Jacques. "Just War." *The Commonweal* 31 (December 22, 1939): 199–200.

Marshall, Charles C. "An Open Letter to Governor Smith." *Atlantic Monthly* 139 (4) (April 1927): 540–49.

Marty, Martin E. *The Irony of It All 1893–1919*. Chicago: University of Chicago Press, 1986.

——. *The Noise of Conflict 1919–1941*. Chicago: University of Chicago Press, 1986.

May, Henry F. *The End of Innocence: A Study of the First Years of Our Own Time, 1912–1917*. New York: Alfred A. Knopf, 1959.

Maynard, Theodore. *The Catholic Church and the American Idea*. New York: Appleton-Century-Crofts, Inc., 1953.

McAvoy, Thomas T., ed. *Roman Catholicism and the American Way of Life*. Notre Dame, Indiana: University of Notre Dame Press, 1960.

McCaffrey, Lawrence J. *The Irish Diaspora in America*. Bloomington: University of Indiana Press, 1976.

——. "Irish Textures in American Catholicism." *Catholic Historical Review* 78 (1) (January 1992): 1–18.

McCann, Dennis P. *New Experiment in Democracy–The Challenge for American Catholicism*. Kansas City, Missouri: Sheed & Ward, 1987.

McClure, Arthur F. *The Truman Administration and the Problems of Postwar Labor, 1945–1948*. Rutherford, New Jersey: Fairleigh Dickinson University Press, 1969.

McCoy, Donald R. *Coming of Age: The United States During the 1920's and 1930's*. Baltimore: Penguin Books, Inc., 1973.

McFaul, James A. "Catholic and American Citizenship." *North American Review* 171 (September 1900): 320–32.

McGinley, A.A. "The Catholic Life of Boston." *Catholic World* 67 (April 1898): 20–36.

McMahon, Francis E. *A Catholic Looks at the World*. New York: Vanguard Press, 1945.

McMahon, Joseph H. "The Battle for Decency." *The Commonweal* 20 (19) (September 7, 1934): 441–43.

McMath, Jr., Robert C. *American Populism: A Social History, 1877–1898.* New York: Hill & Wang, 1993.

McNamara, Patrick J. "A Study of the Editorial Policy of the *Brooklyn Tablet* Under Patrick F. Scanlan, 1917–1968." M.A. thesis, St. John's University, 1994.

McNamara, Sylvester. *American Democracy and Catholic Doctrine.* Brooklyn: International Catholic Truth Society, 1924.

McNicholas, John T. "The Episcopal Committee and the Problem of Evil Motion Pictures." *The Ecclesiastical Review* 91 (2) (August 1934): 113–19.

McShane, Joseph M. *"Sufficiently Radical": Catholicism, Progressivism, and the Bishops' Program of 1919.* Washington, D.C.: The Catholic University of America Press, 1986.

McSorley, Joseph, CSP. *Father Hecker and His Friends.* St. Louis: B. Herder Book Company, 1952.

McVann, James, CSP. "The Beginnings of the Paulist Apostolate to Non-Catholics." Uncompleted STL Dissertation, The Catholic University of America, 1932.

Merwick, Donna. *Boston Priests, 1848–1910.* Cambridge: Harvard University Press, 1973.

Millar, Moorhouse F.X. *Unpopular Essays in the Philosophy of History.* New York: Fordham University Press, 1928.

Miscamble, Wilson D., CSC "Catholicism and American Foreign Policy from McKinley to McCarthy: A Historiographical Survey." *Diplomatic History* 4 (1980): 223–40.

———. *George F. Kennan and the Making of American Foreign Policy, 1947–1950.* Princeton: Princeton University Press, 1992.

———. "The Limits of American Catholic Fascism: The Case of John A. Ryan." *Church History* 59 (4) (December 1990): 523–38.

Moore, R. Laurence. *Religious Outsiders and the Making of Americans.* New York: Oxford University Press, 1986.

Morriss, Frank. "Gillis Legacy." Review of *My Last Book*, by James Gillis. In *The Homiletic and Pastoral Review* 59 (2) (November 1958): 202–03.

Moynihan, F.M. "Father Gillis's Latest." Review of *This Mysterious Human Nature*, by James Gillis. In *The Homiletic and Pastoral Review* 57 (7) (April 1957): 664–66.

Murray, Robert K. *Red Scare: A Study in National Hysteria, 1919–1920.* Minneapolis: University of Minnesota Press, 1955.

Nash, George H. *The Conservative Intellectual Movement in America Since 1945.* New York: Basic Books, Inc., Publishers, 1976.

Nash, Gerald D. *The Crucial Era: The Great Depression and World War II.* New York: St. Martin's Press, 1992.

——. *The Great Depression and World War II: Organizing America, 1933–1945.* New York: St. Martin's Press, 1979.

"Neutrals and the Truth About the War." *Tablet* (London) 174 (December 2, 1939): 631–32.

Nevins, A.J. "The Catholic Press in the United States." In *Twentieth Century Catholicism–A Periodic Supplement to the Twentieth Century Encyclopedia of Catholicism*, Number 3, ed. Lancelot Sheppard, 29–50. New York: Hawthorn Books, 1966.

Nickels, Marilyn Wenzke. *Black Catholic Protest and the Federated Colored Catholics, 1917–1933.* New York: Garland Publishing, Inc., 1988.

Noble, David W. *The Progressive Mind 1890–1917.* Minneapolis: Burgess Publishing Company, 1981.

Nolan, Hugh J., ed. *Pastoral Letters of the United States Catholic Bishops*, Vol. I., Washington, D.C.: National Conference of Catholic Bishops, United States Catholic Conference, 1984.

Norton, Richard. "'Americanism' or The Catholic Church in America." *The Nation* 68 (March 30, 1899): 236–38.

Nuesse, C. Joseph. *The Catholic University of America–A Centennial History*. Washington, D.C.: The Catholic University of America Press, 1990.

O'Brien, David J. *American Catholics and Social Reform–The New Deal Years*. New York: Oxford University Press, 1968.

———. *Isaac Hecker, An American Catholic*. New York: Paulist Press, 1992.

———. *Public Catholicism*. New York: Macmillan Publishing Company, 1989.

———. *The Renewal of American Catholicism*. New York: Oxford University Press, 1972.

Ochs, Stephen J. *Desegregating the Altar: The Josephites and the Struggle for Black Priests, 1871–1960*. Baton Rouge: Louisiana State University Press, 1990.

O'Connell, Marvin R. *John Ireland and the American Catholic Church*. St. Paul: Minnesota Historical Society Press, 1988.

Ogden, August Raymond, FSC. *The Dies Committee: A Study of the Special House Committee for the Investigation of Un-American Activities 1938–1944*. Washington, D.C.: The Catholic University of America Press, 1945.

Olson, James S. *Catholic Immigrants in America*. Chicago: Nelson-Hall, 1987.

O'Neill, James M. *Catholicism and American Freedom*. New York: Harper & Brothers, 1952.

O'Neill, William L. *American High: The Years of Confidence 1945–1960*. New York: The Free Press, 1986.

———. *The Progressive Years: America Comes of Age*. New York: Harper & Row Publishers, 1975.

O'Rahilly, Alfred. "Catholic Origins of Democracy." *Studies* 8 (March 1919): 1–18.

———. "Sources of English and American Democracy." *Studies* 8 (June 1919): 189–209.

———. "The Sovereignity of the People." *Studies* 10 (March 1921): 39–56.

————. "The Sovereignity of the People II." *Studies* 10 (June 1921): 277–87.

Osborne, William. *The Segregated Covenant: Race Relations and American Catholics.* New York: Herder and Herder, 1967.

Oshinsky, David M. *A Conspiracy So Immense–The World of Joe McCarthy.* New York: The Free Press, 1983.

O'Toole, James M. *Militant and Triumphant: William Henry O'Connell and the Catholic Church in Boston, 1859–1944.* Notre Dame, Indiana: University of Notre Dame Press, 1992.

————. "The Role of Bishops in American Catholic History: Myth and Reality in the Case of Cardinal William O'Connell." *Catholic Historical Review* 77 (4) (October 1991): 595–615.

Parsons, Wilfrid, SJ. *The First Freedom–Considerations on Church and State in the United States.* New York: The Declan X. McMullin Company, Inc., 1948.

————. *The Pope and Italy.* New York: The American Press, 1929.

————. Review of *The Key to Peace*, by Clarence Manion. In *America* 84 (March 24, 1951): 728–29.

Perrett, Geoffrey. *America in the Twenties: A History.* New York: Simon and Schuster, 1982.

————. *Days of Sadness, Years of Triumph: The American People 1939–1945.* Madison: University of Wisconsin Press, 1985.

Peterson, Merrill D. *The Jeffersonian Image in the American Mind.* New York: Oxford University Press, 1960.

Phillips, Cabell. *The 1940s, Decade of Triumph and Trouble.* New York: Macmillan Co., Inc., 1975.

Piehl, Mel. *Breaking Bread: The Catholic Worker and the Origin of Catholic Radicalism in America.* Philadelphia: Temple University Press, 1982.

Piper, John F. *The American Churches in World War I.* Athens, Ohio: Ohio University Press, 1985.

Portier, William L. "Isaac Hecker and *Testem Benevolentiae*: A Study in

Theological Pluralism." In *Hecker Studies–Essays on the Thought of Isaac Hecker*, ed. John Farina, 11–48. New York: Paulist Press, 1983.

Rager, John C. "The Blessed Cardinal Bellarmine's Defense of Popular Government in the Sixteenth Century." *Catholic Historical Review* 10 (January 1925): 504–14.

——. "Catholic Sources and the Declaration of Independence." *Catholic Mind* 28 (July 8, 1930): 253–68.

——. *Democracy and Bellarmine*. Shelbyville, Indiana: Quality Print, Inc., 1926.

Ratte, John. *Three Modernists: Alfred Loisy, George Tyrrell, William L. Sullivan*. New York: Sheed and Ward, 1967.

Regan, Richard J. *American Pluralism and the Catholic Conscience*. New York: The Macmillan Company, 1963.

Regier, C.C. *The Era of the Muckrakers*. Gloucester, Massachusetts: Peter Smith, 1957.

Reher, Margaret Mary. *Catholic Intellectual Life in America*. New York: Macmillan Publishing Company, 1989.

——. "The Church and the Kingdom of God in America: The Ecclesiology of the Americanists." Ph.D. diss., Fordham University, 1972.

Reilly, Joseph. "The *Catholic World* in Recent Years." *Catholic World* 151 (April 1940): 17–23.

Reilly, Sr. Mary Lonan, OSF. *A History of the Catholic Press Association, 1911–1968*. Metuchen, New Jersey: The Scarecrow Press, Inc., 1971.

Riach, John, CSP. "'England' or 'The Empire.'" *Catholic World* 153 (April 1941): 72–76.

Rice, Elizabeth Ann. *The Diplomatic Relations Between the United States and Mexico, as Affected by the Struggle for Religious Liberty in Mexico 1925–1929*. Washington, D.C.: The Catholic University of America Press, 1959.

Robichaud, Paul, CSP. "Catholic Total Abstinence." Unpubished Essay, 1994.

——. "Modernist Ghosts in the Halls of St. Thomas: The Paulists in Washington, D.C. 1902–1907." *Journal of Paulist Studies* 1 (1992): 40–53.

——. "The Very Reverend Superior 1858–1978." *Paulist History* 4(1) (May 1994): 3–29.

Rorty, James and Moshe Decter. *McCarthy and the Communists*. Boston: The Beacon Press, 1954.

Ross, Eva J. "Action in the South." *Catholic World* 151 (August 1940): 566–69.

Rossi, Joseph S., SJ. *American Catholics and the Formation of the United Nations*. Washington, D.C.: University Press of America, 1993.

Rovere, Richard H. *Senator Joe McCarthy*. New York: Harcourt, Brace and Company, 1959.

Ryan, Dennis P. *Beyond the Ballot Box: A Social History of the Boston Irish, 1845–1917*. Amherst: University of Massachusetts Press, 1983.

Ryan, John A. *The Catholic Church and the Citizen*. New York: The Macmillan Company, 1928.

——. "Church, State and Constitution." *The Commonweal* 5 (April 1927): 680–82.

——. "Confusion About the War." *The Commonweal* 31(22) (March 22, 1940): 464–67.

——. "An Open Letter to the Editor." *Catholic World* 143 (April 1936): 22–26.

——. *Right of Self-Government*. New York: The Macmillan Company, 1920.

—— and Francis J. Boland. *Catholic Principles of Politics*. New York: The Macmillan Company, 1940.

—— and Moorhouse F.X. Millar. *The State and the Church*. New York: The Macmillan Company, 1922.

Sands, William F. "The Return of the New Deal." *Catholic Digest* 1 (May 1937): 1–5.

Satolli, Archbishop Francis. "The Relations of Church and State." In *Loyalty to Church and State*, 99–111. Baltimore: Murphy & Co., 1895.

Schlesinger, Arthur M. Jr. *The Coming of the New Deal*. Boston: Houghton Mifflin Company, 1959.

——. *The Vital Center: The Politics of Freedom*. Boston: Houghton Mifflin Company, 1949.

Schwarz, Jordan A. *The New Dealers: Power Politics in the Age of Roosevelt*. New York: Alfred A. Knopf, 1993.

Sedgwick, H.D. "The United States and Rome." *Atlantic Monthly* 84 (October 1899): 445–58.

Selner, John, SS. "Father James Gillis, C.S.P." *The American Ecclesiastical Review* 137 (July 1957): 31–38.

——. "Truth and Consequence." *The Voice* 26 (November 1948): 19–20.

Sexton, John E. and Arthur J. Riley. *History of Saint John's Seminary, Brighton*. Boston: Roman Catholic Archbishop of Boston, 1945.

Shannon, David A. *Between the Wars: America 1919–1941*. Boston: Houghton Mifflin Company, 1965.

Shea, John Gilmary. *The Cross and the Flag*. New York: Catholic Historical League of America, 1899.

——. "No Actual Need of a Catholic Party in the United States." *American Catholic Quarterly Review* 12 (October 1887): 705–13.

Sheerin, John B., CSP. "He Fought with a Pen." *Messenger of the Sacred Heart* 84 (March 1949): 56–60.

——. *Never Look Back: The Career and Concerns of John J. Burke*. New York: Paulist Press, 1975.

Shenton, James P. "The Coughlin Movement and the New Deal." *Political Science Quarterly* 73 (September 1958): 352–73.

Shields, Currin V. *Democracy and Catholicism in America*. New York: McGraw-Hill Book Company, Inc., 1958.

Shuster, George N. "Answer to Senator Nye." *The Commonweal* 34 (October 17, 1941): 609–11.

——. *The Catholic Spirit in America*. New York: Dial Press, 1927.

Sirgiovanni, George A. *An Undercurrent of Suspicion: Anti-Communism in America During World War II*. New Brunswick, New Jersey: Transaction Publishers, 1990.

Skillin Jr., Edward. "The Catholic Press and the Election." *The Commonweal* 33 (November 1, 1940): 50–52.

Skinner, James M. *The Cross and the Cinema: The Legion of Decency and the National Catholic Office for Motion Pictures, 1933–1970*. Westport, Connecticut: Praeger Publications, 1993.

Slawson, Douglas. "'The Boston Tragedy and Comedy': The Near Repudiation of Cardinal O'Connell." *Catholic Historical Review* 77 (4) (October 1991): 616–43.

——. *The Foundation and First Decade of the National Catholic Welfare Council*. Washington, D.C.: The Catholic University of America Press, 1992.

Smith, Alfred E. "Catholic and Patriot: Governor Smith Replies." *Atlantic Monthly* 139 (5) (April 1927): 721–28.

Smith, Timothy. *Revivalism and Social Reform in Mid-Nineteenth Century America*. Nashville: Abingdon Press, 1957.

Smith, William Barry. "The Attitude of American Catholics Towards Italian Fascism Between the Two World Wars." Ph.D. diss., The Catholic University of America, 1969.

Spanier, John W. *The Truman-MacArthur Controversy and the Korean War*. New York: W.W. Norton & Company, Inc., 1965.

Stassen, Harold and Marshall Houts. *Eisenhower: Turning the World Toward Peace*. St. Paul, Minnesota: Merrill/Magnus Publishing Corporation, 1990.

Steinberg, Peter L. *The Great "Red Menace": United States Prosecution of American Communists, 1947–1952*. Westport, Connecticut: Greenwood Press, 1984.

Stockley, W.F.P. "As Others See Us." *American Catholic Quarterly Review* 26 (102) (April 1901): 278–86.

Sullivan, Robert E. and James M. O'Toole, eds. *Catholic Boston–Studies in Religion and Community 1870–1970.* Boston: Roman Catholic Archdiocese of Boston, 1985.

Sullivan, William Laurence. *Under Orders: The Autobiography of William Laurence Sullivan.* New York: Richard R. Smith, 1944.

Sunoo, Harold Hakwon. *America's Dilemma in Asia: The Case of South Korea.* Chicago: Nelson-Hall, 1979.

Talbot, Francis X. "Catholicism in America." In *America Now,* ed. Harold E. Stearns, 528–42, New York: The Literary Guild of America, 1938.

Tanquerey, Adolphe. *Doctrine and Life.* Translated by Louis A. Arand, SS. Tournai, Belgium: Desclée & Co., 1933.

———. *The Spiritual Life–A Treatise on Ascetical and Mystical Theology.* Translated by Herman Branderis, SS. Tournai, Belgium: Desclée & Co., 1933.

Tartre, Raymond, SSS. Review of *James Gillis–Paulist,* by James Finley, CSP. In *Emmanuel* 64 (12) (December 1958): 524–26.

Taylor, Hannis. *The Origin and Growth of the American Constitution.* Boston: Houghton Mifflin Company, 1911.

Thaman, Mary Patrice. *Manners and Morality of the 1920s: A Survey of the Religious Press.* New York: Bookman Associates, 1954.

Thernstrom, Stephan. *The Other Bostonians: Poverty and Progress in the American Metropolis, 1870–1970.* Cambridge, Massachusetts: Harvard University Press, 1973.

Tull, Charles J. *Father Coughlin and the New Deal.* Syracuse, New York: Syracuse University Press, 1965.

Valaik, J. David. "American Catholic Dissenters and the Spanish Civil War." *Catholic Historical Review* 53 (January 1968): 537–55.

———. "Catholics, Neutrality and the Spanish Embargo, 1937–1939". *Journal of American History* 44 (June 1967): 73–85.

Van Allen, Rodger. *The Commonweal and American Catholicism: The Magazine, the Movement, the Meaning.* Philadelphia: Fortress Press, 1974.

Vinca, Robert H. "The American Catholic Reaction to the Persecution of the Church in Mexico, 1926–1936." *Records* 79 (1) (March 1968): 3–38.

Wald, Kenneth D. "The Religious Dimension of American Anti-Communism." *Journal of Church and State* 36 (3) (Summer 1994): 483–506.

Walsh, William J. "Catholic Negro Leadership." *The Interracial Review* 12 (8) (August 1939): 123–25.

Warren, Frank A. and Michael Wreszin, eds. *The New Deal: An Anthology.* New York: Thomas Y. Crowell Company, 1968.

Weiss, Nancy. *Farewell to the Party of Lincoln: Black Politics in the Age of FDR.* Princeton, New Jersey: Princeton University Press, 1983.

Wentz, Frederick. "American Catholic Periodicals React to Nazism." *Church History* 31 (1962): 400–20.

Werstein, Irving. *Shattered Decade 1919–1929.* New York: Charles Scribner's Sons, 1970.

Whealon, John F. "The Great 'Preamble': Did Bellarmine Influence Jefferson? A Look at the Record." *The Commonweal* 42 (July 6, 1945): 284–85.

White, Joseph M. *The Diocesan Seminary in the United States: A History from the 1780s to the Present.* Notre Dame, Indiana: University of Notre Dame Press, 1989.

Wilkins, Roy. "Father Gillis's Broadcast." *Interracial Review* 6 (1) (January 1933): 12–13.

Williams, Michael. *American Catholics in the War: National Catholic War Council, 1917–1921.* New York: The Macmillan Company, 1921.

———. *The Catholic Church in Action.* New York: The Macmillan Company, 1934.

——. *Catholicism and the Modern Mind*. New York: Dial Press, 1928.

——. "The Present Position of Catholics in the United States." New York: Calvert Publishing Co., 1928.

Wilson, Francis Graham. *The American Political Mind*. New York: McGraw-Hill Book Company, Inc., 1949.

——. *The Case for Conservatism*. Seattle: University of Washington Press, 1951.

Wolfskill, George. *The Revolt of the Conservatives: A History of the American Liberty League, 1934–1940*. Boston: Houghton Mifflin Company, 1962.

—— and John A. Hudson. *All But the People: Franklin D. Roosevelt and His Critics, 1933–39*. Toronto: The Macmillan Company, 1969.

Zielinski, Martin A. "Working for Interracial Justice: The Catholic Interracial Council of New York." *U.S. Catholic Historian* 7 (2&3) (Spring & Summer 1988): 233–60.

Index